EVENT TOURISM IN ASIAN COUNTRIES

Challenges and Prospects

Advances in Hospitality and Tourism Series

EVENT TOURISM IN ASIAN COUNTRIES

Challenges and Prospects

Edited by
Shruti Arora, PhD
Anukrati Sharma, PhD

First edition published 2022

Apple Academic Press Inc.
1265 Goldenrod Circle, NE,
Palm Bay, FL 32905 USA
4164 Lakeshore Road, Burlington,
ON, L7L 1A4 Canada

CRC Press
6000 Broken Sound Parkway NW,
Suite 300, Boca Raton, FL 33487-2742 USA
2 Park Square, Milton Park,
Abingdon, Oxon, OX14 4RN UK

© 2022 by Apple Academic Press, Inc.

Apple Academic Press exclusively co-publishes with CRC Press, an imprint of Taylor & Francis Group, LLC

Reasonable efforts have been made to publish reliable data and information, but the authors, editors, and publisher cannot assume responsibility for the validity of all materials or the consequences of their use. The authors, editors, and publishers have attempted to trace the copyright holders of all material reproduced in this publication and apologize to copyright holders if permission to publish in this form has not been obtained. If any copyright material has not been acknowledged, please write and let us know so we may rectify in any future reprint.

Except as permitted under U.S. Copyright Law, no part of this book may be reprinted, reproduced, transmitted, or utilized in any form by any electronic, mechanical, or other means, now known or hereafter invented, including photocopying, microfilming, and recording, or in any information storage or retrieval system, without written permission from the publishers.

For permission to photocopy or use material electronically from this work, access www.copyright.com or contact the Copyright Clearance Center, Inc. (CCC), 222 Rosewood Drive, Danvers, MA 01923, 978-750-8400. For works that are not available on CCC please contact mpkbookspermissions@tandf.co.uk

Trademark notice: Product or corporate names may be trademarks or registered trademarks and are used only for identification and explanation without intent to infringe.

Library and Archives Canada Cataloguing in Publication

Title: Event tourism in Asian countries : challenges and prospects / edited by Shruti Arora, PhD, Anukrati Sharma, PhD.
Names: Arora, Shruti, editor. | Sharma, Anukrati, 1981- editor.
Series: Advances in hospitality and tourism book series.
Description: First edition. | Series statement: Advances in hospitality and tourism | Includes bibliographical references and index.
Identifiers: Canadiana (print) 20210290579 | Canadiana (ebook) 2021029065X | ISBN 9781774630044 (hardcover) | ISBN 9781774639481 (softcover) | ISBN 9781003161134 (PDF)
Subjects: LCSH: Tourism—Asia. | LCSH: Tourism—Asia—Marketing. | LCSH: Tourism—Asia—Planning. | LCSH: Tourism—Social aspects—Asia. | LCSH: Special events—Asia. | LCSH: Special events industry—Asia.
Classification: LCC G155.A78 E94 2021 | DDC 338.4/7915—dc23

Library of Congress Cataloging-in-Publication Data

Names: Arora, Shruti, editor. | Sharma, Anukrati, 1981- editor.
Title: Event tourism in Asian countries : challenges and prospects / edited by Shruti Arora, PhD, Anukrati Sharma, PhD.
Description: First Edition. | Palm Bay, FL : Apple Academic Press, [2022] | Series: Advances in Hospitality and Tourism Series / Editor-in-Chief, Mahmood A. Khan, PhD | "Apple Academic Press exclusively co-publishes with CRC Press, an imprint of Taylor & Francis Group, LLC"--T.p. verso. | Includes bibliographical references and index. | Summary: "Events, including repeat annual events, have the unique ability to drive sustainable tourism to certain areas and regions and to generate economic benefits for local communities. The events industry has grown dramatically over the last several decades, and there has been increased participation from governments, local communities, and private sectors. This new volume offers a wide variety of research, experience, and examples of events in Asia, including business meetings and conferences; destination weddings; carnivals; food and art festivals; music festivals and concerts; cultural and traditional events; religious and spiritual gatherings; sports events; and more. The authors, from various parts of Asia, give illustrative examples from various countries, such as India, Sri Lanka, Turkey, Malaysia, Uzbekistan, and Kyrgyzstan. The diverse perspectives are those from stakeholders, travelers, researchers, academicians, professionals in the event and tourism industry, and the community. The chapters in Event Tourism in Asian Countries: Challenges and Prospects cover the changing trends in the event tourism industry, the influence and role of social media and other technology, the contribution of women in events and festivals, and the impact of event tourism in economic development on local communities. Addressing the issues, challenges, and future of event tourism and management, this new volume will valuable addition to the library of event professionals, hospitality and tourism researchers, community development managers, and others in Asia and elsewhere"-- Provided by publisher.
Identifiers: LCCN 2021039180 (print) | LCCN 2021039181 (ebook) | ISBN 9781774630044 (Hardback) | ISBN 9781774639481 (Paperback) | ISBN 9781003161134 (eBook)
Subjects: LCSH: Tourism--Asia--Marketing. | Tourism--Asia--Planning. | Tourism--Social aspects--Asia. | Culture and tourism--Asia. | Special events--Asia.
Classification: LCC G155.A74 E9 2022 (print) | LCC G155.A74 (ebook) | DDC 915.0068/8--dc23
LC record available at https://lccn.loc.gov/2021039180
LC ebook record available at https://lccn.loc.gov/2021039181

ISBN: 978-1-77463-004-4 (hbk)
ISBN: 978-1-77463-948-1 (pbk)
ISBN: 978-1-00316-113-4 (ebk)

ABOUT THE ADVANCES IN HOSPITALITY AND TOURISM BOOK SERIES

Editor-in-Chief:
Mahmood A. Khan, PhD
Professor, Department of Hospitality and Tourism Management,
Pamplin College of Business,
Virginia Polytechnic Institute and State University,
Falls Church, Virginia, USA
Email: mahmood@vt.edu

This series reports on research developments and advances in the rapidly growing area of hospitality and tourism. Each volume in this series presents state-ofthe-art information on a specialized topic of current interest. These one-of-a-kind publications are valuable resources for academia as well as for professionals in the industrial sector.

BOOKS IN THE SERIES:
Food Safety: Researching the Hazard in Hazardous Foods
Editors: Barbara Almanza, PhD, RD, and Richard Ghiselli, PhD

Strategic Winery Tourism and Management: Building Competitive Winery Tourism and Winery Management Strategy
Editor: Kyuho Lee, PhD

Sustainability, Social Responsibility and Innovations in the Hospitality Industry
Editor: H. G. Parsa, PhD
Consulting Editor: Vivaja "Vi" Narapareddy, PhD
Associate Editors: SooCheong (Shawn) Jang, PhD,
Marival Segarra-Oña, PhD, and Rachel J. C. Chen, PhD, CHE

Managing Sustainability in the Hospitality and Tourism Industry: Paradigms and Directions for the Future
Editor: Vinnie Jauhari, PhD

Management Science in Hospitality and Tourism: Theory, Practice, and Applications
Editors: Muzaffer Uysal, PhD, Zvi Schwartz, PhD, and Ercan Sirakaya-Turk, PhD

Tourism in Central Asia: Issues and Challenges
Editors: Kemal Kantarci, PhD, Muzaffer Uysal, PhD, and Vincent Magnini, PhD

Poverty Alleviation through Tourism Development: A Comprehensive and Integrated Approach
Robertico Croes, PhD, and Manuel Rivera, PhD

Chinese Outbound Tourism 2.0
Editor: Xiang (Robert) Li, PhD

Hospitality Marketing and Consumer Behavior: Creating Memorable Experiences
Editor: Vinnie Jauhari, PhD

Women and Travel: Historical and Contemporary Perspectives
Editors: Catheryn Khoo-Lattimore, PhD, and Erica Wilson, PhD

Wilderness of Wildlife Tourism
Editor: Johra Kayeser Fatima, PhD

Medical Tourism and Wellness: Hospitality Bridging Healthcare (H_2H)©
Editor: Frederick J. DeMicco, PhD, RD

Sustainable Viticulture: The Vines and Wines of Burgundy
Claude Chapuis

The Indian Hospitality Industry: Dynamics and Future Trends
Editors: Sandeep Munjal and Sudhanshu Bhushan

Tourism Development and Destination Branding through Content Marketing Strategies and Social Media
Editor: Anukrati Sharma, PhD

Evolving Paradigms in Tourism and Hospitality in Developing Countries: A Case Study of India
Editors: Bindi Varghese, PhD

The Hospitality and Tourism Industry in China: New Growth, Trends, and Developments
Editors: Jinlin Zhao, PhD

Labor in Tourism and Hospitality Industry: Skills, Ethics, Issues, and Rights
Abdallah M. Elshaer, PhD, and Asmaa M. Marzouk, PhD

Sustainable Tourism Development: Futuristic Approaches
Editor: Anukrati Sharma, PhD

Tourism in Turkey: A Comprehensive Overview and Analysis for Sustainable Alternative Tourism
Editor: Ahmet Salih İKİZ

Capacity Building Through Heritage Tourism: An International Perspective
Editor: Surabhi Srivastava, PhD

The Hospitality and Tourism Industry in ASEAN and East Asian Destinations: New Growth, Trends, and Developments
Editors: Jinlin Zhao, PhD, Lianping Ren, D.HTM, and Xiangping Li, PhD

Event Tourism in Asian Countries: Challenges and Prospects
Editors: Shruti Arora, PhD and Anukrati Sharma, PhD

ABOUT THE EDITORS

Shruti Arora, PhD, is currently working as a guest faculty in the Department of Commerce and Management, University of Kota, Kota, Rajasthan, India. She has over 10 years of experience in education. Her core subjects are marketing, general management, international business management, and customer relationship management. She has published several research papers in international refereed journals and one chapter in edited book in the Routledge Advances in Event Research Series in 2018. She has also authored the book *Event Management and Marketing: Theory, Practical Approaches and Planning.*

Anukrati Sharma, PhD, is currently working as an Associate Professor in the Faculty of Commerce and Management, University of Kota, Kota, Rajasthan, India. Dr. Sharma has worked as an internal trainer and teacher in the management arena. In 2015, she received a Research Award from the University Grants Commission (UGC), New Delhi, India, for her project "Analysis of the Status of Tourism in Hadoti and Shekhawati Region/Circuit (Rajasthan): Opportunities, Challenges, and Future Prospects," and she completed her dissertation research on "Tourism in Rajasthan—Progress & Prospects." She has two postgraduate degree specialties—one in International Business (Master of International Business) and the other in Business Administration (Master of Commerce). Her special interest areas are tourism, tourism marketing, strategic management, general management, and international business management. She has edited several books, including *Tourism: Opportunities and Ventures; Maximizing Business Performance and Efficiency through Intelligent Systems* (IGI Global); *Sustainable Tourism Development: Futuristic Approaches* (Apple Academic Press/CRC Press); *Tourism Events in Asia Marketing and Development* (Routledge); and *Sustainable Destination Branding and Marketing: Strategies for Tourism Development* (CABI, UK). She has authored the book *Event Management and Marketing Theory, Practical Approaches and Planning* and the book *International Best Practice in Event Management* (United Kingdom Event Industry Academy Ltd. and Prasetiya Mulya Publishing, Indonesia). She has also edited *The Emerald Handbook of ICT in Tourism and Hospitality*

(Emerald Publishing UK), which is in press now. Dr. Sharma is a member of several professional organizations, and she has attended a number of national and international conferences and presented 45 papers. She has been invited as a keynote speaker for talks, lectures, and panel discussions by several countries, including Sri Lanka, Nepal, Uzbekistan, and Turkey.

CONTENTS

Contributors .... *xiii*
Abbreviations .... *xvii*
Preface .... *xix*

1. Event Tourism: Prospects and Trends 1
   Anukrati Sharma and Shruti Arora

2. Main Tendencies of Historical and Cultural Tourism Development in Uzbekistan 9
   Amonboev Mukhammadsiddik, Tursunov Bobir, and Ruziev Shohruzbek

3. Event Tourism in Turkey 39
   Serap Akdu and Uğur Akdu

4. Tribal Fair and Festival: Context, Examples, and the Interpretation of Technology 73
   Azizul Hassan and Anukrati Sharma

5. The Impact of Modernization on Malay Weddings 87
   Ahmad AlBattat, Trisha Anne Joseph, and Abdul Azim Mazlan

6. Events Tourism in the Eye of the COVID-19 Storm: Impacts and Implications 97
   Priyakrushna Mohanty, Himanshi, and Rashmiranjan Choudhury

7. Business Tourism and Economic Impacts: Evidence from the Malaysian Business Events Industry 115
   Jeetesh Kumar and Kashif Hussain

8. The Effect of Traditional and Modern Events on Students' Psychology and Well-Being: A Case Study on ALLEN 139
   Krishana Kumar Nimbark

9. Travel and Tourism Competitiveness and Cultural Tourism Events in Sri Lanka 151
   D.A.C. Suranga Silva, Kalpani V. Gamage, Manori L. Guruge, and Dulaja N. Silva

10. Future of Food Tourism in India: A Psychographic Overview 171
    Khushboo Gupta and Sarika Mohta

11. Social Media Transforming Tourist Behavior 183
    Ashmi Chhabra

12. Mega-Events Tourism and Sustainability: A Critique 219
    Priyakrushna Mohanty, Oshi Singhania, and Uswathul Hasana

13. Local Economic Incentives of Art Events:
    A Case Study of Kochi–Muziris Biennale 235
    Biju Thomas and A. Vinodan

14. Role of Event Tourism in Economic Development 249
    Melike Sak, Aslı Sultan Eren, and Gül Erkol Bayram

15. Role of Host Communities in Indigenous Cultural Events and
    Tourism Interactions: Challenges Toward Imaging the
    Event Located at Little-Known Destinations 267
    Samik Ray

16. World Nomad Games as an Emerging Large-Scale Event and
    Its Role for Tourism Development in Kyrgyzstan 287
    Azamat Maksüdünov and Kyialbek Dyikanov

17. Participation and Role of Women in Events and Festivals:
    A Study on the Contributions of Women in Revitalizing and
    Sustaining the Folk Potential of Fairs and Festivals in India 309
    Anila Thomas

18. Prospects and Challenges of Event Tourism in
    Bangladesh—Post-COVID-19 327
    Md. Wasiul Islam and Dababrata Chowdhury

19. Challenges for Community Engagement in Event Tourism:
    A Case Study of Bundi Utsav of Rajasthan, India 359
    Anurodh Godha

20. Digital Platforms and Future Challenges of Tourism in
    Asian Countries 373
    Jyoti Chaudhery and Jatin Maniktala

21. The Future of Event Tourism: Path for Sustainable
    Growth Toward 2030 385
    Shruti Arora and Anukrati Sharma

Index *393*

CONTRIBUTORS

Serap Akdu
Associate Professor, Department of Tourism Guidance, Gumushane University, Faculty of Tourism in Turkey

Uğur Akdu
Assistant Professor, Department of Tourism Guidance, Gumushane University, Faculty of Tourism in Turkey

Shruti Arora
Department of Commerce and Management, University of Kota, Kota, Rajasthan, India

Ahmad AlBattat
Post Graduate Centre, Management and Science University, Selangor, Malaysia

Gül Erkol Bayram
School of Tourism and Hospitality Management, Department of Tour Guiding, Sinop University, Nasuhbeyoğlu District, Sinop, Turkey

Tursunov Bobir
Department of Economic Security, Tashkent State University of Economics, Republic of Uzbekistan

Ashmi Chhabra
Department of Management and Commerce, IIS Deemed to University, Jaipur, India

Jyoti Chaudhery
Department of Commerce and Management, University of Kota, Kota, Rajasthan, India

RashmiRanjan Choudhury
North-Eastern Hill University, Shillong, India

Dababrata Chowdhury (Daba)
Suffolk Business School, University of Suffolk (UoS), Ipswich, United Kingdom

Himanshi
Institute of Hotel & Tourism Management, *Maharshi Dayanand* University, Rohtak

Kiyalbek Diykanov
Department of Management, Social Sciences Institute, Kyrgyz-Turkish Manas University, Bishkek, Kyrgyzstan

Ash Sultan Eren
Department of Tourism Guidance, School of Tourism and Hotel Management, Sinop University, Sinop, Turkey

Kalpani V. Gamage
Department of Economics, University of Colombo, Colombo, Sri Lanka

Anurodh Godha
Vardhman Mahaveer Open University, Kota, Rajasthan 324021, India

Khushboo Gupta
Trilok Singh TT College, Sikar, Rajasthan, India

Manori L. Guruge
Department of Economics, University of Colombo, Colombo, Sri Lanka

Uswathul Hasana
Department of Tourism Studies, School of Management, Pondicherry University, Puducherry, India

Azizul Hassan
Tourism Consultants Network, The Tourism Society, London, United Kingdom

Kashif Hussain
School of Media and Communication, Centre for Research and Innovation in Tourism (CRiT), Taylor's University, Malaysia

Md. Wasiul Islam
Forestry and Wood Technology, Discipline of Khulna University, Bangladesh

Trisha Anne Joseph
School of Hospitality and Creative Arts, Management and Science University, Selangor, Malaysia

Azamat Maksudunov
Department of Management, Faculty of Economics and Administrative Sciences, Kyrgyz-Turkish Manas University, Bishkek, Kyrgyzstan

Jatin Maniktala
Department of Commerce and Management, University of Kota, Kota, Rajasthan, India

Abdul Azim Mazlan
School of Hospitality and Creative Arts, Management and Science University, Selangor, Malaysia

Priyakrushna Mohanty
Department of Tourism Studies, School of Management, Pondicherry University, Puducherry, India

Sarika Mohta
OKIMR, University of Kota, Kota, Rajasthan, India

Amonboev Mukhammadsiddik
Department of Tourism and Service, Tashkent State University of Economics, Republic of Uzbekistan

Samik Ray
Department of Tourism (Government of India), Eastern Region, Kolkata 700071, India

Anukrati Sharma
Department of Commerce and Management, University of Kota, Rajasthan, India

Ruziev Shohruzbek
Department of Tourism and Service, Tashkent State University of Economics, Republic of Uzbekistan

Jeetesh Kumar
School of Hospitality, Tourism and Events, Centre for Research and Innovation in Tourism (CRiT), Taylor's University, Malaysia

Krishana Kumar Nimbark
Department of Chemistry, ALLEN Career Institute, Kota, Rajasthan, India

Melike Sak
Department of Tourism Guidance, Sinop University School of Tourism and Hotel Management, Sinop, Turkey

D.A.C. Suranga Silva
Tourism Economics, University of Colombo, Colombo, Sri Lanka

Dulaja N. Silva
Sri Lanka Technological Campus, Padukka, Sri Lanka

Oshi Singhania
Department of Tourism Studies, School of Management, Pondicherry University, Puducherry, India

Anila Thomas
Department of Tourism and Travel Management, Jyoti Nivas College (Autonomous), Bangalore 95, Karnataka, India

Biju Thomas
RLGT – Regional Level Tourist guide, Ministry of Tourism, Government of India, Southern Region

A. Vinodan
School of Commerce and Business Management, Central University of Tamil Nadu, Neelakudy, Tamil Nadu 610005, India

ABBREVIATIONS

ACM	Academy of Country Music
AIS	Australian Institute of Sport
ASEANs	Association of Southeast Asian Nations
ATA	International Air Transportation Association
CA	Central Asian
CIS	Commonwealth of Independent States
DMO	destination marketing organization
EFA	European Festivals Association
EMITT	East Mediterranean International Tourism & Travel Exhibition
GDP	Gross Domestic Product
ICCA	International Congress and Convention Association
ICT	information and communication technology
İKSV	Istanbul Foundation for Culture and Arts
IO	input–output
IPL	Indian Premier League
KMB	Kochi–Muziris Biennale
MGM	Money Generation Model
MICE	Meetings, incentives, conventions, and exhibitions
MWC	Mobile World Congress
NATAS	National Association of Travel Agents Singapore
NPF	National Policy Framework
OECD	Organization for Economic Co-Operation and Development
ROI	return on investment
SIT	Special Interest Tourism
SSNs	social networking sites
TOBB	Türkiye Odalar ve Borsalar Birliği
TSA	Tourism Satellite Account
TTC	Travel and Tourism Competitiveness
TTCI	Global Travel and Tourism Competitive Index
UCI	Union Cycliste Internationale
UGC	Users Generated Content
UNESCO	United Nations Educational, Scientific and Cultural Organization
UNWTO	United Nations World Tourism Organization

WACS	World Association of Chefs' Societies
WHO	World Health Organization
WNG	World Nomad Games
WTO	World Tourism Organization
WTTC	World Travel & Tourism Council

PREFACE

Images of an event have a huge implication for the sustainable development of tourism around the world. This can be any kind of event—religious, cultural, or traditional; sports; music; etc., which also plays a vital role in economic development as well.

Event tourism is a form of tourism that has grown at a fast rate in the last few years. Events are for the short-term occurrence to attract tourists to view or to participate in a particular event and to be entertained. An event has the power to extend the number of tourists and generate additional revenue for the regional population. There are some places are just only visited by tourists because of special events, for example, annual concerts, carnivals, film festivals, or sport events. Every year such events are the main attraction for tourists. In fact, sometimes events are organized for repeat visitors.

Event tourism has had a huge impact on community development in many areas. Event tourism has expanded exponentially. Event tourism creates many jobs that generate millions of dollars in sales or income around the world.

An attempt has been made in this book to discuss aspects from the viewpoints of different people, stakeholders, travelers, researchers, academicians, event organizers, and the tourism industry.

There is no uncertainty in believing that various events enhance the events industry and tourism value, and that much awareness has been given to the economic field of event tourism.

The editors of this volume felt the need for a book that focuses on diverse events in event tourism in Asian countries, such as events on art, sports, food, culture, etc. The book has grown out of the collective experience of many contributors. It provides a broad coverage of event tourism topics that will give a good understanding to academicians, students, and researchers. It will provide information regarding the issues, challenges, and future of event tourism. The book also highlights community development, the participation of women in the event tourism industry, social media, and a new trend of weddings in some unique places.

The chapters of the book reveal the changing trends in the event tourism industry, the contributions of women in sustaining the potential of events and festivals, and the role of event tourism in economic development.

This book is an ambitious effort from professionals in various countries, including India, Sri Lanka, Turkey, Malaysia, Uzbekistan, and Kyrgyzstan. We are thankful to all the contributors.

CHAPTER 1

EVENT TOURISM: PROSPECTS AND TRENDS

ANUKRATI SHARMA[*] and SHRUTI ARORA

Department of Commerce and Management, University of Kota, Rajasthan, India

[*]Corresponding author. E-mail: dr.anukratisharma@gmail.com

ABSTRACT

The tourism and travel industry is such an industry that has developed as the biggest worldwide industry in the 20th century and is anticipated to grow quicker day by day and events have become a big way to gather large amount of media interest, and attracting venture and moreover political interest, and this also lays the role of events combining with tourism. Events are the significant spark in tourism industry. The Asian nations have a wonderful history of showing their societies and cultures through different events and having tourism prospects. Although it is of common knowledge that event tourism as an industry has equally optimistic and pessimistic impacts on destinations and their communities, the impact of properly planned events on tourism has been a reason of escalating significance for destination competitiveness because they add a mixture of attractions to the tourist. Due to this reason only event tourism became established as an independent discipline a few decades ago. The reason behind this study is to assess principally the idea of events and the tourism industry and the connection linking events and tourism through theoretical study. In this chapter, the nature, evolution, growth and expansion of event tourism, and future challenges are discussed.

1.1 INTRODUCTION

Tourism, by and large, is known for its accommodation, hospitality, leisure, and guest attractions. But today event organizers and managers have realized the value of events and this awareness gave birth to the event tourism industry. Going into event tourism it is first and foremost imperative to identify what tourism and event are since they both go connected with each other. The term "event" does not have a universally accepted single definition. The events are extremely flexible or multitalented in nature; as a result the explanation of the events can vary in different situations. Bowdin (2006) observes the word "event" is to reveal particular functions, presentations, performances, or festivities that are deliberately structured and molded to smear special occasions and/or to accomplish particular social, cultural, or corporate objectives and destinations. Events are increasing in recent decades and interest in understanding their importance in the tourism industry has risen accordingly. An occasion or event is happening at a particular point in time and place, or celebrating, or identifying a unique event. An event plays a momentous role in the enlargement of culture, arts, education, and tourism. There are different types of events which are as follows (Figure 1.1):

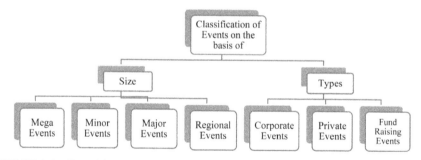

FIGURE 1.1 Types/classification of event, Source: Sharma and Arora (2018).

1. Mega events that are by and large targeted at international markets. They have an explicit acquiesce in terms of enlarged tourism, media exposure, and financially viable impact like the Olympic Games, Commonwealth Games, Maha Kumbh Mela.
2. Minor events include historical, cultural, and musical and dance performance.
3. Major events magnetize considerable local interest and a huge number of participants as well as generating significant tourism income like the Jaipur Literature Festival.

4. Regional events that are designed to increase the appeal of a specific tourism destination or region like Pushkar Mela.
5. Corporate events, such as business dinners, conferences, product launches, and meetings, are used to endorse their company's brand name and products.
6. Private events, such as wedding, birthday parties, and festival gatherings, are used for persons who can book venues.
7. Charity/fundraising events are organized to raise money for a charitable trust such as charitable auctions.

Tourism has a great potential to accelerate progress across sustainable development goals. It can generate quality jobs for durable growth, reduce poverty, and promote fair and inclusive economic growth. Tourism can be explained as an individual traveling to and staying in places outside their normal environment for the purpose of relaxation, business, and different purposes. Events are supportive in destination appearances and attractiveness and on a very basic level, it is useful in advertising and promotion of places that are productive in worldwide competitiveness to pull visitor spending. Combination of event and tourism is explained by Getz (2008) that explains event tourism as an interrelation between tourism management and event management. Tourism management deals with tourism development depending on examining the behavior and motivation of a wide range of sightseers. On the other side, event management transacts with event marketing, blueprint, and supervision of an event. Subsequently, event tourism is in the focal point of these management segments. In other words, event tourism focuses on full use of the abilities of events to accomplish tourism expansion of host communities. Event tourism can be described as planning and advertising of any events, fairs, and festivals to attract more tourist that can act as a technique for financial boom. Present tourism is an increasingly rigorous, commercially structured, and business-related set of activities and as a result, events have gained fame and used efficiently by profit and nonprofit institutions.

1.2 RELATIONSHIP BETWEEN EVENTS AND TOURISM

The rise in per capita income and the necessitate for leisure and pastime activity put up an emergent interest in tourism (Komurcu et al., 2014). In the same way, the demands and needs of the tourists become enlarged and differed. At this point, alternative tourism took place. Event tourism is one of the alternative tourism types that ought to be esteemed by the business endeavors of tourism sector, event managers, and regional authorities as it adds to the advancement of the destination and gives various advantages like economic, sociocultural and environmental development. The rivalry between tourist destinations strengthens and develops day by day. So it is essential to constantly discover the new conduct of diversification of the accessible tourism product and develop new concepts to participate in the market. Event tourism can help destinations to attract more tourists and offers a competitive marketing advantage. Event tourism has been assumed as a strategic approach during the destination management industry and is recognized as a key tourism product (Benur and Bramwell, 2015; McKercher, 2016). Events can act as a final product to destination marketing that will bring opportunities and can create a hugely positive impact on the development of countries as it contributes to the GDP of the country and creates millions of jobs. This development will persist as Asian tourists are increasing in number. For increasing the number of tourists there is a necessity of organizing a planned event that often boosts the development of infrastructure. There are various types of events that are organized in Asian countries and only some of the regions are particularly famed for the meticulous type of event such as:

1. Singapore, Hong Kong, Malaysia especially for MICE tourism
2. Macau for convention and exhibition
3. India for art, religious, and cultural events
4. Thailand for Lantern Festivals—Loy Krathong and Yi Peng
5. Singapore for Neon Lights festival
6. Bali for Gandrung Sewu festival (one of Asia's newer cultural festivals)

The event industry is a vibrant and best ever-growing sector by means of development in tourism. When appropriately facilitated, events have the probability to fabricate the visitor economy, offer media exposure, advance development and improvement, and motivate infrastructure upgrades that incorporate the rise of new associations. According to Lee et al. (2004) on a worldwide scale celebrations, events and occasions with a solid social part are essentially expanding in numbers. According to Milic (2010), the more extensive the range and importance of the events, the higher the level of the global affection and contribution of the worldwide and local celebrities, the larger the awareness of the global media for such an occasion, and simultaneously, the better the promotion of the destination, its culture and traditions, but also its economy, so there is a need to arrange big events and attract the tourist and promote the destinations.

1.3 GROWTH OF EVENT TOURISM IN ASIAN COUNTRIES

The entire area is seeing a sort of blast with certain nations being unquestionably more developed in the curve. Events are an enormous part of the tourism industry and are enduring to grow. Event can be centered on music, sport, learning, or extravagance, they are producing billions of profits and changing the way association, hospitality associations, and resorts work far and wide. At present, there is a vast agreement of rising economies in the area and most of them are currently prepared to understand the capability of event tourism. The Asian countries covered are as follows:

1. *Eastern Asia-Pacific* covers Mongolia, China, Japan, Korea, and Hong Kong.
2. *Southeast Asia* covers Singapore, Philippines, Thailand, Cambodia, Malaysia, Indonesia, Vietnam, Lao PDR, and Brunei Darussalam.
3. *South Asia* covers Sri Lanka, Bangladesh, Pakistan, India, and Nepal.

As per MasterCard Global Destination Cities Index (GDCI) (2017), Asia Pacific destinations finished up half of the world's best 10 most visited urban areas. Besides, the area likewise had the most elevated guest spending among its main 10 cities. The worldwide guest spends in this area shows the area's sturdy developing status (Ho, 2018). Asia and in this way the Pacific (+6%) recorded 343 million worldwide visitor appearances in 2018. The influx in Southeast Asia developed 7%, trailed by Northeast Asia (+6%) and South Asia (+5%). Oceania indicated progressively moderate development at +3% (UNWTO, 2019). Asia's developing economy is positively affecting the business travel showcase. Commencing from January to August 2019, 17% of Asians voyaging overseas were on business/MICE trips, which contrasted with the preceding year and was a better than expected raise of 8% (Rokou, 2019). This development is due to the strategies that are planned to utilize the events in the tourism industry, setting goals and objectives, and discover the possibility to accomplish these objectives in a long run. An event tourism strategy helps to expand the conceivable positive advantages that events can bring to destinations and would prompt progression in the advancement of the event business.

Likewise, Southeast Asia draws in an enormous number of vacationers every year. Its social and cultural history is apparent by means of an abundance of old monuments, legacy sites, brilliant and colorful celebrations, and particular cooking styles and taste that have risen for tourist who look for an inimitable cultural familiarity. Southeast Asia's fairs and social celebrations have come to be the Association of Southeast Asian Nations (ASEANs) best resource for the tourism industry (Shamasundari, 2017). Progressively, nations and territories worldwide assemble together in quest of hosting international sporting events as these bring monetary advantages to the host country; however, these countries are also concerned in gaining elusive outcomes such as stronger networks, sport's culture, expressive dedication, improved identity, and destination promotion. South-East Asia/ASEAN proved it is not simply a dynamic and vibrant location in terms of monetary development however also as a international magnificence venue for many massive worldwide wearing occasions (ASEAN Tourism, 2014). With ASEAN having arranged and being host to such assorted international events, beginning from the Asian games to Commonwealth games; and from worldwide Tennis Tournaments to Asian's biggest Regatta, ASEAN's place a few of the worldwide biggest and most alluring location for overall games is legitimately merited.

1.4 FUTURE CHALLENGE IN THE EVENT TOURISM INDUSTRY

To date, there is hardly a single industry that has not suffered from the fallout of COVID-19. According to the report, as of April 6, 2020, 96% of all international destinations have acquainted travel limitations accordingly with the infection. Around 90 destinations have absolutely or to some degree shut their boundaries to vacationers, whereas a further 44 are shut to specific sightseers depending on country of origin, United Nation World Tourism Organization (UNWTO) said (*Economic Times*, 17th April 2020). Event tourism as an industry would have the hardest impact globally among all economic sectors, due to COVID-19 (Coronavirus) in 2020. Preceding COVID-19, the whole industry, all over the globe, was in spreading out mode from all fronts, that is, international and domestic tourism. However, COVID-19 had slowed down this expansion mode and due to this hundreds of events have been cancelled all over the world, which were planned for tourists. Even for the very first time, the Olympic Games got postponed for an entire year. This is the foremost challenge for the industry to recover post-COVID-19, as people will be very particular while choosing their tourist destinations and the events to be attended. Likewise, they would like to travel such places where travelers are quite less and near the nature like slopes and seashores. In the initial 1–2 years health, hygiene, and safety of tourist will become an important pillar for promoting the destination. And therefore, those who adopt this strategy can be the most honed to recuperate quicker than the others. But presently to stay connected with people various organizers are not cancelling their events instead they are planning virtual events as almost all the world's population is stuck at home. Meetings, gatherings, conferences, and seminars have been overhauled to become virtual events and they are working superbly in keeping individuals associated.

1.5 CONCLUSION

Individuals consistently travel for recreation, diversion, and business reason to attend conference, meetings, and these individuals have added to the development of the destination directly or obliquely and then overall event tourism industry is constructed. Around the world, the events are presently treated as an element of tourism product. Event tourism is concerned with the creation and advancement of events as an ignition for the tourism industry. They offer a unique form of tourist attraction, ranging from simple community festivals to global trade fairs, worldwide sports events like the Cricket World Cup, display shows and exhibitions. More and more events are planned and organized so as to add a value to the tourism industry. Events for the tourist are experiencing an impressive development in number, size, and popularity. Event tourism can be motivated by two reasons: first, dedicated event tourist who especially travel to attend the events and second, tourist attending the events while away from home. It is a testimony that there is a growth and development in the event tourism. Event tourism can probably build up any tourism destination and has an impact on the community through its socio-impact. But due to COVID-19 calamity everywhere throughout the world, it will take effort for the business to recuperate, as the business operations in the event tourism segment should begin at a moderate pace primarily, involving less volume of business and tourist.

KEYWORDS

- **event**
- **tourism**
- **event tourism**
- **inception**
- **Asian countries**

REFERENCES

ASEAN Tourism, 13 October 2014. ASEAN As A Venue For Big International Sporting Events. Retrieved from https://www.aseantourism.travel/articles/detail/asean-as-a-venue-for-big-international-sporting-events, Accessed on 9th May 2020.

Benur, A. and Bramwell, B., 2015. Tourism product development and product diversification in destinations. Tourism Management, 50, 213–224.

Bowdin, G., 2006. Identifying and analyzing existing research undertaken in the events industry: a literature review for People1st. Leeds Metropolitan University: Leeds.

Getz, D., 2008. Event tourism: definition, evolution, and research. Tourism Management, 29 (3), pp. 403–428.

Komurcu, G.B., Boz, M., Tukelturk, S.A., 2014. Festivals as a Type of Event Tourism: Tenedos Local Flavours Festival Sample Case. Istanbul Ticaret Universitesi Sosyal Bilimleri Dergisi. Retrieved from https://www.researchgate.net/publication/312472498_FESTIVALS_AS_A_TYPE_OF_EVENT_TOURISM_TENEDOS_LOCAL_FLAVOURS_FESTIVAL_SAMPLE_CASE.

Lee, C., Lee, Y., Wicks, B., 2004: Segmentation of festival motivation by nationality and satisfaction, Tourism Management, 25 (1), 61–70.

McKercher, B., 2016. Towards a taxonomy of tourism products. Tourism Management, 54, 196–208.

Milic, M., 2010. Significance of events for destination development. SEE Business Travel and Meetings Magazine. Retrieved from https://www.seebtm.com/en/significance-of-events-for-destination-development/, Accessed on 9th May 2020.

Sharma, A. and Arora, S., 2018. Event Management and Marketing: Theory, Practical Approaches and Planning, Bharti Publications. ISBN: 978-93-86608-61-1.

UNWTO, 21st January 2019. Retrieved from https://www.unwto.org/global/press-release/2019–01-21/international-tourist-arrivals-reach-14-billion-two-years-ahead-forecasts, Accessed on 4th May 2020.

Ho, M., 2018. Horwath HTL, Asia Pacific: Regional tourism trends, https://www.hospitalitynet.org/file/152008398.pdf, Accessed on 4th May 2020.

Shamasundari, R., 2017. A cultural journey through Southeast Asia. The ASEAN Post. Retrieved from https://theaseanpost.com/article/cultural-journey-through-southeast-asia, Accessed on 8th May 2020.

Rokou, T., October 2019. Asia remains the largest tourism growth market. In TravelDailyNews.com, Retrieved from https://www.traveldailynews.com/post/asia-remains-the-largest-tourism-growth-market, Accessed on 8th May 2020.

The Economic Times, April 2020. COVID-19 pandemic could cost millions of jobs in global tourism industry: UN body. Retrieved from https://economictimes.indiatimaes.com/news/international/business/covid-19-pandemic-could-cost-millions-of-jobs-in-global-tourism-industry-un-body/articleshow/75194635.cms?from=mdr, Accessed on 16th May 2020.

CHAPTER 2

MAIN TENDENCIES OF HISTORICAL AND CULTURAL TOURISM DEVELOPMENT IN UZBEKISTAN

AMONBOEV MUKHAMMADSIDDIK[1], TURSUNOV BOBIR[2], and RUZIEV SHOHRUZBEK[1]

[1]*Department of Tourism and Service, Tashkent State University of Economics, Republic of Uzbekistan*

[2]*Department of Economic Security, Tashkent State University of Economics, Republic of Uzbekistan*

ABSTRACT

Historical and cultural tourism is one of the main directions of the tourism industry. Determining the role and share of historical and cultural tourism in the development of general tourism, that is, its potential, is one of the main areas of research of representatives of the tourism business and scientists in this field. While many studies focus on the historical and cultural monuments, infrastructure, and geographical location of the country as a potential for historical and cultural tourism, this research on the development of historical and cultural tourism in Uzbekistan offers a new approach to determining the tourist potential of countries to study the largest groups of incoming tourists by country on the basis of a survey and come on this basis jakda compatible focuses on the assessment of the capacity of tourists in the country and compatible as the tourism potential tourists. In economic approaches, the potential is mainly analyzed on the basis of supply factors, whereas in this approach the need to pay special attention to demand factors is put forward. A mathematical formula for assessing the historical and cultural tourism potential is also proposed. This chapter provides the necessary conclusions on the development of historical and cultural tourism in the country.

2.1 INTRODUCTION

In the context of globalization, special attention is paid to the development of tourism services in the economies of developed countries. According to the website of the United Nations World Tourism Organization (UNWTO), in 2018 the number of international tourists worldwide will increase by 6% to a total of 1.4 billion. This means that the number of international tourist visits in 2018 increased by 77 million compared to 2017 (http://www2.unwto.org). Today, historical and cultural tourism, as one of the fastest-growing types of industry, creates opportunities for the creation of new jobs in the economy and the development of related industries.

A number of scientific studies are being conducted to improve the scientific and methodological framework for the innovative development of the market of historical and cultural tourism services in the world. In this process, special attention is paid to identifying development trends in the market of historical and cultural tourism services and developing a model for the development of historical and cultural tourism in the national economy. Among the important issues in the development of historical and cultural tourism is to improve the reception of tourists by tourist facilities and to strengthen cooperation between organizations and intersectoral cooperation in the management of tourist activities.

2.2 LITERATURE REVIEW

Foreigners, Alonso and Ogle (2010), Aminian (2012), Buhalis (2003) on the general economic problems of tourism development in market relations and Azar (2003), Alekandrova (2001), Gulyaev (2003), Avchenko et al. (2010), Zorin et al. (2005), from the Commonwealth countries. Zaytseva (2003), Ismaev (1994), Dmitriev (2013), Skobkin (2011), scholars such as Orlovskaya (2013), Mironenko et al. (2014) have more or less views. Theoretical bases of historical and cultural tourism, practical problems of its development Landry (2013), Pearce (2005), Prentice and Andersen (2003), Richards (2004), Wan Sze and Tony (2006), Genisaretsky (1994) found features of historical and cultural tourism and trends in its development (Genisaretsky, 1994, Gordin and Dedova, 2015, Quarterly, 2002, Kotlyarov, 1978, Podunova, 1999). It is widely covered in scientific research by scientists from Commonwealth countries such as Bereznitskaya (1990).

Theoretical and methodological issues of tourism development in Uzbekistan (Abdurakhmonov, 2013; Boltaboev et al., 2017; Po'latov, 2011; To'xliev and

Abdullaeva, 2006; Pardaev and Atabaev, 2006; Muxammedov and Rakhmatov, 2007; Usmanova, 2009; Adilova, Alimova, Eshtaev, Norchaev, 2004; Khamidov, 2017; Matyokubov, 2011; Ruziev, 2009; Ibodullaev, 2010), widely covered in methodological and research work.

The lack of theoretical and methodological coverage of the issues of improving the organizational and economic mechanism for the development of historical and cultural tourism in Uzbekistan in the abovementioned scientific work of foreign and domestic scientists served as a basis for determining the direction of research.

2.3 ANALYSIS OF THE MAIN TRENDS IN THE DEVELOPMENT OF HISTORICAL AND CULTURAL TOURISM IN UZBEKISTAN

Uzbekistan is one of the countries with rich tourism potential and all the opportunities for tourism development. According to the UNWTO, tourism is the fourth largest exporter of goods and services in the world and the third most profitable. Tourism is one of the fastest-growing sectors of the world economy. Its share in world GDP is about 10%. According to the World Tourism and Tourism Council, Uzbekistan ranks 76th in the world in terms of tourist arrivals in 2018 (www.stat.uz), accounting for 0.2% of the total tourist flow (Uzbekistan's potential in this regard is 2.2%) (www.unwto.org).

Presidential Decree PF-5326 of February 3, 2018 "On additional organizational measures to create favorable conditions for the development of tourism potential of the Republic of Uzbekistan" (2014) and resolutions of February 7, 2018 "On measures to accelerate the development of domestic tourism," all directions of tourism in our country, including historical and cultural tourism, development of pilgrimage tourism, increase in the flow of tourists on inbound tourism, demonstration of the historical and cultural potential of the country to the world and became the main organizational and legal program for the formation of tourism culture.

These approved documents have created a number of opportunities for the effective use of existing historical and cultural resources in the country, demonstrating the potential of historical and cultural tourism, attracting investment in tourism infrastructure, as well as the implementation of innovative directions to promote tourism potential. At the same time, the simplification of the visa regime for foreigners wishing to travel our country, the development of tourism infrastructure in accordance with international standards, and the effective use of information and communication technologies to ensure the completeness of information on each historical and cultural site have also made a big impact on the whole process.

The decree establishes a visa-free regime for citizens of 7 countries for a period of 30 days from the date of entry into the country, abolishes the requirement for tourism vouchers to the Ministry of Foreign Affairs for 39 citizens, as well as the issuance of electronic entry visas for citizens of a number of countries A number of other tasks have been set for the introduction of the tourism system, the preservation of tourist facilities and the development of tourism potential.

"Travel around Uzbekistan!" program for the development of domestic tourism plays an important role in enriching the knowledge and imagination of our compatriots to visit the sights, the holy places, the history of our country. It is also noteworthy that for businesses operating in the field of tourism, a wide range of benefits and preferences are provided for the abolition of certain tax obligations, access to soft loans, attracting foreign investment and other issues.

Tourism is a type of activity that directly affects the social, cultural, educational, and economic spheres of all countries, as well as international economic relations. It is necessary to determine the effectiveness of tourism in the development of the country's economy, based on the characteristics of tourism. The effectiveness of tourism is determined by the number of visitors or the volume of activity of tourist structures that produce a particular tourism product.

Analyzing the effectiveness of tourism in terms of the number of visitors, at the end of 2018 the number of foreigners visiting the Republic of Uzbekistan amounted to 5346.0 thousand people, which is 99% more than the same period last year.

The distribution of foreign citizens arriving in the Republic of Uzbekistan by travel purposes shows that 10.7 thousand of them are for study, 54.0 thousand for commercial purposes, 53.5 thousand for medical purposes, 58.8 thousand for service, 459.8 thousand for service, and 4709.8 thousand came for tourism purposes (Figure 2.1).

The big share of foreign visitors are among the Commonwealth of Independent States (CIS) countries is 1783.8 thousand in the Republic of Kazakhstan, 261.9 thousand in the Republic of Tajikistan, 143.9 thousand in Russia, and 62.5 thousand in the Republic of Turkmenistan. Among foreign visitors, 55.2 thousand went to Turkey, followed by Korea with 37.4 thousand, China with 19.7 thousand, Germany with 7.8 thousand, the United Arab Emirates with 5800, 7000 of which are in France (Figure 2.2).

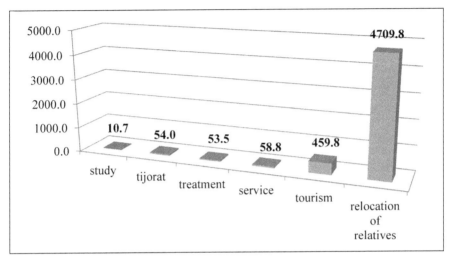

FIGURE 2.1 Distribution of the number of foreigners arriving in Uzbekistan in 2018 by destination.

It is clear from the visit of foreigners to Uzbekistan that the main part of tourists is citizens of CIS countries. This requires the need to improve the mechanisms for promoting the tourism potential of the country in foreign countries.

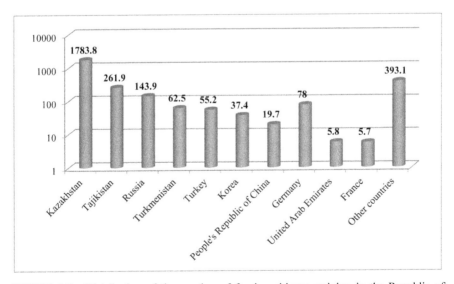

FIGURE 2.2 Distribution of the number of foreign citizens arriving in the Republic of Uzbekistan by country, thousand people.

In 2018, 98.7% (101.7 thousand units) of tourist vouchers were purchased directly by the population. In particular, 44.8 thousand (44%) tickets were sold to citizens of Uzbekistan, 9.9 thousand (9.8%) to CIS citizens, and 31.8 thousand (31.3%) to citizens of other countries. In addition, 15.2 thousand tickets were sold to citizens of Uzbekistan abroad (Table 2.1).

TABLE 2.1 Number and Value of Tourist Vouchers Sold in 2018

	Number, unit	Value, million, Sum
Total of Tourist Vouchers Sold	**105,093**	**140,906, 1**
From them directly to the population including:	101,703	99,971, 3
To the citizens of Uzbekistan on the territory of Uzbekistan	44,800	18,996, 3
To citizens of Uzbekistan by foreign countries	15,194	15,797, 4
To the citizens of the CIS on the territory of Uzbekistan	9900	12,971, 0
To foreign citizens on the territory of Uzbekistan	31,804	57,966, 6

Uzbekistan has created favorable conditions for business activities engaged in tourism services. According to 2018 data, there are 914 hotels, tourist buses, and campsites in the country, as well as 983 tour operators (www.stat.uz).

To continue increasing the flow of tourists, Uzbekistan is actively developing cooperation with many countries around the world. In this regard, intergovernmental and interagency agreements have been signed with a number of foreign countries. Cooperation with international organizations specializing in tourism is also very important.

In particular, since 1993, Uzbekistan has been a member of the UNWTO. It unites more than 150 countries of the world. Since 2004, the UNWTO Regional Office for the Great Silk Road has been operating in Samarkand. It coordinates the support of tourism development on this transcontinental route. Recognizing the contribution of our country to the development of this sector, the member states of this international organization have repeatedly elected the Republic of Uzbekistan to the governing body of this organization—the Executive Council. In 2004 99th session of the Council in Samarkand was organized. The holding of this conference in our country has once again confirmed the effectiveness of comprehensive measures taken to develop the tourism sector in the country by the international community (www.unwto.org).

At the present stage, the regular holding of major events in the country, which bring together representatives of the tourism industry of many countries, plays an important role in ensuring the rapid development of tourism in Uzbekistan. At such international events, experts in the field of tourism discuss the main principles of the industry's development, establish practical contacts.

Since 1995, the Tashkent International Tourism Fair has been held annually. This forum is a good platform for constructive dialogue between partners working in this field.

Since 2013, Uzbekistan has been hosting the International Tourism Exhibition of Uzbekistan "Holiday World," which opens the spring-summer tourist season. This event demonstrates the brightness and diversity of cultures of the regions of the republic, their tourist potential. The exhibition provides an opportunity for local and foreign tour operators to promote their products and services at the beginning of the new season, to conclude contracts with major customers.

The favorable geographical location of Uzbekistan on the Great Silk Road, the fact that the country has more than 7000 monuments of different periods and civilizations, and many of them are included in the UNESCO World Heritage List are the important factors in the consistent development of this industry.

In Samarkand—the capital of the state of the great Amir Temur—many attractions are famous all over the world. The Registan architectural ensemble, the Ulugbek Observatory, the Bibi Khanum Mosque, and the mausoleum of Amir Temur, which rightly contain the most beautiful examples of medieval Eastern architecture, have become the city's visiting cards.

In terms of the number and importance of historical monuments and shrines, Bukhara is not inferior to Samarkand. Mosques and madrassas, trade domes and markets, swimming pools and squares testify to the 2500-year history of Bukhara. In addition, Khiva, Shakhrisabz, and Termez amaze their ancestors with their rich and centuries-old history and unique architectural monuments, as well as inspire such feelings in the hearts of contemporaries (www.unwto.org).

There are 7160 historical and cultural sites (archeological sites, sights, architectural objects, works of art) in the Republic of Uzbekistan, including 1657 in Samarkand region, 1256 in Kashkadarya region, 982 in Bukhara region, 484 in Jizzakh region and Surkhandarya region, 465,370 in Fergana region, 352 in the Republic of Karakalpakstan, 319 in Tashkent, 311 in Khorezm region, 296 in Namangan region, 264 in Tashkent region, 203 in Andijan region, 169 in Navoi region, and 32 in Syrdarya region. fuels (Figure 2.3).

FIGURE 2.3 List of historical and cultural sites (archeological sites, sights, architectural objects, and works of art) located in the Republic of Uzbekistan.

Today, widespread tourism in foreign countries requires the widespread introduction of new forms of tourism, creating the necessary conditions for the development of tourism in our country.

Event tourism, in turn, will allow us to attract more tourists through the coverage of spiritual, educational, cultural, and sports events organized in our country. These include national holidays and festivals, theatrical performances, film and theater festivals, flower festivals, fashion shows, auctions, various music competitions and festivals, and sporting events (Resolution of the Cabinet of Ministers of the Republic of Uzbekistan, 2014).

According to experts' thought, the development of this form of tourism in the near future will lead to a sharp increase in the number of tourists compared to other forms of tourism.

In order to ensure sustainable development of tourism in all regions of the country, the State Committee for Tourism Development and the Ministry of Culture organized the Sharq Taronalari Music Festival, Asrlar Sadosi Festival of Traditional Culture, Tashkent International Photo Exhibition, Teatre. Uz International Theater Festival, Maqom International Festival, Tashkent International film forums, gastronomic events, and other international and national cultural events.

In particular, the Decree of the President of the Republic of Uzbekistan dated May 19, 2017 and the Cabinet of Ministers of the Republic of Uzbekistan dated June 30, 2017. According to the Resolution No. 450 (Resolution of the Cabinet of Ministers of the Republic of Uzbekistan, 2017), measures to accelerate the development of tourism potential of Bukhara and Samarkand regions were approved. The resolution provides for the organization and holding of annual thematic festivals in Samarkand region, such as "Samarkand breads," "Samarkand craftsmen," "National dishes," "Oriental sweets," the organization of information tours for foreign tour operators and the media, preparation of tourist maps of excursions, as well as the promotion of the tourism potential of Samarkand on popular foreign TV channels, information about the sights and rich history of the region on the World Wide Web and social networks through extensive advertising and promotion of the brand of the city of Samarkand is shown.

Carrying out a large-scale advertising campaign and promotion of the Bukhara brand through the festivals "Silk and Spices," "Melon Festival," "City Day," "Oriental cuisine," "Craftsmen of Bukhara" on the basis of Bukhara region, organization of info-tours for foreign tourism organizations and Representatives of the mass media, as well as the promotion of tourism potential on popular foreign TV channels, placement on special sites of the Internet and popular social networks, writing articles on historical and landmarks The smell is focused.

All regions of the country have a rich historical and cultural heritage. Systematic holding of various cultural events and festivals in all regions with the use of event tourism leads to the socioeconomic development of the regions. At the same time, the holding of cultural events through real tourism will allow to demonstrate the tourism potential of our country to foreign citizens, as well as to coordinate organizational and intersectoral relations between the entities engaged in tourism.

2.4 ANALYSIS RESULTS OF HISTORICAL AND CULTURAL TOURISM POTENTIAL IN UZBEKISTAN

Factors of development of historical and cultural tourism, based on the analysis of the results of the study, will allow identifying the first target groups of historical and cultural tourism in our country.

Methods for determining the demand for historical and cultural tourism potential are different from each other at each stage and require special consideration. The use of the most basic and simple methods of sociological research from a methodological point of view. Because at this stage, the need to visit the country needs to be clear enough. Modern communication technologies make it possible to conduct sociological surveys that cover not only specific regions, but also a number of sociodemographic characteristics. The disadvantage of these approaches is that the probabilities of selection are distorted, and sociological research may not reflect the social structure of the choices being studied. However, given the description of our study, there is no reason to assume that the results obtained for different social groups will vary significantly. Nevertheless, goal-oriented questions can be supplemented with questions about the social and demographic characteristics of the respondents in order to correct the alleged violations. Therefore the survey included a study of the following characteristics: age, nationality, type of professional activity, gender, marital status, level of education, contact with the local diaspora, presence of acquaintances or relatives in Uzbekistan (Appendix 1).

The first group of questions revealed the awareness of the respondents about Uzbekistan and its historical attractions. The results are shown in Figure 2.4.

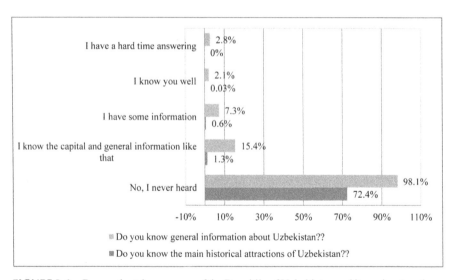

FIGURE 2.4 Respondents' awareness of the Republic of Uzbekistan and its main attractions.

Despite the country's efforts to gain recognition in the global tourism market, there is a low level of public awareness of Uzbekistan. Less than 10% have enough imagination about the country. At the same time, the work on the level of awareness of the most important historical attractions of the

Main Tendencies of Historical and Cultural Tourism 19

country does not meet the demand. Only 3% of respondents have a level of awareness of Gina historical attractions. It is very important for tourists to be informed about the country and its historical and cultural tourism opportunities so that it can be considered as an alternative in the choice of travel destinations.

Based on this data, there was no point in assessing the tourism potential. Because even in a large general selection, the number of respondents who were aware of the historical and cultural monuments was less than 50 people. Based on these data, an error in estimating tourism potential would have led to a large statistical error. At the same time, there is no trend in terms of dependence on demographic data.

We narrowed the selection of historical and cultural tourism potential to be assessed on the basis of demographic factors, based on the theory of spatiality, on the principle of belonging to the region. According to this method, the greatest demand for attracting tourist flows existed in the regions directly adjacent to the tourist area. Repeat selection was determined on the example of the People's Republic of China, Kazakhstan, the Russian Federation, Turkey, and India. The results are shown in Figure 2.5.

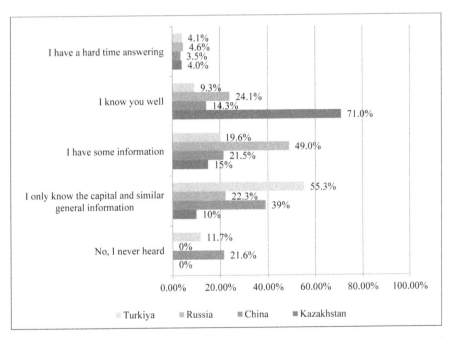

FIGURE 2.5 The level of awareness in the nearby major countries about the country and its main attractions.

As can be seen from Figure 2.5, the level of awareness among the population of large countries in the vicinity of the country and its main attractions is much higher, which confirms the theory of spatiality. But the level of awareness varies significantly depending on which country it is. Residents of neighboring Kazakhstan are familiar with Uzbekistan. The reason for this is not in the neighborhood, but in the unity of customs and traditions. It was found that 71% of the selected population of Kazakhstan is familiar with the historical and cultural attractions of Uzbekistan.

It was found that the level of awareness of the citizens of the Republic of Turkey about the sights of our country is low. However, Turks also belong to the family of Turkic peoples. However, Turkey is far from Uzbekistan compared to the countries studied. Only 9.3% of respondents in Turkey said they were familiar with the country's historical and cultural attractions.

Russia and China are at a moderate level of awareness of Uzbekistan's historical and cultural sites. In Russia, the population with some information about the main attractions of Uzbekistan is 73.1%. In the PRC, this group includes only 35% of respondents. More than 60% of respondents in this country either have no idea about the historical and cultural heritage of Uzbekistan or only have a general idea. The second survey found that respondents had a higher level of knowledge about attractions in the country than those who took part in the first survey.

The main conclusion of this part of the analysis is that the demand for the main tourist potential of Uzbekistan is concentrated in the neighboring countries. Because the level of recognition of historical and cultural attractions outside the region is relatively low.

The main countries with the main potential for outbound tourism in the region are China, India, Russia, Kazakhstan, and Turkey. The assessment of tourism potential under the first stage will be carried out for this group of countries. To do this, the level of awareness of the historical and cultural attractions of Uzbekistan will be assessed across each country. Among the groups familiar with the cultural sites of Uzbekistan, the share of those who consider Uzbekistan as an option to visit will be determined. Then the assessment of historical and cultural tourist potential is carried out according to the following formula:

$$TP_1 = \sum_{i=0}^{n} F_i \times W_i \times O_i \qquad (2.1)$$

where

TP_1—demand for the overall potential of historical and cultural tourism in Uzbekistan in the first stage;

Main Tendencies of Historical and Cultural Tourism

i – the serial number of the country sending the tourists;
F_i – The share of citizens of the country who are aware of the historical and cultural sites of Uzbekistan;
W_i – The share of citizens of Uzbekistan who are considering the possibility of visiting historical and cultural sites;
O_i – The total number of outbound tourist flows out of the country.

The results of the assessment of awareness of historical and cultural sites of Uzbekistan for citizens of all countries, except India. The assessment for India showed that 5.1% of respondents said they were aware of cultural sites. The peculiarity is that most of the respondents in this country mentioned religious objects, especially objects related to the history of Buddhism and Islam.

The share of those who are aware of the historical and cultural sites of the country, considering the possibility of visiting Uzbekistan, according to formula 2.1, and the results of the general assessment of tourists are given in Table 2.2.

TABLE 2.2 Demand for Historical and Cultural Tourism Potential of the Republic of Uzbekistan for First-Stage Tourists

Country	Awareness of Historical and Cultural Sites of the Republic of Uzbekistan (%)	Considering the Possibility of Visiting Uzbekistan (%)	Total Mobile Tourist Flow (million)	Demand for Tourist Potential Is One Thousand People
China	14.3	0.2	142	40.6
India	5.1	0.4	40	8.9
Russia	24.1	1.6	42	162.0
Kazakhstan	71.0	4.1	10	291.1
Turkey	9.3	0.4	8	2.8
Overall				**507.4**

The demand for tourism potential at this stage is limited by the low level of awareness of the opportunities for historical and cultural tourism in Uzbekistan. As these opportunities are better known to Kazakhstan and the Russian Federation, these two countries form the basis of tourists at this stage. Only 2–4 people out of a thousand in the major Asian markets of China and India consider Uzbekistan as an travel option. In the first case, this is due to the proximity of the regions of Western China. Low level of awareness and lack of reasons to travel to Uzbekistan are of great importance for the development of historical and cultural tourist attractions of the country.

The second stage of determining the demand for historical and cultural tourism potential has not yet identified a specific tourist destination, but the demand includes tourists defined by the similarity of the culture. The research methodology in this case may be the same as that used in the previous step. All tourists in this group also form a demand for tourist potential. Theoretically, the region could attract all the tourists in this group. The tourist is less likely to meet the need as they can choose other destinations that meet their selection criteria.

Therefore the method of assessing tourism potential is divided into two periods. In the first period, an assessment of the demand for travel in the tourist destinations of a particular cultural group will be conducted. In the second period, it is necessary to separate this potential between the countries that demand it.

In the first phase, it is necessary to identify a group of cultures that can be included in Uzbekistan. In practice, this refers to destinations that are similar in their historical and cultural value to tourists. In many ways, the historical and cultural heritage of Uzbekistan is compared by foreign tourists to the culture of the Middle East and Central Asia. This includes Turkish-speaking countries such as Turkey and Azerbaijan, as well as Arab countries. Because there is no clear distinction between these two cultures, with which most tourists are closely intertwined.

In the second stage, an assessment of tourism potential for the Middle East and Central Asia was conducted. An additional similarity here is that in this case the application of filtering according to the spatial model of the countries sending tourists is unreasonable. The countries of the Middle East and Central Asia are generally well known to many tourists from all over the world. Therefore the assessment was conducted separately for the countries under study. Accordingly, it is necessary to first assess what percentage of the world's population is aware of the region's major historical and cultural sites. The results are shown in Figure 2.6.

It was found that the level of awareness of the Middle East and Central Asia as a whole is many times higher than in Uzbekistan in particular. Only 8.2% of respondents are not familiar with the region at all due to the fact that the general level of information in the selection varies.

After that, the tourist potential of the whole region was assessed. According to the assessment, 5.7% of respondents consider the possibility of traveling to the country. We calculate the demand for tourist potential according to the formula (2.1):

$$ТП_2 = 0.201 \times 0.057 \times 580 = 6.64 \; млн. киши. \tag{2.2}$$

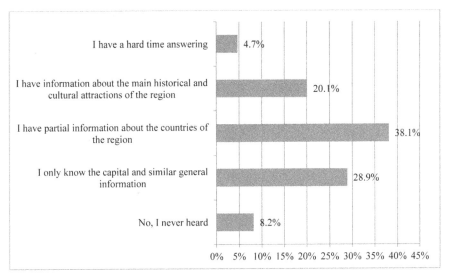

FIGURE 2.6 Respondents' awareness of the Middle East and Central Asia and its main attractions.

Thus the demand for the total tourist potential of historical and cultural tourism in the region is 6.64 million constitutes a person.

In the second period, it is necessary to distribute the demand for the historical and cultural tourism potential of the region to determine its share in the Republic of Uzbekistan. In other equal conditions, the same value of historical and cultural potential and the effectiveness of the implementation of tourism potential are distributed equally among all areas of tourism potential.

In practice, this does not happen because different countries realize their tourism potential with different efficiencies, as well as display different values from a historical and cultural point of view.

Much of the scientific work in the field of assessment of historical and cultural tourism potential depends on the effectiveness of its implementation. At the same time, tourist resources such as historical and cultural sites are considered on an equal footing with the development of transport infrastructure, security, quality of services provided in tourist accommodation. Such an approach, in our view, is completely fair. Historical and cultural tourism meets the demand for historical and cultural sites of the peoples living in the territory of our country. Transport infrastructure and accommodation do not meet these requirements but rather the requirements that arise in the process of meeting the basic needs for historical and cultural sites. Satisfaction of these requirements will affect the implementation of this basic requirement but will not replace it. It is necessary to distinguish the tourist factors that shape the factors influencing the implementation of the proposal for historical and cultural tourism.

Based on these initial conditions, the assessment of the tourist potential is the number of objects, the assessment of historical and cultural value of the tourist potential. But according to the methods we have considered before, the material objects of historical and cultural tourism are only part of the problem. The second part is the spiritual heritage and culture of the people.

The lists of UNESCO cultural heritage sites are the most convenient for the assessment of tangible and intangible heritage. These lists bring together the most important cultural sites located in the country or on the territory of a number of countries. The number of countries and facilities on their territory is given in Table 2.3.

TABLE 2.3 Number of UNESCO Historical and Cultural Sites in the Region (https://ich.unesco.org)

Country	Material Objects	Nonmaterial Objects	Overall
Uzbekistan	4	7	11
Turkey	17	16	33
Turkmenistan	3	3	6
Eron	21	13	34
Iraq	5	3	8
Jordan	5	1	6
Syria	6	1	7
Azerbaijan	2	11	13
Kazakhstan	3	8	11
Tajikistan	1	3	4
Kyrgyzstan	2	8	10
Afghanistan	2	1	3

The general distribution of UNESCO cultural heritage sites is shown in Figure 2.7.

Most of the cultural heritage sites are in the two countries in the region, namely Turkey and Iran. They account for 46% of the facilities. Azerbaijan and Kazakhstan and Uzbekistan are in the second group of the share of historical and cultural tourism potential of the region with 8%. The share of this region in the total tourist potential is 531,000 tourists. But if countries with war, international isolation, or other factors characterized by a very low level of security are excluded, the picture will be even better. That is, the historical and cultural tourism potential of the region in these countries cannot be realized from a security point of view. The tourism business is in them, practically nonexistent or very poorly developed. Such countries in the region include Afghanistan, Iraq, Syria, as well as Jordan, which borders Syria, Tajikistan due to its proximity to Afghanistan, and Iran, which has conflicting relations with a number of countries at high risk of tension. In this case, the share of Uzbekistan in the demand for historical and cultural tourism potential of the region is 13.1%, which is equal to 870 thousand.

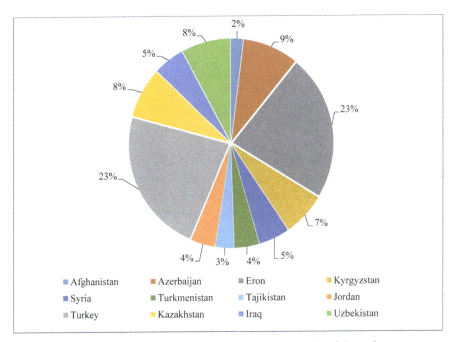

FIGURE 2.7 Distribution of UNESCO cultural sites by countries of the region.

The third stage is the simplest in terms of determining the demand for historical and cultural tourism potential. It is determined by the total number of tourists coming to the country for purposes other than historical and cultural tourism. Therefore it is not difficult to evaluate it.

The total number of foreigners visiting Uzbekistan in 2018 will reach 5 million. More than 346,000 people. But traditionally the main share in this figure falls not on tourist trips but on trips made for personal purposes. Figure 2.8 shows statistics on target agreements for Uzbekistan.

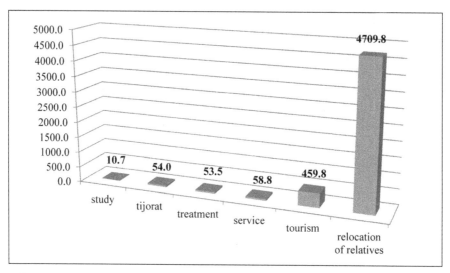

FIGURE 2.8 Distribution of the number of foreigners arriving in Uzbekistan by destination in 2018 by destination.

The data show that the growth observed in 2018 was mainly due to visits for personal purposes, whereas the development dynamics of visits for tourist purposes was not so positive and did not exceed 459.8 thousand people. If the number of tourist visits to Uzbekistan is excluded from the total number of visits, the demand for tourism potential at this level will reach 2 million.

The total demand for historical and cultural tourism potential in Uzbekistan is 5.57 million soums. constitutes a person. But these numbers should not be confused. Because they reflect a large influx of people coming to the country for personal purposes. This is due to the fact that many millions of Uzbek families currently living in other countries come to Uzbekistan to see their relatives and friends. Visits to relatives are a factor in shaping the demand for historical and cultural tourism potential. When tourism products are constantly updated and new activities are developed, historical and cultural tourism is one of the favorable factors of development because it can attract this group of tourists.

In addition, this group of tourists is well acquainted with our country and does not feel the need to invest in infrastructure and services. On the other hand, the economic efficiency of this type of tourism is much more limited for the country, and such tourists spend less on accommodation, meals, excursions, the main items of tourist spending.

The main requirements for the development of historical and cultural tourism are countries with historical ties, located near or on the borders of Uzbekistan. In the territory of these countries, Uzbekistan is well known and can be considered by tourists as one of the options for visiting historical and cultural sites. At the same time, there is a low level of representation of the Republic of Uzbekistan in the world community as a rich historical and cultural center. This is a clear shortcoming.

Between 531,000 and 870,000 tourists may be attracted to the country, primarily at the expense of Turkey and Iran, based on their similarity to the cultures of the Middle East and Central Asia. In terms of security concerns in many parts of the world, the country needs to offer cheaper and safer routes for tourists to visit. This, in turn, could be an alternative to countries with developed historical and cultural tourism destinations, such as Iran and Turkey.

In the analysis of the demand for the potential of historical and cultural tourism, it is necessary to pay special attention to the large number of endogenous and exogenous factors identified in the first chapter of the work. For example, the development of tourist infrastructure, the level of security, the development of the catering system, car rental, the availability of guides and the level of professional training, natural climatic conditions, and ecology. It is important to understand that all these factors do not constitute, expand, or shrink the historical and cultural potential but affect its realization. However, this approach can be applied in the context of analyzing the potential of historical and cultural tourism.

For example, if the stock of hotel rooms and apartments is full during the high season, from the point of view of historical and cultural tourism, this will not affect the demand for potential, but may make it difficult to realize. On the other hand, in terms of developing tourism potential in general, the number of hotel rooms is a potential limiting factor.

Prior to the declaration of independence, tourism in Uzbekistan was organized in Moscow, and contacts with foreign tourism organizations were carried out through the firm Intourist, which has offices in all allied republics. Transportation was provided by Moscow Aeroflot and all financial information was coordinated through Moscow. After gaining independence, Uzbekistan has the opportunity to establish not only transport links but also relations with the world tourism market.

The creation of its own organizational and economic mechanism of the tourism industry began with the creation of the national company "Uzbektourism." The national company has become the main coordinating body in the territory of the Republic of Uzbekistan, forming a single state policy in the field of tourism.

Uzbekistan has modernized its airport, air fleet, railways, and highways. Some major projects have been implemented, Tashkent airport has been modernized. Regional airports have been modernized.

Enterprises engaged in tourism in Uzbekistan have received benefits, the licensing of tourism activities has been liberalized and facilitated in order to stimulate tourism activity. Companies providing tourist and excursion services are exempt from VAT. At a certain stage, there was a significant increase in the activity of tourism, and by 2009, the annual inflow of tourism amounted to 1 million. The number of tourists has stabilized.

As a result of parliamentary control, it was noted that the law "On Tourism," adopted in 1998, did not meet the requirements of the time and some of its norms should be harmonized with modern requirements. In 2017, it became clear that the level of tourist inflows into the country does not correspond to the existing tourist resources at all. This is especially true of the rich historical and cultural heritage that can be compared to the cultural heritage of Ancient Greece and Rome. Suffice it to say that the UNESCO World Heritage list includes more than 4.5 thousand sites located in the territory of the Republic of Uzbekistan.

In this regard, the president of the Republic of Uzbekistan Sh. Mirziyoyev decided to develop a concept for the development of tourism in Uzbekistan in the medium term, as well as developed a program of measures to implement this concept. Within the framework of this Concept, the Uzbektourism National Company was liquidated and the State Committee for Tourism Development of the Republic of Uzbekistan was established. The organizational structure of the State Committee for Tourism Development is formed on the principle of functionality. With the exception of the Silk Road Office, it brings together all international affairs under the Silk Road Restoration Program. In addition, the structure is divided into regional structures for several major tourist regions of the country. Within the functional structure, each department of the Committee is responsible for its own functional area.

Coordination between the various functional units is carried out at the level of the central administrative apparatus of the Committee. The central office focuses on the coordination of most of the state units. Coordinates foreign and domestic tourism, which is part of separate organizational units, as well as issues of standardization and certification.

Within this organizational structure, a whole range of issues is carried out, from attracting tourists to providing services by types of tourist activities. It is noteworthy that the Central Office is organized as a separate department in the organizational structure of the Department of Marketing Research and National Tourism Product Promotion.

The distribution of the mutual functions of attracting and serving tourists cannot be said to be fully justified. Because the functions of attracting and serving tourists are so closely intertwined, each of the two independent structures attracts powers. At the moment, none of them directly responds to the results of tourist trips. If the level of service is unsatisfactory, efforts to attract tourists and improve the level of service will be ineffective. In this case, the description of the category of tourists and the system of services must be mutually agreed. If the routes developed by the department attract tourists who are not interested in them and are not satisfied with the price or quality of service, the result of the work will also be unsatisfactory.

Today, tourist service has a detailed nature, ranging from attraction and service to communication to feedback. The organizational structure of the Committee should include these tasks in the list of important tasks.

The development of the institutional structure of tourism management has been considered by scientists of the republic as a matter of development of the tourism sector. In particular, studies have shown that there are no priorities in the field of tourism. The program of measures developed in accordance with the concept of tourism development in Uzbekistan in the medium term has a general character and covers many factors that affect tourism. However, this concept does not clarify the main issues of positioning in the world tourism market, the main directions and categories of tourists, certain indicators for assessing the effectiveness of tourism activities, the mechanism of impact of activities on tourism activities. The business processes within the framework of the implementation of the concept are also not defined.

This problem is caused by the lack of organizational and intersectoral coordination between government and tourism enterprises, as noted in scientific research.

Along with the Tourism Development Committee, the Ministry of Foreign Affairs, the Ministry of Culture, the Ministry of Internal Affairs, the Customs Committee, Uzbekistan Airways, Uzbekistan Railways and a number of other structures are involved in tourism. Today, each of these structures fulfills its functions in the framework of the implementation of the concept of medium-term development of tourism in Uzbekistan. A mechanism of cooperation between this agency and government agencies is developing.

Statistics of visits for historical and cultural purposes show that the majority of tourists visit several sites located in several regions. Cheapness and adequate development of transport infrastructure serve this purpose. At the same time, the territorial principle of governance leads to a greater separation of affairs in the regions. As a result, it hinders the dissemination of the best knowledge. At the same time, the competition between the regions does not always correspond to the tasks of developing the general system of tourist services.

Prior to the implementation of the concept, the national company Uzbektourism was operating in the country, which had a number of state-owned facilities on its balance sheet, combining administrative and economic functions. Such a system would ensure the integration of administrative and economic structures. But practice has shown that such integration leads to the negative consequences associated with the monopolization of the market. In addition to integration issues, it is necessary to address the issue of creating and developing an appropriate competitive environment.

The ongoing work on the promotion of the tourist brand of the country abroad shows that the integrated approach is not fully formed. Accepting a trademark is a complex and lengthy process. It is more difficult to emphasize the uniqueness of a country in terms of the number of Middle Eastern countries that have much in common with the population of the Far East, Europe, and America. The country's position through the Silk Road approach cannot be considered successful. A number of countries in the region are making use of this historical direction. This does not help to emphasize the uniqueness. Uniqueness can be achieved through a unique experience and the formation of tourist impressions. In the process of defining a strategic path on the basis of promotional activities and following it at all stages of communication with tourists, not only government agencies and tour operators but also the entire information space where tourists receive secondary information should be involved and based on it. The process of visiting the country should take into account the formation of an authentic image.

In line with modern approaches to shaping the image of a tourist destination, tourists use a variety of methods to obtain information. Official information often does not play a significant role in this process. Much of the information used by tourists is decentralized. These are various reviews on specialized sites, reviews from acquaintances, colleagues, and relatives. At the same time, this information may not be about the general journey but its individual aspects. For example, accommodation, catering, transportation infrastructure, and more. It is not possible to control the dissemination of relevant information by administrative means. Every enterprise and government agency involved in the provision of tourist services should have mechanisms to provide information to tourists and control information, the dissemination of positive information, and the rapid response to negative reviews.

The system of information support of the organizational and economic mechanism should be studied independently. In the current situation, the availability of complete and objective information is a necessary condition for timely and reasonable decisions, both at the state level and by individual economic entities in the field of tourism. Modern information technologies offer a wide range of opportunities to collect and process information, thereby determining the amount of valuable information. For the successful development of business in the field of tourism, all decisions by tourism enterprises should be made on the basis of generalized and verified experience, an extensive and objective database. Studies have shown that the majority of tourism enterprises do not rely on such integrated data, forming a unique information system based on their own experience. Another way for them to develop is to learn from the experience of other businesses that are demonstrating efficiency.

The only subject of tourism activity that seeks to integrate and process large amounts of data is the State Committee for Tourism Development.

The first problem is the lack of necessary computing resources, software and hardware for the given tasks. The existing organizational structure does not have the necessary staffing and funding.

The second problem is the quality of the information. First of all, it is unknown to what extent the data obtained and the completeness and reliability of the research commissioned by the Committee are within the scope of the statistical report. According to the results of our research, the majority of tourism businesses consider the work of data collection to be unimportant and often present it with little clarity. The data collection methodology also does not take into account the possibility of data distortion. The attitude of the committee itself to the collection of statistical information is not uniform. There is an opinion that information is not in demand, the tasks of collecting and processing it are seemingly formal.

The third problem is the lack of mechanisms for disseminating the results of analytical data processing in the network. Even the information currently provided to tourism enterprises, according to the survey, is not available to all organizations involved in tourism. However, it is observed that the information is provided in a form that is less suitable for use by small businesses, which form the basis of the tourism industry. This, in turn, shows that companies do not have the knowledge and resources needed to process this data and turn it into management decisions.

Currently, the development of tourism is one of the priorities of the Republic of Uzbekistan. The concept of medium-term development of tourism in Uzbekistan and a set of measures for its implementation covers virtually all aspects of tourism. These activities also include marketing research, but the concept is not fully focused on marketing research. This can make it difficult to achieve the goals of the concept and reduce the effectiveness of the activities carried out.

The starting point for tourism development is the assessment of tourism potential. Tourism potential is considered in terms of available resources that can attract tourists. These include historical and cultural sites, natural resources, and more. But these facilities are considered to have no potential if they are not focused only on resources, specific segments of the tourism market, and to meet specific needs.

This had a fundamental impact on the definition of measures for the development of tourism. The program of measures for the development of tourism is aimed at the development of these resources without a clear understanding of the relationship between this activity and the increase in tourist flows as a key criterion for the development of the tourism market.

Without a clear understanding of the target travel group and the mechanism of attracting tourists, the development of the resource base presents several important shortcomings.

First, at least part of resource development will not be rational because these resources are not evaluated by tourists. Since the development of the entire resource base of tourism is carried out without taking into account the need for it, certain improvements do not affect the development of the tourism industry or their impact is inconsistent with development. For example, the greatest interest in tourist facilities is formed by relatively low-income tourists who prefer to use public transport or public taxis. The development of car rental services, on the other hand, may depend mainly on the premium category cars for the needs of medium and high-class tourists.

Second, the distribution of resources between different directions can be characterized by significant disproportions, as each of them is not based on what goals need to be achieved. Disproportions can occur between individual components of the tourism infrastructure. For example, high-class hotels of international standards are built, but the system of domestic service or accommodation is not unlikely to be inconvenient for this group of customers.

Disproportions can also occur at different stages of a tourist's planning and implementation of a trip. The greatest interest and attention is paid to capital-intensive projects related to the modernization of infrastructure and hotel complex. At the same time, if the attraction of tourists is not achieved, these measures will be meaningless. It will not be enough to simply form the tourist reception infrastructure and provide informational materials. In order to attract tourists, many factors need to be matched and the impact of the information must be strong enough. At the same time, it will be necessary to provide it against the background of intensive marketing companies from competing countries, which have a reputation as a reliable tourist destination in the market. This work represents a more difficult and costly type of tourism development activity than the construction of hotels, landscaping of monuments, and historical monuments. It is also important to control the number of tourists visiting Uzbekistan and ensure the formation of their positive role models. Otherwise, all efforts to develop the resource base of tourism will be ineffective. All areas of development within the tourist service cycle must develop in a balanced way.

The third type of disproportion is related to the time distribution of events. It is clear that the promotion of a tourism product, for example, takes more time than the construction of hotels or the organization of exhibitions, events, artisan workshops. If a large number of hotels are built at the same time, their occupancy will be low. This leads to bankruptcy, deterioration of service and savings on repairs, meals, other types of hotel expenses that directly affect the level of service. Incoming tourists may face a low level of service and the mass influx of tourists to the country will never increase. The implementation of appropriate measures for the development of tourism must be interconnected. In order to form a positive image and attract new groups of tourists, it is important to provide a high level of service to a limited number of tourists in the early stages.

In general, the modern organizational and economic mechanism of tourism development in Uzbekistan should focus on the development of specific measures for the organization of tourist resources in the target groups in the development of tourism. At the same time, the need to coordinate the types of tourism entities and establish horizontal links between them, as well as the relationship between tourism entities and other foreign enterprises, is relevant.

Building trust in tourists is becoming a very serious factor in promoting in the tourism market in an environment where the amount of information is too large. The process of assessing the reliability of the data obtained is becoming increasingly difficult and complex. Tourist confidence is built on the subject's interaction with the region's tourist environment. This cannot be done on the basis of administrative methods.

At a time when the influence of individual tourism entities is growing and the participation of government agencies is declining, the lack of knowledge, competencies, and resources to address the growing level of tasks and responsibilities in tourism enterprises (many of which are small businesses with limited financial resources) is obvious. is happening. This risks being a significant constraint on tourism development, as these enterprises now have the necessary knowledge (marketing, communication, linguistics) to form a large-scale positive information flow, which allows them to create a problem-solving framework with many other participants to attract mass tourists. etc.) do not have.

2.5 CONCLUSIONS

Based on the above discussion, the following conclusions can be drawn:

1. All regions of our country have a rich historical and cultural heritage. The systematic holding of various cultural events and festivals in all regions with the use of event tourism leads to their socioeconomic development. At the same time, the holding of cultural events through real tourism will allow us to demonstrate the tourism potential of our country to foreign citizens, as well as interorganizational and intersectoral coordination between the entities engaged in tourism activities.
2. The main requirement for the development of historical and cultural tourism are countries with historical ties, located near or on the borders of Uzbekistan. Uzbekistan is well known in these countries, and the fact that tourists visit it for historical and cultural purposes determines their main goals. At present, our country is emerging in the world community as a rich historical and cultural center. This, in turn, shows that with the need to demonstrate the historical and cultural potential of our country to the world through information technology, it is possible to offer safe and affordable destinations for tourists in our country.
3. In the development of historical and cultural tourism in our country, it is necessary to pay special attention to the country's position in the world tourism market, important segments of tourists and mechanisms for attracting them, to develop performance indicators necessary for important business processes and cross-sectoral cultural events.
4. The starting point for tourism development is the assessment of tourism potential. Tourism potential is considered in terms of available resources that can attract tourists. These include historical and cultural

sites, natural resources, and more. But these facilities are considered to have no potential if they are not focused only on resources, specific segments of the tourism market and to meet specific needs.
5. If demographic factors are not taken into account in the development of measures for the development of historical and cultural tourism, the resources invested in this area are inefficiently distributed, as these measures indicate the satisfaction of tourists and whether the services invested meet demand.

KEYWORDS

- tourism
- Uzbekistan
- cultural tourism
- history
- traditions
- tourist

REFERENCES

Abdurakhmonov, K.Kh. (2013). Tourism Management: A Study Guide. Branch of FSBEI HPE "REU named after G.V. Plekhanov" in Tashkent, 248c.

Alexandrova, A.Y.U. (2001). International Tourism: Textbook. Manual for Universities. M.

Alonso, A.D., and Ogle, A. (2010). Tourism and hospitality small and medium enterprises and environmental sustainability. Management Research Review, 33.

Aminian, A. (2012). Environmental performance measurement of tourism accommodations in the pilgrimage urban areas: the case of the Holy City of Mashhad, Iran. Procedia—Social and Behavioral Sciences, 35, 514–522.

Avchenko, P.V., Pogosov, I.A., Zhiltsov, E.N. (ed) (2010). Public Sector Economics, Textbook, P.V. Savchenko, I.A. Pogosova, E.N. Zhiltsova. (Eds).-M.:, INFRA,-M.–763 p.-(Higher education).

Azar V.I. (2003). Economics and Organization of Tourism,-M.: Aspect-Press, p. 439.

Bereznitskaya, H.J.I (1990). Tourism as a Factor of Intercultural Communication. Diss.. Cand. Culturology. St. Petersburg, p. 156.

Boltaboev, M.R., Tukhliev, I.S., Safarov, B.Sh., Abdukhamidov, S.A. (2017). Electronic textbook on "Tourism: Theory and Practice."

Buhalis, D. (2003). eTourism: information technology for strategic tourism management, Pearson; Smith, S. (2010) Practical Tourism Research, CABI.

Dmitriev, M.N. Economics of the tourist market. In Textbook for University Students Studying in the Areas of Service and Tourism M.N. Dmitriev, M.N. Zabaeva, E.N. Malygina. (Eds.)-M.:, UNITY-DANA, 2013,–311 p.

Genisaretsky, O. I. (1994). Design and Culture.–M.

Gordin, V. E., Dedova, M. A. (2015). Comparative study of the role of cultural events in the development of small cities. In: XV April International Scientific Conference on the Problems of Economic and Social Development: in 4 books / Otv. Ed.: E. G. Yasin. Prince 2. M.: HSE Publishing House., S. 471–480;

Gulyaev V.G. (2003). Tourism: economics and social development. M.: In Finance and Statistics.

Hamidov O. (2017). Improving the management mechanism for the development of ecotourism in Uzbekistan. I.f.d. ... diss. Avtoref, Samarkand.

http://www2.unwto.org

https://ich.unesco.org.

Ibadullaev N. Opportunities 2010 to increase the efficiency of tourism resources (on the example of Samarkand region). Iqt. fan. ... diss. Avtoref, Samarkand.

Ismaev, D. K. (1994). Fundamentals of Strategy and Marketing Planning in Foreign Tourism. M.

Kotlyarov, E.A. (1978). Geography of recreation and tourism. In Formation and Development of Territorial Recreational Complexes, E.A. Kotlyarov (Ed.), Moscow: Thought,-238 p.: ill., 16 hp;.

Kruzhalin, V.I., Mironenko, N.S., et al., (2014). Geography of Tourism. Textbook. N.V. Siegern-Korn, N.V. Shabalina (Eds.).-M. Federal Agency for Tourism, 336 p.

Landry, Charles (2013). Culture and Commerce: The Royal Academy and Mayfair. Stroud: Comedia. ISBN 978-1-908777-03-4.

Matyakubov U. (2011). Directions and prospects for improving the efficiency of tourism, taking into account the environmental situation (on the example of Khorezm region). Iqt. fan. nomz. (Diss.), Samarkand.

Muxammedov M., Rakhmatov F. Formation of market relations in the field of tourism and its impact on network efficiency indicators. Service and tourism: Problems of management and development. Proceedings of the International Conference. Samarkand, 2007;

Norchaev A. (2004). The impact of the development of international tourism on economic growth. Economics. PhD (Diss.), -120 p.

Orlovskaya, V.P. Economics of the Tourism Industry: Textbook, E.I. Bogdanov, E.S. Bogomolova, V.P. Oryol; (Eds.) Prof. E.I. Bogdanov, SIC INFRA-M, 2013. 318 p.

Pardaev M., Atabaev R. (2006). Basics of tourism.-Samarkand, SamISI.-74 p.; Tuxliev I. (2010). Basics of tourism.-Samarkand, SamISI. 271 p., To'xliev I., Qudratov F., Pardaev M. (2008). Tourism planning. Textbook. T.: "Economics and Finance". 262 p.

Pearce, D. G. (2005). Distribution channels for cultural tourism in Catalonia, Spain. Current Issues in Tourism 8(5).

Podunova, N.I. (1999). Tourism and Environment. Cultural and environmental aspects of tourism. Ecology of Culture. Research Institute of Culture.

Po'latov, M.E (2011). Modern models for calculating the integrated criteria for assessing business activity // Economic Bulletin of Uzbekistan, Tashkent, no. 4. pp. B.23–B.26.

Prentice, R., V. Andersen (2003). Festival as creative destination, Annals of Tourism Research 30 (1).

Quarterly V.A. (2002). Tourism. Textbook.-M.: Finance and Statistics,-320 p.

Resolution of the Cabinet of Ministers of the Republic of Uzbekistan dated December 5, 2014, No 335 "On approval of the list of objects that cannot be used as collateral and mortgage due to historical, artistic or other cultural value," Annex 1. www.lex.uz

Resolution of the Cabinet of Ministers of the Republic of Uzbekistan dated May 19, 2017 No pp. 2980 "On measures to accelerate the development of tourism potential of the city of Bukhara and Bukhara region in 2017–2019," www.lex.uz

Resolution of the Cabinet of Ministers of the Republic of Uzbekistan dated June 30, 2017 No 450 "On measures to accelerate the development of tourism potential of the city of Samarkand and Samarkand region in 2017–2019," www.lex.uz

Richards, G. (2004). Cultura popular, tradición y turismo en las Festes de la Mercè de Barcelona. In Font, Joseph (ed.) Casos de turismo cultural: de la planificación estratégica a la evaluación de productos. Barcelona: Ariel, McKercher, B.

Ro'ziev S. (2009). Uzbekistan's cultural tourism market and its prospects. Iqt. fan.... diss.-Tashkent.

Skobkin, S.S. Economics of the enterprise in the industry of hospitality and tourism (IGiT): Textbook/S.S. Skobkin.-M.: Master, INFRA-M, 2011 431 p.

To'xliev N., Abdullaeva T. (2006). Management and organization of business in tourism in Uzbekistan. -T.: Gos. Nauch. Izd. "National Encyclopedia of Uzbekistan," 386 p.

Usmanova, D. (2009). Features of the formation of a tourist product and promising directions for its development. It. fan. ... diss.-Samarkand, SamISI,–25 b.

Wan Sze Mei and Tony S. M. Tse (2006). Are short duration cultural festivals tourist attractions? Journal of Sustainable Tourism 14(1).

www.stat.uz

www.unwto.org

Zaitseva, N.A. (2003). Management in Socio-Cultural Service and Tourism, Textbook for Students of Higher Educational Institutions.-M.: Publishing Center "Academy," 224 p.

Zeppel, Heather (2002). Cultural tourism at the Cowichan native village, British Columbia. Journal of Travel Research, 41.

Zorin, I.V., Kaverina, T.P., Kvartalnov, V.A. (2005). Tourism as an Activity, Textbook. M.: Finance and Statistics. 288 p.

CHAPTER 3

EVENT TOURISM IN TURKEY

SERAP AKDU* and UĞUR AKDU

Department of Tourism Guidance, Gumushane University, Faculty of Tourism in Turkey

*Corresponding author. E-mail: serapakdu@gmail.com

ABSTRACT

Turkey is a country with many natural, cultural, and historical attractions, as well as many infrastructure and superstructures such as transportation, accommodation facilities, food and beverage businesses, and communication infrastructure. These features increase the event tourism potential of Turkey as in many types of tourism. Offering unforgettable event tourism opportunities by combining all its touristic supplies, Turkey hosts many different events from music festivals to shopping festivals. There are many national, international, and local events organized in Turkey, and most of these events are followed by large masses. In this chapter, event tourism activities and event tourism potential in Turkey, which connects the Asian and European continents, have been written.

3.1 INTRODUCTION

Tourism movements, which have turned into mass participation with the trilogy of sea, sun, and sand, have directed the visitors, who are in search of difference, to the search for an alternative holiday and over time, alternative types of tourism have emerged. Over time, there has been a great interest in alternative tourism types. Accordingly, there has been an increase in the number of tourists traveling around the world in line with their personal tastes, wishes, and expectations. Alternative tourism types, which provide important experiences for visitors, have provided a significant opportunity to destinations especially have no touristic source as sea, sand, and sun. In this way, the destinations increase the types of tourism and the number of tourists thus increasing the tourism revenues. These alternative tourism types have been differentiated by marketing natural, cultural, and historical values of destinations such as health tourism, sports tourism, farm tourism, cave tourism as tourist products. Event tourism is one of these alternative tourism types and events are an important motivation factor in tourism. Events organized with different themes and contents have become an important touristic source for many destinations. Events have become a major value of economic development for many regions. In addition to reviving the region's economy, the events organized in any destination also have important contributions to the promotion of the region and the revival of touristic resources such as natural attractions, social and cultural activities in the destinations. Event tourism means that various activities such as shopping and culture for destinations, art festivals, sports events, religious events, fairs, and exhibitions are used as a tourist attraction. These events, which increase the number of visitors, also provide significant contributions to the tourist destination. Events organized in a destination provide many advantages such as extending the tourism season, diversifying tourism, strengthening infrastructure activities in the region, creating new sources of income, and contributing to the image of the region. For example, it is known that approximately 7 million tourists visited the region during the 2014 World Cup held in Rio De Janeiro, Brazil. During this 1-month event, Brazil earned approximately $30 billion. Apart from this, Olympic Games, Formula 1, FIFA World Cup, UEFA Champions League, Eurovision song contest, Oscar award ceremony, Grammy award ceremony, Cannes film festival, Rio carnival are examples of big events that have an important potential for event tourism. Millions of people around the world are following these events and making efforts to participate in them. All these events organized internationally, nationally, regionally, or locally have been a significant tourism type that invigorates both domestic and foreign tourism activities of the countries. Event tourism is an important tourism type that is growing rapidly in the world tourism mobility (Getz, 2008: 405). Based on this importance, many destinations around the world try to gain favor from event tourism by organizing various activities. In this context, Turkey's current situation has been discussed in terms of event tourism activities in this chapter.

3.2 EVENT TOURISM MARKET IN TURKEY

Special events are an important tourist attraction and an important part of tourism development and tourism marketing (Yoon et al., 2000: 33).

Correspondingly to the development activities and tourism market in the world, Turkey is an important destination that continues to develop in this type of tourism with organized events that local, national, and international scope. Important events organized until now in Turkey have been presented in Table 3.1. These events in Table 3.1 have made a significant contribution to the tourism of the country. Event tourism that develops with the quantitative and qualitative increase of the events organized continues to benefit the tourism of Turkey.

TABLE 3.1 Examples of International Events Organized in Turkey

Event's Name	City	Year
East Mediterranean International Tourism and Travel Exhibition (EMITT)	Istanbul	Every Year
Formula 1, Grand Prix	Istanbul	2005–2011
International Basketball Federation (FIBA) World Olympic Qualifying Tournament for Women	Istanbul	2012
Winter World University Games	Erzurum	2011
European Youth Olympic Festival	Trabzon	2011
Eurovision Song Contest	Istanbul	2004
U23 World Wheelchair Basketball Championship	Adana	2013
UEFA Champions League Final	İstanbul	2004–2005
FIFA U-20 World Cup Turkey	Istanbul, Bursa, Antalya, Trabzon, Gaziantep, Kayseri and Rize	2013
Summer World University Games	Izmir	2005
Special Athletes Alpine Ski Racing Championship	Erzurum	2012
World Athletics Indoor Championships	Istanbul	2012
WTA World Women Tennis Championship	Istanbul	2013
World Chess Olympiads	Istanbul	2012
World Water Forum	Istanbul	2009
17th Mediterranean Games	Mersin	2013

Table 3.1 shows the international events organized in Turkey. When the table is examined, it is seen that different activities are organized in different provinces in Turkey. This shows that Turkey's event tourism potential and the effort made for event tourism. These events are followed by a wide audience worldwide and are realized with a wide participation. For example, the 17th Mediterranean Games in Mersin between June 20

and 30, 2013 organized with the participation of 3,000,069 athletes and 187 officials in 31 branches (Harman et al., 2013: 1401). There was a high demand for tickets at the stadium with a capacity of 25,000 people, and the tickets were sold out within the first 10 min of the sale. In addition, East Mediterranean International Tourism and Travel Exhibition (EMITT) fair organized in Istanbul has hosted 44,000,321 visitors from 103 countries and 200 tour operators met with exhibitors and visitors in 2020 (EMITT, 2020). These events have made a significant contribution to Turkey's tourism and economy. For example, total spending by foreign visitors coming to Istanbul for the Turkey F1 Grand Prix event organized in 2005 has provided 8 million 232,000 Turkish Lira (TL) direct economic contribution (Karagöz, 2006: 109; Akdu, 2016). In addition, these events are also very effective in terms of destination promotion and marketing. For example, 24 countries participated in the Eurovision song contest organized in Turkey in 2004. Song contest broadcasted live both participating countries and many countries outside of them and Turkey also had an opportunity to make an important promotion in the international arena.

The congress and meeting organization market, which is discussed within the scope of event tourism and which has developed greatly due to the development of technology and science after the Second World War, increased investment and production, and the type of transportation and opportunities, is also an important opportunity for a destination. Especially the financial supports for these events which offer information and experience sharing opportunities for the participants by the institutions and organizations represented by the participants is an important factor that facilitates the development of this market. It is stated that congress and meeting organizations held around the world have doubled every ten years, that is, approximately 10% increase every year in the research reports of International Congress and Convention Association covering the years between 1963 and 2012. It is said that congress and meeting organizations account for about 30% of world tourism income and about 10% of people travelling around the world travel for congress and meeting organizations (KUTO, 2016; ICCA, 2016). In general, when evaluated in terms of conventions and meetings organization, it said that the continued systematic development and growth in Turkey. Concordantly, the first international event is held in 1969 named World Red Cross Congress in Turkey with 1300 delegates participation. Also, it is known that another organization has organized under the name of the World Chambers of Commerce on the same dates with World Red Cross Congress and approximately 1200 international delegates are hosted in this congress

(Arslan, 2008:25; Aksu et al., 2004; Atabaş, 2008: 41). The United Nations Conference on Human Settlements (Habitat II) organized between June 1 and 15, 1996 in Istanbul is known as the largest international organization in the last 20 years and one of Turkey's largest organization for international congresses. For this congress, Istanbul Lütfi Kırdar Sports and Exhibition Palace which was used as a sports and exhibition space between 1988 and 1996 is renamed as "International Convention Centre" and started to serve under the name "Istanbul Lutfi Kırdar International Convention and Exhibition Centre" in the Turkish meeting and convention market (İCEC, 2016). UNICEF, United Nations Educational, Scientific and Cultural Organization (UNESCO), UNIDO organizations which are forming this system, nongovernmental organizations, local administrations, private sector, union representatives, and academicians participated in the HABITAT II Conference with the official delegations of the United Nations. During the 2-week organization, approximately 25,000 participants were hosted in Istanbul (KUTO, 2016: 21; Arslan, 2008: 25; Akdu, 2016: 168). Although there is no steady growth due to the flexible structure of the meeting and congress events, organizing ongoing meetings and congresses in another destination each period, participants' preferences, Turkey has an important place in the event tourism market and has proved that with a lot of international major events. Turkey hosted 221 international congresses in 2013 and showed a significant growth in 2013 through its share of congress tourism. Turkey became the 18th country in the world and the 10th in Europe in 2013. Unfortunately, Turkey could not continue the success in 2014 and 2015 as the number of congresses achieved in 2013. Turkey hosted 190 congresses in 2014 also hosted 211 congresses in 2015 because of the incidents encountered in the world and cancelation the preapproved 69 congresses. Owing to the events around the world affected all countries negatively, Turkey did not experience a great decrease in the general ranking. Turkey was ranked 19th in the world and 11th in Europe in 2014. In 2015, it increased to 18th place in the world and maintained its place in the ranking in Europe. Istanbul became the 8th city in the world with 148 congress organizations in 2015 the ranking of the cities where congresses held. Due to the reasons explained above, Istanbul which failed to achieve the same success in 2018 with 33 organizations, decrease to 46th in Europe and decrease to 84th in the world. Similarly, Turkey decreases 52nd in the world and decrease 26th in Europe with 55 congress organizations in 2018 compared to previous years (İCVB/1, 2016; ICCA, 2013; ICCA, 2019). Statistics are located about domestic and foreign participants of the congress organized in Turkey in 2015–2019 years in Table 3.2.

TABLE 3.2 Statistics About Participants of the Congress Held in 2015–2019 in Turkey

		Year	Number of Participants
Number of participants of the training, task, congress and meeting organization	Total number of participants	2015	2,212,327
		2016	1,810,536
		2017	1,780,820
		2018	1,902,089
		2019	1,850,208
	Republic of Turkey citizens	2015	246,559
		2016	264,728
		2017	228,649
		2018	220,265
		2019	232,646
	Participants of other countries	2015	196,5768
		2016	1,545,808
		2017	1,552,171
		2018	1,681,825
		2019	1,617,561

Source: Republic of Turkey, Ministry of Culture and Tourism (2020).

When Table 3.2 is analyzed, changes are seen in the number of participants every year. However, considering the type of meeting and its structure, it can be said that the number of participants hosted each year is close to each other when evaluated depending on the type and structure of the meeting. Although this situation seems stable, it is, unfortunately, difficult to make a mention about a stable development and standards due to the variable structure of the congress and meeting organization market. Significant developments are seen in the congress and meeting market in big cities such as Antalya, İzmir and Ankara additionally İstanbul. A research report has prepared to point out the Meeting, Incentive, Congress, Events industry market volume in Turkey containing 270 meetings management company by Tourism Media Group. According to the chart showing the top five cities where participants organized the most events in the report, it is seen that Antalya is the city where meeting and event management companies organized the most activities with the rate of 24.3%. Antalya is followed by Istanbul with 22.9%, İzmir with 14.2%, and Ankara with 12.9%. Accordingly to the report, events are organized in May (19%), October (16.4%), April (13.7%) and September (13%) in Turkey. July is the month in which the activities are organized less frequently with 1% (Ataman, 2016; Akdu, 2016). Events organized in Turkey grouped in the chart in Figure 3.1 according to the scopes.

FIGURE 3.1 Events organized in Turkey.

3.2.1 MUSIC FESTIVALS AND CONCERTS

As it is known, music festivals are important events that can be easily integrated with many types of tourism. Visitors can go from where they reside to music festivals or concert events, even outside the country's borders. Although the basis of these visits is music, it can be integrated with many different activities such as culture, health, shopping, museum, and ruins.

Turkey has hosted many national and international music festivals and concerts in many musical genres like Latin, jazz, hip-hop, blues, dance, rock, or electro-music in an extended period of time up to one week in one night. There are examples of the ongoing and previously organized music festivals in Turkey below.

3.2.1.1 ROCK'N COKE MUSIC FESTIVAL

The Rock'n Coke music festival is the biggest music festival that took place at Hezarfen Airport in Istanbul in 2003. Rock'n coke music festival hosted the most famous performers such as Pet Boys Shop, Suede, and The Cardigans. It is the most comprehensive music festival in Turkey owing to the participation of rock singers, famous music groups of the world, and other festival lovers. The second year of the festival, 2004, was very important to lay the foundations for the international recognition and identification of the festival. Rock'n Coke festival reached the international level and had significant followers worldwide by gathering together international and national famous singers and music group such as Mazhar Fuat Özkan (MFÖ), Özlem Tekin, Erkin Koray, Kurban, Athena, Kargo also 50 Cent, Rebel Moves Fun Lovin' Criminals, The Orb, Spiritualized and others. The festival, which is organized regularly by national and international famous performances every year until 2007, continued to be organized every 2 years after this date. Unfortunately, the festival has been organized for the last time in 2013 and it is said that it will start to be organized again soon. The Rock'n Coke music festival takes an average of three days. Participants stay in the camping area opened from Friday by setting up tents daily or two days. Apart from the big stage, there have been various places such as car park, alternative stages, camping area, the amusement park, where the participants can provide all kinds of needs—entertainment needs and shopping area (Akdu, 2016; Binici, 2018).

3.2.1.2 ISTANBUL INTERNATIONAL MUSIC FESTIVAL

Istanbul Music Festival is among the most respected and well-established classical music events in Turkey. The Istanbul Music Festival has played a major role in building up an appreciation for classical music more than 40 years in Turkey. Festival held by the Istanbul Foundation for Culture and Arts (İKSV) first named "İstanbul Festival" in 1973, after renamed as

"İstanbul Music Festival" in 1994. Festival have been hosted Famous chefs such as Kurt Masur, Mariss Jansons, William Christie, Daniel Barenboim and Gustavo Dudamel. Moreover, many celebrity international soloists such as Fazıl Say, Kathleen Battle, Suna Kan, Anne Sophie Mutter, Ayla Erduran, İdil Biret, Shlomo Mintz, and Juan Diego Flore have been hosted by Istanbul Music Festival. The Istanbul Music Festival, the 48th of which will be organized in 2020, has been a member of the European Festivals Association (EFA) since 1977 (İKSV/1, 2020).

3.2.1.3 INTERNATIONAL ANTALYA PIANO FESTIVAL

International Antalya Piano Festival has been organized by Antalya Metropolitan Municipality and continues to held regularly every year since 2000. The festival, which hosted successful names such as İdil Biret, Ayşegül Sarıca and Aris Garrufalis for the first time in 2000, continues to host successful artists with national and international reputations every year. The International Antalya Piano Festival will be held for the 21st time in 2020. It is a member of EFA (APF, 2020; Event Türkiye, 2020).

3.2.1.4 ISTANBUL JAZZ FESTIVAL

The Istanbul Jazz Festival has been held by İKSV since 1994. It is organized in different concert and event venues in Istanbul every year in the first half of July. The Istanbul Jazz Festival covers a very wide geography from Latin America to Northern Europe. Festival offers a wide selection of different music style including pop music, rock, funk, blues, reggae, and so on music to their participators. While this diversity gives audiences different concert experiences, it allows the city to be experienced with another eye by blending the historical and natural texture of Istanbul with its cultural heritage with music. The Festival is carried out in private venues and hosted numerous participants each year. Festival is organized in different places asides from Cemil Topuzlu Open Air Stage such as historical places are Hagia Eirene Museum, Istanbul Archeology Museums, Esma Sultan Mansion also parks all around the city and open spaces such as gardens of private buildings and Camialti Shipyard, ruins of Şan Theater, Beykoz Kundura factory. Istanbul Jazz Festival is one of the first members of the International Jazz Festivals Association (İKSV / 2, 2020).

3.2.1.5 AKBANK JAZZ FESTIVAL

Akbank Jazz Festival is one of Turkey's oldest jazz festivals began with concerts organized in Istanbul for the first time in 1991. Aside from the most important jazz musicians of the world, this festival has supported the new shining stars of new generations. Today it has become a versatile organization with panels, workshops, film screenings, concerts and social responsibility projects. Akbank Jazz Festival, which includes classical and modern jazz as well as electronic and world music projects within the scope of its expanding musical range over the years, is an event that not only jazz music lovers but also many music lovers cannot give up. Akbank Jazz Festival organized since 2006 besides of Istanbul with jazz concerts in Ankara, Eskisehir, Gaziantep, Izmir, Eskisehir, Trabzon, Adana, Erzurum, Kayseri was held in Turkey in many cities such as Kars. The Akbank Jazz Festival held annually with the motto of the "jazz version of the city" and will be organized 30th time on October 8–18, 2020, it is a member of the European Jazz Festival Association (AkbankSanat, 2020).

3.2.1.6 IZMIR EUROPEAN JAZZ FESTIVAL

The aim of the event that organized 26th time in March 2019 is to bring together jazz masters and jazz lovers in Europe and Turkey in the attempt of generating feelings of love, peace and friendship. While jazz artists from Switzerland, France, Austria, Luxembourg, Poland, Slovakia, and Italy meet jazz audiences, many young jazz lovers have the opportunity to listen, love, and learn the jazz music of Europe. The biggest difference of Izmir European Jazz Festival is that it organizes an intensive training program at the festival. The artists, who come to give a concert to the festival, transfer their knowledge to young artists from Izmir with their workshops and master classes. Two successful young people participating in the workshops attend the Siena Summer Jazz Master Classes courses with a scholarship, in cooperation with the Siena Jazz Foundation and İKSEV. To date, 21 young people have taken advantage of this opportunity. In addition, for the last 17 years, the festival's official poster is determined with the Poster Competition of Jazz. Young designers in talents from all over Turkey could join the competition. İzmir European Jazz Festival is a member of the European Jazz Network (EJN) (İKSEV, 2020).

3.2.1.7 KONYA INTERNATIONAL MYSTIC MUSIC FESTIVAL

The International Mystic Music Festival has been organized every year in Konya since 2004 by the Provincial Culture and Tourism Directorate of Konya Governorship. The festival, which has become the meeting point of the traditional mystical music of the world peoples, aims to introduce traditional music and to provide a cultural environment where they can be exhibited as they are, without interaction with popular elements, by preserving their authentic structures and features. Concerts of the festival, where traditional, mystical or religious mystical music of the world peoples are exhibited, are free and open to the public. The concerts are organized in the Konya Metropolitan Municipality Mevlana Culture Center Sultan Veled Hall, and the Semâ Ceremony is performed in the Mevlana Culture CenterSemâ Hall. "Konya International Mystic Music Festival," organized as part of the Anniversary of Hazrat Mevlana's Birth Anniversary Events, is considered as the most respected festival in the world of mystical music. Konya Mystic Music Festival, which has been registered as one of the world's most important mystical music festivals (the 8th best festival in the world) for a long time in terms of its own history, is known all over the world and competes with major organizations now. To date, 129 bands and 785 artists from 45 countries have participated in the Mystic Music Festival and performed for a total of 15.480 min. The last festival was organized for the 16th time on September 22–30, 2019, and organization works are ongoing for the 17th (Konya İKTM, 2020).

3.2.1.8 CHILL-OUT FESTIVAL

Organizers summarize the Chill-out festival as "Started as the 'uncompromising dream' of a boutique team that has remained the same to a large extent and has been bringing the refined style of Lounge FM 96 to life since 2006." The festival, which continues regularly every year, has a relaxing effect in the simplicity of nature. Festival is hosted to national and international soloists and music groups focusing on different music styles. Besides the unforgettable music experience, the festival offers cheerful activities, interesting workshops, and delicious food alternatives. The festival is aimed to develop and increase the number the cultural festival in Turkey to global standards and creating a character in the festival's participants. Chill-out festival is met music lovers in Bodrum and Çeşme besides Istanbul (Chilloutfest, 2020).

Besides of the above-described music festivals, there are lot of ongoing major music festivals organized regularly in Turkey. Some of these festivals are listed below:

- Zeytinli Rock Festival
- Cappadox/Cappadocia Music Festival
- Mersin International Music Festival
- One Love Festival
- International Gaziantep Opera and Ballet Festival
- Gümüşlük International Classical Music Festival
- International Ankara Music Festival
- Ankara International Jazz Festival

3.2.2 SHOPPING AND LIFE FESTIVALS

Shopping festivals are one of the most important events of recent times, which allow people to gain different experiences while shopping. Shopping and life festivals are a type of festival that can be integrated with different events such as concerts and exhibitions and contribute to the region, where many companies such as shopping malls (AVM), streets and streets shops, restaurants and entertainment centers participate, and various discounts are applied during the festival (Akdu, 2016; Tayfun and Arslan, 2013: 195). Life festivals are organized with the participation of all age groups and many different sectors in many themes such as home decor, entertainment and education, which can be called life events together with shopping festivals. Examples of these festivals are given below.

3.2.2.1 IZMIR INTERNATIONAL FAIR

Izmir international fair, bringing together different sectors of Turkey's first and most comprehensive exhibition will be organized on September 3–12, 2021, 89th times. Izmir International Fair, which is a trade fair has more than 1000 companies, and 60 countries, in many different product groups such as health, food, automotive, commercial vehicles, business machines, general machinery, furniture, finance, communication technologies and telecommunications are participated. In conjunction with economic empowerment and increase trade facilities, the fair hosts many events every year. All activities besides the trade fair are followed with interest and eagerly awaited by many people every year from concerts to theatres, from cinema shows to musical shows, from conversation to street shows, and appealing to every segment. The fair, which is open for 10 days, is visited by approximately 1.5 million people every year.

3.2.2.2   ISTANBUL SHOPPING FESTIVAL

The festival combines culture, important historical past, gastronomy, the art of Istanbul with shopping and amusement. Istanbul Shopping Fest has been organized every year since 2011. In addition to discounts and campaigns, the festival includes events that will allow you to live and explore Istanbul with pleasure. The festival is organized not only in shopping malls but also in various central points of the city, modern shopping malls that offer many products at discount prices. It is also wide participation festival that continues with various streets, with concerts, competitions, special fashion shows, colorfully decorated streets.

3.2.2.3   ANKARA SHOPPING FESTIVAL

Ankara shopping festival organized in Ankara is capital of Turkey for the first time in 2012 and continues to be organized on the same dates every year. Among the strategic partners of the festival are the Ministry of Culture and Tourism, Ankara Governorship, Ankara Metropolitan Municipality, Ankara Chamber of Commerce and Clothing Industrialists Association. Apart from these, many companies provide sponsor support for the festival (Tayfun and Arslan, 2013: 194). In addition to shopping opportunities, the festival also includes events such as concerts, exhibitions and shows. The festival renamed as fashion and shopping festival and continues to be organized today.

3.2.2.4   ISTANBUL INTERNATIONAL PUPPET FESTIVAL

The International Istanbul Puppet Festival, which brings together the world's most colorful and successful puppet games every year in Istanbul and organized by the Istanbul Karagöz Puppet Foundation was organized under the general art direction of Cengiz Özek who is 22nd UNESCO Cultural Heritage Carrier and International Puppet and Karagöz artist between October

24 and November 3, 2019. Total nine groups from seven countries exhibited their games at the festival. Besides the puppet games, the festival includes movie screenings, workshops, and exhibitions (Kukla Festivali, 2020).

3.2.2.5 ISTANBUL INTERNATIONAL DANCE FESTIVAL

Istanbul International Dance Festival held with the motto of "Dance for Peace and Goodness" with the participation of more than 5000 social dancers from more than 80 countries from America to Africa, from Europe to the Far East for the 8th time in 2019. One hundred and twenty hours Salsa LA-NY-Cuba, Cha, Zouk, Bachata, Kizomba, Semba, Tango, Hip Hop Vals, Afro House, Tarraxinha, Zumba Classes such as Modern Dance, Reggaeton, Swing, Lindy Hop, Flamenco, Afro Rumba, Urban/Street, Funky, Jazz, Ballet, Oriental, Body Isolation, Sirtaki, Roman Air, Zeybek, Caucasian Dances are taught from the world's most famous dance instructors at the beginning, intermediate, and advanced levels in eight separate halls in 4 days. Within the scope of the dance festival, there are many amusing events such as the performances of Foreign and Local Latin, Hip Hop, Modern Dance groups, workshops, and themed dance parties that will last until the morning accompanied by well-known DJs in five evenings (Dance Fest, 2020).

Besides the shopping and living festivals summarized above some of the events and festivals organized in Turkey are listed below:

- Istanbul International Puppet Festival
- Istanbul Boat Show
- Bodrum International Yacht Show
- Izmir International Puppet Festival
- Istanbul Design Week
- Istanbul Fashion Week

3.2.3 GASTRONOMY EVENTS

3.2.3.1 INTERNATIONAL GAZIANTEP GASTRONOMY FESTIVAL

GastroAntep gastronomy festival is an international festival that has been organized since 2015 after Gaziantep became the city of gastronomy within the scope of UNESCO Creative Cities Network. Gaziantep, located on the northwestern end of the Mesopotamia region where humanity started to live together, be engaged in agriculture and husbandry for the first time, is located in a unique geography that features the characteristics of the Mediterranean and land climates in the region. With the effect of its physical geography, Gaziantep has different diversity of agricultural products and this situation makes a significant contribution to the food and gastronomic product variety of the province and region. All these features have increased the international recognition of the city's gastronomy. Gaziantep, which is the first UNESCO Gastronomy City within the scope of UNESCO Creative Cities Network of the three gastronomic cities in Turkey, exhibits rich local gastronomy with a great festival all over the world. GastroAntep realizes Gaziantep's unique cuisine with the participation of gastronomy professionals, the world famous Michelin star restaurant chefs, academicians, students and residents, local, and international visitors, with the cooperation of Gaziantep Metropolitan Municipality and Gaziantep Development Foundation. Food presentations in various concepts, workshops, workshops for children and adults, animations, cooking competitions in various categories, concerts, and amusement events are organized within the scope of the gastronomy festival (GastroAntep, 2020).

3.2.3.2 ISTANBUL INTERNATIONAL GASTRONOMY FESTIVAL

It is an international gastronomy competition besides gastronomy festival. It is aimed to meet Turkish cuisine with other culinary cultures of the world, the collaboration and information exchange between Turkey's and the world's leading chefs and cooks. Festival held in 2019 for the 17th times following to acceptance of membership in the World Association of Chefs' Societies (WACS) of Chefs and Cooks Federation of Turkey in 2008 an important event in the international sense. International Istanbul Cuisine Days which have "Continental" title by WACS due to successful organizations in the past, provides competition opportunities at an international level to Turkey's young chefs and students. The chefs who succeed in the competitions to be held within the framework of the standards set by the WACS are the owners of both medals and certificates that are valid worldwide. Approximately 30 different countries attend the festival every year (TAŞFED, 2016).

3.2.3.3 ISTANBUL COFFEE FESTIVAL

The Istanbul Coffee Festival was organized for the first time in 2014 at Galata Greek Primary School with more than 14,000 participants. The festival, which continues this journey in Haydarpaşa Station in its second year, continues to be held in KüçükÇiftlik Park as of the third year. The organization emphasized it is not a coincidence for the festival starts and continue in locations bearing collective city memory and culture aims to offer a new festival experience to the consumer combining the speciality coffee and its life culture with the city's texture. As part of the festival, concerts, workshops, seminars, panels and many entertaining activities are organized (ICF, 2020).

3.2.3.4 URGUP INTERNATIONAL GRAPE HARVEST FESTIVAL

Urgup International Grape Harvest Festival held for the 48th time in 2019 is organized by District Governorship, Municipality, nongovernmental organizations, tourism professionals, and farmers. The harvest festival is a cultural and gastronomy festival that focuses to promote the grape of Urgup and its by-products like pekmez (grape molasses), which is one of the most important features of Urgup in addition that call attention to the importance of tourism and agriculture for Urgup (NevşehirValiliği, 2020; Akdu, 2016).

3.2.3.5 HATAY GASTRONOMY ACTIVITIES

Hatay was awarded the title of "City of Gastronomy" in 2017 within the scope of the UNESCO Creative Cities Network. Hatay, which is an important flavor destination of Turkey, reinforces this title with the gastronomy events and hosts many domestic and foreign visitors. For example, a dessert called kunefe is made to share out with visitors within the scope of Hatay Kunefe Festival, which is organized every year between July, 21 and 23. The last dessert made was 75 m long. Apart from this, various events are organized on the gastronomy values of the region such as Local Desserts and Local Soups Competition, Altınözü Olive and Olive Oil Festival, Payas Caravanserai Festival (1st September), İskenderun Fish and Bread Festival (28 March), International Erzin Citrus Festival (November), Erzin Olive and Olive Oil Festival (15–16 October), Hatay Daphne Festival (14th-16 October), International İskenderun Tourism and Culture Festival (1–5th July), International Arsuz Culture and Art Festival (9–16 August), International Samandağ Silk Festival, Kırıkhan Spring Festival (9 May), Samandağ July Festival (11–14 July), Akçalı Egg Festival (30 March), Local Products Fair (18–23 April), Kırıkhan Liver Festival (14 May), Dörtyol Food Festival, Altınkep Competition (Fish-themed) Screening-Hatay-2016, Altınkep Gastronomy Competition, Local Appetizers, Local Desserts and Local Soups Competition (Hatay, 2020).

3.2.4 CULTURE AND ART FESTIVALS

Turkey hosts so many national and international cultural and artistic events each year. These festivals, which include events such as cinema and theater festivals, ballet, book fairs, are generally organized in big cities such as Istanbul, Antalya, Izmir, Ankara, Bodrum, Konya. Below are the examples of events organized in Turkey.

3.2.4.1 ASPENDOS INTERNATIONAL OPERA AND BALLET FESTIVAL

Aspendos International Opera and Ballet Festival is the first opera and ballet festival in Turkey organized in the Aspendos ancient theatre which is about 2000 years since 1994 by Republic of Turkey Culture and Tourism Ministry general directorate of state opera and ballet. Aspendos International Opera and Ballet Festival is attracted intense interest along the Mediterranean coastline, especially in the city of Antalya is hosted local and foreign audiences reaching about 60,000 people each year. Aspendos Opera and Ballet Festival is one of the significant art events held by the State Opera and Ballet. Five years after its start, it gained an international identity and was accepted to the EFA, which is among the respected institutions of Europe. International Aspendos Opera and Ballet Festival is the festival that received the world's first and only "Quality Management Certificate" award (TS-EN-ISO 9001: 2000) in 2015 (Devlet Opera ve Balesi Genel Müdürlüğü, 2020)

3.2.4.2 ANTALYA INTERNATIONAL GOLDEN ORANGE FILM FESTIVAL

The International Antalya Film Festival, which started with concerts and theaters that started to be organized in the mid-1950s in the historical Aspendos Ancient Theater, is one of the well-established film festivals in Europe and Asia, Also, the oldest and longest-running film festival in Turkey. The shows, which have shown intense interest by the public and held every year in the summer, continue to be organized in a festive atmosphere until the beginning of the 1960s. Antalya Golden Orange Film Festival, which started in 1964 under the leadership of Doctor Avni Tolunay has turned into an event where the heart of national cinema beats over the years. The festival is the most important event in the cinema journeys of many master names of Turkish cinema so far. The International Antalya Film Festival, which has been moved to the international platform since 2005 and has become a big cinema event, is a wide-participation festival and is on the way to become an ambitious film festival on the world cinema platform. Films of important and respected figures of world cinema, including Asian and European cinema, also meet movie lovers. Antalya Golden Orange Film Festival, which will be held for the 57th time in 2020, is organized by ANSET under the auspices of Antalya Metropolitan Municipality. Today, Antalya Golden Orange Film Festival, which hosts many national and international famous names, is a member of the Federation of International Filmmakers Associations (FIAPF) (Akdu, 2016; AltınPortakal, 2020).

3.2.4.3 ISTANBUL INTERNATIONAL SHORT FILM FESTIVAL

It is notable as the longest-lasting and most experienced event among the international short film festivals organized in Turkey. This event is organized in order to support the short film, which is based on telling a lot in the context of cinema art in a short time, and which allows its directors to reflect their talents in the most original way, and to prepare an environment for young directors to make their voices heard nationally and internationally. The festival launched in 1978 at the national level, including only films produced in Turkey at the beginning. The festival created an international identity since 1988 above the major interest it received. To date, around 6000 short films have been shown; approximately 1600 foreign guests have been hosted; and 530 interviews and 65 workshops have been launched. The films are presented to the audience in three separate halls, twice, with the participation of the director. In the national section, there is a competition section where fiction, documentary, animation, and experimental films are evaluated separately. All national films that apply to the festival are watched by the selection committee, the films to be included in the screening program are determined, and the best of each branch is awarded by the same committee (İFF, 2016).

3.2.4.4 INTERNATIONAL ISTANBUL THEATER FESTIVAL

Istanbul Theater Festival organized for the first time in 1989. The festival, which is organized every year until 2002, is an international event where local and foreign theaters and dance groups meet with the audience for three weeks in May every 2 years between 2002 and 2017. The productions and societies within the scope of the festival, which continues to be organized every year since 2017, bring different perspectives both to the audience and the art world; national and international, classical and contemporary interpretations are staged within the scope of the Istanbul Theater Festival. Offering a Lifetime Achievement Award to a Turkish and a foreign artist every year since 1997, the Istanbul Theater Festival continues to carry new orientations and works at the national and international level in the field of performing arts each year with its program focusing on educational projects, co-productions and themes related to today's social problems (İKSV/3, 2020).

3.2.4.5 ANKARA ACCESSIBLE FILM FESTIVAL (AFF)

The festival is based on the fact that everyone has the right to participate in cultural life. It was organized for the first time in 2013 to remind that it is a must to create conditions where individuals with disabilities can exercise their social and cultural rights. All film screenings, side events, and workshops within the scope of AFF, which defends that individuals with disabilities should have the opportunity to watch movies with their relatives to participate in a cultural and social event, to develop and use their creative, artistic, and intellectual capacities, not only for themselves but also to enrich the society they are part of are presented as accessible. Current cinema examples are shown with audio description for the visually impaired individuals, sign language for the hearing impaired and detailed subtitles, and post-movie interviews are translated into Turkish sign language. Workshops and all side events within the scope of the AFF are organized with the infrastructure that individuals with visual and hearing disabilities can also participate. These films are compiled in the Library of Disabled Movies and an accessible cinema archive is created (EF, 2020).

3.2.4.6 INTERNATIONAL ISTANBUL BIENNIAL

İKSV has been organizing the Istanbul Biennial since 1987 that aims to create a meeting point in the field of visual arts among artists and viewers of different cultures. Biennial is the most comprehensive international art festival organized both in Turkey and its geographical environment. International Istanbul Biennial plays a major role in the promotion of contemporary artists all over the world besides Turkey. It also offers the opportunity to follow the artistic developments and current discussions in the world and supplementary training in this way both general attendees and the art students through conferences, exhibitions, panel and workshops within the scope of the biennial applied in simultaneous translation. The 17th of the Biennial will be organize in 2020 (İKSV/4, 2020).

3.2.4.7 SEB-I ARUS (VUSLAT (REUNION) COMMEMORATE OF HAZRAT MEVLANA)

Mevlâna Celâleddin-I Rumi, who adopted that everyone understands each other and treats each other with tolerance and frequently emphasized that his view of life was also in line with the Quran and the Prophet Hazrat Muhammed, passed away on Sunday, December 17, 1273, when he was 66 years old. MevlânaCelâleddin stated his death day as the moment of Vuslat (reunion) to Allah, whom he knows as the greatest lover, hence, he accepts that night as "Seb-I Arûs," that is, "Wedding Night." The 746th commemorate ceremony of Şeb-i Arus, which has been organized regularly for 82 years, was organized in 2019 with the motto "VEFÂ VAKTİ (Faithfulness Time)." In addition to the events such as Merasimi, Nevbe (Nevbe is the name of special rhythms performed in the Dervish lodges with the participation of specific rhythm instruments and sounds, and also a special rhythm instrument used during some religious orders.), Tekke pilaf, mesnevi conversation, Gülbank prayer (the name given to stereotyped takbirs, prayers, sung with one mouth by a community), sema (Ayin-i Şerif), Sufi music concert, many events such as exhibitions, photography competitions, and workshops are organized at the commemoration ceremonies (Konya Valiliği, 2020).

It continues to be held regularly in many activities outside of culture and art activities outlined above in Turkey. Some examples are listed below:

- Istanbul International Opera Festival
- İzmir International Film Festival
- İzmir International Short Film Festival
- Antalya State Opera and Ballet Festival
- Antalya International Choir Festival
- Antalya International Folk Music and Dance Festival
- Bodrum International Ballet Festival

3.2.5 SPORTS EVENTS

Many national and international sports events and competitions such as athletics football, tennis, basketball, motor racing, cycling, volleyball, rowing races, regattas, winter sports, and extreme sports are organized in Turkey. Within the scope of these events, many domestic and foreign visitors are hosted every year. Investments such as stadiums and tracks, which are required for the fulfillment of these events, have been made and new infrastructure investments continue to be made according to the need. In this context, it can be said that Turkey is one of the world's most important destinations in national and international sporting events. For many sports that have important resources in terms of natural features sporting events held in Turkey are listed below.

3.2.5.1 PRESIDENTIAL CYCLING TOUR OF TURKEY

Presidential Cycling Tour organized first launched in 1963 under the name "Marmara Tour" by Turkey Cycling Federation and gained International status in 1965. The Tour was taken under the auspices of the Presidency in 1966. The tour was organized for the first time in the "Union Cycliste Internationale (UCI) World Tour" category in 2017. The tour was organized for the second time in 2018 in the "UCI World Tour" category with the participation of a total of 20 teams, 9 of which are "World Tour" teams. Presidential Cycling Tour which is the world's unique intercontinental bike tour reaches a wide access network worldwide including more than 120 countries through national and international television channels primarily Eurosport with live and recorded broadcasting (Tour, 2020).

3.2.5.2 KIRKPINAR OIL WRESTLING CHAMPIONSHIP AND FESTIVAL

Kırkpınar Oil Wrestling is a traditional Turkish oil wrestling sports tournament organized by Edirne municipality every year in Edirne in late June and early July. Kırkpınar Oil Wrestling Festival, one of the well-established sports activities of the world, won the "European Distinguished Destinations" award in 2008 and was accepted to the "Intangible Cultural Heritage Representation List of Humanity" by UNESCO on 16 November 2010. The history of Kırkpınar oil wrestling is based on different legends. One of these legends is as follows: During the conquest of Rumelia, Orhan Gazi's brother Süleyman Pasha, conquered several castles along with Domuzhisarı Castle with 40 soldiers. While these armed forces are returning, they wrestle during their breaks in Samona which are within the borders of Greece today. Two of them cannot beat each other. Then two wrestlers bout again on a Hıdırellez day (6 May). Wrestling starts early in the morning and lasts until midnight until the death of two wrestlers. They are buried under a fig tree in there by their friends. Years later, when their friends come back to the same place, they have found that clean and lush fountains flow in a place where their two wrestlers are buried. Thereupon, this place is called "Kırkpınar" and thus the Kırkpınar Oil Wrestling tradition begins. Wrestlers are fighting for three days in the square at the festival, which has been held every year since then. In the finals made on the last day, the first, second, and third wrestler of each category (boyun) are determined. The most important of these is the chief veteran (başpehlivan). During the wrestling, Kırkpınar Festival is organized and various events are held within the scope of this festival. Kırkpınar Oil Wrestling and Festival will be held 659 times in 2020 (Akdu, 2018; Boyacıoğlu, 2013; Edirne İKTM, 2020).

3.2.5.3 ISTANBUL INTERCONTINENTAL SWIMMING RACE

Boğaziçi Intercontinental Swimming Races, which have been continuing in different style and categories for 32 year. Swimming races will be organized 33rd times with 12 different age categories according to their age range in 2021. The Unique event is intercontinental swimming race from Asia to Europe in the world, organized by Turkey's National Olympic Committee (TOC), Also it is held without interruption since 1989. The Bosphorus Intercontinental Swimming Race is organized with great social and institutional support under the auspices of the International Olympic Committee (IOC) (TMOK, 2020).

3.2.5.4 ISTANBUL MARATHON

It is an important sports event in Istanbul. The idea of running from Asia to Europe, which was brought to the agenda in 1973 by *Tercuman* newspaper, was realized with the initiative of a group of German tourists in 1979. The Istanbul Marathon, which has been developing year by year, has been brought to the top with the organizations of the Istanbul Metropolitan Municipality. Asia-Europe Run which is the first name of the event was changed to name as Eurasia Marathon in the following years. Subsequently the name of the Eurasia Marathon was changed to Istanbul Marathon in 2013. The aims of Istanbul Marathon are to promote the city and its name. The Istanbul

Marathon continues to be organized in an indispensable feast for Turkish sports and Istanbul residents over the years (IM, 2016). The Istanbul Marathon takes place every year on the second Sunday of November in Istanbul, and three different race as 10, 15, and 42 km are organized within the scope of the marathon (Istanbul Maraton, 2020).

Sporting events samples which regularly organized in series across the globe, Turkey or under the sponsorship of Turkey apart from the above-outlined sporting events held in are listed below:

- TEB BNP Paribas Istanbul Cup
- Extreme Sailing Series
- PWA World Windsurf Competitions
- Gallipoli Marathon
- CEV Women's Volleyball Champions League
- Turkish Airlines Euroleague Basketball

3.2.6 TRADITIONAL TURKISH FESTIVALS (LOCAL EVENTS)

Turkey is a very rich country in terms of local events and over a thousand events are organized on different topics and contents during the year. A total of 1188 local events were identified in a study conducted by the Ministry of Culture and Tourism of Turkey and Kızılırmak (2006) and 1254 local events were identified in a study conducted by Giritlioğlu et al (2015). Local events organized under different names in all months of the year in Turkey and reflecting the tradition and tradition, culture, life and commercial life of the region where it is organized are an important touristic potential. Kızılırmak (2006) has sorted 1188 local events organized in Turkey and determined by the Ministry of Culture and Tourism according to their topics in his study. Local events according to their subjects are given in Table 3.3.

When table 3.3 is examined, is seen that quite varied events organized from mining events to agricultural products have been realized for much different mass in Turkey. Giritlioğlu et al. (2015) explained that the local events in Turkey are organized in spring and summer rather than winter. The general purpose of the local events organized is to promote regional, national, and international value of the region-specific value that organizes the event, to keep the traditions and culture alive, to transfer it to future generations, and to increase the tourism mobility in the region. Examples of local events in Turkey are given below.

TABLE 3.3 The Local Events Organized by Topics in Turkey

Event Topics	Number of Events
Activities related to agricultural products	132
Activities related to culture and art	130
Liberation Day celebrations of provinces and districts	129
plateau festivals	110
Sports Events	103
Special day and week celebrations	74
Commemoration of historical and religious people	70
Provincial and district festivals	63
Activities related to Bahar, Nevruz and hıdrellez	54
Expo and Fairs	50
Music, dance, opera, ballet and folklore events	49
Recreational activities	35
Activities related to food and beverage types	35
Tourism festivals	29
Youth and children's activities	28
Celebration of Atatürk's arrival in provinces and districts	26
Sunnah Feasts	20
Handicraft activities	17
Activities related to Animal husbandry	16
National holidays	11
Friendship and solidarity activities	5
Mining related activities	1
Total	**1188**

Source: Kızılırmak (2006).

3.2.6.1 MANISA MESIR PASTE FESTIVAL

The wife of Yavuz Sultan Selim, Hafsa Sultan, opened the Sultan Mosque and Complex built in her name in 1523 and appointed Merkez Efendi as the head of the hospital. Sometime after the opening, the Governor of Manisa informs Şehzade Mustafa with an urgent letter that Hafsa Sultan had a disease but could not be treated well despite the efforts of all doctors. The situation is communicated to Merkez Efendi. Merkez Efendi prepares a special paste with a mixture of 41 kinds of spices. This special paste heals Hafsa Sultan in a short time. Hafsa Sultan, who finds healing from this special paste, which is known as mesir paste, informed Merkez Efendi that the paste should be known to the public and that she wants them to bring health. Mesir paste, prepared upon this request, is wrapped in small papers and distributed to the public by spreading from the Sultan Mosque, built on behalf of Hafsa Sultan on March 21 (on Nevruz). This festival, which is organized as the ManisaMesir Paste Festival now, is a well-established event celebrated for 479 years. The event, which has not lost its cultural and historical texture over the years, includes health and faith tourism activities in addition that artistic and cultural features. Mesir paste, which is the main theme of the festival, contains 41 kinds of spices, begins to be prepared with a prayer ceremony held in Sultan Complex on the day of Nevruz and spreads from the Sultan mosque and its complex at the scattering ceremony, coincide with the third or fourth Sunday of April. The International Manisa Mesir Paste Festival was included in the "Intangible Cultural Heritage Representation List of Humanity" in 2012 by UNESCO (Döner and Tepeci, 2014: 786; UNESCO, 2020).

3.2.6.2 CAMEL WRESTLING

Camel wrestling is the wrestling that is generally organized in the Aegean (Denizli, Selçuk, İzmir, Muğla, Germencik, Aydın), Marmara (Balıkesir, Çanakkale), and Mediterranean (Burdur, Antalya, Isparta) regions and is related to the Yörük culture. Camel wrestling takes place in open squares. It is said that traditional camel wrestling probably started in Hıdırbeyli village of Germencik, Aydın about two hundred years ago. However, it is stated in the "End of Camels" section of the book *Interesting Events in Western Anatolian History* by A. Münis Armağan, camel wrestling was organized in Tire and its vicinity during 2nd Mahmut period. In camel wrestling festivals, as in other major festivals, the public is not only spectators, they do play themselves, wrestle themselves, and enjoy. In this festival, the public shows their culture, art, and character. Camel wrestling is a real public festival and cultural exchange center where it is organized (Çulha, 2008: 1835).

3.2.7 FAIRS AND EXHIBITIONS

According to İçöz (1998), one of the important types of event tourism is the exhibitions and fairs, where many products or services come together under the same roof, where they are exhibited and where the professionals or the public are invited. According to Hacıoğlu (2015), exhibitions are like a prestige, information, and education show and are generally not organized periodically. Exhibitions and fairs, where the promotion rather than sales are carried out intensely, create the opportunity to exchange ideas with the current and potential customers (Tavmergenve Aksakal, 2004: 40). Fairs and exhibitions can be made as integrated with each other or can be made separately and it constitutes an important potential in terms of tourism activities in Turkey. According to statistics of Türkiye Odalar ve Borsalar Birliği/the Union of Chambers and Commodity Exchanges of Turkey (TOBB), fairs held in Turkey in 2015 are shown in Table 3.4.

TABLE 3.4 Fairs Organized in Turkey in 2019

Number of Fairs 2019	Number of Fairs	Total Number of Participators	Total Number of Visitors	Number of Foreign Visitors
Fairs	482	62.293	25.828.251	719.267
		By Fair Types		
Specialized Fairs	475	61.286	25.373.267	713.767
General Fairs	7	1.500	454.379	5.500
Total	482	62.786	25.828.251	719.267
		By Fair Size		
National Fairs	349	26.942	19.703.099	284.560
International Fairs	133	35.351	6.125.152	434.707
Total	482	62.293	25.828.251	719.267

Source: TOBB (2020)

Looking at the fairs in Turkey in 2019, it is seen that about 62.2 million people hosted in total 482 fairs. These statistics prove the importance of fairs and exhibitions in terms of event tourism market. Referring to the planned exhibition list reported to the TOBB in Turkey, it is expected to be held in 136 international, a total of 450 fairs in 2020. Examples of the fair held in Turkey are listed below:

- Travel Turkey Izmir Tourism Fair and Conference
- EMITT (Eastern Mediterranean International Tourism and Travel Fair)
- Satef (Travel Agents and Suppliers Fair)
- Tourism Fair (World Tourism Forum and Fair)
- ACE OF M.I.C.E. (Congress, Meeting, and Event Fair)
- FETEX (Fethiye Tourism, Tourism Suppliers and Food and Beverage Fair)

- Eurasia Boat Show (Sea Vehicles, Equipment and Accessories Fair)
- Exposhipping EXPOMARITT International Maritime Exhibition and Conference

Fine arts in different kinds of art that is closely watched by art lovers and exhibitions organized in Turkey is very important in terms of event tourism. These exhibitions, which are organized intensely in big cities such as Istanbul, Ankara, Izmir, Antalya, are organized in a wide range from personal painting exhibitions of a painter to design exhibitions, from exhibiting photographs of a photographer to sculptures exhibitions (Akdu, 2016).

3.2.8 CONGRESS AND MEETING EVENTS

Turkey is a world-class convention center with accessibility, quality, and a number of meeting and congress centers, service quality, price and congresses, and reference to the meeting. Turkey continues to serve in these various types of tourism with investments in hotels congress tourism with its big convention centers established for conventions and meetings organization. Important congress and convention centers with a capacity of more than a thousand people in Turkey are shown in Table 3.5.

TABLE 3.5 Important Meeting and Convention Centers in Turkey

Congress and Meeting Center Name	City	Capacity (Person)
Ephesus Convention Center	Kuşadası	12.000
WOW Hotels and Convention Center	Istanbul	6.500
LütfiKırdar International Convention and Exhibition Center	Istanbul	5.000
Istanbul Congress Center	Istanbul	3.700
Grand Cevahir Hotel and Convention Center	Istanbul	3.513
Hilton Hotel	Istanbul	3.450
Feshane Congress Center	Istanbul	3.420
Sabanci Congress and Exhibition Center (Glass Pyramid)	Antalya	3272
Haliç Congress Center	Istanbul	3.000
Hilton Bomonti	Istanbul	2.900
Divan Talya Congress and Conference Center	Antalya	2.500
Harbiye Military Museum and Culture Center	Istanbul	1.821
Sheraton Çeşme Hotel Congress Center	Izmir	1.600

Source: TÜRSAB (2013).

When Table 3.5 is analyzed, it is seen that the largest capacity congress center is the Ephesus Congress Center in Kuşadası, Aydın. This is an important indicator that the investments made for the congress tourism market are considered both nationally and regionally.

3.2.9 FAITH EVENTS

Faith events in Turkey are organized in certain periods according to various religions and beliefs. Ramadan bairam (Eid al-Fitr) and sacrifice bairam (Eid al-Adha) and various events organized in the country during these bairams be an example of religious events which celebrate the great enthusiasm of Muslims in Turkey. In addition, "St. Nicholas Day" for commemorate to St. Nicholas known Santa Claus worldwide in Demre, Antalya in December since 1983 with the participation of religion and scientists from different parts of the world, Akdamar Church ritual held on the second Sunday of September every year in the Akdamar church in Van after 95 years, Şeb-iArus (Wedding Night), organized every year on 17 December, which is the anniversary of the death of MevlânâCelâleddîn-î Rûmî, to commemorate Mevlana and the ritual performed by the Christian Orthodox in the historical Sumela Monastery in Trabzon can be given as an example for belief events. These religious events constitute an important potential in terms of event tourism (Akdu, 2016).

3.2.10 NATIONAL HOLIDAYS

National holidays celebrating in the big cities to the smallest villages everywhere in Turkey with great enthusiasm and excitement and various events organized within the scope of these national holidays are very important in terms of event tourism. National festivals and events held in Turkey dates are listed below (Akdu, 2016).

Republic Day: National Day commemorates the proclamation of the Republic of Turkey on October 29, 1923. Republic Day is one of the most important national holidays celebrated every year on 29 October.

August 30 Victory Day: It is an official and national holiday, celebrated on 30 August in Turkey Republic and Turkish Republic of Northern Cyprus each year to commemorate the battle of Dumlupınar, which led to victory under the command of Mustafa Kemal.

National Sovereignty and Children's Day: The National Sovereignty and Children's Day, which was given to the children of the world by Mustafa Kemal Atatürk, is celebrated every year on 23 April with festivals and joviality organized for children.

Commemoration of Atatürk, Youth and Sports Day: In Turkey, May 19, 1919, Mustafa Kemal Atatürk came to Samsun, is recognized as the day of the liberation struggle began. It is celebrated with state ceremonies and sports events throughout the country under the name of Atatürk Commemoration, Youth and Sports Day on 19 May every year.

3.3 CONCLUSION

Activities organized in a destination are an important motivation factor for both local people and visitors. At the same time, the activities that provide an important competitive advantage for the destination also strengthen infrastructure activities in the region, create new sources of income, and contribute to the image of the region. This movement, which is analyzed as event tourism in the tourism literature, is an important tourism type that is growing rapidly within the world tourism mobility (Kömürcü, 2013: 23; Getz 2008: 405). Many destinations around the world make investments to increase their event tourism activities and strive to maximize the benefit they will get from event tourism. Turkey also organizes many different activities at national, international, and local levels and invests to get more share from the event tourism market. In this context, it hosts events that have continuity worldwide and have a significant follower mass and supports these events with important infrastructure and superstructure investments. For example, the 25th winter Universiade organized in Erzurum province has invested more than 600 million (TÜSF, 2020). Turkey is a country that has many infrastructure and superstructure for successfully manage the many types of tourism with natural, cultural, and historical attractions also many transportations, accommodations, food and beverage companies, communications. The features that are accepted as an important factor in increasing the satisfaction of the visitors and increasing the efficiency of the activities organized for the event tourism increases the potential for event tourism as in many other types of tourism in Turkey. There are many activities organized at national, international, and local levels in Turkey. Many of these events are followed by a wide audience. Music festivals, shopping festivals, culture and arts festivals, religious events, traditional Turkish festivals (local events), sports events, national festivals, fairs with these events congresses, meetings organizations allow for the acceptance of Turkey as an important destination in event tourism. These events complement and develop the event tourism due to infrastructure and superstructure ownership and working coordinately of transportation, communication, congress centers, meeting halls, accommodation facilities, organization companies, travel agencies, congress offices, universities, and other organizations. Turkey has tourism activities with all these features provide a significant competitive advantage over their competitors in the event tourism market.

KEYWORDS

- **Turkey**
- **event tourism**
- **congress tourism**
- **alternative tourism**

REFERENCES

Akbank Sanat, Akbank Caz Festivali, https://www.akbanksanat.com/caz/30-akbank-caz-festivali (Accessed, Feb. 04, 2020).

Akdu, U. Türkiye'nin Etkinlikve Kongre Turizm- Potansiyeli in Kongreve Etkinlik Yönetimi, Özel, Ç.H. and Sezerel, H. Ed. Anadolu University Press, Eskişehir, 2016, pp. 162–195.

Akdu, U. *Kırkpınar Yağlı Güreşleri-2010, Manisa Mesir Macunu Şenlikleri-2012 VeNevruz Kutlamaları—2009* in Türkiye'nin Unesco Değerlerive Turizm Potansiyeli, Karaman, A.; Ateş, A. and Sayın, K. Eds., EğitimYayınevi, Konya, 2018.

Akın A. A., Erdinç Ö. V., Sinan, V. and Özcan, C. Evaluation of congress tourism development in the world and in Turkey, *Tourism Review*, 2004, 59(1), 44–46. https://doi.org/10.1108/eb058429.

Altın Portakal, 2020; About the Festival, https://www.antalyaff.com/tr/page/index/1/61 (Accessed, Feb. 04, 2020).

APF, International Antalya Piano Festival, https://apf.com.tr/ (Accessed, Feb. 04, 2020).

Arslan K. *Türkiyède Kongre Turizmini Geliştirme İmkânları*, İTO Yayınları, İstanbul, 2008.

Atabaş, A., Kongre Turizmi Bağlamında Şehir Markalaşması: Trabzon İncelemesi, Master Thesis, T.C. Kültür ve Turizm Bakanlığı, Tanıtma Genel Müdürlüğü, Ankara. 2008

Ataman, V. Araştırma. A: http://www.turizmguncel.com/haber/turkiyenin-kongre-toplanti-ve-etkinlik-sektorune-iliskin-onemli-arastirma-h22360.html (Accessed, Nov. 20, 2016).

Binici, V. Bir Zamanlar Türkiye: Rock'n Coke, https://www.wannart.com/bir-zamanlar-turkiye-rockn-coke/ 2018 (Accessed Feb. 20, 2020).

Boyacıoğlu, Z. Dünya Turizminde Yükselen Trend Marka Kentler: Yeni Bir Destinasyon Olarak Marka Kent Edirne, Proceedings of 14th. National Tourism Congress, 2013, 99–120, Kayseri.

Chilloutfest, About Chill-Out Festival, http://www.chilloutfest.com/index.php/about/ (Accessed, March. 14, 2020).

Çulha, O., KültürTurizmi Kapsamında Destekleyici Turistik Ürün Olarak Deve Güreşi Festivalleri Üzerine Bir Alan Çalışması, Journal of Yasar University, 2008, 3(12), 1827–1852

Dance Fest, Istanbul International Dance Festival, https://www.istanbuldancefestival.net/ (Accessed, March. 14, 2020).

Devlet Opera ve Balesi Genel Müdürlüğü, International Aspendos Opera Ballet Festival, https://www.operabale.gov.tr/aspendos2019/Sayfalar/tarihce.aspx (Accessed, Feb. 04, 2020).

Döner, Z. G. and Tepeci, M, Manisa Mesir Macunu Festivali Ziyaretçilerinin Festivale Katılım Nedenleri VeMemnuniyet Düzeylerini Etkileyen Unsurların Belirlenmesi, Proceedings of 15th National Tourism Kongress, 2014, 782–795, Ankara.

Edirne İKTM, Geleneksel Kırkpınar Yağlı Güreşleri, https://edirne.ktb.gov.tr/TR-76392/kirkpinar-yagli-guresleri.html (Accessed, March. 14, 2020).

EF, About Festival, http://www.engelsizfestival.com/en/36146/ABOUT (Accessed, Feb. 04, 2020).

EMITT, EMITT 2020 Welcomed 44,321 Visitors And Close To 1000 Exhibitors From 103 Countries! http://www.emittistanbul.com/Articles/emitt-2020-welcomed-44321-visitors-and-close (Accessed, February 20, 2020)

Event Türkiye, 18. Uluslararası Antalya Piyano Festivali'ne Muhteşem Final, http://eventturkiye.com/18-uluslararasi-antalya-piyano-festivaline-muhtesem-final/ (Accessed, Feb. 04, 2020).

Gastro Antep, International Gaziantep Gastronomy Festival, http://gastroantepfest.com/tr/Manage/GastroAntep (Accessed, March. 14, 2020).

Getz, D. Event tourism: Definition, evolution, and research, *Tourism Management,* 2008, Volume: 29, Issue: 3, 403–428

Giritlioğlu, İ., Olcay, A., and Özekici, Y. K. Bir Turizm Çeşitliliği Olarak Festival Etkinliklerinin Sınıflandırılması: Türkiye Üzerine Bir Değerlendirme. *ODÜ Sosyal Bilimler Araştırmaları Dergisi (ODÜSOBİAD),* 2015, 5(13), 306–323.

Hacıoğlu, N. *Turizm Pazarlaması,* Nobel Akademik Yayıncılık, Ankara, 2015.

Harman, S.; Duran, E. and Kaya, O., Bağımsız Seyahat Eden YerliGezginlerinSeyahatAlışkanlıklarıveSeyahatGüzergâhlarıÜzerine Bir Araştırma, Proceedings of 14th National Tourism Congress, Proceeding Book, 429–448, Kayseri, 2013.

Hatay, Hatay Gastronomi Şehri, http://hataygastronomi.com/(Accessed, March. 14, 2020).

ICCA, ICCA Statistics Report Country and City Rankings Public Abstract, https://www.iccaworld.org/dcps/doc.cfm?docid=2082 (Accessed, Nov. 24, 2016)

ICCA, A Modern History of International Association Meetings: 1963–2012 http://www.iccaworld.org/knowledge/benefit.cfm?benefitid=5180, 2013, (Accessed: Nov. 24, 2016).

ICCA, The International Association Meetings Market 2018 ICCA Statistics Report - Public Abstract file:///C:/Users/akduu/Downloads/2018-Country-and-City-Rankings_Public-Abstract%20(2).pdf (Accessed, March 10, 2020).

ICF, Istanbul Coffee Festival, https://www.istanbulcoffeefestival.com.tr/festival/ (Accessed, March. 14, 2020).

İCEC., İstanbul Lütfi Kırdar, http://www.icec.org/tr/kurumsal/tarihce (Accessed: Nov. 24 2016)

İCVB/1, Statistics, http://tr.icvb.org.tr/icca-istatistiklerine-gore-turkiye-3/#sthash.M3XRGlL2.dpuf (Accessed: Nov. 24, 2016).

İFF, Istanbul International Short Film Festival, http://www.istanbulfilmfestival.com/hometurkish.html (Accessed, Feb. 04, 2020).
İKSV/1, İstanbul Kültür Sanat Vakfı, Tarihçe, https://muzik.iksv.org/tr/festival-hakkinda/tarihce (Accessed, Feb. 04, 2020).
İKSV /2, İstanbul Kültür Sanat Vakfı, Tarihçe, http://caz.iksv.org/tr/festival/tarihce (Accessed, Feb. 04, 2020).
İKSEV, İzmir Kültür Sanatve Eğitim Vakfı, http://www.iksev.org/tr/caz-festivali (Accessed, Feb. 04, 2020).
İKSV/3, History, https://tiyatro.iksv.org/en/the-festival/history (Accessed, Feb. 04, 2020).
İKSV/4, History, https://bienal.iksv.org/en/biennial/history(Accessed, Feb. 04, 2020).
İstanbul Maraton, Tarihçe, https://www.maraton.istanbul/tarihce(Accessed, Feb. 04, 2020).
Karagöz, D. Etkinlik Turizmive Etkinlik Turizmi Bağlamında Yabancı Ziyaretçi Harcamalarının Ekonomiye Etkisi: Formula 1 2005 Türkiye Grand Prix Örneği, Master Thesis, Anadolu Üniversitesi, Sosyal Bilimler Enstitüsü, Turizm Otel İşletmeciliği Anabilim Dalı, Eskişehir, 2006
Kızılırmak, Türkiye'de Düzenlenen Yerel Etkinliklerin Turistik Çekicilik Olarak Kullanılmasına Yönelik Bir İnceleme, *Sosyal Bilimler Dergisi*, 2006, Sayı: 15.
Konya İKTM, Konya İl Kültürve Turizm Müdürlüğü, http://mistikmuzik.com/?page_id=1455 (Accessed, Feb. 04, 2020).
Konya Valiliği, Şeb-I Arus Hazreti Mevlana'nın Vuslat Yıldönümü, https://sebiarus.gov.tr/ (Accessed, March. 14, 2020).
Kömürcü, G. B., Etkinlik Turizmi Çeşidi Olarak Festivaller: Bozcaada Yerel Tatlar Festivali Örneği, Master Thesis, T.C. Çanakkale Onsekiz Mart Üniversitesi Sosyal Bilimler Enstitüsü Turizm İşletmeciliği Anabilim Dalı, Çanakkale, 2013.
Kukla Festivali, Istanbul International Puppet Festival, http://www.istanbulkuklafestivali.com/tr/ (Accessed, March. 14, 2020).
KUTO (Kuşadası Ticaret Odası). Dünyadave Türkiye'de Kongre Turizmi, Kuşadası-Efes Kongre Merkezi, Kongre Ve Ziyaretçi Büroları, http://www.kuto.org.tr/img/kuto/raporlar/26.pdf Erişim Tarihi: 24 Kasım 2016.
Nevşehir Valiliği, Ürgüp Bağ Bozumu Festivali, http://www.nevsehir.gov.tr/rgp-bag-bozumu-festivali (Accessed, March. 14, 2020).
Republic of Turkey, Ministry of Culture and Tourism, Tourism Statistics, https://www.ktb.gov.tr/EN-249283/tourism-statistics.html (Accessed, March. 05, 2020).
TAŞFED, About Festival, http://www.istanbulgastronomyfestival.com/tr/hakkimizda.aspx?id=5 (Accessed, March. 14, 2020).
Tavmergen, İ. and Aksakal, E. G. *Kongreve Toplantı Yönetimi*, SeçkinYayıncılık, Ankara, 2004.
Tayfun, A. and Arslan, E. Festival Turizmi KapsamındaYerli Turistlerin Ankara Alışveriş Festivali'nden Memnuniyetleri Üzerine Bir Araştırma, *İşletme Araştırmaları Dergisi*, 2013, 5/2, 191–206.
TMOK, 2020, Türkiye Milli Olimpiyat Komitesi, Samsung Boğaziçi Kıtalararası Yüzme Yarışı, http://bogazici.olimpiyatkomitesi.org.tr/Anasayfa (Accessed, March. 14, 2020).
Tour, History, https://www.tourofturkey.org.tr/en/history (Accessed, March. 14, 2020).
TOBB, 2020, İstatistikler, https://www.tobb.org.tr/FuarlarMudurlugu/Sayfalar/Istatistikler.php (Accessed, March. 17, 2020).
TÜRSAB (Türkiye Seyahat Acentaları Birliği), Türkiye Kongre Turizmi Raporu, 2013, http://www.Tursab.Org.Tr/Dosya/12188/Tursab-Kongre-Turizmi-Raporu_12188_5546141.Pdf (Accessed, March. 17, 2016).

TÜSF, Üniversite Sporları Federasyonu, Sonuç Raporu, (http://www.univspor.org.tr/images/stories/universiade/kis/2011.pdf (Accessed, March 05, 2020).

UNESCO, 2020, Mesir Macunu festival, http://www.unesco.org/culture/ich/en/RL/mesir-macunu-festival-00642 (Accessed, March. 17, 2020).

Yoon, S., Daniel, M., Spencer, D., and Dae-Kwan, K., A Profile of Michigan's Festival and Special Event Tourism Market, *Event Management An International Journal*, 2000, 6(1).

CHAPTER 4

TRIBAL FAIR AND FESTIVAL: CONTEXT, EXAMPLES, AND THE INTERPRETATION OF TECHNOLOGY

AZIZUL HASSAN[1*] and ANUKRATI SHARMA[2]

[1]*Tourism Consultants Network, The Tourism Society, London, United Kingdom*

[2]*Department of Commerce and Management, University of Kota, Rajasthan, India*

*Corresponding author. E-mail: azizulhassan00@gmail.com

ABSTRACT

Tribal fairs are the mirror of the cultural and historical bequest of the community. Geographically and socially isolated, these fair are linked with visualizing tribal cultural diversities. Their customs, traditions, attires, music, and dance are the keys of their social and economic development where their originality and authenticity are preserved in a respectful manner. In reality, these fair are also positively contributing the country's development process. Thus this research aims to study the impact of tribal festivals on the local and wider the socioeconomic well-being in a city. The endeavor is to find out the role of tribal fairs in their social and economic development and to dig out the possibility of involvement with the mainstream of the society. Rajasthan is a state of India that reflects various colors of cultures and traditions. It is also comprised of many tribes having their identity and authenticity. This research analytically explains the tribal fairs of Rajasthan. The "Baneshwar" fair by the Bhil tribes and the Sitabari Mela by Saharia tribes are dominant in this area and our target group. This research on the basis of arguments made on available literature studies confirms that each tribe individually has its own traditions, customs, and lifestyles. Tribal fairs are the showcase of their complete culture and cultural tourists always admire the originality. So it can be a tool for their social and economic development. Many strategies need to create the environment for tribal fairs capitalizing opportunities. Finally, this study suggests the need to preserve the intangible tribal heritage of tribal fairs of Rajasthan with the support of effective technologies.

4.1 INTRODUCTION

Tribal tourism is a new and expanding addendum to such postmodern travel modes as ecotourism, nature, and wilderness travel. For the tourists, these new destination concepts speculate an indistinguishable attentiveness of losing ground resources that individuals should see while they still can (Smith, 1996). "Tribal tourism" is defined by Terry Ward (2010) as *"a novel type of travel in which tourists visits tribal villages in order to be showing to a culture entirely diverse from their own" (p. 1)*. For tribal tourism, some states of Orissa, Jharkhand, Madhya Pradesh, Chhattisgarh, and Himachal are famous. Conventionally, tribal tourism is believed as instrumental for creating diverse financial opportunities for both in and around the selected tribes. This supports for fostering awareness about the Indian tribal people to fight against lack of opportunities, oppression, and social exclusion. Any form of tourism can benefit the society, in general. Also, tourism can create psychological and social values for the relevant tribal population. Still, tourism activities can lead to negative consequences and harmful effects on society. In earlier decades, many tourism initiatives like tours in tribal areas produced negative and harmful effects on the tribal people.

Many researchers, NGO workers, and social activists are working for tribal development, upliftment, and inclusion in the society. Providing basic facilities to the needed community is never a solution. Keeping this observation in mind, tribal tourism theory came into the mind of many researchers. Indigenous tribes are relatively rich in ethnic features and cultural resources. Many of the remote tribes are retaining some significant number of cultural and social systems, rituals, and handicrafts. These tribes also both directly and indirectly can influence people that live in the city by forming a strong attraction. Chang and Huang (2009) directed that the indigenous culture can be a valuable and important indicator of tourism products. These researchers reflected that in aboriginal tourism regions, indigenous mostly stay as the prime content of goods. These have turned into a relatively newer economic source type. Hinch and Butler (2007) argued that indigenous tourism represents the indigenous people that are directly attached to the tourism industry's operation or performs in the tourism industry as a mean for attracting tourists to visit the aboriginal culture. The research is conducted mainly from literature review and on-site visits so as to achieve the set objectives of the topic (i.e., tribal fairs and festivals can be a tool for social and economic development; the preservation of their customs and traditions with the application of effective technologies are important). Outcomes of this study can explore whether tribal festivals can back the economic development initiatives. The outcome can also support their traditions and customs' preservation.

4.2 INDIGENOUS TOURISM

Whitford and Ruhanen (2016) explored that sustainability issues can both shape and underpin a considerable proportion of Indigenous tourism research that is published to date. The present challenge is to achieve a better and comprehensive understanding of Indigenous tourism on the Indigenous stakeholders' context. Also, to approach its complexity in a flexible, adaptive, and iterative style coupled with the affected stakeholders that are attached to the research process and knowledge creation as well as the conclusion.

Carr et al. (2016) emphasized on tourism capacities as beneficial elements for realizing sustainable Indigenous development in "Indigenous peoples and tourism: the challenges and opportunities for sustainable tourism." This research reviewed in the contents in details. The research reminded the readers both of the pessimistic and constructive authenticity of Indigenous tourism.

"The Commodification and Management of Culture" is a volume published in *Advances in Tourism Research* in 2005. Through *Tourist-Host Nexus-Research Considerations* by Ryan (2005) examined the nexus of researcher and researched within the framework of the association between tourism and indigenous peoples. It was debated that the academy, the local outlook, and the imperative tourism are the most important three elements subsist in this association.

Notzke (1999) explores the present trends of indigenous (aboriginal) tourism development in Canada's Western Arctic region in the research titled "Indigenous Tourism Development in the Arctic." In the North, aboriginal tourism is featured as a resource-based industry, conventionally in the big game hunting form, and in a more recent perspective, evolves into ethnic, cultural, and ecotourism. Few of the indigenous people tend to explore innovative ways for harnessing tourism for supporting the conventional elements of the land-based economy. The validity of such tourism know-how shows a major advantage as well as foremost challenges for the management.

In their publication titled *Indigenous Tourism Research, Past and Present: Where to from Here?*, Whitford and Ruhanen (2016) explored that sustainability issues can both shape and underpin a considerable proportion of Indigenous tourism research that are published to date. The present challenge is to achieve a better and comprehensive understanding of Indigenous tourism on the Indigenous stakeholders' context. Also, to approach its complexity in a flexible, adaptive, and iterative style coupled with the affected stakeholders that are attached to the research process and knowledge creation as well as its conclusion. This is both a moral essential and a realistic approach to make sure the results of investigated assist the sustainability of Indigenous tourism.

4.3 TRIBE AND THE HISTORICAL CONTEXT

The English word "tribe" is derived from the Latin word "Tribus" which means a specific common and political organization type functioning in almost all societies. The notion of "tribe" denotes a category of people and entitles a developmental step in the society. In ancient time, tribes were heavily reliant on the forest for their daily needs like shelter, food, treatment, medicine, and clothes. However, as time moved, these tribes became able to control the forest with capacities to grow the required foods. In such ways, the tribes became able to meet their demands at the time of their needs. Thus the forest offered the tribal people complete support for generating their livelihoods. In the last seven to eight decades, manufacturing industries and mining coupled with the use of power hugely accelerated resource collection from forests. These activities in return led to the loss of indigenous cultures and resources. Vidyarthi and Rai (1977), in their research titled *The Tribal Culture of India* have well documented such transformations of the indigenous sociocultural and economic systems. This research featured vital issues that are attached to the indigenous cultural lifestyle. Modernization and industrialization, with their significant roles in the human kind actually allowed people to realize the importance to preserve tribal culture and social systems.

In the last few decades, Special Interest Tourism (SIT) has appeared as a rapidly growing approach and concept in tourism that presents a strong people-focused and sustainable model. This model searches for generating authentic experiences in line with interacting the host communities in fair manners. Hall and Weiler (1992) recommended that SIT can be enriching, rewarding, adventuresome, and a journey to learn. According to them, these are the main four elements of SIT. The product and service offers of SIT can be customized with an aim to generate experiences for niche markets (Douglas et al., 2001). Such products and services offer both unique and useful insights into specific communities, destinations, or knowledge. In SIT, indigenous people turn to become a major element of the tourism industry. Such tourism type is named "Indigenous Tourism" that is formed by special interest areas for tourists where these tourists like to experience authentic indigenous ethnicity and culture.

Indigenous tourism is rather a resource-based tourism type where indigenous traditions as a main tourist desirability, the expansion of tourism in accumulation to the local attractive natural landscapes, and unusual extraterrestrial scene, the more tourists the "Man" as a very important purpose. Numerous scholars have defined for aboriginal tourism diverse definitions: Ryan and Huyton (2002) defines that "Aboriginal Tourism" is a tourist imaginative acts by aboriginal culture, celebrations, attractions, chronological heritage, and customs magnetize while traveling to tourist activities occupied in aboriginal areas. Wu (2003) argues that the notion of "Aboriginal Tourism" is somehow dissimilar from the common tourism activity patterns. The reason is the associates are not rigid rides or not capable to converse with natural resources, but people who live, reliable cultural traditions. "Aboriginal Tourism" is defined as the expansion of Aboriginal cultural resources as a spindle, the changed things; activities implications include Aboriginal arts and crafts, clothing, architecture, and music, dance, cultural traditions, and so on (Wu, 2003). As a result, indigenous tourism can have a linkage with the small businesses that are based on inherited tribal knowledge of nature and culture. This enhances at the time when indigenous people initiate to operate tours, guiding, and cultural centers. As well as these people stated providing relevant facilities to visitors and controlled the access of tourists to homelands and cultural events (Zeppel, 2006).

Smith (1996) suggested the four H's (i.e., habitat, heritage, history, and handicrafts) to define indigenous tourism. Accordingly, the visitor industry's segments directly attach native people in the way to attract tourists.

Indigenous tourism is outlined as a means toward the survival of the culture of many native communities while this offers a path for overcoming social isolation. The cultures of the tribal people are mostly of particular interest types. This is the basic and preliminary motivational factor for tourists to travel to exotic regions, destinations, events, and attractions. These normally include cultural villages, local museums, indigenous festivals, nature-based tours, indigenous art galleries, and events. The attractions in indigenous tourism can be located both in remote and rural regions having inadequate infrastructures and facilities (Getz and Jamieson, 1997). The essential parts of indigenous tourism are formed by spiritual, environmental, and cultural aspects of indigenous traditions and heritage (Zeppel, 2006). The preliminary capacities and strengths of tribal tourism stay in its ability to draw tourists' attention and creating their interests for experiencing the local cultures in the most authentic settings.

Tourist participation in interactive activities with aboriginal people is the other basic strength of indigenous tourism (Imtiaz and Hassan, 2016; Hassan, 2016). Thus the preference in such a market remains more to offer both spontaneous and intimate cultural experiences. The prime reason for this is the strong affinity between the natural environment and the aboriginal cultures. Tribes generally behold an inheritance of customs, traditions, and rituals that are deeply rooted in their conventional lifestyle and culture.

4.4 TRIBAL DIVERSITIES OF RAJASTHAN

India is considered as the land cultural diversities, festivals, and many different seasonal celebrations. Such fairs and festivals support in reinforcing cultural values and roots. These also enable communities for preserving their customs, traditions, and to ensure economic values. All of such promising fair and festival roots are attached to the economic agents like business prosperity, agricultural bliss, social benefits, and entrepreneurship development. Tribal fairs and festivals permit the local tribes to be connected to their foods, arts, crafts, talents, dance, and relevant cultural landscape forms as well as promoting significant livelihoods through entrepreneurial activities. They lead to economic development through gifts, fruits, and sweets exchange as elements of cultural richness. Also, these are commonly attached to economic agents such as consumer, entrepreneur, and producer. In each festive season, the demand for particular services and goods increases mainly owing to tribal festivals and fairs where the supplies are also met. Many hundreds of the tribal shopkeepers make temporary shops across the streets and take the new opportunities of such festivals and fairs. Tribal peoples in Rajasthan have created interests in the world. Tourists have special interests in them mainly for their attractive dwellings, occupations, customs, and costumes. Tribes in Rajasthan make a wide range of customs, lifestyles that range from aristocratic, nomadic, farmers, shepherds, camel-herders, craftsmen, traders, and so on. These tribal peoples comprise homogeneity in both socioeconomic status and customary living patterns. Conventional tribal dresses identify the local communities of Rajasthan where modernization becomes an unavoidable tool. Tribal dresses and costumes have differences even with similarities in clothing, jewelry, and adornment types. These tribal peoples like to wear their conventional outfits.

The Bhils: Bhils are commonly known and popular as the bowmen of Rajasthan. The Bhils are known as the tribe that spread across the whole India. This tribe forms the largest tribal group not only in India but also in South Asia. The Bhils usually dwell in the Western region of Madhya Pradesh. This region adjoins Gujarat, Maharashtra, and Rajasthan, and some Bhils also live in the northeastern part of Tripura.

The Bhil tribe belongs to the race of the pre-Aryans. The name "The Bhil" is believed as derived from "billu" or "villu." Following the Dravidian language, this name meant bow. They are possibly the most ancient tribe of India and mentioned in Hindu mythology and also believe Valmiki and Eklavya as their ancestors. In earlier centuries, they were believed and well known as the great warriors. They used to fight against the Marathas, the Mughals, and the British. The Language and Costumes of the Bhil tribe are too attractive. Apart from other states, the Bhils comprise 39% of Rajasthan's total population. They speak the "Bhili," which is an Indo Aryan language.

The Bhils are well known for their simplicity and truthfulness. The Bhils are also brave at the same time. The bow is their traditional and national weapon that is made from bamboo. In earlier ages, the Bhils were the greatest hunters but these days they mostly live on agriculture as the main source of their livelihood.

Religious beliefs and practices of the Bhils mostly differ between themselves and from place to place. Approximately all of the Bhils adore the local deities. These deities are named as "Sitalmata," "Kanhoba," "Khandoba" and "Bahiroba." The worshipped tiger is named "Vaghdev." The Bhils do not have any temple owned by them. The Bhils have "Gurus" or "Bhagat" to execute their religious rites.

The Bhils have an enriched cultural history that emphasizes on music and dance. "Ghoomar" is said to be the most popular and well-known dance of the Bhils. The "Gair" is the dance drama on the religious ground as performed by the male members in "Sharavana" months (July and August). They have talents in making clay sculptures and make beautiful elephants, horses, tigers, and their deities.

The "Baneshwar" fair is the major festival that the Bhils celebrate during the "Shivratri" (in January or February). This fair is to "Baneshwar Mahadev," who is also known as "Lord Shiva." Actually, two fairs are conjoined in one fair. One of these two fairs takes place in reverence of "Lord Shiva" while the other is commenced after setting the "Vishnu temple" by Jankunwari. During this fair, on the banks of the Som and Mahi river, they gather together to set up camps. They sing conventional songs and dance around the fire. They perform a dance around the fire and sing traditional songs. At the Lakshmi Narayan temple and at night, they enjoy "Raslila." Animal shows, cultural shows, magic shows, and acrobatic feasts are the popular and major attractions of these fairs.

The "Dusshera" and the "Holi" are the other major festivals that are celebrated by the Bhils in all over India. During these two festivals also, the Bhils sing their traditional songs and dance around the fire. The whole night they spend at the "Lakshmi Narayan temple" to enjoy "Raslila." The rituals and celebration styles of these two festivals have similarities with the "Baneshwar" fair.

The use of color varieties tends to make Bhil dresses more attractive and appealing. The Bhil women like to wear their traditional dress that is the "Sarees" when the Bhil men like to wear pyjama with a loose long frock and the farmers wear turbans. During the festivals, the costumes of the Bhil men and women can be featured as traditional. During these festivals, the Bhil women wear "Ghaghra," "Odhna" as well as "Kapada," an upper cloth piece. In ancient times, the Bhils women used to wear short skirts of knee-length for better movements. With "Odhna" and "Lugda," the Bhil women cover up their torso and head. "Pejania," an ornament that is worn on hand, leg, and arm offers safety and protections from thorns and animals. On the other side, the Bhil men wear "Tunic," turban, "Angi," and "Potario" (a lower garment). All of the Bhils also love to wear brass ornaments and jewelry. They generally wear beautiful jewelry that matches their customs, sentiment, costumes, and ethnicity. Few of the widely popular pieces of jewelry worn by the Bhil women are "Bichiya," "Dhimmna," "Beenti," "Oganiya," "Pejania," "Hansli," "Kasla," "Haar," "Bidi," "Tagli," and "Kamkada." They also use silver brass and white metal in jewelry.

The Saharia: The Saharia tribe is only prehistoric tribal group in Rajasthan. They are intensed in the Shahbad and Kishanganj Panchayat Samities of Baran district. Tod (1881) mentioned them along with Minas, the Bhils, and Gujjars as the ancient residents of the region. The word Saharia emerged from the Persian World, Sehi, meaning jungle. The Saharia were counted by the Muslim rulers as the forest inhabitants. The Saharias' customs and manner bear a great resemblance to caste Hindus with whom they live in their present habitat and who consider them to be untouchable. The costume of the Saharia men was a short-length Dhoti, Salook (shirt), and turban. The Saharia women wore Ghagra, Lungra, and Choli (bodice). Young boys wore Pancha (small piece of dhoti) and Salook and the girls wear dressed in Ghaghria, Palka, and Faria. Very small children moved without any clothes and were seen nude. In general, the Sahariyas reside in separate village "Basti" that is called "Saharana." These people follow the religious practices of the Hindu and speak the dialect that is influenced by Hadoti. Over the years, the Sahariyas have been maintaining ecological stability with the environment they live. These people have very inadequate dependency on technology.

Commonly, the Sahariyas get themselves engaged in collecting minor products of the forest and they live as agricultural laborers. Their main trading and selling commodities are gum, forest wood, honey, vegetables, fruits, "Tendu" leaves, etc. The Shariyas are believed as primitive. However, a good number of them are not primitive and rely on agriculture to live on. Some of them are also forest product collectors and landless laborers.

For the Shariyas, the "SitaBari Mela" is traditionally famous. SitaBari is a holy place located near "Kelwara Kasba," which is about 45 km from Baran City. On "Jeshta Amavasya," a large tribal fair is organized. A number of "Kunds" are situated in this place that attribute to "Laxman," "Sita," "Kush," "Surya," and "Lav." All of these are religiously important and auspicious to the Sahariyas. Millions of people visit this fair titled the "Kumbh." In this fair, the "Swyambar" or marriage function of the Sahariya tribe is organized. People come from many different areas of Rajasthan and adjoined Madhya Pradesh. In this fair, the Sahariya boy drops a handkerchief as a ritual to propose the Sahariya girl. Accepting this handkerchief by this Sahariya girl establishes that the marriage is agreed. The groom and the bride perform the "Sat phere" that is a ritual of seven round of the Barnawa tree. With the blessings of their parents the bride and groom are accepted as a married couple. This fair is also known as the animal fair where buffalo, cows, and other animals are bought and sold. These fairs are the good presentation of customary living styles.

4.5 SOME INSIGHTS OF PRESERVING THE TRIBAL FAIR AND FESTIVAL WITH EFFECTIVE TECHNOLOGY APPLICATION

Rajasthan is well known and famous for having places that are both culturally and religiously important. Rajasthan also has tribes with ritual and are cultural richness and diversities. The "Baneshwar" fair is relatively a popular tribal fair that aligns both with religious and traditional rituals. This fair is important because the Bhils visit this fair from many neighboring states like Gujarat and Madhya Pradesh and pray to the "Lord Shiva." This fair does not merely have cultural or religious values but also exhibits frolic and fun of the general lifestyles and acts as a place to sell or buy local items. This fair becomes popular with folk dances, songs, animal shows, magic shows, or acrobatic feats. With the priest, a massive parade disembarks at the fair. This is named "Mathadhish." The myth is that the river water becomes purer and holier at the time the "Mathadhish" takes bath and thus the people bathe at the same time in the river. The "Sitabari" fair that is held annually at "Sitabari" celebrates the place's sacredness with its historical and religious significance. In Hinduism, the "Sitabari fair" at Sitabari shows the Sitabari town's religious importance. This fair is celebrated and enjoyed by the people with a variety of events, activities, and rituals.

The "Swyambar" ceremony is organized for offering enjoyment of the people with their family members. This fair turns into a major visitor attraction in Sitabari town with the participation of people residing in nearby areas like Kota, Nagaur, Bundi, Aklera, Jhalawar, the Bhilwara, and others.

In each fair, many people are gathered to visit and enjoy the activities and performances. The commodification of these fairs is also strong when people sell and buy essential and fancy goods and commodities. Stalls and shops bring attractive readymade and handmade products. Also, the cultural shows that are arranged mainly by the youngsters welcome the local villagers to attend.

All these activities are boon for economic development of these tribes and villagers. These fairs and festivals of the two different tribes of the same state deserve promotion and marketing. The application of effective technologies can help in this regard. However, this application is rather a subject for further research. The Bhil community is socially and economically better in position as compared to the Sahariyas. After visiting such villages, it had been realized that the reason of poverty and illiteracy is not lack of regular source of income. They are the community who feels themselves differently and detached from the rest of the society. They believe in their traditions and customs and never think beyond that. But few young tribal groups, who already performed as a folk artist at many places, wanted their community to more educated and civilized. Past studies have already shown (Ryan, 2005) that tribal tourism development has two aspects (i.e., Capacity building and Commodification). Capacity building is one of the main optimistic characteristics and the other one which reflects as their living style is being presented for the tourism development. The present study further offers tribal tourism fairs in place of tribal tourism and tribal fairs. This may eradicate the ill effects of commoditization and augment the preferences of the source of income. Very few tourism researchers tend to meet the tribal people to take their opinion about tribal fair development.

Organizing tours, exhibitions, drama, etc., in a sequence at their villages during the fairs and festivals could be a great idea (Sharma, 2018). Kota city of the Hadoti region is primarily known as an education city. Lots of institutions and universities are located here. The education institutes, universities, colleges, and coaching centers can play a vital role in supporting the Tribe fairs and festivals. In the opinion of the researchers, the artist of the fairs and festivals must be invited during MICE events for their performances. The tribe artists should also be encouraged and financially supported by the Universities for exchange programs in different states and countries. It will give their art due weightage in the various nook and corners of the country. The website of different hotels may also highlight these fairs and festivals.

Moreover, research in this area is required to know more about tribal fairs and festivals. The government universities may keep a provision for the admissions at school, college, and university level for the children of the artists who belong from these tribes. This will support them and keep them associated with their beliefs, art, and culture.

They responded in a very positive manner but they never took their religious customs or fairs with economic benefits. Most of the villagers perceive their fair as social or religious customs. Though many of them were economically involved with these fairs but they took fairs as their way for economic benefits. Associating these fairs and festivals with technology could be a great idea to provide recognition on a global level. Not only this, more of education tourism in these areas, particularly at the time of fairs and festivals, can work as a boon for the villagers and develop a new way to earn more (Sharma, 2015).

4.6 CONCLUSION

This research aimed to explain and analyzes the effects of tribal festivals on the local and wider socioeconomic well-being in a city. There is a huge potential that tribal tourism and festivals can have positive effects on the local livelihood. Strategic policy interventions are required for ensuring commercial viability of presenting tribal traditions, cultures, and customary living styles. This is one of the influential ways to empower the tribes and their performers on the socio-economic context. This research stress on taking all of the necessary efforts for ensuring sustainable inherent quality, innate beauty and fundamental tribal ideology, traditions, cultural forms, and art. Also, the general people of the society are required to be well aware about the styles, values, diverse tribal performing arts. In this regard, effective publicity and campaign of the tribal festival elements become beneficial to attract more general tourist audience. The presentation of tribal and folk cultural forms, arts, and festivals before the tourists needs careful attention. For the reason, useful strategic policies application also becomes relevant for meeting the tourist demands. This chapter concludes and justifies with its primary and secondary data analyses that tribal tourism development is a tool for their economic and social development but their religious and social fairs are the strongest instrument for their overall development. Through these fairs, their handicrafts, customs and rituals, cuisines, attires, and other articles could be exhibit and sell to a large number of people. This way, they will not feel as commodity or strange. The State Government and local authorities need to make new policies and planning to highlight the said fairs and festivals of the region. The involvement of more local people and artists in fairs and festivals will not only support them economically but also boost up their morale to associate the coming generations with their culture and tradition. One of the key limitations of this study is not to incorporate primary data. Thus future studies should cover aspects of religious, social customs, rituals, and traditions of a festivals and fairs on the context of effective and useful technology application.

KEYWORDS

- Rajasthan
- tribe
- tourism
- fair
- culture

REFERENCES

Carr, A., Ruhanen, L. and Whitford, M. (2016) (eds.). *Sustainable Tourism and Indigenous Peoples*. Oxon: Routledge.

Chang, H-M. and Huang, H.C. (2009). A study of indigenous tribe tourism planning and developing case by Huanshan in Taiwan. *The Journal of International Management Studies*, 9(1), pp. 146–155.

Chang, J. (2006). Segmenting tourists to aboriginal cultural festivals: An example in the Rukai tribal area. *Tourism Management*, **27**(6), pp. 1224–1234.

Douglas, N., Douglas, N. and Derrett, R. (2001). *Special interest tourism*: Context and cases. *John Wiley & Sons Australia, Ltd*. Brisbane: *Australia*.

Getz, D. and Jamieson, W. (1997). Rural tourism in Canada: Issues, opportunities and entrepreneurship in aboriginal tourism in Alberta. In S. Page and D. *Getz* (eds.) *The Business of Rural Tourism: International Perspectives*. London: International Thomson Business Press, pp. 93–107.

Hall, C. M. and Weiler, B. (1992). Introduction: What's so special about s*pecial interest tourism*? In *B. Weiler* and *C. M.* Hall (eds.) *Special Interest Tourism, London: Belhaven Press*, pp. 1–14.

Hassan, A. (2016). A composition of variable economic activities: Cases of three groups of indigenous of peoples of South Asia. In K. Iankova, A. Hassan and L. A. Rachel (eds.), *Indigenous People and Economic Development: An International Perspective*. Oxon: Routledge, pp. 267–282.

Hinch, T. and *Butler, R.* (2007) (eds.). *Tourism and Indigenous Peoples: Issues and Implications*. *Oxford*: Butterworth-Heinemann.

Imtiaz, M. and Hassan, A. (2016). The urges of language adaptation for economic development within the Garos of Bangladesh. In K. Iankova, A. Hassan and L. A. Rachel (eds.), *Indigenous People and Economic Development: An International Perspective*. Oxon: Routledge, pp. 307–324.

Liao, C-C. and Lin, Y-X. (2013). A study of indigenous tribes tourism developing-case by Lilang, Tbulan, and Hrung in Taiwan. *International Scholarly and Scientific Research & Innovation,* **7**(11), pp. 2945–2951.

Notzke, C. (1999). Indigenous tourism development in the Arctic. *Annals of Tourism Research*, **26**(1), pp. 55–76.

Ryan, C. (2005). Tourist-host nexus—research considerations. In C. Ryan and M. Aicken (eds.) *Indigenous Tourism: The Commodification* and M*anagement* of C*ulture,* Amsterdam: Elsevier, pp. 1–11.

Ryan, C. and Huyton, J. (2002). Tourists and aboriginal people. *Annals of Tourism Research*, **29**(3), pp. 631–647.

Sharma, A.(2015). Educational tourism: Strategy for sustainable tourism development with reference of Hadauti and Shekhawati Regions of Rajasthan, India (Romania). *Journal of Knowledge Management, Economics and Information Technology*, **2**(4), pp. 1–17.

Sharma, A. (2018). Festivals for sustainable tourism development: A case study of Hadoti region, Rajasthan. *Handbook of Festivals*, Routledge, pp. 366–373.

Smith, V.L. (1996). The four Hs of tribal tourism: Acoma—a pueblo case study. *Progress in Tourism and Hospitality Research*, **2**(3–4), pp. 295–306.

Vidyarthi, L.P. and Rai, B.K. (1977). *The Tribal Culture of India*. New Delhi: Concept Publishing Company.

Ward, T. (2018). *Tribal Tourism: Ethical or Exploitative?* Retrieved from: https://www.aol.com/2010/12/08/tribal-tourism-ethical-or-exploitative/ (accessed: the 22nd December, 2018), p. 1.

Whitford, M. and Ruhanen, L. (2016). *Indigenous tourism research, past and present: Where to from here? Journal of Sustainable Tourism*, **24**(8–9), pp. 1080–1099.

Wu, Z-Q. (2003). Tribal tourism and eco-tourism. *Agricultural Management Newsletter*, **35,** pp. 15–18.

Zeppel, H. (2006). *Indigenous Ecotourism: Sustainable Development and Management.* Oxford: CABI.

CHAPTER 5

THE IMPACT OF MODERNIZATION ON MALAY WEDDINGS

AHMAD ALBATTAT[1*], TRISHA ANNE JOSEPH[2], and ABDUL AZIM MAZLAN[2]

[1]Post Graduate Centre, Management and Science University, Selangor, Malaysia

[2]School of Hospitality and Creative Arts, Management and Science University, Selangor, Malaysia

*Corresponding author. E-mail: dr.battat@msu.edu.my

ABSTRACT

Marriage is one of the most notable moments for humans regardless of their social status. Stylish, high ended, and expensive weddings have become a passionate issue in Malay modern society. This study determines that the ever-growing desires of the 21st-century bride and groom could be a factor of pricey consumption activities of commodities and services to fulfil the dream wedding, brides are highly desirous in realizing their unique wedding dreams caused the waste of money. The traditional way in planning and executing a wedding ceremony that used to be anchored in religion and frugal value is currently facing massive challenges due to the trendy and high-cost wedding dream concept. The modern Malay community facing a wedding expenses issue following the existence of various new kind of preparations, including the demand of customer wants, needs, and trends. Thus it could influence the managing of expenditure by not prioritizing matters that might be the source of expenditure.

5.1 INTRODUCTION

Events are generally known as moments that happen or take place especially with one or more important reasons or celebrations. Events are mostly a planned public or social occasion. There are various types of events that have been determined and can be found in this whole wide world such as conferences, seminars, meetings, team building events, incentives events, dinners, trade shows, press conferences, networking events, opening ceremonies, product launches, theme parties, trade fairs, shareholder meetings, award ceremonies, birthdays, festivals, weddings, and many more (Bowdin, Allen, O'toole, Harris and McDonnell, 2012).

A wedding is a ceremony where or a couple of people are united in marriage. Wedding traditions and customs vary greatly between cultures, ethnic groups, religions, countries, and social classes. There is a specialist or a specific organizer for weddings who is called a wedding planner. Wedding planner is a professional event consultant who would offer to assist bride-grooms-to-be with the design, planning, and management of the weddings according to the package chosen. Weddings are significant and memorable events in people's lives and due to this reason, couples are often willing to spend considerable or a big amount of money to turn their dream weddings into reality (Husin et al., 2018).

Modernization has come across all aspects in life including marriage in this millennial era. Most of the people in these days tended to have their wedding theme slightly or more different apart from their original culture, influenced by social media or circles where they find it is "rare" to have such wedding. Many wedding planners nowadays have the capability of realizing their clients' dreams, even, offering more packages to fulfil the desire of having a modern wedding (Khairuddin, 2016).

Wedding services were described as part of the consumption activities carried out by the middle class in urban areas as Fatimah Abdullah (2009), but now the culture of consumption and the use of these commodities and services has transmitted to the bridal couple from the low-income family. This situation proves that there has been a high level of taste among the bride's informants in fulfilling the form of their dream wedding. An important factor affecting the use of goods in capitalist society is the production of new goods referring to the struggle for good standing (Hirsch, 1976). This causes the subordinate social group to endeavor to have certain goods in order to pursue the upper class but at the same time the upper group will continue to invest in order to possess certain goods to reinforce the existing social distance

(Featherstone, 1991). In this context, knowledge of new items, social values, culture, and how to use them becomes very important.

The rising of various modern wedding trends in Malaysia has gone more or slightly astray from the traditional concept of Malay weddings. Also, to analyze how the dream wedding desires would affect the value of traditional weddings to realizing them. Trends will somehow affect the actual culture, but the value of a culture must be kept and preserved despite that it is adaptive. Hence, wedding planners need to amend the concept carefully according to the modernization yet, the preservation of cultural values are not to forget. We will also be identifying the types of wedding packages that are available and used by the majority of newlywed bride and grooms (Khairuddin, 2016).

Nowadays, trends have been leaving more and more impacts and influences in wedding planner market of concepts. The wedding planner must compete in parliamentary procedure to remain profitable. Nowadays, with the increasing recognition of the importance of customer retention and loyalty, companies now understand the importance of their assistance. Nowadays, the dream weddings of every Malay couple is very diverse and different from the traditional Malay wedding. Obviously, the perception of society toward the wedding is changing according to the season; previously where a person plays a role in controlling a wedding party, now, the ringgit becomes a bet for the occasion. The concept of simplicity has been ignored to keep the name and status in society (Khairuddin, 2016). This research problem in relation with the modernization of Malay weddings is that it disrupts a few factors such as the cost of weddings planned out by wedding planners (Suraya, 2016). The modernization of Malay weddings has pulled apart the traditional cultures when it has been affected by modern cultures in time to come. The aims of this study are to understand the effects of modernization on Malay weddings, to determine the ever-growing desires of bride and grooms in the 21st century, and to examine why Malay wedding traditions have evolved into a modernized version of what it is today.

5.2 IMPORTANCE OF THE CHAPTER

The importance of this chapter is to know how modern trends have affected Malay weddings. These days, there are various wedding trends in the industry that are competing. Marriage is the Rites de Passage for most people regardless of their social status. However, costly wedding ceremonies have become a heated issue in Malay contemporary society. This chapter examined how bridal wedding desires were heavily influenced by pricey consumption activities of marketed commodities and services to be fulfilled. The Malay brides were highly desirous of realizing their unique wedding dreams, which were entrenched in heavy, overt consumption of commodities and services provided by the modern wedding industry players. This means that the traditional wedding ceremony that used to be anchored in religion, customs and frugal attitudes is facing tremendous challenges due to the prevalence of the new market and consumption-driven wedding dream concept, and that this phenomenon is rendering contemporary Malay Wedding ever more costly.

The chapter identifies how to overcome the changes against the traditional Malay Wedding culture and at the same time, understand why it has evolved from a traditional Malay Wedding culture to a modernized version of what it used to be and what it currently is now. And to highlight how bridal wedding desires were heavily influenced by pricey consumption activities of marketed commodities and services to be fulfilled. Along with keeping three aspects in mind that are the Wedding Attires, Wedding Rituals, and Wedding Packages.

It is very important to know how modern trends have affected Malay weddings. These days, there are various wedding trends in the industry that are competing, and how bridal wedding desires are heavily influenced by pricey consumption activities of marketed commodities and services to be fulfilled. There are several key terms used in this chapter such as consumerism, Malay wedding ceremony, modern brides, Rites de Passage, wedding dream, wedding products, services, and finally, modernization. Modernization has overcrossed boundaries across all aspects in tradition; in this case we will be specifying the "Effects of Modernization on Malay Weddings." The majority of people these days tend to have their wedding themes in a wide scale of difference or "upgrade" from their original culture that is heavily influenced by social media and the public. Wedding planners in this 21st century have developed the capability and variation of realizing their clients' dream wedding and thus offering more packages to fulfill the desire of having a wedding in a unique modernized aspect.

5.3 MODERNIZATION

Modernization is a global phenomenon. It has altered many phases of lifestyle and yet, the culture that has long been practiced and ritualized by the Malay community that includes certain aspects of Wedding Events should be preserved. This research that we have carried out brings focus and sheds the light on the effects of Modernization on Malay Weddings specifically at Mahligai Creative Weddings and Laman Kayangan, Shah Alam in the possibilities and hopes of understanding the position that newlywed bride and grooms of this modernized era; and understand why Malay Weddings have evolved into a modernized version of what it is today.

An event functions within society purposely to share the joy of celebrations and declare identities with others. According to Raj (2009), events have played an important role in portraying cultures and contributing a major part in economic development. Social and cultural requirements are fully accepted by citizens, as well as the production of economic welfare because such cases will grasp attention to various people from a various foreign region, local citizens, and many more (Raj et al., 2002). For instance, global joint ventures can also be shown through events on both local and international scales. Event planning is meant for determination. Events were created from individual and community initiatives back then, meanwhile, these days the event management is commonly operated by entrepreneurs and professionals from the event industry for the only reason that events are purposeful, organized for specific goals, and probably a high chance of risks to be assigned to the nonspecialists (Bowdin et al., 2012).

An event can be defined as a public assembly for the purpose of celebration, entertainment, education, marketing, or reunion. Getz in his book *Event Management and Event Tourism* (1997) stated that events are temporary occurrences, either planned or unplanned, and they usually have a finite length that is normally fixed or publicized for planned events. They can be classified or organized in different ways based on their size, form, and content. Examples of the various types are special events, hallmark events, mega events, community events, sports event, and many more. Different typologies of events have been established worldwide depending on the purposes of events. Events have been part of any nation's culture and traditions (Raj, 2009). These groupings seem to be appropriate as they encompass all sorts of events and allow the researcher to give the audience a more specific, categorized overview of events (Arcodia and Barker, 2003). Furthermore, to the local people, they can learn more about their own identity in-depth as well as boost up their sense of pride (Raj, 2009) (Figure 5.1).

Typologies of Events

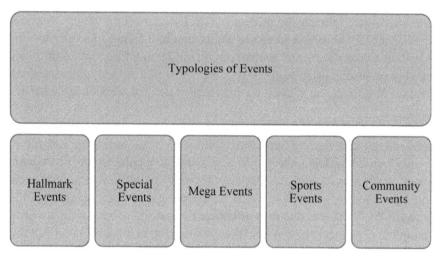

FIGURE 5.1 Typologies of events (Raj et al., 2009).

Community events are known to be laden with traditional and cultural elements. A wedding is a ceremony and associated rituals by which two people vow to spend their lives together in marriage. The wedding ceremony, for example, is among the most significant and fundamental of the religious and sociocultural traditions and events. According to Sneizek (2005), the wedding ceremony involves processes, procedures, and substantial number of meanings that are significant toward forging social community relationships and bonding. Shone and Parry (2004) argued that weddings can be the most complicated events to organize as they involve family and friends a wide range of inspection and repair-related activities ranging from catering to entertainment as easily as the formal aspect of the wedding itself. Planning a wedding calls for multiple tasks and times that may be intertwined in ways that realize both their means and their carrying out extremely complex (McKenzie and Davies, 2010). However, the day of the actual event may consist of the wedding ceremony itself followed by a reception and buffet planning may take several months and affects large numbers of people (Shone and Parry, 2004). Because of such complications and due to the growing length of days, size of budgets, widened scope, and limited time availability, people are turning to event planners to coordinate this important milestone (Goldblatt, 2005).

Modernization through its elements namely social advancement and trends gradually alter the practices in one of the most popular Malay social events that is wedding as modernization gradually touches the periphery of rural area, the axis which discerns between urban and rural is becoming fader. In the midst of modernization, the dream weddings of every Malay couple are diverse and different from the traditional ones and the perception of society toward the wedding change according to the season as now the wealth becomes a bet in order to execute the occasion successfully instead of the role of key people in the weddings (Khairuddin, 2016).

5.3.1 WEDDING ATTIRES

The theme of marriage refers to the identity or certain elements chosen by the couple for their wedding ceremony. Krishnan (2008) mentioned that the theme can be created like other community; for example, western, Japanese, Minang, Javanese, and so on; colors with the use of one or a combination of two or three colors; environment such as garden wedding and so on, all of which rely on the bride's brilliance to create the atmosphere of their unique wedding ceremonies and to make it memorable; not only to the couple but also to the guests (Otnes and Pleck, 2003; Dee, 2006).

The main purpose of selecting and using the concept and color of the theme in their wedding ceremony is to make the wedding look more beautiful and interesting, following the current trends, and to obtain uniqueness and differs their big day from others. In the context of this chapter, the use of concepts or themes of weddings indirectly affects the overall structure of a wedding, especially in terms of commodities and materials to be used. This is because all sorts of commodities and services in a wedding ceremony must be in line with the "requirements" of the concept or theme that has been chosen. The more complex and sophisticated the concept or theme chosen, the higher the cost the couple will have to bear for the necessary goods and services.

5.3.2 WEDDING RITUALS

The choice of lifestyle could differentiate and classify the "taste of choice" of an individual. A high percentage of the respondents said they tend to choose branded goods due to the influences of their peers especially to avoid the feeling of "inferior and shame" (Rokiah Ismail, 2003). The inseparability of concept or "theme" and weddings is since both are embroidered to each other in the implementation of the wedding events in Malay community these days and the usage of highly costly and branded goods in weddings are following the currents standards. The dream and desire to use commodities or services is essentially created, formed, and in the end, it is developed socially in the modern Malay community. The more complex or high-end concept of the wedding theme, the brides and grooms will have to bear the higher costs to get the necessary commodities and services that suits chosen concepts and themes.

5.3.3 WEDDING PACKAGES

Wedding packages are one of the most important commodities in today's weddings as most wedding commodities such as the complete set of seals including bridal beds, chandelier lamps, and decorative ornaments, bridal room decoration, make-up and grooming, and the entrance arch have been assembled under one package and at a certain price offered by the wedding boutiques in accordance with the budget allocation. Khairuddin (2016) stated that the choices of wedding packages from his informants based on the perfection of existing wedding commodities, according to the chosen concept or theme and the commodities and services required for their wedding receptions. In addition, the selection of wedding packages under the same boutique also indirectly help them to save their time, energy, and money as all the necessities for their wedding ceremony they find under the same roof and source. The findings show that expensive price factor is not a barrier for informants to cater their desires as they have provided enough budget allocation to ensure that their wants and needs are fulfilled. Obviously, they are willing to spend a huge amount of money to achieve their desires and thus to satisfy them.

5.4 CONCLUSION

Marriage can be considered as one of the most memorable and happiest moments in a person's life. Hence, the desire to have a beautiful, grand, and a lively wedding is indeed a must. Although the current weddings are still in place to meet religion and cultural demands, at the same time it is also being implemented in order to fulfill the dream weddings through consumption on the commodities and wedding packages and services provided by the events industry. Desire and dreams are a form of personal development that has sociological dimensions and social identity created or extracted through experience, reading, and advertising and so on from various media to the point that the consumption of commodities and services is considered as a standard. In making sense, the consumption pattern is considered as a symbol of relationship and individual's responsibility to fulfill it as a symbol of status and identity (Gell, 1986). Identity is important to emphasize "who you are" and it could be constructive and dynamic. It can be related to such factors, relationship, power, class, gender, and education level. In the context of this research, personal identity and dreams are formed and influenced by new culture intermediaries, especially magazines.

KEYWORDS

- modernization
- Malay wedding
- events
- consumerism
- ceremony
- brides
- Rites de passage

REFERENCES

Allen, J. (2000). Events beyond 2000: Setting the agenda: Proceedings of Conference On Event Evaluation, Research and Education: Sydney July 2000. Sydney: Australian Centre for Event Management.

Creswell, J. W. (2018). Qualitative inquiry at research design: Choosing among five approaches. Los Angeles; London; New Delhi; Singapore; Washington DC: SAGE Publications.

Denzin, N. K., and Lincoln, Y. S. (2013). The landscape of qualitative research. Los Angeles: SAGE Publications.

Event Management—theseus.fi. (n.d.). Retrieved from https://www.theseus.fi/bitstream/handle/10024/82944/event management - official version.pdf?sequence=1

Getz, D. (2008). Event tourism: Definition, evolution, and research. Tourism Management, 29(3), 403–428. doi:10.1016/j.tourman.2007.07.017

Gill, P., Stewart, K., Treasure, E., and Chadwick, B. (2008). Methods of data collection in qualitative research: Interviews and focus groups. British Dental Journal, 204(6), 291–295. doi:10.1038/bdj.2008.192

Harrell, M. C., and Bradley, M. (2009). Data collection methods: Semi-structured interviews and focus groups. Santa Monica, CA: RAND.

Husin, S. N. M. S., Azahari, R., and Rahman, A. A. (2018). Wedding expenses by the Malay Muslim community: An investigation into the sources of expenditure. International Journal of Academic Research in Business and Social Sciences, 8(10), 481–499.

Karipis, K. I., Tsimitakis, E. N., and Skoultsos, S. G. (2009). Contribution of Visitor Information Centers to promoting natural and cultural resources in emerging tourism destinations. International Journal of Tourism Policy, 2(4), 319. doi:10.1504/ijtp.2009.028717

Khairi, and Bin, H. (2019, February 22). A studio research project: Malay celebration as a cultural expression in creating sculpture utilizing an up-cycle approach. Retrieved from https://monash.figshare.com/articles/A_studio_research_project_Malay_celebration_as_a_cultural_expression_in_creating_sculpture_utilizing_an_up-cycle_approach_/4664356

Maxwell, J. A. (2013). Qualitative research design: An interactive approach. Thousand Oaks, CA: SAGE Publications.

Muhammad, R., Zahari, M. S., Kamaruddin, M. S., and Ahmat, N. C. (2013). The Alteration of Malaysian Festival Foods and Its Foodways. Procedia—Social and Behavioral Sciences, 101, 230–238. doi:10.1016/j.sbspro.2013.07.196

Newman, L. F. (1999). Introduction to qualitative research methods: A guidebook and resource, Third Edition. The Journal of Nervous and Mental Disease, 187(9), 587. doi:10.1097/00005053-199909000-00011

Omoregie Etiosa The Impacts of Event Tourism on Host ... (n.d.). Retrieved from https://www.theseus.fi/bitstream/handle/10024/43714/omoregie_etiosa.pdf?sequence=1

Planning expertise, variables influencing performance ... (n.d.). Retrieved from https://pdfs.semanticscholar.org/1799/ce6125dc6d61f0b6f617fa4a5be470aae658.pdf

Ranjani, C. V. (2017). Wedding insurance acceptability and promotional strategies (6th ed., Vol. 3). Retrieved May 16, 2019.

Richards, G., and Palmer, R. (2010). Why Cities Need to be Eventful. Eventful Cities, 1–37. doi:10.1016/b978-0-7506-6987-0.10001-0

Sallehuddin, M. K., and Sukimi, M. F. (2016). Dreams and reality in contemporary Malay wedding ceremonies: A case study from suburban Kuala Lumpur. Geografia 12(7).

Iverman, D. (2017). Doing qualitative research. London: SAGE Publications.

Smith, M. K. (2010). Cultural tourism in a changing world: Politics, participation and (re)presentation. Clevedon, UK: Channel View Publications.

Teoh, G. K., Tan, M. P., Tan, J. S., and Chong, M. C. (2018). Conducting community-based participatory research in an urban Malaysian community: Lessons learned and challenges in establishing partnerships. Journal of Community and Applied Social Psychology, 28(3), 156–168. doi:10.1002/casp.2348

CHAPTER 6

EVENTS TOURISM IN THE EYE OF THE COVID-19 STORM: IMPACTS AND IMPLICATIONS

PRIYAKRUSHNA MOHANTY[1*], HIMANSHI, and RASHMIRANJAN CHOUDHURY

[1]*Department of Tourism Studies, School of Management, Pondicherry University, Puducherry, India*

[2]*Institute of Hotel & Tourism Management, Maharshi Dayanand University, Rohtak, Haryana, India*

[3]*Department of Tourism & Hotel Management, North-Eastern Hill University, Shillong, Meghalaya, India*

*Corresponding author. E-mail: pkmohanty90@gmail.com

ABSTRACT

Events are considered to be integral parts of global tourism and currently they are experiencing massive turmoil in the form of cancellations or postponements thanks to the recent outbreak of the coronavirus disease (COVID-19) which has been declared as a pandemic of the 20th century. Despite its multifaceted nature, the implications of COVID-19 on various events have been understudied thanks to the novelty of the severe acute respiratory syndrome coronavirus 2 (SARS-CoV-2). This paper undertakes a systematic review of scientific literature to discuss the recent developments in various global events amidst COVID-19 and the implications of the disease on event management.

6.1 INTRODUCTION

Travel and Tourism is considered as a sunrise industry that accounted for 10% (8.9 trillion US$) of the global GDP, 330 million jobs (one in every ten jobs), 6.8% (1.7 trillion US$) of total global exports, and 4.3% (940 billion US$) of total investments in the year 2019 (WTTC, 2020a). Events constitute a critical part of tourism systems as they function as major elements both at the origin point (events as push factors to travel) and at the destination point (event as a pull factor) in the marketing and development of the destination (Getz and Page, 2016). Events show a wide spectrum of types based on its nature, size, professionalism, and volume (Bouchon, Hussain, and Konar, 2017). In recent times, many tourism service providers and organizations are specializing in organizing and conducting special events like community fairs and local festivals, thereby attracting local communities and visitors while providing social and economic benefits to the local communities (Getz, 2005, 2008; Hanrahan and Maguire, 2016; Maguire and Hanrahan, 2017).

With the advent of 2020, the travel and tourism industry has experienced massive turmoil in the face of a never before health emergency, that is, the COVID-19 outbreak across the globe (Barua, 2020). The impacts of this unparalleled disease on the travel and tourism sector are unprecedented and fast-changing in nature (UNWTO, 2020). It is believed that the tourism industry is going to be the hardest-hit industry in this pandemic scenario with negative impacts spread on to both demand and supply of tourism products (WTO, 2020). It has been estimated that the travel and tourism sector will take a dip of 20%–30% in the international tourism arrivals (UNWTO, 2020) and a loss of 50 million jobs throughout the global industry (WTTC, 2020b). Consequently, the recent outbreak of COVID-19 has had devastating effects not just on the tourism industry, but also on events all across the world (Gautret et al., 2020). May it be the postponement of the Summer Olympics in Tokyo and the Cannes Film Festival or the cancellation of Wimbledon in the UK and Metropolitan Opera in New York, the impact of COVID-19 was all-prevailing with multifaceted socio-economic and geopolitical implications (Chin, 2020; Garcia et al., 2020).

Though literature concerning tourism or destination management in the context of an infectious disease outbreak is in plenty (*see* Chen et al., 2007; Dwyer et al., 2006; Gössling, 2002; Gu and Wall, 2006; Hall, 2011; Hall et al., 2004; Hodges and Kimball, 2012; Rosselló et al., 2017), only a few of them deal with the management of events in the infectious disease outbreaks (Baker, 2015; Memish et al., 2014), Further, the severity of COVID-19 is unparallel and superior when compared to the outbreaks of other coronaviruses like SARS and MERS (Mahase, 2020; Sun et al., 2020). Due to these multifaceted implications, the current situation demands a special investigation into the various ways in which COVID-19 has impacted the aspect of event management, to prepare well and mitigate any potential risk to the audience or organizers in the post-COVID-19 period.

The current work has attempted to fill the above-mentioned gap by performing a systematic review of the literature of the works concerning COVID-19 and event management. The study discusses two major aspects of event tourism. In the first section, an overview of the status of events tourism before COVID-19 has been briefly discussed. The question of why events remain as a critical factor in the context of COVID-19 has been narrated as the second objective. The third objective deals with the assessment of the impacts of COVID-19 on tourism and events.

6.2 REVIEW METHODOLOGY

Given the novelty and unprecedented nature of COVID-19, research articles discoursing the impact of COVID-19 on events are scarce. Therefore this study can be classified as exploratory research. Due to the scarcity of scientific works on the said subject, the authors of this paper have taken cues from "gray literature," *which includes unpublished studies and studies published outside widely available journals* (Conn et al., 2003, p. 256) and are rich sources of information. In this context, to make the study more robust searches with the same predefined parameters were conducted to trace out the Government and international agency reports, press briefings, preprints, newspaper articles that dealt with the aspect of tourism event management in the context of COVID-19. Thematic content analysis was performed on the sources of data collected through searching the keywords on academic and general search engines. Following the tracing of the themes, the draft of the paper was designed and grammatical and typographical errors were rectified by reviewing by each author.

6.3 STATUS OF EVENTS BEFORE COVID-19 PANDEMIC: AN OVERVIEW

Events are considered essential motivators in the tourism business and they play a major role in the marketing and development of a destination (Getz, 2008). According to Salem, Jones, and Morgan (2004, p. 19), events are "a unique blend of activities, which are the tools for achieving the overall event aims and satisfying customer needs." However, Brown and James (2004) argue that the definition of events varies from one textbook to another. Van der Wagen (2007, p. 5) opines that the event can be best described as: "An event is generally a complex social endeavor characterized by sophisticated planning with a fixed deadline, often involving numerous stakeholders."

Events Tourism is registered as the fastest growing sector in the tourism industry and currently undergoing a dramatic change due to the sudden outbreak of COVID-19. Events play a crucial role in the development of the tourism industry and economic benefits (Seraphin, 2020). Every year, a large number of attendees participate in events that contribute to the promotion of the destination, cultural awareness, employment opportunities, and economic growth (Lee et al., 2013; Lee et al., 2017). As per the study by Oxford Economics (2018), the annual participation only in business events alone was around 1.5 billion visitors worldwide while the share of the global event industry in the global GDP was 1.5 trillion USD with direct and indirect spending constituting a staggering figure nearing 2.5 trillion USD. The global event industry also provided direct and indirect employment opportunities to 26 million peoples (Gössling et al., 2020; Ozili and Arun, 2020). Festivals make a huge contribution and act as an integral part of the tourism industry in different ways, including tourism promotion and cultural offering (Rowen, 2020; Sigala, 2020). Festivals are divided into varied ranges such as food festivals, theater, dance, music, and art. Music events of the United Kingdom contribute £17.6 billion to the economy of the nation and recorded a hike of 22% in the last 2 years and 57% interested in participation in tourism activities (Bas and Sivaprasad, 2020; Davies, 2020).

6.4 EVENTS AND COVID-19: EXPLORING THE LINKAGE

On December 31, 2019, a case of pneumonia with unrecognizable cause was detected in Wuhan, the capital city of Hubei province, and reported to the country office of the World Health Organization (WHO) in China (WHO, 2020c). By January 3, 2020 44 patients with similar symptoms were reported to the national office in China and on January 5, 2020 the news of disease outbreak was flashed on the WHO website (WHO, 2020b). Within a month of its detection, WHO flagged the disease outbreak as *Public Health Emergency of International Concern* on January 30, 2020 (WHO, 2020c) and on February 11, 2020 the disease and the virus causing the disease was officially named as COVID-19 and SARS-CoV-2, respectively (WHO, 2020a). By March 11, 2020, the world witnessed the COVID-19 outbreaks in 114 countries and given its outreach. WHO characterized COVID-19 as a *pandemic* (WHO, 2020d). The disease is having a catastrophic effect on varied spectrums of economic activity and in particular on global tourism. With massive changes in work-life patterns, this pandemic has been promoting an environment of the biggest depression of the 1930s (Rappeport and Smialek, 2020, April, 14).

As the biggest pandemics of the 21st century, the COVID-19 outbreak has had catastrophic impacts on almost all spheres of economic activity (Fernandes, 2020; McKibbin and Fernando, 2020). Global events as one of the crucial wings of tourism have been among the hardest-hit sectors (Ahmed and Memish, 2020; Ebrahim and Memish, 2020; McCloskey et al., 2020). The massiveness of the events in terms of the volume, size, and scope makes them a potentially easy target for not just COVID-19, but also any infectious disease outbreaks. Events suffer from the innate disadvantage of higher vulnerability to internal or external disturbances meaning any small disturbance in the internal and external environment causes catastrophic impacts on any event no matter how neatly the action plan for the event is designed. For example, the Hajj pilgrimage conducted annually in the Kingdom of Saudi Arabia. Even if being the biggest mass gathering annual event in the world, Hajj has been experienced major disturbances not just by COVID-19 outbreak but also by the outbreak of SARS, the rift valley fever (RVF), H1N1 pandemic, Ebola, MERS and Zika (Ahmed and Memish, 2020).

Furthermore, events are considered as one of the biggest sources for transmission of infectious disease (Ishola and Phin, 2011). Therefore cancellation or postponement of the events is always considered as the preferred decision when it comes to a pandemic situation (Ahmed and Memish, 2020; McCloskey et al., 2020). Events and festivals, conducted without any proper regulation can become "super spreading" events. In the recent past, India experienced a sharp surge in the number of COVID-19 infections thanks to the lack of measures taken at religious congregation like Tablighi Jamaat (BBC, 2020).

6.5 COVID-19 AND EVENTS: IMPACTS AND IMPLICATIONS

Amidst the COVID-19 crisis, immediate restrictions were imposed by the government on travel activities and event gatherings. This resulted in irreparable loss to the events tourism sector. According to a report by OSAKA (2020), Meetings, Incentives, Conferences, and Exhibitions events which play a crucial role in the economic growth registered unprecedented cancellations and postponement of events. Almost all events were canceled and postponed by the organizers as per the guidelines announced by the government—exhibitions, concerts, conferences, sports events, marriages, and trade shows (Gössling et al., 2020; Ozili and Arun, 2020). All kind of events across the world whether cultural, business, sports or mega events like Olympic 2020, Indian Premier League (IPL), IIFA 2020, ITB-India, India Fintech Festival, Ultra Festival, Goa Fest, FDCI India Fashion Week, Marathon, META Theater Awards, E3, SXSW tech event, and many more have got affected due to the pandemic (Gössling et al., 2020; Ranasinghe et al., 2020).

Mega events not only have a mass popular appeal but as well as boost the tourist expenditures, provide income sources, and employment. The event provides a platform for promoting and creating awareness regarding the host region. COVID-19 leads to the postponement of two mega events in the world, that is, Olympics 2020 and EURO 2020 Union of European Football Associations (Ludvigsen and Hayton, 2020). Many global events are delayed or canceled due to COVID-19 and few of them are Singapore Airshow 2020, IT and CM China and CTW China, International Exhibition Logistics Associations, National Association of Travel Agents Singapore (NATAS), and ISPO Beijing.

According to Event and Entertainment Management Association, COVID-19 has adversely impacted the events industry in India with incurred losses of Rs. 40,000 crore and estimated approx. Rs. 3000 Cr impact in the first two months based on 100 MSMEs survey projection (reported by Javeri, 2020, June 25). According to the recent release, the event industry is expected to bear a loss of approx. Rs. 20,000 in the first quarter of the financial year 2021 and the industry has planned to postpone events till the third or fourth quarter of the year 2020. If extend to another quarter then events will be canceled for the particular year (Mahendra, 2020, April 10). The impact of Covid-19 disease on sporting event is unprecedented and uncertain. The world never experienced a pandemic of this scale in the century (Ludvigsen and Hayton, 2020). To mitigate the chance of shut down or collapse, event industry may lay off employees or deduct salaries.

The outbreak of COVID-19 has knocked down the event industry around the world. There is a long list of events for which attendees congregate as participants or spectators in the event. A few of the major events have been categorized into five segments and the impact of COVID-19 on each segment has been discussed below (Table 1).

TABLE 6.1 Impact of COVID-19 on Major Events Across the Globe

Type of Events	Name of the Event	Hosting Country	Status
Business/Corporate Meetings	2020 Geneva Motor Show	Switzerland	Canceled
	Google I/O	California, United States	Canceled
	ITB Berlin	Germany	Canceled
	London Book Fair	United Kingdom	Canceled
	2020 North American International Auto Show	Michigan, United States	Canceled
	St. Petersburg International Economic Forum 2020	Russia	Canceled
	Wikimania 2020	Thailand	Postponed
	Computex 2020	Taiwan	Postponed
Religious Events	Christian Holy Week events in Rome	Italy	Canceled
	Easter fires	Multinational	Canceled
	Umrah pilgrimage	Saudi Arabia	Canceled
	New Orleans St. Joseph's Night and Parade	Multinational	Canceled
	Holy Week in Spain	Spain	Canceled
	Vesak	Thailand	Canceled
	Buddha's Birthday	Multinational	Canceled
	Etekaf and *Mid-Sha'ban*	Iran	Canceled
	Passion Play of Iztapalapa	Mexico	Moved to undisclosed location
Sports Events	2020 Arctic Winter Games	Yukon, Canada	Canceled
	Monaco Grands Prix	Monaco	Canceled
	2020 Rome Marathon	Italy	Canceled
	2020 Summer Olympics	Japan	Postponed
	2020 FIFA U-20 Women's World Cup	Panama	Postponed
	La Liga	Spain	Suspended
	2020 Indian Premier League	India	Postponed
	44th Chess Olympiad	Russia	Postponed
	2020 PGA Championship	California, United States	Postponed
Award Functions	47th Daytime Emmy Awards	United States	Postponed
	55th Academy of Country Music Awards	Nevada, United States	Postponed
	Cannes Film Festival	France	Postponed
	L.A. Screenings	California, United States	Canceled
Geopolitical Meetings	36th ASEAN Summit	New Zealand	Rescheduled
	2020 Indian Rajya Sabha elections	India	Postponed
	2020 United Nations Climate Change Conference	Scotland	Postponed

Source: Authors' own work.

6.5.1 IMPACT ON BUSINESS/CORPORATE EVENTS

Business and corporate events have a substantial share in the tourism industry. Business events need a wide range of facilities like convention and exhibition centers, different range of hotels with banquet facilities, and several private and public amenities. Globally most of the business events occur at the city level because of service availability (Getz, 2004). The corporate events have been largely affected by the COVID-19 as almost all services have got hampered because of the precautionary measures taken for the pandemic. Governments worldwide have banned international and domestic travel and halt on mass gathering as the first action when COVID-19 declared as a pandemic (Jamal and Budke, 2020).

The renowned global events having enormous tourism potential have seen an uncertain situation and some of them get canceled as well. Though the financial losses are irreversible, the decision is appreciable on account of the saving of mankind. One of the leading travel and trade show ITB Berlin, 2020 was canceled due to the rapid spread of the COVID-19 (ITB Berlin, 2020, February 28). ITB Berlin is a major tourism corporate event with 10,000 exhibitors from over 180 countries and expected more than 160,000 visitors (ITB Berlin, 2020, February 28; TTR Weekly, 2020, February 29). Though the business firms, ticket buyers will get a refund, it is a massive loss for the organizers as well as the business firm who expected a bunch of trade from the event.

Some of the large technological business meets and conferences also canceled in the due course of COVID-19 situation. The Google I/O developers meet was scheduled in May was canceled by the authorities (Google, 2020; Warren, 2020, March 3). The Mobile World Congress (MWC) one of the biggest events that were planned in Barcelona in February also canceled for the same. The MWC a mega event for partnership, deals, and product launch was expected more than 1200 mobile companies across the globe, with thousands of gathering (Warren, 2020, March 3). Prioritizing the health and safety of the concerned people Facebook also canceled its event developer conference F8. An annual event running since 1988, the Game Developers Conference has been postponed to the next year (Farokhmanes and Statt, 2020, February 28).

One of the largest book fairs, which would have celebrated its 50th anniversary this year, the "London book fair" was canceled over the COVID-19 outbreak. The book fair gathers more than 25,000 numbers of people including the publishing industry to promote, sell, and negotiate their products (BBC, 2020, March 4). Some other book fair events like Paris book fair, book fair in Germany faced the same while Bologna book fair in Italy was initially postponed to May but in later situation organizers called off the event (Nawotka, 2020, March 11). The publication industry faces the indirect impact of the COVID-19.

6.5.2 COVID-19 AND RELIGIOUS EVENTS

COVID-19 pandemic has had a devastating impact on religious festivals across the world. However, as religious events are celebrated only on a fixed date of the year, postponement or cancellation was mostly no option for policymakers. While many religious events were celebrated with minimum devotees, others were celebrated in a secluded environment. Below, the impact of COVID-19 on some of the major religious events has been discussed; Hajj is considered as the fifth pillar of Islam religion. In this annual pilgrimage in the month of Ramadan, millions of Muslims around the world visit Mecca and Medina pilgrimage. Hajj is mandatory for Muslims to visit once in a lifetime (Abuznaid, 2006). In 2019, around 2,400,000 pilgrims congregated at Hajj. The COVID-19 crisis has adversely impacted Hajj pilgrims this year. As per the guidelines set by WHO, restrictions are imposed on event gatherings. In consideration of the COVID-19 impact, UMRAH and the ministry of Hajj announced strict precautionary measures for Hajj Pilgrimage 2020. The Ministry of Hajj and UMRAH had also imposed limits on the pilgrim allowed in the premises, that is, only 10,000 Saud Arabian pilgrims while pregnant, older, and sick pilgrims were advised for not attending the congregation (AFP, 2020, July 30). As per the guidelines all the mandatory measures were taken care of like COVID test before arriving Mecca, quarantine after attending the hajj, regular sanitization of premises, and maintenance of social distancing. As per the new normal of the current situation, a kit having all necessary items was provided to every pilgrim.

The Islamic spiritual event Itikaf is especially known for the seclusion in the mosque during Rajab month. The event believed that it purifies heart, repent, and provides opportunities to work on self-improvement. However, the official announced the cancellation of Itikaf this year due to the COVID-19 outburst (Khamenei, 2020, March 9).

Similarly, after the permit of the Supreme Court, Jagannath Rath Yatra was commenced midst COVID-19. The holy festival is connected with the beliefs and faith of thousands of people across the world. The Rath Yatra was allowed by Supreme Court with the strict guidelines and measure as only 500 peoples were allowed to pull the gigantic chariot of Lord Jagannatha, Balbhadra, and Subhadra. Millions of the devotees take a glimpse of the holy event on television (Sharma, 2020, June 24)

The Holy week is event is a blend of mourning and joy both, which is mostly celebrated by Christians worldwide. Due to the outburst of COVID-19 and imposed restrictions on the mass gathering, Holy week was celebrated without attendees. As per the past events, Holy week drew 10,000 attendees but this time coronavirus came into existence. Hence, it becomes necessary to take needed measures (Burke, 2020, March 14).

New Orleans parades were known for their unique culture. The COVID pandemic and shutdown had a major impact on the annual mega-events like St. Patrick's Day. 34th Joseph St. Patrick Parade was canceled because of COVID. Many events of New Orleans got affected due to the sudden outbreak epidemic. A large number of workers working in the hotel lost their jobs and as per the estimated the budget deficit for next year was $100 million (WDSU Digital, 2020, March 10).

The COVID-19 led to the cancellation of events like Parade and incurred the loss. As per the earlier records, Holy week contributes around 1.3% to GDP, while the expenses incurred in Holy week were 9 million and generated around 400 million in return. The events suspended were Andalusia, processional parades, La Linea e la Conception, Castilla Y Leon. Semana Santa (Holy Week) is among the big businesses which contribute to economic development as well. The study revealed that the suspension of festivals and events could cost more than €102 to the Malaga economy.

The annual event Passion Play of Iztapalapa is celebrated during the Holy Week and held in Iztapalapa borough of Mexico City. It is one of the oldest and elaborate passion plays in Mexico and covered by media. About 3 to 4 million spectators are drawn by these plays. After the COVID-19 crises, the Mayor of Iztapalapa declared to cancel the open space play of Passion of Jesus Christ and announced to celebrate the Passion Play in close space with minimum involvement and stream on televisions and social network platform. The commercial activities fairs and pilgrimage had also registered the adversely hit of COVID-19 (Redacción, 2020, March 17).

For more than 1000 years, Holy Fire is celebrated in Jerusalem and symbolizes the "Jesus" resurrecting. Every year approx. 10,000 Christian pilgrims assemble and celebrate Holy Fire in Jerusalem. This year the Holy Fire was celebrated in an unprecedented way due to the enforced strict restrictions. The virtual platforms like Facebook live and other websites were used for sermons and Seders to the pilgrims. Not only had the gathering registered fall even though the chocolate demand also recorded a decline. Every year Belgium noticed a hike in chocolate demands during this week but this time coronavirus hit harder to the Belgium confectioners (Report, 2020, March, 21).

Keeping in mind the increasing cases of COVID-19, the upcoming Vesak event was canceled by International Council Vesak. United National Day of Vesak event is an international event and commemorated Buddha's birth, enlightenment, Mahaparinirvana. The 17th United Nation Day to be held in Thailand in May but later canceled as a precautionary measure (Lewis, 2020, March 10).

6.5.3 SPORTS EVENTS AMIDST COVID-19

The pandemic has put restrictions on public movements and limited the functionalities which have affected all sectors including sports. The sports industry which is estimated at an annual global value of US$ 756 billion is facing the threat of COVID-19. Economic consequences have been observed as millions of jobs not only related to sports but several associated sectors are also at risk in the ongoing pandemic situation (United Nations, 2020). Likewise, other sports companies and clubs have been exposed to economic and financial problems that may lead to the shutdown of businesses. In this pandemic situation, the sports event with no spectators (ghost game) is losing its credibility as the fan support affect results and generates revenue for the team as well as for broadcasters (Drewes, Daumann, and Follert, 2020). Few professional sports have resumed including team sports with a mutual understanding of concerned authorities with permission of national to regional Governments. The IPL will be played in UAE from September to November with certain guidelines. On the other side, the cancellation of IPL tournament could have resulted in a loss of Rs 4000 crores of revenue for the BCCI (Majumdara and Nahab, 2020).

Certainly, it cannot be recommended to immediately return to the pre-COVID-19 as the situation may turn to be fatal. Most governments and sports organizations need to adopt a few measures and WHO guidelines to effectively manage sports activities. For example, the Australian Institute of Sport (AIS) in consultation with other institutes and Governments has developed a framework for rebooting sports in the COVID-19 environment (Hughes et al., 2020). The AIS framework suggests three levels of activities with a minimum baseline for different high-performance/professional sports.

6.5.4 COVID-19 AND AWARD FUNCTIONS

Major global award ceremonies saw a series of cancellations because of the COVID-19 pandemic. Some of the major award functions have been discussed below:

47th Daytime Emmy Awards is presented by NATAS to the best US daytime television for outstanding achievements. Earlier the events were scheduled on June 12–14, 2020 but later on postponed to June 26, 2020. However, COVID-19 was the route cause for the postponement of the event. Finally, on June 26 the results were announced and awards were felicitated to the winners (Hill, 2020). Similarly, the COVID-19 led to the rescheduling of the 55th Academy of Country Music (ACM) awards. As earlier, it was scheduled to be held on April 5 but later decided to postpone. On Sep 16, 2020, Keith Urban will host the ACM awards that will be held in Nashville, Tennessee (Levenson and Forrest, 2020).

Cannes Film Festival, an annual film festival organized at Cannes, was announced to be held on May 12–13, 2020 but then postponed due to midst breakdown of the pandemic (Marshall, 2020, March 19). L.A screening is another independently developed television markets that attract the prominent T.V program buyer. As per the recorded data, there are about 1500 buyers from 70 countries for hosting L.A screening in Los Angeles. Nowadays, US Television distributors are searching for the best alternatives to cope up with COVID-19 (Videoage, 2020, March 12).

6.5.5 COVID-19 AND GEOPOLITICAL EVENTS

Similar to other events, many geopolitical meetings got suspended amidst COVID-19 keeping in mind the safety and security of politicians and bureaucrats. The ASEAN summit was planned to be commenced on April 8–9 but then the members of ASEAN postponed the event to the end of June 2020 (ASEAN, 2020, March 20). The 26th United National climate change conference, also known as COP26, was to be hosted by Britain this year and was scheduled to be held in November 2020, but because of the ongoing COVID pandemic, the date shifted to 1–12 November 2021 (Lawless and Jordan, 2020, April 1).

There is a further long list of events affected by COVID, but discussing the impact on every event is beyond the scope of the study. However, there is one trend that has caught the attention of the authors. When the physical events have seen a massive downfall in the time of COVID-19, the use of the online or virtual medium of events has experienced remarkable growth. The corporate and academic firms adopted a virtual medium to run the business, new product launch, and to strive during the global crisis. Some of the virtual media platforms, as well as mobile applications, have achieved substantial growth in the last few months. A virtual event platform 6Connex has reached 1000% growth by organizing 52,000 events and subevents in the COVID-19 times (John, 2020, May, 27). YouTube and Facebook are the preferred platforms for new product launch while other platforms like Google meet, Hangout, Zoom, WebX are some concurrent meeting platforms that got a rapid response in the pandemic period.

6.6 CONCLUSION

Events Tourism constitutes the fastest-growing segment in the tourism market and its growth before the COVID-19 pandemic has been discussed in the initial part of this paper. In the second part, it is argued that due to their massiveness and higher vulnerability, events suffer from an innate disadvantage in the COVID-19 context. Furthermore, events have the potential to become the superspreading sources of infection if not organized with proper guidelines and apt measures. Lastly, the impact of the pandemic on various segments of the events has been discussed in detail. It can be concluded that events tourism has experienced "never seen before" loss in this COVID-19 pandemic. While corporate and sports events conceded the biggest losses in the form of cancellations, religious events were carried out with precautionary measures and minimum devotees. The status of other forms of events like academic and award ceremony events in the COVID-19 pandemic have been discussed in this paper.

KEYWORDS

- COVID-19
- events
- event tourism
- sports
- religious events

REFERENCES

Abuznaid, S. (2006). Islam and management: What can be learned? *Thunderbird International Business Review, 48*(1), 125–139.

AFP. (2020, July 30). Only 10,000 Muslims allowed Hajj amid Covid-19 fear. *The Deccan Herald*. Retrieved from https://www.deccanherald.com/international/only-10000-muslims-allowed-hajj-amid-covid-19-fear-867498.html

Ahmed, Q. A., and Memish, Z. A. (2020). The cancellation of mass gatherings (MGs)? Decision making in the time of COVID-19. *Travel Medicine and Infectious Disease, 34*, 101631.

ASEAN. (2020, March 20). Prime Minister's Letter on Rescheduling the 36th ASEAN Summit handed to ASEAN Ambassadors. Retrieved from https://www.asean2020.vn/xem-chi-tiet1/-/asset_publisher/ynfWm23dDfpd/content/prime-minister-s-letter-on-rescheduling-the-36th-asean-summit-handed-to-asean-ambassadors.

Baker, D. M. A. (2015). Tourism and the Health Effects of Infectious Diseases: Are There Potential Risks for Tourists? *International Journal of Safety and Security in Tourism and Hospitality, 1*(12), 1.

Barua, S. (2020). Understanding Coronanomics: The Economic Implications of the Coronavirus (COVID-19) pandemic. Available at SSRN: https://ssrn.com/abstract=3566477 or http://dx.doi.org/10.2139/ssrn.3566477

Bas, T., and Sivaprasad, S. (2020). The Impact of the COVID-19 Pandemic Crisis on the Travel and Tourism Sector: UK Evidence. Available at SSRN 3623404. doi: https://dx.doi.org/10.2139/ssrn.3623404

BBC. (2020, 31 March 2020). Coronavirus: Search for hundreds of people after Delhi prayer meeting. *BBC*. Retrieved from https://www.bbc.com/news/world-asia-india-52104753

BBC. (2020, March 4). London Book Fair cancelled over coronavirus fears [Online]. Retrieved from https://www.bbc.com/news/entertainment-arts-51735208

Bouchon, F., Hussain, K., and Konar, R. (2017). Event management education and event industry: A case of Malaysia. *MOJEM: Malaysian Online Journal of Educational Management, 3*(1), 1–17.

Brown, S., and James, J. (2004). Event design and management: Ritual sacrifice. In I. Yeoman, M. Robertson, J. Ali-Knight, S. Drummond, and U. McMahon-Beattie (Eds.), *Festivals and Events Management* (pp. 53–64): Elsevier Butterworth-Heinemann.

Burke, D. (2020, March 14). The great shutdown 2020: What churches, mosques and temples are doing to fight the spread of coronavirus. *CNN*. Retrieved from https://edition.cnn.com/2020/03/14/world/churches-mosques-temples-coronavirus-spread/index.html

Chen, Y.-C., Kang, H.-H., and Yang, T.-C. (2007). A Study on the Impact of SARS on the Forecast of Visitor Arrivals to China. *Journal of Asia-Pacific Business, 8*(1), 31–50.

Chin, K. (2020, 13 March, 2020). Coronavirus Fallout: A Roundup of Canceled Events. *The Wall Street Journal*. Retrieved from https://www.wsj.com/articles/coronavirus-fallout-a-roundup-of-canceled-events-11583943224

Conn, V. S., Valentine, J. C., Cooper, H. M., and Rantz, M. J. (2003). Grey literature in meta-analyses. *Nursing Research, 52*(4), 256–261.

Davies, K. (2020). Festivals Post Covid-19. *Leisure Sciences*, 1–6. doi: https://doi.org/10.1080/01490400.2020.1774000

Drewes, M., Daumann, F., and Follert, F. (2020). Exploring the sports economic impact of COVID-19 on professional soccer. *Soccer and Society*, 1–13.

Dwyer, L., Forsyth, P., and Spurr, R. (2006). Effects of the SARS Crisis on the Economic Contribution of Tourism to Australia. *Tourism Review International, 10*(1–2), 47–55.

Ebrahim, S. H., and Memish, Z. A. (2020). COVID-19–the role of mass gatherings. *Travel Medicine and Infectious Disease*.

Farokhmanes, M., and Statt, N. (2020, February 28). GDC postponed to later this year over coronavirus concerns San Francisco's biggest gaming event won't take place next month [blog post]. Retrieved from https://www.theverge.com/2020/2/28/21156037/gdc-2020-canceled-coronavirus-gaming-event-san-francisco

Fernandes, N. (2020). Economic effects of coronavirus outbreak (COVID-19) on the world economy. Available at SSRN 3557504.

Garcia, S. E., Mzezewa, T., Vigdor, N., Zaveri, M., Zraick, K., Sisario, B.,...Padilla, M. (2020, 1 April, 2020). A List of What's Been Canceled Because of the Coronavirus. *The New York Times*.

Gautret, P., Al-Tawfiq, J. A., and Hoang, V. (2020). COVID 19: Will the 2020 Hajj pilgrimage and Tokyo Olympic Games be cancelled? *Travel Medicine and Infectious Disease*, 101622.

Getz, D. (2004). *Bidding on events: Identifying event selection criteria and critical success factors.* Paper presented at the Journal of Convention and Exhibition Management.

Getz, D. (2005). *Event Management and Event Tourism.* New York: NY: Cognizant Communication Corporation.

Getz, D. (2008). Event tourism: Definition, evolution, and research. *Tourism Management, 29*(3), 403–428.

Getz, D., and Page, S. J. (2016). Progress and prospects for event tourism research. *Tourism Management, 52*, 593–631.

Google. (2020). Google I/O. Retrieved from https://events.google.com/io/

Gössling, S. (2002). Global environmental consequences of tourism. *Global Environmental Change, 12*(4), 283–302.

Gössling, S., Scott, D., and Hall, C. M. (2020). Pandemics, tourism and global change: a rapid assessment of COVID-19. *Journal of Sustainable Tourism*, 1–20.

Gu, H., and Wall, G. (2006). The effects of SARS on China's tourism enterprises. *Turizam: Međunarodni Znanstveno-stručni Casopis, 54*(3), 225–234.

Hall, C. M. (2011). Health and medical tourism: a kill or cure for global public health? *Tourism Review, 66*(1/2), 4–15.

Hall, C. M., Timothy, D. J., and Duval, D. T. (2004). Security and tourism: towards a new understanding? *Journal of Travel and Tourism Marketing, 15*(2–3), 1–18.

Hanrahan, J., and Maguire, K. (2016). *Local authority planning provision for event management in Ireland: A socio-cultural perspective.* Paper presented at the Journal of Convention and Event Tourism.

Hill, L. (2020). Work on 47th Annual Daytime Emmy Awards Will Continue, Despite Postponement. Retrieved from https://www.indiewire.com/2020/03/47th-annual-daytime-emmy-awards-postponed-1202219232/

Hodges, J. R., and Kimball, A. M. (2012). Unseen travelers: medical tourism and the spread of infectious disease. *Risks and Challenges in Medical Tourism: Understanding the Global Market for Health Services.* Santa Barbara, CA: Praeger, 111–137.

Hughes, D., Saw, R., Perera, N. K. P., Mooney, M., Wallett, A., Cooke, J., et al. (2020). The Australian Institute of Sport framework for rebooting sport in a COVID-19 environment. *Journal of Science and Medicine in Sport, 23*(7), 639–663.

Ishola, D. A., and Phin, N. (2011). Could influenza transmission be reduced by restricting mass gatherings? Towards an evidence-based policy framework. *Journal of Epidemiology and Global Health, 1*(1), 33–60.

ITB Berlin. (2020, February 28). ITB Berlin 2020 cancelled [Press release]. Retrieved from *https://www.itb-berlin.com/Press/PressReleases/News_73794.html*

Jamal, T., and Budke, C. (2020). Tourism in a world with pandemics: local-global responsibility and action. *Journal of Tourism Futures, 6*(2).

Javeri, L. G. (2020, June 25). Reeling under COVID-19 impact, India's live events giants mull future approach for audience changed by pandemic. *Firstpost*. Retrieved from https://www.firstpost.com/entertainment/reeling-under-covid-19-impact-indias-live-events-giants-mull-future-approach-for-audience-changed-by-pandemic-8437481.html

John, K. (2020, May, 27). Virtual Events Up 1000% Since COVID-19, With 52,000 On Just One Platform. *Forbes*. Retrieved from https://www.forbes.com/sites/johnkoetsier/2020/05/27/virtual-events-up-1000-with-52000-on-just-one-platform/#2aeaffd37a23

Khamenei. (2020, March 9). Imam Khamenei's recommendation following the cancellation of Itikaf due to the Coronavirus outbreak. Retrieved from https://www.jornada.com.mx/ultimas/capital/2020/03/17/cancelan-viacrucis-de-iztapalapa-5742.html

Lawless, J., and Jordan, F. (2020, April 1). UN climate summit postponed until 2021 because of COVID-19AP. *AP NEWS*. Retrieved from https://apnews.com/c0be712432e3443cbe819629f4407047

Lee, C.-K., Lee, M., and Yoon, S.-H. (2013). Estimating the economic impact of convention and exhibition businesses, using a regional input–output model: A case study of the Daejeon Convention Center in South Korea. *Asia Pacific Journal of Tourism Research, 18*(4), 330–353.

Lee, C.-K., Mjelde, J. W., and Kwon, Y. J. (2017). Estimating the economic impact of a mega-event on host and neighbouring regions. *Leisure Studies, 36*(1), 138–152.

Levenson, E., and Forrest, S. (2020). Academy of Country Music Awards postponed because of coronavirus. *CNN*. Retrieved from https://www.cnn.com/2020/03/15/us/academy-country-music-awards-coronavirus/index.html

Lewis, C. (2020, March 10). 17th United Nations Day of Vesak Event Canceled over Coronavirus Risk. Retrieved from https://www.buddhistdoor.net/news/17th-united-nations-day-of-vesak-event-canceled-over-coronavirus-risk

Ludvigsen, J. A. L., and Hayton, J. W. (2020). Toward COVID-19 secure events: considerations for organizing the safe resumption of major sporting events. *Managing Sport and Leisure*, 1–11.

Maguire, K., and Hanrahan, J. (2017). Assessing the economic impact of event management in Ireland: A local authority planning perspective. *Event Management, 21*(3), 333–346.

Mahase, E. (2020). Coronavirus: covid-19 has killed more people than SARS and MERS combined, despite lower case fatality rate. In: British Medical Journal Publishing Group.

Mahendra, V. (2020, April 10). Coronavirus Impact: As events move online the industry stands to lose Rs 20,000 crore in Q1FY21. *The Financial Express*. Retrieved from https://www.financialexpress.com/brandwagon/coronavirus-impact-as-events-move-online-the-industry-stands-to-lose-rs-20000-crore-in-q1fy21/1924634/

Majumdara, B., and Nahab, S. (2020). Live sport during the COVID-19 crisis: fans as creative broadcasters. *Sport in Society*, 1–9.

Marshall, A. (2020, March 19). Cannes Film Festival Postponed Over Coronavirus Concerns. *The New York Times*. Retrieved from https://www.cnn.com/2020/03/15/us/academy-country-music-awards-coronavirus/index.html

McCloskey, B., Zumla, A., Ippolito, G., Blumberg, L., Arbon, P., Cicero, A.,...Borodina, M. (2020). Mass gathering events and reducing further global spread of COVID-19: a political and public health dilemma. *The Lancet, 395*(10230), 1096–1099.

McKibbin, W. J., and Fernando, R. (2020). The global macroeconomic impacts of COVID-19: Seven scenarios.CAMA Working Paper No. 19/2020, Available at SSRN: https://ssrn.com/abstract=3547729 or http://dx.doi.org/10.2139/ssrn.3547729

Memish, Z. A., Zumla, A., Alhakeem, R. F., Assiri, A., Turkestani, A., Al Harby, K. D.,... Barbeschi, M. (2014). Hajj: infectious disease surveillance and control. *The Lancet, 383* (9934), 2073–2082.

Nawotka. (2020, March 11). 2020 Bologna Children's Book Fair Is Canceled. Retrieved from https://www.publishersweekly.com/pw/by-topic/international/trade-shows/article/82659-bologna-children-s-book-fair-is-canceled.html#:~:text=The%20book%20fair%20issued%20a,Trade%20Fair%20has%20been%20cancelled.%22

OSAKA. (2020). *Guidelines for Infectious Disease Control.* Retrieved from https://cdn.osaka-info.jp/page_translation/content/07833fc0-c56e-11ea-af36-06326e701dd4.pdf

Oxford Economics. (2018). *Global Economic Significance of Business Events.* Retrieved from https://insights.eventscouncil.org/Portals/0/OE-EIC%20Global%20Meetings%20Significance%20%28FINAL%29%202018-11-09-2018.pdf

Ozili, P. K., and Arun, T. (2020). Spillover of COVID-19: impact on the Global Economy. *SSRN Electronic Journal.* doi: https://doi.org/10.2139/ssrn.3562570

Rappeport, A., and Smialek, J. (2020, April, 14). I.M.F. predicts worst downturn since the great depression. *New York Times.* Retrieved from https://www.nytimes.com/2020/04/14/us/politics/coronaviruseconomy-recession-depression.html

Redacción, M. (2020, March 17). Stations of the Cross in Iztapalapa are suspended; events behind closed doors and via TV. Retrieved from https://www.jornada.com.mx/ultimas/capital/2020/03/17/cancelan-viacrucis-de-iztapalapa-5742.html

Report, T. (2020, March, 21). Checkpoints disappear in Wuhan, Easter fires canceled. Retrieved from https://www.tellerreport.com/news/2020-03-21-checkpoints-disappear-in-wuhan-easter-fires-canceled-.rkKG4AQ8U.html

Rosselló, J., Santana-Gallego, M., and Awan, W. (2017). Infectious disease risk and international tourism demand. *Health Policy and Planning, 32*(4), 538–548.

Rowen, I. (2020). The transformational festival as a subversive toolbox for a transformed tourism: lessons from Burning Man for a COVID-19 world. *Tourism Geographies,* 1–8.

Salem, G., Jones, E., and Morgan, N. (2004). An overview of events management. In I. Yeoman, M. Robertson, J. Ali-Knight, S. Drummond, and U. McMahon-Beattie (Eds.), *Festival and Events Management* (pp. 14): Elsevier Butterworth Heinemann.

Seraphin, H. (2020). *COVID-19: an opportunity to review existing grounded theories in event studies.* Paper presented at the Journal of Convention and Event Tourism.

Sharma, S. (2020, June 24). With masked priests and minimum public attendance, this is how the Jagannath Yatra looked like amid the pandemic. *Times Now.* Retrieved from https://www.timesnownews.com/india/article/with-masked-priests-minimum-public-attendance-this-is-how-the-jagannath-yatra-looked-like-amid-the-pandemic/611080

Sigala, M. (2020). Tourism and COVID-19: impacts and implications for advancing and resetting industry and research. *Journal of Business Research, 117,* 312–321.

Sun, P., Lu, X., Xu, C., Sun, W., and Pan, B. (2020). Understanding of COVID-19 based on current evidence. *Journal of Medical Virology, 92*(6), 548–551.

TTR Weekly. (2020, February 29). ITB Berlin 2020 cancelled. Retrieved from https://www.ttrweekly.com/site/2020/02/itb-berlin-2020-cancelled/

United Nations. (2020). *The impact of COVID-19 on sport, physical activity and well-being and its effects on social development.* Retrieved from https://www.un.org/development/desa/dspd/wp-content/uploads/sites/22/2020/05/PB_73.pdf

UNWTO. (2020). Impact Assessment of the Covid-19 Outbreak on International Tourism. Retrieved from ttps://www.unwto.org/impact-assessment-of-the-covid-19-outbreak-on-international-tourism

Van der Wagen, L. (2007). *Human resource management for events: Managing the event workforce*: Routledge.

Videoage. (2020, March 12). The L.A. Screenings Update.

Warren, T. (2020, March 3). Google cancels I/O 2020, its biggest event of the year: Google's developer event scrapped due to coronavirus spread Retrieved from https://www.theverge.com/2020/3/3/21163553/google-io-2020-cancelled-coronavirus-tech-developer-conference

WDSU Digital. (2020, March 10). New Orleans St. Patrick's parades, Super Sunday, large events canceled because of coronavirus concerns. Retrieved from https://www.wdsu.com/article/new-orleans-st-patricks-parades-super-sunday-large-events-canceled-because-of-coronavirus-concerns/31365373

WHO. (2020a). Naming the coronavirus disease (COVID-19) and the virus that causes it [Press release]. Retrieved from https://www.who.int/emergencies/diseases/novel-coronavirus-2019/technical-guidance/naming-the-coronavirus-disease-(covid-2019)-and-the-virus-that-causes-it

WHO. (2020b). Pneumonia of unknown cause—China [Press release]. Retrieved from https://www.who.int/csr/don/05-january-2020-pneumonia-of-unkown-cause-china/en/

WHO. (2020c). Rolling updates on coronavirus disease (COVID-19). Retrieved from https://www.who.int/emergencies/diseases/novel-coronavirus-2019/events-as-they-happen

WHO. (2020d). WHO Director-General's opening remarks at the media briefing on COVID-19-11 March 2020 [Press release]. Retrieved from https://www.who.int/dg/speeches/detail/who-director-general-s-opening-remarks-at-the-media-briefing-on-covid-19-11-march-2020

WTO. (2020). Tourism and COVID-19. Retrieved from https://www.unwto.org/tourism-covid-19

WTTC. (2020a). Economic Impact. Retrieved from https://www.wttc.org/economic-impact/

WTTC. (2020b). Open Letter from WTTC to Governments. Retrieved from https://www.wttc.org/about/media-centre/press-releases/press-releases/2020/open-letter-from-wttc-to-governments/

CHAPTER 7

BUSINESS TOURISM AND ECONOMIC IMPACTS: EVIDENCE FROM THE MALAYSIAN BUSINESS EVENTS INDUSTRY

JEETESH KUMAR[1*] and KASHIF HUSSAIN[2]

[1]School of Hospitality, Tourism and Events, Centre for Research and Innovation in Tourism (CRiT), Taylor's University, Malaysia

[2]School of Media and Communication, Centre for Research and Innovation in Tourism (CRiT); Taylor's University, Malaysia

*Corresponding author. E-mail: Jeetesh.kuamr@taylors.edu.my

ABSTRACT

The business event industry has grown enormously since the 1980s. Though the downturn has hit it in national and international economic activity in the first half of the 1990s, it continues to grow faster than tourism as a whole. With business tourism, there is a significant financial gain for the host community. Moreover, business tourists contribute to the host community by exploiting hotels, restaurants, shopping avenues, and collaborating in different varied activities. Also, these events bring status and stand for the host destination. According to United Nations World Tourism Organization for the projection of long-term tourism, the international arrivals (overnight) rate increased by an average of 3.5% from 2010 to 2030. The market share of emerging economies increased from 30% in 1980 to 45.6% in 2018 and is expected to reach 57% by 2030, equivalent to over 1 billion international tourist arrivals. World Travel and Tourism Council mentioned in their business travel report that the total amount spent by business tourists was US$ 1,283 billion and 182 million business tourists travelled worldwide in 2019. Due to such demand and favorable conditions, several trends can be seen in the event industry including continued growth of the overall industry, boost in fuel costs affects the travel industry, source of travel planning and purchasing, development and expense management, geo-tourism, generational shifts, crises and disaster planning, and family and friends reunion travel. There are several impacts of the business event industry on the host economies. This chapter has looked forward as the impacts, particularly economic impacts, and the suitable model/ways to estimate the economic impacts of business events. This chapter is helpful for academics as well as for industry personal linked with business tourism.

7.1 INTRODUCTION

Meetings, incentives, conventions, and exhibitions (MICE) sector has been identified as a fast-growing segment of the tourism industry in the past decade. Wootton and Stevens (1995) mentioned that "business tourism has grown strongly since the 1980s and through the downturn has hit it in national and international economic activity in the first half of the 1990s, it continues to grow faster than tourism as a whole." Hence, this chapter had been dedicated to research on the business events industry and the economic value of business events.

Tourism is a significant source of foreign exchange earnings, a generator of personal and corporate incomes, a creator of employment, and a contributor to government earnings. It is a dominant international activity, surpassing even trade oil and made product. Economists study the results of the tourism industry in the economy. The economic importance of the tourism industry cannot be underestimated. Besides, Travel and Tourism has been set for a milestone year as the industry's total (direct, indirect, and induced) contribution to the global economy, contributed US$ 8.9 trillion to GDP and 330 million jobs globally in 2019 (World Travel and Tourism Corporation (WTTC), 2020).

Business tourism can be defined in many ways, as different authors have different perspectives on business tourism. Business tourism consists of business events, including MICE. MICE business has matured, developed, and reflected the changes of the cordial reception business (Montgomery and Strick, 1995; Rogers, 2008). It is a vital growing segment in the area of business. With business tourism, there is significant financial gain for the host community. Moreover, business tourists contribute to the host community by exploiting hotels, restaurants, shopping avenues, and collaborating in different varied activities. Furthermore, being chosen as a conference host brings status and stands for the host destination (Rogers, 2008; Kumar and Hussain, 2013).

Further, the literature supports that the business tourism industry is one of the critical sectors in the worldwide tourism industry that is growing and maturing fast. It is the sector that pulls remunerative direct and indirect revenues for host destinations. Besides, it conjointly creates employment opportunities and generates exchange. Because of these significant characteristics, the quantity of destinations vying for this young and dynamic trade is extraordinarily increasing.

7.2 REVIEW OF LITERATURE

7.2.1 MICE INDUSTRY

The MICE Industry, also known as the business events industry, is one of the fastest-growing types of tourism and is turning into an effective standard method to regenerate native economies. While adapting to the International Congress and Convention Association (ICCA) (2012, 2013) concept, tourism can be divided into leisure tourism and business tourism. Similarly, Haven-Tang et al. (2007) and Hankinson (2005) mentioned that business tourism encompasses all visits associated with a tourist's employment or business interest like meetings, conferences, and exhibitions. Furthermore, business is global, whereby every industry/business wants to explore more and needs to get into new markets. The exhibition is one of the key business events, whereby companies use the exhibition as a market diversification (marketing strategy) to exhibit new products and capture new markets.

Therefore the economic importance of business events cannot be underestimated. Nevertheless, it is quite necessary within the MICE business to identify the total expenditure from the views of each organizer and participant. As a result, business events have become key players that attract businesses. Based on an analysis carried out by the World Travel and Tourism Council (WTTC, 2020), the worldwide travel and business enterprise trade grew by 3.5% in 2019, marginally quicker than the global rate in the economic process, which was expected to be 2.5%.

The year 2019 was another year of strong growth for the global Travel and Tourism sector reinforcing its role as a driver of economic growth and job creation. This rate of change means that the travel and business enterprise trade had been predicted to a total contribution of US$ 8.9 trillion to the worldwide economy. Besides, when the impact of the broader economy on the trade area unit (visitor exports) was taken into consideration, the travel and tourism industry has injected US$ 1.7 trillion into the worldwide economy and generated 330 million jobs—or one in ten of all jobs on the earth (WTTC, 2020). Therefore tourism is a significant driver of growth and prosperity, and significantly in developing countries, it offers employment to eradicate impoverishment.

According to United Nations World Tourism Organization (UNWTO, 2013) "tourism includes the activities of persons travelling to and staying in places outside their usual atmosphere for less than one consecutive year for leisure, business, or different functions not associated with the exercise of an activity compensated from the place visited." Also, based on United Nations World Tourism Organization (UNWTO) (2019), arrivals of international tourists in Asia-Pacific reached historically high, which was 348 million in 2018, 7% more than the year 2017. Most destinations posted double-digit growth, boosted by the healthy development of local economies in the region. Receipts grew, accordingly, by 7% in real terms to US$ 435 billion for the year 2018.

On the other hand, ICCA's (2012) custom-made definition of business tourism is that "business tourism is providing facilities and services to the big number of tourists World Health Organization annually attend conferences, congresses, exhibitions, business events incentive travel, and company hospitality." International congress and convention associations additionally highlight that there is not usually used or universally accepted definition obtainable for the term business tourism (ICCA, 2012).

Besides, the UNWTO also did not describe business tourism specifically (UNWTO, 2012). From past literature on business tourism, researchers represented it by keeping it within its scope of business activities concerning tourism. For example, Haven-Tang, Jones, and Webb (2007) mentioned that business tourism consists of all visits associated with a tourists' employment or business interest, e.g., conferences and meetings; exhibitions and trade fairs; and company hospitality and events. Similarly, Hankinson (2005) cited business tourism as travel-related to group action at conferences, exhibitions, and incentive events. These previously mentioned ideas are essential to determine why the UNWTO might not think about it as an entirely business tourism industry; instead, classified it as a meeting industry.

On top of that, UNWTO (2011, 2012, 2013) defines the conference industry as a visit with the primary purpose that could be a business/professional schedule that includes attending conferences, congresses, trade fairs and exhibitions, and different businesses and professional activities. Furthermore, the term meeting industry is most popularly applied by ICCA, Meeting Professionals

International, and Reed Travel in the form of MICE that does not acknowledge the economic nature of such business (UNWTO, 2012).

Several studies have commented on the confusion surrounding the utilization of specific term within the field of business tourism or meeting trade associated with MICE. Therefore the concept of business events in this study was derived. The MICE industry is also known as the convention and meeting industry, where conferences and exhibitions are the most critical types of business events. Several studies have mentioned that business meetings always occur for a shorter time or on the same day, so tourists do not spend much time the local tourism products like hotel/lodging and F&B (UNWTO, 2006). Besides, minimal data are available for the incentive group and the organizers (PCOs), which had been very reluctant to provide data (expenditure). The market is highly monopolistic in competition and has intense rivalry in the industry. Therefore all the data had been kept private and confidential (Riandey and Quaglia, 2008; Singer, Groves, and Corning, 1999). Hence, the current chapter elaborated business events from two (2) dimensional perspectives: Conferences and Exhibitions.

Conferences: It is usually a short duration of gathering for discussing relevant topics, resolution issues, or only consulting with the individuals working within the same field. Organizations organize conferences to create a platform and network for discussion, to require a more in-depth examination for their industry, to exchange views, to convey vital messages, to dialogue crucial queries, or to provide subject matter to some relevant areas (Rogers, 2008). Conferences are being organized around different cities, and countries called rotating conferences and conferences might be managed at similar destinations called annual conferences. A conference is a meeting activity/event of individuals, who "confer" a couple of topics of common interest. It includes the organizer and the attending tourists. The World Health Organization has organized the event regionally or internationally, private companies, educational establishment, trade or professional association, and also the independent attending participants coming from different regions or countries to participate in the event.

Exhibitions: Events to which businesses send staff to display their product to potential customers. They attend to shop for and receive professional information regarding the products being exhibited, mainly straight from the manufacturers.

An exhibition is a professionally organized event that facilitates the meeting of buyers and sellers efficiently. An advert exhibition includes trade fairs, trade shows, or expos that are usually scheduled for a particular interest or the industry will showcase and demonstrate their latest products, services, and examine recent trends and opportunities. It includes the organizer, and the World Health Organization organizes the event locally or internationally, which can be a private company or association with independent buyers and sellers coming from different regions or countries to attend/join the event.

Therefore the business events industry is recognized as a high-yield element of the tourism industry with direct connections to alternative vital areas, such as conferences, incentive groups, and exhibitions. It has great potential for additional expansion (Wooton and Stevens, 1995). Global business events have contributed US$ 1.07 trillion in terms of direct spending, 26 million jobs globally and generated US$ 1.5 trillion of GDP in 2017 (Events Industry Council. 2018). Hussain et al. (2017) reported in their research for the year 2016, an average expenditure per business tourist per event was found to be MYR 6271 (US$ 1918), whereas conference delegates and exhibition buyers had an average spending of MYR 7426 (US$ 2271) and MYR 5114 (US$ 1564), respectively. Total direct economic value contributed to the local economy through the business tourism market in Malaysia was MYR 4.7 billion (US$ 1.44 billion). The overall economic multiplier was found to be 2.1, which accounts for MYR 9.7 billion (US$ 2.96 billion) of total economic impact (direct, indirect and induced). Research also mentioned about contribution to employment that one FTE for every MYR 29,806 of total economic value created 325,437 job opportunities to the Malaysian economy. In 2014, the business tourist market supported the local economy by MYR 416 million (US$ 127.2 million) of contribution to tax revenue.

7.2.2 BUSINESS EVENTS, SIZE, AND ECONOMIC VALUE

"Business Tourism is concerned with people travelling for purposes which are related to their work. As such, it represents one of the oldest forms of tourism, a man having travelled for this purpose of trade since very early times" (Davidsons, 1994). The tourist who travels for business purposes is called a business tourist, and according to the standard definition of tourism, the business tourist has to stay at least one night away from home. Business tourism is business to business activity. This industry encompasses organizers and delegates of the conferences, exhibitors, and visitors at the trade fairs and exhibitions, incentive travels, and individual business tourists.

Cope (2006) claimed that business tourists could be divided into two categories: individual business tourist and business tourist. Individual tourist could be the person who is travelling regularly because of his job/employment. On the other hand, Davidson (2001, p. 73) mentioned that tourists participate in occasional group events. Business tourism and the MICE industry are closely related. Business tourist earns more significant revenue for the host destinations as compared to other tourism types. Business tourism can be described from two different perspectives: demand and supply sides (Mc Niccoll, 2004). Demand perspective looks at the money spent by the inbound tourists who came for business purpose and supplies side of business tourist looks into the number of activities and products designed and supplied to the business tourists.

Swarbrooke and Horner (2001) mentioned that business tourists are the ones who spend double or triple to leisure tourists and use top-class hotels, transport, and restaurants during their stay. Furthermore, Swarbrooke and Horner (2001) elaborated that business tourism works at a high peak in the winter and usually four days of the week, from Monday to Thursday. MICE industry extended its business to some sun destination for their off-peak season. Business tourists have more chances to return in the future for business or leisure purposes if they enjoy and are satisfied with the destination; plus, they will do word of mouth to their fellow friends and family, which has a direct positive effect on the future host destination. Free marketing and satisfied tourists have become ambassadors for the destination.

Most of the time, all business tourists enjoy the same services and facilities as leisure tourists. Business tourists spend more than leisure tourists and sometimes, business tourists become leisure tourists. Business tourists extend their stay for a few more days at the destination for a holiday, leisure purpose, pre- or post-event they were participating in. Business tourists also bring their companion, friend, or spouses for leisure purpose and business trip. The companion will be accessible during the business events and these ads on the leisure tourist numbers due to business events. Similarly, the airlines also used to combine tourists, business, and leisure together, except charter flights. Hotels also use to accommodate all types of tourists and the venue, conference halls/building that also can serve different occasions like one day concert and on another day, the same venue to be used for an international conference (Swarbrooke and Horner, 2001).

According to the ICCA statistics, 400,000 business events (conferences and exhibitions) are being held every year with an average output of US$ 280 billion. Similarly, the Global Association of Exhibition industry mentioned that the annual output of the MICE industry is US$ 1.16 trillion, which includes US$ 400 billion from conferences and US$ 760 billion from exhibitions. UNWTO (2012) mentioned in their report that by 2030, there will be US$ 2 billion of new middle-class business tourists available, created throughout the world and led by India and China.

7.2.3 SPENDING PATTERNS AMONG BUSINESS TOURISTS

It is challenging to assess real economic impact because there is no standard method to measure how much a tourist spends, except by surveying detailed information of goods and services and their prices that the tourist used and paid (Lovejoy, 2003). Hence, it is significant to survey the actual tourists who spend. Still, most of the time, tourists spend through different channels like TSAs or other accounting models, creating an estimate of the sending directly (Okubo and Planting, 1998). Moreover, literature shows that many studies have looked into tourists' spending; however, most of the time, visitors' spending is reported in a lump sum—the whole group or per trip or day expenditure. Chhabra (2002) explained the expenditure pattern for tourists, where it was found that tourists spent more money on lodging/hotel, followed by shopping, food and beverages, and travel expenditure.

Meanwhile, Stynes (1998) particularized the technical aspects of measuring tourists' spending, primarily focused on collecting data and accurate visitors data, region/area should be defined clearly, spending area/categories, and only for visitors to a particular region. Furthermore, Stynes illustrated that the survey questionnaire should be precise to reduce biases and recall bias. It is also essential to survey within a few days of the spending; otherwise, there are chances of recall bias. Many researchers have concluded that recall bias error occurred due to underestimating spending (Frechtling, 1994; Howard et al., 1991; Stynes, 1998; Stynes and Mahoney, 1989).

As mentioned earlier, business tourists spend almost double/triple compared to leisure tourists. Therefore, several tourism organizations have highlighted these high expenditures and intend to revisit a leisure trip to have a positive economic impact.

Wang et al. (2006) classified the tourist's expenditure regarding identifying the major significant factor influencing the expenditure categories. It is essential to point out the main category—the most spending area by collecting expenditure data from the sample to understand destination planners' wide-ranging understanding. Another study by Brida et al. (2012) stated that demographic factors (type, age, gender, nationality, economic, purpose, and social-cultural) also affect tourists' expenditure. Income level and prices can be significant factors to determine the demand for leisure tourism. Therefore, both factors can have a negative effect on business tourism.

Later, it was found by Downward and Lumsdon (2003) and Lehto et al. (2004) that income is not a significant factor for business tourists, especially same-day tourist, as most of the expenses done by business tourists are covered by the company, or the organization they are working for. Hence, it is substantial to understand the business tourists' spending patterns, which have potential economic benefits rather than leisure tourists. According to Chi and Qu (2009), tourists' satisfaction is measured by tourism experience in the destination. A good tourism experience is significant to influence the tourists for future purchase and recommendations to their friends (Choi and Chu, 2001; Yoon and Uysal, 2005).

Furthermore, tourists' spending consists of pre- and post-business trip expenditure activities, which are very helpful for planning for the growth of the business tourism industry. Regular data collection, monitoring activities, and destination-based surveys every year allow one to keep track of the time-series data. The most important consequence from the business tourists' spending each dollar in the MICE tourism initiates the broad, comprehensive set of economic inter- reactions that influences other sectors for additional spending in the economy (Lubbe; Douglas; Wieme and Fabris-Rotelli, 2013).

TABLE 7.1 Business Events Activity 2017

	Direct Spending (US$-Billion)	Participants (Million)	Average Spending (US$)	Direct GDP (US$ Billion)	Direct Jobs (000s)
Global Total	$1,071.2	1,520.7	$704	$621.4	10,308
North America	$381.0	329.7	$1,156	$221.6	3,234
Western Europe	$325.0	444.4	$731	$182.5	2,595
Asia	**$271.4**	**482.7**	**$562**	**$165.1**	**3,175**
Latin America and the Caribbean	$33.0	91.2	$362	$20.6	494
Central and Eastern Europe	$24.6	66.0	$373	$12.5	345
Africa	$23.4	80.6	$290	$11.7	328
Middle East	$12.8	26.1	$488	$7.5	136
Top 50 countries	$1,033.7	1,409.0	$734	$602.3	9,824

Source: Events Industry Council. 2018.

7.2.4 MICRO AREAS OF EXPENDITURE—BUSINESS TOURISTS

There is no standard measure to categorize the exact areas for business tourists' spending and the amount. Besides, economic impact studies are beneficial for future development. Therefore data used in these estimates must be accurate as a small error can be the reason for a big difference in economic estimation (Howard et al., 1991; Kumar and Hussain, 2014). Earlier, several studies used the self-administrative expenditure survey to assess economic impacts, but none of the study assigned any specific category for the expenditure. The expenditure category could vary from 4 to 20. Walsh (1986) mentioned that an increase in the number of a category would lead to accurate estimation of economic impacts, as accurate expenditure data can increase the validity and the reliability of the economic estimates (Figure 7.1).

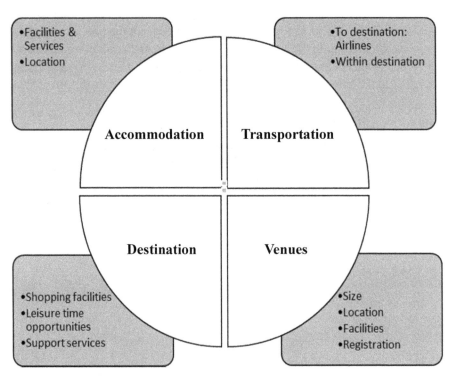

FIGURE 7.1 Micro Areas of Spending for Business Tourist.
Source: Swarbrooke and Horner, 2001.

An increase in the expenditure category can reduce the response rate and data accuracy (Walsh, 1996). Surveys with 20 expenditure categories typically have a small sample size that cannot be explicitly used in the analysis. Still, it can be used as a cumulative to develop new categories with a reasonable sample size (Moisy et al., 1990). Literature has proven that studies with seven expenditure categories represented almost 85% of all expenditure in the economy. To measure the business tourists' spending in different areas during their business trip, it is essential to know where tourists wish to spend. Sometimes, tourists can spend unknowingly, which does not come under economic impact research.

Therefore, Swarbrooke and Hornor (2001) came up with four factors that influence the tourists' spending pattern in different areas: environment, location, experience, and the other aspects where micro expenses can range from 4 to 20. Meanwhile, from the technical point of view, Stynes (1998) considered that location strongly influences business tourists' expenditure. Spending areas can differ from site to site, which can help define the expenditure categories. As mentioned earlier, including too many types in the survey and measuring too many varieties can confuse and reduce the response rate (Walsh, 1986).

7.2.5 ECONOMIC IMPACT ASSESSMENT

Han and Fang (1997) stated that tourism is an important economic activity in most countries worldwide and has a direct economic impact. The tourism industry has tremendous indirect and induced impacts. An easy way to summarize all these three impacts is that tourists, participants, delegates in the restaurants, hotels, or any of the tourism products can be referred to as the direct effect. Restaurants also buy products, such as vegetables and other ingredients from other businesses, which can be called an indirect impact. Meanwhile, the induced effect occurs due to additional income of the restaurants and hotel employee, and they spend money in the local economy by purchasing goods and services (Vogelsong and Graefe, 2001; Santos and Vieira, 2012). Economic impact studies are very beneficial because they illustrate the benefits of travel and tourism. Several studies for economic impacts assessment were conducted and varied in the methodological part of the information level gathered. That is one reason that makes every study different.

There are different factors for the studies of the economic impact, like the tourism industry, that is always studied and shows the positive economic effects of the tourism, but on the other hand, residents always come up with the negative economic impacts of tourism (Fleming and Toepper, 1990). An economic impact study can be carried out for a city, region, state, country, or a particular convention center by surveying the total expenditure done by the tourists in the area. Studies are instrumental in educating people and in developing economy. Economic analyses can be used as a planning tool and policy for the government and private sector to make promotional activities and set their goals. An economic assessment identifies the level of contribution of tourism toward the local economy. It also shows the relationship between different economic segments. It comes up with the approximate necessary changes, which can take place in the economy due to existing or possible available actions. Antigua and Barbuda Tourism Development Programme (2003) mentioned that the economic impacts of tourism go up due to demand and supply relationship in the industry. The demand–supply factors influence the number of visitors, their length of stay, and their expenditure patterns. At the same time, the economy's structural characteristics of the economy and its natural tendency recirculate all those expenditures internally in the economy done by the tourist. This circulation system is an ongoing process, so the more rounds the circulation in the economy, the greater the multiplier effect and the tourism multiplier for tourism spending can be estimated using ratios (Santos and Vieira, 2012).

Furthermore, Stynes (1997) revealed a variety of economic impacts of business tourism, tourists' contribution to sales, profits, job opportunities, tax revenue, and additional income for employees in the local economy. The most common direct impacts arise within the primary tourism sectors, like lodging, restaurants, transportation, retails trade, and amusements. Meanwhile, through secondary effects (indirect and induced), tourism affects most of the sectors in the economy. In general, an economic impact analysis of the tourism industry focuses on the increase in sales, income, and job opportunities in the local economy (area, and region), resulting from the tourism practices. Also, Jago (2012) mentioned in a report "The value of business events" for Tourism and Business Events International for Joint Meetings Industry Council that benefits for assessing business events are described in two parts:

- Return on investment (ROI) for delegates and their employers
- Other delegates and host destination benefits

ROI is a well-known procedure. It has been used by many industries, including business events, as it helps to estimate all the benefits for delegates (attendees) and their employers. Second, ROI also estimates the benefits for the host destination for hosting and inviting a significant number of delegates to attend and participate in the event.

7.2.5.1 DIRECT AND INDIRECT POSITIVE ECONOMIC EFFECTS

Direct positive economic impacts are the ones that occur as a direct result of the travel and tourism activity in a region, such as employment. Indirect positive economic impacts occur when residents spend to buy goods and services to supply travel-related. At the same time, the effects induced include spending of the resident who gets a job, wages, or salary from the tourism-related activity, and they spend on their own. Besides, there are some other positive impacts on the environment/physical, such as constructing new facilities, improving local infrastructure, and preventing heritage. Concerning residents, an increase in local pride, community spirit, and awareness increase nonlocal's perception.

7.2.5.2 DIRECT AND INDIRECT NEGATIVE ECONOMIC EFFECTS

Direct and indirect negative economic impacts lead toward the development of the economy and tourism industry. Such results include inflation (price increases during the MICE event), congestion, environment degradation, real estate speculation, failure to attract targeted tourists, better alternative investments, inadequate capital, and short estimation of the costs of events. There are some other negative impacts of tourism from social and cultural points of view like, modification of nature or the activity to accommodate tourism, chances of increase in crime rate, social dislocation and changes in community structure, and promotion of the activities, which may be of private/personal nature. There could be some negative impacts from the political or administrative point of view as the use of the event to a legitimate unpopular decision, failure to cope, inability to achieve aims, and economic exploitation of local population to satisfy the political elite (Janeczko, Mules, and Ritchie, 2002).

7.2.6 DIRECT, INDIRECT, AND INDUCED EFFECTS

According to Stynes (1997), an ideal economic impact analysis uncovers the money from the tourism industry, first to the businesses and governmental agencies, where tourists spend their money and then, other companies who are supplying goods and services to the businesses, who are offering services to the tourists. Employees get their income by working in the tourism industry or business related to the tourism industry, while the government, through different taxes and other charges on tourists.

Indirect and induced effects are also known as secondary effects by some authors. Economic effects change region to region and all the three types of impact. But surely the total economic effects should be equal to the sum of direct, indirect, and induced effects within the region.

7.2.6.1 DIRECT ECONOMIC EFFECTS

These effects are production changes related to the immediate effects of changes in tourism expenditures. For instance, a rise in the number of tourists staying longer in hotels would directly yield multiplied sales within the hotel sector. The addition of extra sales and associated changes in hotel payments for wages and salaries, taxes, and services directly affect tourist spending.

Some researchers have identified the economic impacts of the convention by totaling the expenditure related to the business event. The gross expenditure of the convention also includes all buying of goods and services related to the convention and the buyers like delegates, organizers, and accompanying persons. We can measure the overall effects of not direct and indirect effects for the region through gross profit. Besides, it is crucial to develop the basic information related to tourist's expenditure within the host destination to identify the direct effects. Meanwhile, Tyrell and Johmston (2001) came up with a few points to avoid confusion between gross and net expenditure while doing economic impact analysis in the region,

- Source of the expenditure
- The starting point of the expenditure
- Reason for expenditure
- End of the expenditure

Business tourism is known as a high-quality tourism segment, and the expenditure of business tourists is always higher than an average leisure tourist. As in Malaysia in 2012, many tourists have spent an average of 346 RM per day, and compared to all other types of tourists, it was almost triple. It had been the same in the UK in 2001, as business tourists spent an average of 146 £ per day compared to other visitors with average spending of only 56 £ per day (International Passenger Survey, 2000). So, we can say that all the expenditures done by delegates and organizers represent the total expenditure in different tourism sectors, such as

- Accommodation
- Transportation
- Shopping
- Food and beverages
- Entertainment
- Pre or post-tour

7.2.6.2 INDIRECT ECONOMIC EFFECTS

These effects are the production changes resulting from numerous rounds of respending of the hotel industry's receipts in different backward-linked sectors (i.e., enterprises supply products and services to hotels). Changes in sales, jobs, and income within the linen supply company, for example, represent indirect effects of changes in hotel sales. Businesses that supply products and services to the linen supply company represent another round of indirect effects, eventually linking hotels to varying degrees to several alternative economic sectors in the region.

7.2.6.3 INDUCED ECONOMIC EFFECTS

Induced effects are the changes in economic activity ensuing from household spending of income earned directly or indirectly due to tourism spending. For example, hotel and linen supply workers supported directly or indirectly by tourism, spending their payment within the local region for housing, food, transportation, and the usual array of household product and service needs. The sales, income and jobs that result from household spending of additional wage, salary, or proprietor's income are induced effects.

Economic studies tell the state government, bureau, and business officials regarding the net benefits of promoting the destination, tourism, and recreational activities. Reviews also help the local public (household) to underrate the benefits for the local economy and ultimately to the local people to reassure or stop repelling the tourism marketing activities. Last but not least, economic impact assessment studies also educate the local, state, and national level officials to develop laws and policies to promote economic, social, and cultural tourism to attract a significant number of tourists and ensure their safety (Frechtling, 1994). In Malaysia, Shuib et al. (2013) studied at direct expenditure effects of a particular event (Rainforest world music festival 2009 in Santubong, Sarawak). Money Generation Model (MGM) was used to look at direct effects of the event, an average total expenditure per participant was about RM 334 per day, a festival created RM 7.4 million in sales, 117 new FTE, RM 3.3 million as income to the region and RM .69 million as tax revenue.

7.2.7 MULTIPLIERS EFFECT

A multiplier is a tool that helps to measure the spending amount, which is not leaked out of the local economy due to further spending on good and services. As direct economic impacts of the business tourism can be measured by surveying the participants or measuring the overall business sales, to measure the secondary economic impacts (indirect and induced), we can use a multiplier that calculates the leakages of new expenditure in the area, as it is very important to measure the secondary impacts because these give an accurate assessment. Multiplier works with the amount of leakages and the amount as revenue in the local region. Leakages include taxation, foreign company, and importing goods and services. Meanwhile, tourism expenditure is an invisible kind of export that creates an inflow of foreign currency in the local economy of the particular destination. Like other exports, this export also has a big number of positive like, additional business turnover that leads to additional revenue, income of household, and revenue for government in terms of taxes. This export also helps to create a huge number of jobs.

The multipliers used for economic impact assessment are output, income, value-added, and employment multipliers. An increase in the level of economic activity due to direct tourist expenditure can be measured with an output multiplier. Employment multiplier helps to count the number of jobs created due to extra spending by tourists. On the other hand, value-added and income multiplier measures the total income left in the economy after all leakages, and it is the essential multiplier for the economy because only this measures the income left in the economy after the increase due to tourist spending.

> *Sales Multiplier:* Sales multiplier is also known as output multiplier; the total value of sales by all sectors/industries of the economy is compulsory to satisfy the final demand for the industry output.
>
> *Sales multiplier* = Direct sales + indirect sales/ Direct sales
>
> *Sales multiplier* = Direct sales + indirect sales + induced sales/ Direct sales
>
> *Income Multiplier:* Income multiplier translates the effects of changes in final demand in household income.
>
> *Income multiplier* = Total direct, indirect, and induced income/ Direct sales
>
> *Employment Multiplier*: The number of jobs created during an economic change, if the relationship between the value of the industry's output and its employment level can be estimated, then the employment multiplier can be calculated.
>
> *Employment multiplier* = Total direct, indirect and induced income/ Direct Sales

Multiplier changes over time, and in several economic impact studies, multipliers are generated by using past year data. It is costly to develop a new Input-Output coefficient, and it may take several years to complete the Input-Output Table. Besides, many existing models have been often used to conduct economic impact studies.

Also, there are a few reasons why the input–output relationship changes over time, such as technological changes and the invention of new products over time, which varies the producers' buying behavior. Besides, more changes in price across commodities induce substations of the relatively cheaper input for the more expensive items.

7.2.8 TOURISM SATELLITE ACCOUNT

The main objective of the TSA is to create and maintain a standard database for all to evaluate the economic impact of tourism-related activities, in particular region or country. Travel and Tourism Satellite Accounting, as defined by WTTC (2010):

"The standardised United Nations measurement of travel and Tourism's economic impact on the economy's consumption, business spending, capital investment, government expenditure, gross domestic product, and employment is perhaps the most important recent development in the quest for recognizing Travel and Tourism's contribution and future potential". As mentioned above the awareness regarding the economic importance of tourism has begun since the start of the Travel and Tourism Conference in 1990 held in Ottawa. Developed countries like France and Canada started summarizing the point to come up with a standard guideline for the tourism satellite account with the help of a few international organizations, including Organization for Economic Co-Operation and Development (OECD) and World Tourism Organization (WTO) so that international comparability can be carried out, and each country can create and maintain tourism statistics. Finally, in 1999, during the Enzo Paci World Conference on the Measurement of Economic Impact of Tourism in Nice, international groups of organizations, including the OECD, WTO, and Eurostat (European Commission), were established and acknowledged. Tourism Satellite Account shows the relationship between demand for products and services by tourism and their supply. UNWTO has acknowledged a range of twelve (12) tourism characteristics/subsectors for TSA (UNWTO, 2006).

- Hotels
- Second Home
- Restaurants
- Railways passenger transport services
- Road passenger transport services
- Air passenger transport services
- Water passenger transport services
- Transport supporting services
- Transport equipment rental
- Travel agencies
- Cultural services
- Sporting/ recreational activities

All the characteristics/subsectors help to design tourism-related products. The TSA products can be purchased by or for tourists. These products can be categorized into three types, as depicted in the following:

1. *Tourism Characteristic Products*: These products whose consumption goes down significantly once tourists visit the destination in the correct quantity.
2. *Tourism Connected Products:* These products known as tourism-related in the country, but not worldwide.
3. *Tourism Specific Products:* These are also known as tourism-related products and are the combination of tourism characteristic and tourism-connected products.

Expenditure by business tourists is related to business trips when tourists visit places on a business trip for their own or public or private companies. In the System of National Accounts, these expenditures named as secondary consumptions. Still, in TSA, these expenditures are treated as primary, and tourism final consumptions to reflect the full value of tourism demand (UNWTO, 2006).

7.3 ECONOMIC ASSESSMENT MODELS

Several models have been discussed in the literature on economic impact assessment in tourism—business tourism or other events. Economic impact assessment cost can range from US$ 500 to US$ 50,000 or more. Cost depends on the size and the scope of the study covered in the research, the size of the study region, and how the primary data can be collected.

Klijs et al. (2012) mentioned that several models could be divided by 52 potential criteria and subdivided into ten groups. Groups of criteria can be identified as—efficiency, data used as input into models, comparability—standardization, transparency and simplicity, trust in the models—validation and familiarity, sensitivity in the analysis, underlying analyses, expenditure categories, Output indicators, and externalities (Blake et al., 2001; Dwyer et al., 2004). There are several models available for economic impact assessments includes IO, Computable General Equilibrium Model, Social Accounting Matrix, Impact Analysis for Planning (IMPLAN) Model, Random Effects Model (REM) I & II, and MGM.

7.4 DISCUSSION AND CONCLUSION

The MICE industry is also known as the business events industry, and it is one of the fastest-growing types of tourism and turning into significantly common as a method to regenerate native economies. Business tourism encompasses all visits associated with a tourist's employment or business interest like meetings, conferences, and exhibitions (Hankinson, 2005). The business events industry recognized as a high-yield element of the tourism industry. Hunt (1989) and Swarbrooke and Horner (2001) found that business tourists spent double/ triple compared to the leisure tourists and a shorter average stay than other types of tourists. The worldwide business travel market had been taken into account to be huge, approximately 750 million trips with an estimated value in far more than US$ 320 000 million accounted for last few years (UNWTO, 2018).

Besides, economic impact studies are very useful for future development (Howard, Lankford and Havitz, 1991). In the past, so many studies had looked into the economic impact with self-administrative expenditure surveys, but none of the study assigned any specific category for expenditure.

However, in the Malaysian context, limited literature is available on the business tourism industry and none of the research focused on economic value of business events. Furthermore, Malaysia is facing a decline in international business tourists' arrival ranking for worldwide and Asia Pacific. Moreover, the Ministry of Tourism has been using the IO Tables, which is quite outdated and have a lot of restrictions (Briassoulis, 1991; Fletcher, 1989; Johnson and Moore 1993).

Therefore the current research has given a brief discussion of the literature related to MICE/ business events industry and its impacts specifically in Malaysia scenario. The current research discussed microareas of business tourists spending, including business event registration fees, cost of international airline, cost of domestic airline, cost of hotel/accommodation, cost of local cultural tours, money spent on local transportation, money spent on food and beverages, money spent for shopping, money spent on leisure activities, and other expenses along with economic impact assessment studies to predict the impacts of these spending on the host economy. Furthermore, the study discussed major economic assessment models available to assess the impacts and also recognized the importance of the business events industry in the Malaysian context. All the findings of the study have substantial theoretical, managerial, and contextual contributions.

KEYWORDS

- event
- business tourism
- business events
- tourist arrival
- tourist spending
- economic impacts
- Malaysia

REFERENCES

Antigua and Barbuda Tourism Development Programme. (2003). *Tourism's Economic Impacts Increasing the Contribution to Prosperity*. http://www.antigua-barbuda.org/ (accessed March 29, 2019).

Blake, A., Durbarry, R., Sinclair, M. T., and Sugiyarto, G. (2001). Modelling Tourism and Travel Using Tourism Satellite Accounts and Tourism Policy and Forecasting Models. *TTRI Discussion Paper*, 2001(4), Nottingham, UK.

Brida, J. G., Disegna, M., and Scuderi, R. The Visitors' Perception of Authenticity at the Museums: Archaeology Versus Modern Art. *Current Issues in Tourism*. 2014, 17, 518–538.

Chhabra, D., Sills, E., and Rea, P. Tourist Expenditures at Heritage Festivals. *Event Management*. 2000, 7(4), 221–230.

Chi, C. G. Q. and Qu, H. Examining the Structural Relationships Destination Image, Tourist Satisfaction and Destination Loyalty: An Integrated Approach. *Tourism Management*. 2008, 29, 624–636.

Choi, T. Y., and Chu, R. Determinants of Hotel Guests' Satisfaction and Repeat Patronage in the Hong Kong Hotel Industry. *International Journal of Hospitality Management.* 2001, 20, 277–297.

Cope, B. *Marketing in Tourism.* New York: Prentice-Hall. 2006.

Davidson, R. Distribution Channel Analysis for Business Travel. In *Tourism Distribution Channels: Practices, Issues and Transformations;* D. Buhalis, and E. Laws, Ed.; Continuum: London, 2001, pp. 73–86.

Davidson, R. *Business Travel.* London: Longman, 1994.

Dwyer, L., Forsyth, P., and Spurr, R. Evaluating Tourism's Economic Effects: New and Old Approaches, *Tourism Management.* 2004, 307–317.

Events Industry Council. https://www.eventscouncil.org/ (Accessed February 2, 2019).

Fleming, W. R., and Toepper, L. Economic Impact Studies: Relating The Positive and Negative Impacts To Tourism Development. *Journal of Travel Research.* 1990, 29, 35–42.

Frechtling, D. C. Assessing the Impacts of Travel and Tourism. In *Travel, Tourism, and Hospitality Research: A Handbook for Managers and Researchers;* J. R. B. Ritchie and C. R. Goeldner, Eds.; John Wiley and Sons: New York, 1994, pp. 367–391.

Han, X., and Fang, B. Measuring the Size of Tourism and its Impact in an Economy. *Statistical Journal of the UN Economic Commission for Europe.* 1997, 14, 357–378.

Hankinson, G. Destination Brand Images: A Business Tourism Perspective. *Journal of Services Marketing.* 19, 2005.

Haven-Tang, C., Jones, E., and Webb, C. Critical Success Factors for Business Tourism Destinations: Exploiting Cardiff's National Capital City Status and Shaping its Business Tourism Offer. *Journal of Travel and Tourism Marketing.* 2007, 22, 109–120.

Howard, D., Lankford, S., and M. Havitz. A Method for Authenticating Pleasure Travel Expenditures. *Journal of Travel Research.* 1991, 29, 19–23.

Hussain, K., Kumar, J., Kannan, S., and Nor, M. Investigating the Size and Economic Value of Business Tourist Market in Malaysia. *Event Management.* 2017, *21*, 997–514.

International Congress and Convention Association (ICCA) Country and City Rankings Report. 2012.

International Congress and Convention Association (ICCA) Country and City Rankings Report. 2013.

Jago, L. *The Value of Business Events.* 2012.

Janeczko, B., Mules, T., and Ritchie, B. Estimating the Economic Impacts of Festivals and Events: A Research Guide. Australia, CRC for Sustainable Tourism Pty Ltd. *Journal of Services Marketing.* 2000, 19, 24–32.

Klijs, J., Heijman, W., Maris, D. K., and Bryon, J. Criteria for Comparing Economic Impact Models of Tourism, *Tourism Economics.* 2012, 18, 1175–1202.

Kumar, J., and Hussain, K. Review of the Book Overbooked: The Exploding Business of Travel and Tourism by Becker, E. (2013). *Asia Pacific Journal of innovation in Hospitality and Tourism.* 2013, 2, 243–245.

Kumar, J., and Hussain, K. Evaluating Tourism's Economic Effects: Comparison of Different Approaches. *Procedia—Social and Behavioural Sciences.* 2014, 144, 360–365.

Lehto, X. Y., Cai, L. A., O'Leary, J. T., and Huan, T. C. Tourist Shopping Preferences and Expenditure Behaviours: The Case of the Taiwanese Outbound Market. *Journal of Vacation Marketing.* 2004, 10(4), 320–332.

Lovejoy, K. Putting Out the Welcome Mat. *Regional Review.* 2003, 13, 6–8.

Lubbe, B., Douglas, A., Wieme, L., and Fabris-Rotelli, I. Frequent-Flier Programs as a Determinant in the Selection of Preferred Airlines by Corporations. *Transportation Journal.* 2013, 52, 344–364.

Mc Nicoll, I. Issues Arising Concerning the Treatment of Business Tourism in UK Tourism Satellite Account. London: DCMS. A Briefing Paper for Department for Culture, Media and Sport, 2004.

Moisey, N., Yuan, M., and McCool, S. Estimates of Economic Impact of Non- Resident Travellers to Montana: A Technical Report. Research Report 11. Missoula: University of Montana, Institute for Tourism and Recreation Research, School of Forestry. 1990.

Montgomery, R., and Strick, S. *Meetings, Conventions and Expositions.* John Wiley and Sons: New York, 1995.

Office for National Statistics International Passenger Survey. In Business Tourism Partnership 2000. www.businesstourismpartnership.com (accessed March 29, 2019).

Okubo, S., and M. A. Planting. *U.S. Travel and Tourism Satellite Accounts for 1992. Survey of Current Business*, Bureau of Economic: Washington DC, 1998.

Riandey and Quaglia. Resource Paper: Surveying Hard to Reach Groups, 8th international Conference on Survey Methods in Transport: Harmonisation and Data Comparability, Annecy, 2008.

Rogers, T. *Conferences and Conventions: A Global Industry* 3rd ed.; Elsevier Ltd: Burlington, MA, 2008.

Santos, C., and Vieira, J. C. An Analysis of Visitors' Expenditures in a Tourist Destination: OLS, Quantile Regression and Instrumental Variable Estimators. *Tourism Economics.* 2012, 18, 555–576.

Shuib, A., Edman, S., and Yaakub, F. Direct Expenditure Effects of the Rainforest World Music Festival 2009 in Santubong, Sarawak. *International Journal of Business and Society.* 2013, 14, 287–298.

Singer, E., Groves, R., and Corning, A. Differential Incentives: Beliefs About Practices, Perceptions of Equity, and Effects on Survey Participation, Public Opinion Quarterly. 1999, 63, 251–260.

Stynes, D. J. *Economic Impacts of Tourism, A Handbook for Tourism Professionals, Illinois Bureau of Tourism, Illinois Department of Commerce and Community Affairs.* Prepared by the Tourism Research Laboratory at the University of Illinois at Urbana-Champaign, 1997.

Stynes, D. J. *Guidelines for Measuring Visitor Spending. East Lansing, MI: Department of Park, Recreation and Tourism Resources.* Michigan State University, 1998.

Stynes, D. J., and Mahoney, E. *Measurement and Analysis of Recreational and Travel Spending.* In Abstracts of the 1989 Symposium on Leisure Research. Alexandria, VA: National Recreation and Park Association, 1989.

Swarbrooke, J., and Horner, S. *Business Travel and Tourism,* Butterworth Heinemann: Oxford, 2008.

Tyrell, T. J., and Johnston, R. J. A Framework for Assessing Direct Economic Impacts of Tourist Events: Distinguishing Origins, Destinations and Causes of Expenditure, *Journal of Travel Research,* 2001, 40, 94–100.

UNWTO. Tourism Highlights: Facts and Figures, United Nation World Tourism Organization; Madrid, 2006.

UNWTO. Tourism Highlights: Facts and Figures, United Nation World Tourism Organization; Madrid, 2011.

UNWTO. Tourism Highlights: Facts and Figures, United Nation World Tourism Organization; Madrid, 2012.
UNWTO. Tourism Highlights: Facts and Figures, United Nation World Tourism Organization; Madrid, 2013.
UNWTO. Tourism Highlights: Facts and Figures, United Nation World Tourism Organization; Madrid, 2019.
Vogelsong, H., and Graefe, A. R. Economic Impact Analysis: A Look at useful Methods. *P and R Magazine*. 2001, 3, 28–36.
Walsh, R. G. *Recreation Economic Decisions: Comparing Benefits and Costs*, Venture Publishing, Inc: USA, 1986.
Wang, Y., Romp, P., Severt, D., and Peerapatdit, N. Examining and Identifying the Determinants of Travel Expenditure Patterns. *International Journal of Tourism Research*. 2006, 8, 333–346.
Wooton, G., and Stevens, T. Business Tourism: A Study of the Market for Hotel Based Meetings and its Contribution to Wale's tourism. *Tourism Management*. 1995, 16, 305–313.
World Tourism and Travel Corporation. Travel and Tourism Competitiveness Report, WTTC: London, 2010.
World Tourism and Travel Corporation. *Travel and Tourism—Economic Impact*, WTTC: London, 2020.
Yoon, Y., and Uysal, M. An Examination of the Effects of Motivation and Satisfaction on Destination Loyalty: A Structural Model. *Tourism Management*. 2005, 26, 45–56.

CHAPTER 8

THE EFFECT OF TRADITIONAL AND MODERN EVENTS ON STUDENTS' PSYCHOLOGY AND WELL-BEING: A CASE STUDY ON ALLEN

KRISHANA KUMAR NIMBARK

Department of Chemistry, ALLEN Career Institute, Kota, Rajasthan, India; E-mail: krishanakumarnimbark@gmail.com

ABSTRACT

Education is an integral part of one's development as a human. The purpose and the process of it become quite stressful along the way. This study is done to understand and analyze how educating can be eventful and enriching with infusing culture and commitment. Being a teacher myself, it is very much visible how a student's life has been shaping up and how the community can help them. The problems in this could be geographical, ethnic, financial, and emotional. I researched in the Mini Kashi of India, that is, Kota and the Institute, which has been shaping the future of students since 1988, named ALLEN Career Institute. Kota-coaching for IIT JEE and Medical NEET UG has been a pioneer and their methods have been an inspiration. ALLEN Career Institutes has four Directors and faculty members (ALLEN Family) worked toward students' development and making their life eventful. I did interview the students as well as the Director for getting the data regarding the study. The KoCa (Kota Carnival) festival, the Sanskar Mahotsava, the Open Sessions, The Happiness card and online career, and personal guidance programs have been few events that were making a difference in students' life.

8.1 INTRODUCTION

Education completes every individual. However, the process of educating one has been having different turns over the decades. In ancient times we had gurukuls, then came the Pathshalas and schools, colleges, and now online classes. During these Sessions, the goal was to make a person knowledgeable and ready for life. In the whole idea of education we hardly thought about the life of the student who has been going through the ups and downs of his own. What is the area of education he wants to attend? How is he coping with the different stages of it? How can he learn and grow better of himself? These are the few of the concerns that we are going to analyze here.

India has millions of people who fall in the range of 15–25 years of age and they come from middle-class families. In India, the general idea of being educated is to get an excellent job as an engineer or a doctor or something related to the same. As above its' the largest population, which means the resources are limited and the numbers of people to use them are higher as the same goes with the educational institutes. Every student has to perform at highest level of his/her to get into an engineering or medical college. All students undergo centralized common entrance exam for this. When the numbers are higher, the competition is also cutthroat. Student and parents to attain their desires prepare themselves for the best. So they turn to institutes that can help them in the cause. Now we come to the place where these dreams and desires come closure is Kota. A tier 2 city in the state of Rajasthan in India, which is also called Mini Kashi. The place is like a Mecca for the students who want to get into IIT (Best of the Engineering Institute in India) or Medical colleges. They study in the institutes here and prepare themselves for the national level exams. In this city, we have almost 150 thousand students from across the country. The institutes here are like ALLEN Career Institute, Resonance, Bansal Classes, which help students in their respective fields.

Now we come to the life of a student in this process. We have almost 2–2.5 million students every year appearing for the IIT or NEET exam. The number of seats is nearly 15%–20% of the total students appearing. This means every year, nearly 1.8–1.9 million students do not get into their desired field. Few try again and few change their direction or compromise. The above data tells a little about the stressful life of a young student can be. The students come to Kota from different demographical and financial backgrounds. Every individual is different from another in terms of emotional, language, and mental abilities. Only good education or books will not be sufficient for a student, as he is going through a lot of different concerns at a time. Education cannot just be telling what needs to be read, write, or learn. He needs more and different things that can help him through this. I have taken the case from the best of the institute named ALLEN Career Institute, which has helped almost 1 million students over the years in education. They are almost 32 years old. With 4 directors and almost 3000 faculty members, who are working in creating a better life for the students during their promising years.

Student from a very early age start preparing in Kota for IIT and medical, they come from different places and meet at one city; they have a lot difference like cultural, food habits, and common goal. For achieving their ambition student travel through various mental and emotional zones and educational institute support by just not teaching the textbooks, different needs of students are done by various methods of teaching life and making them better in this. The environment of students has been challenging and this affects their study and behavior. These concerns can be from parents, society, food, culture, financial, or emotional. So the development or education of students cannot happen by classrooms or text reading, it has to be something more. Teaching has to be like living life, as an event, or like a festival, which everyone wants to enjoy, everyone wants to be part of it. Study as a life event sounds good. But is it feasible? Yes, it is, and it has been done in this Kota city. We are going to understand how it has been done and what benefits it has given to society and the students. How ALLEN career institute has done it, we are going to understand the same in this study.

8.2 REVIEW OF LITERATURE

The aspect of this study is to understand how making education as an event or saying eventful education is helping the student to grow in life and reach their goals. ALLEN Career Institute has been working toward educating India since 1988 in Kota city, and they have almost taught 1 million students since their early days. A student attends almost 6–7 hours classes every day, every 3 weeks he needs to attend a test to review his study and see where does he/she stand among others. Living in a new place and without parents at the age of approx 14 years, onward lives a total change of life cycle for him/her. Their life becomes quite a same routine day after day and this circle of habits may hamper one's mental and physical health.

According to Seligman and Csikszentmihalyi (2000) well-being is a vital part of optimistic psychology. When we talk about the youngsters who are staying away from their families and a native place, it is more important to focus on their well-being. It is very well said by MacLeod and Conway (2005) giving anticipation of encouraging events is a solution of well-being. The same is reflected in the vision of the directors of ALLEN Institute at Kota city. The significance of foreseeing future constructive results is symbolized by approaches that view the prosperity and well-being as the consequence of individuals being occupied with endeavoring toward esteemed objectives that they accept are probably going to occur (Schmuck and Sheldon, 2001).

Higher Education Research Institute (Astin, 2004; HERI, 2005) states spirituality and religion help students to become compassionate and caring individuals, results in procommunity and selfless human being. Howe and Strauss (2003) also experienced similarities in their research on developing student as a whole. ALLEN Institute works on development of student from cultural and spiritual levels by providing Yoga Session, Sanskar Mahotsva, and guiding the students for a brighter future including society and themselves. These sessions connect the students as one and approach of humanity and care.

Elliott and Hufton (2005) talked about stress and emotional expectation on kids in Asian countries. Education is first priority for Indian households and Indian parents always look toward the best outcome for their kids. The untold pressure to perform on students becomes part of their life. Having invested a lot of years in preparing students, ALLEN Kota and their team maps the syllabus and helps them to overcome these hurdles by organizing Open Sessions and Personal Guide and Mentorship Projects. Students always have access to their faculties and mentors for emotional and educational well-being.

Perry, Deborah L. (What makes Learning fun? 2012) suggested that learning in a manner when it becomes fun gives brighter results. Something new always attracts and desire to know that puts us in a drive mode toward understanding it. Visiting a carnival or a gathering gives an opportunity of meeting people and understand the environment with various aspects of life. This gives impulse to learn more. City administration in tandem with ALLEN for students organizes Kota Carnival (KoCa Festival), which results in the indulgence of almost 150 thousand students for 3 days. Meeting new students, having different opinions toward similar goals, knowing more about the challenges they might face, and fun activities sessions give them a new perspective toward their way of learning and studying. This also rejuvenates students to reach their respective goals.

According to Ertem (2006), motivation is an inner state uncovering individuals behavior and directing them to these behaviors; however, according to Baumeister and Vohs (2007), it is a state where the individual displays various attitudes voluntarily in order to achieve a certain goal. According to Ertem (2006), motivation is an inner state uncovering individuals' behavior and directing them to these behaviors; however, according to Baumeister and Vohs (2007), it is a state where the individual displays various attitudes voluntarily in order to achieve a certain goal. According to Ertem (2006), an internal status of a persons' behavior is called motivation. This is the factor that actually decides and reflects where an individual is focusing. Baumeister and Vohs (2007) said motivation is a state where the personage shows different approaches willingly to attain a certain goal. Thus the researcher states that motivation is an inimitable gift of any individual that actually assists him or her to select a particular path of work. ALLEN faculties with the able guidance of the directors are putting their best efforts to take the students on the right path which is certainly an added value to their motivation level.

Spirituality and religiosity that can contribute to helping students overcome the challenges of transitioning and achieving academic success (Rennick et al., 2013). The years are considered to be formative times for students as they are expected to learn who they want to be as adults, and become more independent and responsible (Arnett, 2000). Arnett (2000) further stated that students are expected to develop better time management and analytical skills. Moreover, for the students, it is required to see the balance between academics and social life.

Lots of learning to be done by the student in a short span of time and to master all alone is looks like A Herculean task. They master the art of divide and rule in a cooperative group study manner. Cooperative learning involves students dividing roles and responsibilities between group members, so learning becomes fun an independent process. On the other hand, collaborative learning develops sharing knowledge, meaning, and developing social responsibilities (Dillenbourg et al., 1996; Dillenbourg, 1999). This makes them habitual to work together and get the best result out of anything in every situation. This makes the learning uplifting and eventful.

The outcomes and the efforts of the teachers and educators decide what kind of person one becomes.

"The foundation is a successful teacher–student bond that allows other aspects to work good" (p. 91) Marzano (2003). Wherein Hallinan (2008) writes: "Learning is a method that involves cognitive and social psychological proportions, and both processes should be considered if academic attainment is to be maximized" (p. 271). The teacher can help the student to become what he himself might not have dreamt of. Successful and measured teaching skills required to outline the future of a student. A teacher is a person who comes with experiences of all obstacles and achievements a student can get in his career.

Teachers at the Institute know about these things and they try to work upon better routine and breaking this circle of habits. As they agree, education needs to be fun and joyful and enriching the soul not corrupting it by stress, and unidirectional. Few of the events are here we will discuss:

1. Open Session

The event is to recognize the efforts of a student in their academia and prize them with medals. This also encourages others to do more and at the same time, they are guided not to fall in the wrong direction The open session gives students to talk to their faculties as well as mentors of the education institute to help them in the study and other areas.

2. Happiness Card

This is the event where student comes for other than text and books discussion, they are loyalty cards which are for discounts in daily needs, fun activities, clothing, and food. This motivates them to go for recreational activities as well as give them financial benefits.

3. Sanskar Mahotsava

It is a cultural event that gives a pit stop the students from their study schedule and rejuvenates them. This is an informal event for both faculties and students, which involves religious activities, motivational speakers, and talent showcase from students.

4. Kota Carnival (KoCa)

It is a cultural and educational event which is organized by the city administration along with the involvement of educational institutions. The event

The Effect of Traditional and Modern Events

sees the externals from diverse areas of work like Music, Education, Sports. This 2–3 day event helps students to bond on various aspects.

Clicked for researcher—Sanskar Mahotsava Nov 2018.

5. Career Counseling

Institute organizes the event where different colleges or educational institutes contribute and helps Students how they can shape their careers. They are also supported in how their way of study needs to be for the future classes as well as current.

6. Yoga Session

Health is very important for each one. The stressful mind cannot perform to desired levels. Students are guided how this practice helps them and how it can be helpful for their studies. One of the sessions, holds the Guinness world record for 100,984 participants on 21st June 2018.

As per the above ways we are finding learning is made eventful by different ways. A student does find himself lost in textbooks but he sees there are ways to do this and which keep him motivated. A student has the confidence to lead a better life always with the education and cultural support he gets in this.

8.3 RESEARCH METHODOLOGY

To understand how exciting education can occur the researcher took the survey and interview method in the ALLEN Institute. Interviews with students and the directors and teachers were done.

Sample size: 120 students, 10 teachers, and director.

Sampling method: The convenience method of sampling is used to collect data from the respondents.

Data collection: The data is collected from both primary and secondary sources. Primary data is collected through structured, questionnaire and secondary data is collected from personal events participation.

8.3.1 ASPECTS OF THE SURVEY

Sr. No.	Question Asked
1	How stressful you feel during studies?
2	Is eventful study is more appealing than regular study?
3	If not selected still I am becoming a better person?
4	Different events kept me motivated toward my goal
5	Education Institutes helped in their personal and educational as well as psychological
6	Do spiritual and cultural activities help in their goal achievement?

Apart from these, their cultural and financial standings were also taken into consideration.

Tier-1 city student and tier-3 city student will have different mental status same for the LIG, HIG, or MIG family member.

8.3.2 RESULTS AND INTERPRETATION

The study was done to analyze the interference of eventful study in students life and his future. The research was conducted in the city of Kota, Rajasthan, at ALLEN Career Institute, which is having the highest number of students across the country for IITJEE and NEET UG.

1. Almost 70% students accept that they are very stressed in their studies, out of which 64% were girls and rest were boys.

2. Almost 91% students agree that studies have to be eventful, which gives them easier approach to learn. Out of these, 89% girls agreed for eventful studies, whereas 93% boys agreed upon eventful studies.
3. 97% of students agree that they are becoming a better person during their stay here, however, they do agree selection disappoints them.
4. 92% agreed on something new (events/seminar) that keeps them going toward their goal.
5. 98% students appreciate the efforts put in by the Institute.
6. 96% students agreed that spiritual and cultural enriching sessions help them motivated and make them connected with family and society.

8.3.3 ASPECT OF SURVEY (INTERVIEW METHOD)

In this personal observation and the interview with one of the directors, Mr. Rajesh Maheshwari (RM), is being studied.

Q What made you start the Institute?
RM In India, we are an education-driven society; getting proper education is not possible for everyone. To help the students to reach and become better in his life gives me satisfaction.
Q How long you have been working in this?
RM I started this in the year of 1988. With time my brothers (the other directors) also joined. It has been 32 years and almost 1 million students have been with us one way or the other.
Q Why the different events like Open Sessions, or Sanskar Mahotsava, and other?
RM I am a firm believer of God almighty. I always look toward soul enrichment on everyone. Once it is done, he/she will reach their goal. Talking about the open session, students need to be encouraged for their efforts and a small token of appreciation will make them go the extra mile. Sanskar Mahotsava is a cultural event where we try to connect god almighty and seek their blessings for future endeavors.
Q In your experience, what are the challenges the students face and how are you going to help them?
RM These students come from different places and a variety of families. First, their families are concerned over well-being, then study, food, lodging, and their friends. They are to help mentally and emotionally as they many times feel lost among a number of students. They need to think that their studies are just not a job, it is fun, it is life experience, it is a way to live, it is a way to connect to oneself and the world.

8.3.4 RESULTS

ALLEN institute and their Director Mr. Rajesh Maheshwari has been working toward the betterment of student since 1988, they have to help students by making the education as a path to living life and adding to that few of life-changing events.

8.4 CONCLUSION

When we talk about students, the image that comes to us a stressed individual with a lot of potential and expectations, this is how the journey begins however it has a happy ending when they get the support, suggestions, motivations, empathy, and personal care. Student teacher relationship is one of the cores of development as well as the environment. The strengths of emotions, culture, spirituality, and text and combining them and becoming a great individual should be the primary goal of education. These aspects are well-taken care by the ALLEN Institute at Kota in the guidance of a large team of faculty members and their directors. The city of Kota has been experiencing the warmth of its good deeds done to students who came here from different areas, societies to learn and become better.

KEYWORDS

- **Kota coaching**
- **ALLEN**
- **KoCa**
- **event**
- **event management**

REFERENCES

Arnett, J. J. (2000). Emerging adulthood: A theory of development from the late teens through the twenties. *American Psychologist*, 55(5), 469.

Baumeister, R. F., and Vohs, K. D. (2007). Self-regulation, ego depletion, and motivation. *Social and Personality Psychology Compass*, 1(1), 115–128.

Dillenbourg P., Baker M., Blaye A., O'Malley C. (1996). The evolution of research on collaborative learning, In *Learning in Humans and Machines: Towards an Interdisciplinary Learning Science*, eds Reimann P., Spada E. (Oxford: Elsevier) 189–211.

Elliott, Hufton, Willis and Illushin (2005) Motivation, Engagement and Educational Performance: Introduction, p. 3.

Ertem, H. (2006). Investigation of secondary education students' motivation types (intrinsic and extrinsic) and levels towards chemistry course based on some variables (Unpublished Master dissertation). Balıkesir University, Balıkesir, Turkey.

Hallinan, M.T. (2008). Teacher influences on students' attachment to school. *Sociology of Education*, 81(3), 271–283.

MacLeod, A. K., and Conway, C. (2005). Well-being and the anticipation of future positive experiences: The role of income, social networks and planning ability. *Cognition and Emotion*, 19, 357374.

Marzano, R. J. and Marzano, J.S. (2003). Building classroom relationships. *Educational Leadership*, 61:1, 6–13.

Perry, Deborah L. (2012) What makes learning fun? Visitors, Conversation and Learning, 11.

Rennick, L. A., Smedley, C. T., Fisher, D., Wallace, E., and Kim, Y. K. (2013). The effects of spiritual/religious engagement on college students' affective outcomes: Differences by gender and race. *Journal of Research on Christian Education*, 22(3), 301–322.

Schmuck, P., and Sheldon, K. M. (eds.). (2001). Life goals and well-being. Towards a Positive Psychology of Human Striving. Seattle, WA: Hogrefe and Huber.

Seligman, M. E., and Csikszentmihalyi, M. (2000). Positive psychology: an introduction. *American Psychologist*, 55, 5–14. doi: 10.1037/0003-066x.56.1.89

CHAPTER 9

TRAVEL AND TOURISM COMPETITIVENESS AND CULTURAL TOURISM EVENTS IN SRI LANKA

D. A. C. SURANGA SILVA[1], KALPANI V. GAMAGE[2],
MANORI L. GURUGE[2], and DULAJA N. SILVA[3]

[1]*Tourism Economics, University of Colombo, Colombo, Sri Lanka*

[2]*Department of Economics, University of Colombo, Colombo, Sri Lanka*

[3]*Sri Lanka Technological Campus, Padukka, Sri Lanka*

ABSTRACT

This study explains the relationship of culture tourism attractions, more specifically cultural events and their impact on destination competitiveness and attraction focusing on Sri Lanka tourism. It has been evident from the finding of this study that the cultural attractions and cultural events have significantly influential to determine the travel and tourism competitiveness of Sri Lanka as a prominent tourist destination in the region. The study investigates how such cultural impact has influenced on the competitiveness of Sri Lanka tourism by analyzing data collected from the Global Travel & Tourism Competitiveness Index and the other relevant secondary data sources. The findings of this study clearly indicate that among all other cultural attractions, cultural events and the related culture tourism related activities are highly decisive to enhance the cultural attraction of each cultural tourism sites of the country and consequently it can increase the travel and tourism competitiveness of Sri Lanka tourism. Furthermore, this study emphasizes the importance of developing the effective policies and providing the necessary incentives for the key stakeholders to improve cultural events of the country by using untapped potential available in different parts of the country with attractive cultural diversification among different communities living in the country.

9.1 SRI LANKA TOURISM: AN *"EXTERNAL ECONOMIC STRESS BUSTER"*

Sri Lanka Tourism has evidently displaced its great contribution to the economic growth and development of the country as being one of the most successful industries during the postwar economy of Sri Lanka. Its direct and indirect, even induced, contributions with its strong backward–forward linkages have been a major reason for such impressive performance of the industry.

During the past decade, from 2009 to 2018, tourist arrivals increased by nearly 475% while foreign exchange earnings of tourism increased by nearly 1150%. On the similarly, level of direct and indirect employment (total employment) increased by nearly 200% while formal accommodation capacity increased by approximately 70% (Silva Suranga, 2020). As a result of this impressive performance, Sri Lanka Tourism has now become the *3rd Highest* Foreign Exchange Earner of the country becoming an *economic resilient builder* or an *external stress buster* against the detrimental impact of the current burning deficit of the *trade account in the balance of payment* of the country.

Lonely Planet's Best in Travel—2019:
Sri Lanka has claimed the top spot in the world's leading travel guide, the Lonely Planet as the best travel destination in 2019

USNEWS.COM:
Sri Lanka ranked one of top countries for travel in 2019

BBC.COM—2019:
Good Food team has named Sri Lankan cuisine as the No.1 trending cuisine in 2019 on their list.

TRAVEL LEMMING READER AWARDS—2019:
World's Top Destination

I ESCAPE WEB SITE UK—2019
Sri Lanka 10 Best Places to Visit in 2019
Source: https://www.srilanka.travel/international-endorsements and other sources

With the accolades given by the Leading global travel indicators and various travel magazines, including Lonely Planet and National Geographic Traveler, Sri Lanka has been recognized as the *best destination or one of the best tourist destinations in the world.*

Tourist attractions in Sri Lanka have been fascinated in *so much in so little,* including UNESCO heritage sites, sandy beaches, attractive wildlife parks, and hill country sceneries, as an island of its size—undoubtedly one of the best tourist destinations in the world of its entire size.

The astonishing wildlife attractions (such as the world's highest elephant gathering at Minneriya national park), 1000-year old Buddhist monuments representing one of the highest numbers of the UNESCO World

Heritages in the region, hiking, train travels through the Hill Country's tea plantations, Enjoyable tropical glamorous beaches including Sun bathing, Surfing, Corel watching, Diving, preserved unique Sri Lankan identity, Colonial Heritance and Legacies, Authentic Sri Lankan Cuisine, and much more provide tourists with "Unforgettable Travel Experiences" alone with the mesmeric socio-cultural diversity and warm friendliness of people of Sri Lanka.

TABLE 9.1 Tourism Contribution for the GDP and Level of Employment by Selected Asian Countries

Country	Contribution of Travel and Tourism Industry to GDP (% of Total)	Contribution of Travel and Tourism Industry to Employment (% of Total)
India	• US$ 41,582.4 million	• 23,454,400
	• 2% of GDP	• 5.5% of Total Employment
Indonesia	• US$ 28,208.9 million	• 3,468,440
	• 3.3% of GDP	• 2.9% of Total Employment
Sri Lanka	• US$ 3,546.9 million	• 344,852
	• (4.6% of GDP)	• 4.2% of Total Employment
Thailand	• US$ 36,407.1 million	• 2,402,320
	• 9.3% of GDP	• 6.3% of Total Employment

Source: Silva Suranga, https://www.ceylondigest.com/people-centric-sustainable-tourism-development-and-entrepreneurial-new-public-service-in-sri-lanka/, 2020, Central Bank of Sri Lanka (2019)

9.2 TRAVEL AND TOURISM COMPETITIVENESS INDEX (TTCI)

Increasing the travel and tourism competitiveness over the other destinations has been considered as a fundamental strategy to increase the attractiveness of a country—Higher the competitiveness of a tourist destination, the Greater is the attractiveness of tourists to such destination.

Consequently, the industry could generate higher tourism receipts, employment opportunities, and other possible positive socioeconomic impacts on the economic growth and development of the country. The Global TTCI provides a set of factors and policies which empower the sustainable development of the travel and tourism sector, which consequently lead to the development and competitiveness of the tourism industry of a country.

TTCI measures the tourism competitiveness among 140 countries of the world considering of 4 subindexes, 14 pillars, and 90 individual indicators distributed among these 14 pillars, which analyzes the factors that enable the sustainable development of both travel and tourism, in term of contributing to higher standards of tourism development of a country. The TTCI considers four main components: (1) enabling environment, (2) travel tourism policy and enabling conditions, (3) infrastructures, and (4) natural and cultural resources. The TTCI highlights the strong and weak areas of the destination country in order to enhance the competitiveness of the tourism industry.

9.3 COMPONENTS OF TRAVEL AND TOURISM COMPETITIVENESS INDEX

According to the TTCI 2019 (http://www3.weforum.org/docs/WEF_TTCR_2019.pdf), *Spain* is the first in this ranking of TTCI-2019 as the best competitive country, followed by France, Germany, Japan, the United States, the United Kingdom, Australia, Italy, Canada, and Switzerland (http://www3.weforum.org/docs/WEF_TTCR_2019.pdf /).

Regional wise, Asia-Pacific is the second most competitive region only behind Europe and Eurasia. In the Asia-Pacific region, several countries like Japan, Australia, China, Singapore, Malaysia, New Zealand, Thailand, and India have been able to show their high competitiveness rather than most of the destination countries in the region. Previous year, Sri Lanka was ranked as the 77th out of 140 countries. This rank was reduced by *13 ranking positions* from the last survey in 2017 (64th place in 2017).

9.4 RELATIVE COMPETITIVENESS OF "SO-SRI LANKA"

One of the major factors determining the growth of Sri Lanka Tourism is the relative competitiveness over the other competitive destination countries in the region.

Recently, Sri Lanka Tourism has shown a slow progress in its performance in increasing its competitiveness with the other tourist destinations in the region. This is obviously visible when Asia-Pacific region has become the *Second Most Competitive Region* in global tourism.

Furthermore, *India* and *Bangladesh* have become one of the fastest-growing competitive destination countries in global tourism when considering the recent performance of its overall TTCI scores. Bangladesh has moved up *five places* to the *TTCI ranking* by obtaining *120th* place at TTCI-2019. Similarly, India has moved up *six places* to the *TTCI ranking* by obtaining *34th* place at TTCI-2019.

TABLE 9.2 Sri Lanka in the Asia-Pacific Travel and Tourism Competitiveness Index—2019

Country	Global Rank	Score
Japan	4	5.4
Australia	7	5.1
China	13	4.9
Hong Kong	14	4.8
Korea. Rep.	16	4.8
Singapore	17	4.8
New Zealand	18	4.7
Malaysia	29	4.5
Thailand	31	4.5
India	34	4.4
Taiwan, China	37	4.3
Indonesia	40	4.3
Vietnam	63	3.9
Brunei Darussalam	72	3.8
Philippines	75	3.8
Sri Lanka	77	3.7
Mongolia	93	3.5
Lao PDR	97	3.4
Cambodia	98	3.4
Nepal	102	3.3
Bangladesh	120	3.1
Pakistan	121	3.1

Source: Compiled from http://www3.weforum.org/docs/WEF_TTCR_2019.pdf /.

Several factors have caused to decrease the level of travel and tourism competitiveness of Sri Lanka tourism from 2017 to 2019.

Among these factors, decrease the level of *Competitiveness in business environment* (50th–79th), *safety and security* (59th–78th), *international openness* (67th–100th), *price competitiveness* (20th–74th), and *natural resources* (31st–43rd) have been the major reasons for such a decrease by *13th ranking positions* in Global TTCI.

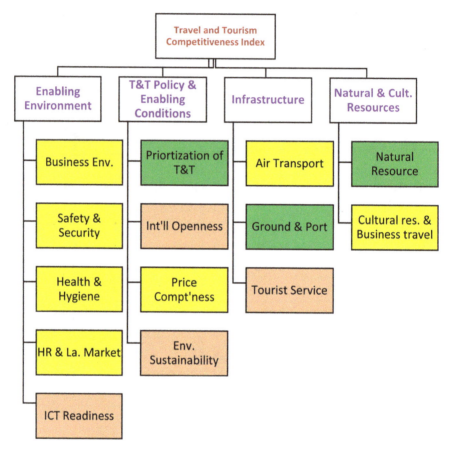

- *Declining price competitiveness of Sri Lanka tourism:* In particular, an increase the requirements to obtain Sri Lankan visa (16th–50th), increase the taxes for air tickets and airport chargers (45th–132nd), higher prices of hotels (compare to the destinations in the region), higher Fuel price levels were major reasons to reduce the *Price Competitiveness of Sri Lanka Tourism.*

    These indicators are further aggravated when considering average cost for Hotel Construction (by different graded hotels).
- Though the competitiveness of Sri Lanka Tourism is higher than Vietnam and Nepal, it is far below than the travel and tourism competitiveness of India, Singapore, Thailand and Malaysia. However, Sri Lanka's Safety and Security, Human Resource and Labor Market, Environment Sustainability and Tourist Service Infrastructure are relatively better than India and few other competitive countries in the region.

TABLE 9.3 Average Estimated Investment Per Hotel Room (in Rs. Million)

Average Estimated Investment Per Hotal Room (in Rs. Million)		
Hotel category	**Actual (Without land cost)**	**Actual (Without land cost)**
City/Budget hotels	10-11	11-12
Hotels and resorts	21-23	24-25
3 Star	13-14	14-15
4 Star	20-22	22-24
5 Star	24-26	29-31
Boutique hotels	19-20	21-22
Villa/Chalets	32-35	35-38

Source: Board of Investment of Sri Lanka; www.investstrilanka.com

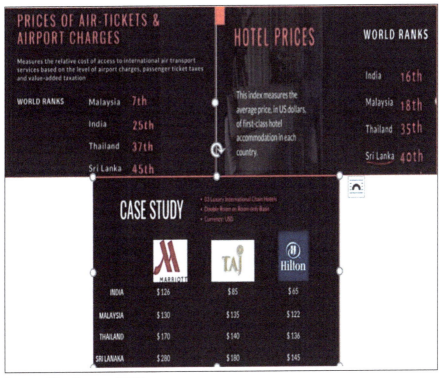

Source: Silva Suranga (2020).

- *Decreasing quality of the infrastructure:* Poor Conditions of the roads and railroads and lack of accessibility of destination sites have reduced the Quality of the Infrastructure in the TTCI.

- *Declining the TTCI's value of natural resources in Sri Lanka tourism*: The major reasons to reduce the TTCI Ranking of *natural resources in Sri Lanka tourism* (39th–112th) were lower the Percentage of Total Protected Areas, Reducing the advantage of natural assets, Less no of Number of World Heritage Natural Sites, Poor Knowledge of Total Known Species, and Less Development of Natural Tourism Digital Demand.

Furthermore, the competitiveness of Sri Lanka Tourism can be summarized into Five Levels of Success at the Global TTCI. In this context, Sri Lanka Tourism is neither representing the lowest performance of TTCI nor at the highest Performance of TTCI.

Higher National Prioritization of Travel and Tourism Development, Ground & Port Infrastructure Facilities and Natural Resource Attractions are the three major categories creating higher overall values of Sri Lanka Tourism in the Travel and Tourism Competitive Index at present.

TABLE 9.4 Key Factors Reducing the Position of Sri Lanka Tourism at the Global Travel and Tourism Competitiveness Index

Major Components of TTCI	2017	2019	Change (2017–2019)
Business Environment	4.7	4.4	Decrease
Safety and Security	5.5	5.4	Decrease
Health and hygiene	5.3	5.3	No Change
Human Resources & Labour Market.	4.5	4.4	Decrease
ICT Readiness	3.7	3.9	Increase
Prioritization of T&T	5.2	5.2	No Change
Int'l Openness	3.1	2.7	Decrease
Price Competitiveness	5.6	5.4	Decrease
Environ. Sustainability	3.9	4	Increase
Air Transport Infrastructure	2.6	2.8	Increase
Ground and Port Infrastructure	3.9	3.7	Decrease
Tourist Service Infrastructure	3.2	3.3	Increase
Natural Resources	4.1	3.6	Decrease
Cult. Res. and Business Travel	1.6	1.7	Increase

Therefore Sri Lanka tourism must focus on several areas to enhance its competitiveness:

- *Business environment*: Lower value of *global ease of doing business index* is also indicating the negative setting of the business environment of the country. Mainly, Lack of property rights and High taxes are two key factors behind such dismal business environment. In addition, the indicators of Ease of Doing Business can be highlighted in this context. Such underperformance and inefficiencies have created in Sri Lanka due to: (1) Difficulties of Getting Electricity for Business operation, (2) Inefficiencies of Registering Property, (3) Difficulties of Getting Credits, (4) Complication of Paying Tax and (5) Problems of Enforcing contracts are several reasons for keeping Sri Lanka at 99th Position of Ease of Doing Business Index (Silva Suranga, 2020).

- *Safety and security:* Even though Sri Lanka has a moderate performance on it, the competitiveness of Sri Lanka Tourism has decreased over the last few years due to the several incidents of attacks on tourists and the sexual assault of women travelers.

  This score can be further decreased due to the impact of Easter Sunday attack. Currently, there are a growing number of *solitary travelers* and many of them are *Women Solitary Travelers*. This market segment would be a *niche market segment* with great potential for Sri Lanka Tourism. Ensuring the security of women must be a main concern for tourism promotion in Sri Lanka.

- *International openness and price competitiveness:* This is one of most detrimental factors to create less competitiveness in Sri Lanka Tourism. Although the *price competitiveness* of Sri Lanka Tourism is relatively at a satisfactory level of the global Travel Tourism Competitiveness, it is highly detrimental when considering the price competitiveness of regional destinations, more specifically at the competitive destinations of Sri Lanka Tourism in the region (India, Thailand, Malaysia, Indonesia, Vietnam).

- Poor attention on *environment sustainability and natural resources* can impede the attraction of international travelers and their memorable experience. At present tourists, more specifically, *Millennials and Generation Z* are seeking opportunities to escape from the hectic city life in *Concrete Jungle.* They greatly value the attraction of natural environment due to the therapeutic capacity of natural environment to restore their inner peace.

  Sri Lanka has a great potential to attract such tourist flows. Policymakers and practitioners should focus to ensure the sustainability of natural environment. Thailand can be a role model for Sri Lanka as it has higher ranking values of Environment Sustainability and Natural Resources in its TTCI. Furthermore, Thailand has stop tourist arrivals to the famous *Maya Beach* due to over tourism. Thailand has banned the usage of single use plastic bags as well. Government of Thailand

has amended its consumption laws in order to help to increase forest cover targeting to increase forest cover from 31.6% to 55% by 2037.
- *Improvement of infrastructure and tourist service facilities:* Countries like Spain, Thailand, Vietnam and India are continuously making a huge investment to improve the tourist infrastructure and basic service facilities. Recently Vietnam has funded heavily on developing on infrastructure facilities in respect of transport, energy, water supply, drainage and information and communications to ensure convenient, quality and modern service to the tourists. In India, augmentation of quality tourism infrastructure throughout the country is a key area of functioning of the Ministry of Tourism. More than fifty percent of the Ministry's expenditure on Plan schemes is incurred for development of quality tourism infrastructure at various tourist destinations and circuits in the States/Union Territories.

Public and private partnership has to be strongly emphasized for tourism infrastructure investments as it can leverage an "exponential growth" in tourism development. With this Public–Private Partnership, India is to reintroduce Ramayana Circuit Tours connected to the *story of Lord Rama* by developing the road and other kinds of accessibility of these circuit tours.

Sri Lanka should develop of both physical and digital infrastructure facilities to increase its travel and tourism competitiveness.

9.5 OUTCOME-DRIVEN POLICY-MEASURES AND RESULT-BASED DEVELOPMENT STRATEGIES

Policy-measures and development strategies taken by different destination countries to increase their travel and tourism competitiveness can be highlighted as global best practices learnable to Sri Lanka Tourism to enhance its competitiveness at global and regional levels.

9.6 ENTERING THE FUNDAMENTAL CORRECTION: STOPPING THE BEGINNING OF "RIP-OFF SRI LANKA"

The National Policy Framework (NPF) of new government constitutes of *Ten (10) Key Policies* aiming to achieve the *Fourfold Outcome:* (1) A Productive Citizenry, (2) A Contented Family, (3) A Disciplined and Just Society, and (4) A Prosperous Nation.

TABLE 9.5 Key Policies in Best Practices

Major Pillars of TTCI	Identified Best Practices Implemented for Improving Travel and Tourism Competitiveness
Business Environment	• **Singapore**: Electronic Tax Payments, Online Business Registrations, More Attractive Corporate Tax Structures • **India**: Improving the Legal Frameworks for Settling Disputes, Abolishing of Some Registration Fees, Lowering the Time Needed for and Cost of Seeking the Construction Permits • **China**: Strengthening Procedures for Enforcing Contracts to Improve the Protections for Minority and SME Investors
Safety and Security	• **Finland**: Maintaining an Independent Judicial System, Good Governance and Rule of Law • **Iceland**: Commitments to Safeguard the Human Rights • **Oman, UAE**: Maintaining Sever Punishments for Any Kind of Crimes
Health and Hygiene	• **Austria**: Maintaining a Good Health Insurance System, Direct Access to Specialists and Well-Organized Medical Emergency Services • **Bulgaria, Lithuania, Czech Republic**: Implementing Social Insurance Systems, Improving the Availability of Basic Healthcare
Human Resources and Labor Market	• **India and Bangladesh**: Increasing the Primary and Secondary Education Enrollment, Continuous Professional Development Programs, Improving the Productivity of Labour Force—***"Skill India"***
ICT Readiness	• **Hong Kong, Singapore**: Maintaining Sophisticated and Advanced ICT Infrastructure Facilities • **Austria and China**: Digitalization of Tourist Enterprises and Development Of E-Government Services
Prioritization of T&T	• **New Zealand**: Effective and unique marketing and branding strategies specially via digital platforms: ***"100% Pure New Zealand."*** • **Malta**: Formulating and implementing long term tourism policies based on a suitable sustainable framework with the principle of maintaining an acceptable rate of progress—***"Malta Tourism Vision to 2030"***
International Openness	• **Japan, Bolivia, and Serbia**: Lowering the visa requirements
Price Competitiveness	• **Bolivia, Serbia, and China**: Lowering the air ticket taxes and airport charges • **Brunei**: Maintaining low fuel prices and high purchasing power

TABLE 9.5 (Continued)

Major Pillars of TTCI	Identified Best Practices Implemented for Improving Travel and Tourism Competitiveness
Environmental Sustainability	• **Japan**: Improving the environmental standards and more commitment to environment treaties • **Denmark**: Direct commitments to clean and efficient energy • **Switzerland**: Implementing proper recycling waste management systems, *"Waste to Energy Plants"* • **Thailand**: Establishing the standards and laws on tourism consumption and employing new technologies for environmental protection
Air Transport Infrastructure	• **Malta**: Improving the airline connectivity by government schemes to attract airline service, introduce new routes and to expand the accessibility, Introduction of low-cost carriers
Ground and Port Infrastructure	• **Spain**: Improving the road and railway systems – Spain's high-speed rail networks and toll road franchises • **Thailand**: Improve domestic land transport by extensions and improvements of roads to promote safety in traveling for tourists, stablish shuttle bus systems and train transportation networks that cover key tourist attractions
Tourist Service Infrastructure	• **Canada and Portugal**: Maintaining quality tourism infrastructure, highest number of ATMs per capita, car rental companies • **Malta and Thailand**: Regular maintenance of public convenience facilities • **Spain**: Improve tourism information services
Natural Resources	• **German**: Expanding the protected lands and habitat protection • **Thailand and Brazil**: Improving the accessibility to the natural resources • **Saudi Arabia**: Improving the environmental regulations
Cultural Resources and Business Travel	• **Japan, Spain and Brazil**: Hosting significant number of international association events and sports events • **Japan, New Zealand and Spain**: Marketing the unique cultural, environment and historical attractions

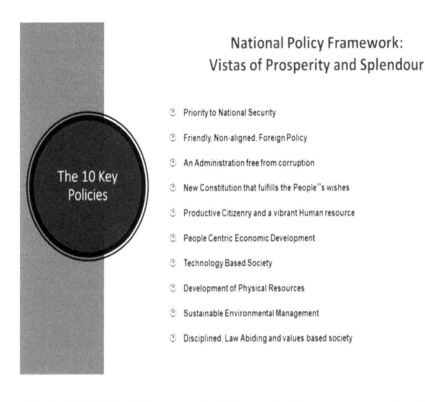

Under this NPF and the *sectoral policies and policy components of tourism development* clearly indicate that its main purpose is to develop Sri Lanka tourism as an *environmental and domestic-culture friendly industry with extensive people's participation*, targeting to attract 7 million tourist arrivals by generating 10 US $ billion income to the nation.

Therefore to achieve such national targets, the Proposed Sectoral Policies & Policy Components with Relevant Strategies for Tourism Development under the *NPF* should be connected with the Major Pillars of Global TTCI.

9.7 EVENT TOURISM DEVELOPMENT IN SRI LANKA

At present, major purposes of generating a significant number of tourists at global level are not purely dependent only on conventional *4Ss Tourism* (Sun, Sea, Sand, and Sex). Tourism products have been significantly diversifying into different specific directions since recent years due to emerging demand-driven market trends and patterns. One important growing segment in global tourism is Meetings, Incentives, Conferences, and Exhibitions (MICE) Tourism.

TABLE 9.6 Major Policies and Strategies with Major Pillars of TTCI

Major Pillars of TTCI	Sectoral Policies and Policy Components with Relevant Strategies for Tourism Development under the National Policy Framework
Business Environment	• Identify new attractions of the country for foreign tourists • Facilitate to hold business conferences, festivals, exhibitions and seminars to attract tourists • Initiate a strategic marketing and advertising programs to promote tourism • Develop household related and community-based tourism
Safety and Security	• Establish Tourist Police Service near tourist centers • Register, train and certify all tourist guides and drivers to prevent unnecessary harassment of tourists, ensure security and protection for the tourists
Health and Hygiene	• Connected with the Ten (10) Key Policies with the Sectoral Policies and Policy Components of Other Sectors of Sri Lankan Economy
Human Resources and Labor Market	• Establish tourism training schools in main tourism cities and also introduce attractive skill development courses • Increase the numbers of workers up to one million in the tourism industry • Revise labor laws governing tourist sector workers
ICT Readiness	• Introduce e-based facilities for reservation of hotels, transport, guides, domestic air tickets and admission card (Single booking software system and Electronic gate systems
Prioritization of T&T	• Increasing annual tourist arrivals to 7 million people. Our aim is to annually add a foreign exchange inflow of USD 10 billion to the domestic economy from tourism
International Openness	• Connected with the Ten (10) Key Policies with the Sectoral Policies and Policy Components of Other Sectors of the Economy
Price Competitiveness	• Provide investment and other facilities to the private sector to develop tourism • Provide incentives to set up high-quality tourist hotels and increase number of Hotel rooms currently available up to double.

TABLE 9.6 (Continued)

Major Pillars of TTCI	Sectoral Policies and Policy Components with Relevant Strategies for Tourism Development under the National Policy Framework
Environmental Sustainability	• Environmental and Domestic-Culture Friendly Industry with Extensive People's Participation • Connected with the Ten (10) Key Policies with the Sectoral Policies and Policy Components of Other Sectors of Sri Lankan Economy
Air Transport Infrastructure	• Introduce More Efficient Immigration and Migration Process Modernize Internal Airports • Connected with the Ten (10) Key Policies with the Sectoral Policies and Policy Components of Other Sectors of the Economy
Ground and Port Infrastructure	• Introduce More Efficient Immigration and Migration Process Modernize Internal Airports • Connected with the Ten (10) Key Policies with the Sectoral Policies and Policy Components of Other Sectors of the Economy
Tourist Service Infrastructure	• Set up tourist service centers at the road junctions connecting main tourist cities • Streamline the processes of approval of tourist facilities while setting up regional offices • Connected with the Ten (10) Key Policies with the Sectoral Policies and Policy Components of Other Sectors of the Economy
Natural Resources	• Environmental and Domestic-Culture Friendly Industry with Extensive People's Participation • Connected with the Ten (10) Key Policies with the Sectoral Policies and Policy Components of Other Sectors of the Economy
Cultural Resources and Business Travel	• Initiate an enable environment for local performers to attract tourist • Environmental and Domestic-Culture Friendly Industry with Extensive People's Participation

MICE Tourism is defined by some scholars as Business Tourism as well. Nevertheless, MICE tourism provides a bountiful incentives and opportunities to make use of leisure time of people to explore the possible gainful business development opportunities during their travelling in destinations and also making a platform through tourism for business knowledge acquisition to the tourists who might not have a clear-cut business development idea before such experience obtaining in their travel destination, otherwise. MICE tourism has become one of the most decisive source generators for the development of *Event Tourism* in many destination countries through its four segments.

9.7.1 PROMOTION OF EVENT TOURISM AND INDUSTRY COMPETITIVENESS: TURNING THE UNTURNED

Both major types of events—Planned and Unplanned Events can be promoted into Event Tourism if proper tourism management is implemented. Planned Tourism Events is to be created by event management organizations or destination countries for tourism promotion or any other purposes that can be used to promote tourism in those particular countries. Such events require a gamut of skills and expertise in setting up, operation, and management with a certain length of time. *Unplanned Events* could be natural events and perhaps the events related Dark Tourism promotion.

On the other hand, Planned Tourism Events can be (1) Mega events, (2) Hallmark events, (3) Major events, and (4) Local events. These events are also related to Cultural and Arts Festivals, Entertainment, Business and Trade, Sport competitions, Recreational, Educational and Scientific, and even Political events.

It is high time we have been convinced that despite a significant number of events happening in Sri Lanka, an insignificant contribution for tourism application and opportunities have been capitalized out of the potential which is a tip of the iceberg, even though the majority of such events are tourist-attraction driven.

One simple reason decisive in this context is no proper relationship established between specific events and tourism development. Most of the attractive cultural festivals and local events are organized primarily for local residents and often with the help of devotees and volunteers. Although in the majority of the cases these events are very local-centric and small with the limited or none tourist attractiveness, the potential to make a significant contribution to tourist attraction and consequent benefits to the local community itself is uncountable. The direct and indirect contribution of these events could be manifold, but not yet unfold to the industry at its great potential. The various types of festivals and events have been long existing in different parts of the country, more specifically rural areas with uniqueness and authenticity.

9.8 TOURISM COMPETITIVENESS AND CULTURAL TOURISM EVENTS

According to the Global TTCI, the *Cultural Resources and Business Travels* are considered under its *Fourth Major Category: Natural and Cultural Resources*. Furthermore, the Pillar Fourteenth (Pillar 14th) of TTCI is the Cultural Resources and Business Travel. Under the Pillar 14th, Five Indicators are considered when calculating the Travel and Tourism Competitiveness Index:

- 14.01: Number of World Heritage cultural sites;
- 14.02: Oral and intangible cultural heritage expressions;
- 14.03 Number of large sports stadiums;
- 14.04 Number of international association meetings and
- 14.05: Cultural and entertainment tourism digital demand.

It is obvious factor that the Pillar 14 and its indicators are vital factors in deciding the level of competitiveness of the destination. For an instance, one of the major reasons for India to obtain higher values of the TTCI is its Cultural Resources and promotion of cultural events in its tourist attraction.

Therefore cultural events and festivals can have a significant and important influence on not only the development of the local communities and their well-being but also to create higher competitiveness of Sri Lanka Tourism.

9.9 SUSTAINABLE APPLICATION AND PROMOTION OF CULTURAL TOURISM EVENTS IN SRI LANKA

Their utilization of the local resources for cultural tourism events can create a significant positive impact on the local economy. However, utilization of such resources should not raise the concerns regarding cultural degradation of local community involved with cultural tourism events.

Most of the cultural events in local areas are community and culturally oriented. Variety and diversity of local culture is a prime power for tourist attraction. It is favorable to enhance the tourism competitiveness of Sri Lanka Tourism. Keeping the authenticity of these events with regional and provincial significance must be maintained for tourist attraction. The important identities of these local events should be protected. Massive tourism promotion with these events would create negative impacts and destroy the authenticity of these events. Making these events at a bigger and larger scale can also destroy the real values of its identity. Value addition of these events must not damage the authenticity of these events. The so-called rapid improvement of these events should not marginalize the local communities and their involvement, more specifically when increasing the number of local and international tourists to these cultural events.

The promotion of cultural event tourism in Sri Lanka can be sustainable not only through the continuous improvement of the offerings of such tourism to enhance the economic standards and capabilities of the local community but also how far such tourism development can protect the cultural identity and authenticity of those cultural events.

9.10 APPLICATION OF RIGHT-POLICY MIX

Innovative creation and efficient delivery of unique and authentic tourism experiences to the tourists can mainly determine whether Sri Lanka Tourism reaches a higher level of competitiveness as a growing top tourist destination country in the world.

Instead of Over-Promising and Under-Producing, Sri Lanka Tourism must produce more and better-quality tourism services to meet current trends and patterns of travel and tourism demand. Tourists are now Discerning Customers. They are asking more *Distinctive* and *Heterogenous* nature and culture-based tourist attractions and services.

Understanding the great variety of tourist sensitivities over the prices of tourism products and services is essential to create an effective marketing of Sri Lanka Tourism. If Sri Lanka Tourism provides only ordinary or sameness products and services, then such tourism demand must be highly priced sensitive. The opposite can be realized if Sri Lanka Tourism can produce unique and memorable travel experiences for tourists.

Therefore focusing on high-quality experience-based tourism products and services is decisive for making Sri Lanka Tourism to be competitive and to create a greater ability to consistently generate more tourism revenues to the country.

Sri Lanka Tourism must find a most suitable combination of the *Right-Policy Mix* in both assets and process of tourism development. The tourism assets are the tourism resources created by the nature and culture and also the man-made attractions and facilities made by Sri Lankan (e.g., infrastructures, marketing). Sri Lanka Tourism must retain its competitive position by satisfying the expectations of tourists and all other stakeholders of the industry while constantly eliminating the threats and exploiting the opportunities arising from the competitive environment in global tourism.

Competitiveness of Sri Lanka Tourism can only be sustained by continuing improvement of the offerings and capabilities of the industry. Certainly, consistent marketing plans and promotional strategies through the price, quality, image, and ensuring the sustainable tourism practices must be focused through a holistic approach.

The Right-Policy-Mix is more applicable when considering the promotion of Cultural Event Tourism in Sri Lanka. It needs more proficient culture tourism management, well knowledgeable workforce, innovative entrepreneurship, robust and responsible marketing, use of new technologies and responsible industry leadership to promote culture tourism events.

In other words, both "Doing the Right Things" *Things Right* are vital importance for great success in promoting cultural tourism events in Sri Lanka.

KEYWORDS

- global travel and tourism competitiveness
- untapped potential
- cultural diversification
- cultural tourism events

REFERENCES

Central Bank of Sri Lanka (2019), Annual Report—2018, https://www.cbsl.gov.lk/en/publications/economic-and-financial-reports/annual-reports/annual-report-2019.

Sri Lanka Tourism Development Authority (2019), Annual Report—2018, https://sltda.gov.lk/storage/documents/0cb228cd03762f638bd515fe83edd453.pdf.

Sri Lanka Tourism Development Authority (2020), Annual Report—2019, https://www.sltda. gov.lk/storage/common_media/Annual%20Statistical%20Report%20219%20Word%20 13.7.20%20(1)789700659.pdf

Suranga, Silva, D.A.C (2020) (https://www.ceylondigest.com/people-centric-sustainable-tourism-development-and-entrepreneurial-new-public-service-in-sri-lanka/, 2020).

UNWTO (2019), 'UNWTO Tourism Data Dashboard', https://www.unwto.org/unwto-tourism-dashboard.

Wimalarathana W. Rev and Silva, D.A.C. (2009) Tourism Resources in Sri Lanka, Western Province-I, ISBN: 9789555119511, Published by Olanda Publisher.

World Economic Forum (2018) Travel and Tourism Competitiveness Index—2018, http://www3.weforum.org/docs/WEF_TTCR_2019.pdf

World Economic Forum (2019) Travel and Tourism Competitiveness Index—2019, http://www3.weforum.org/docs/WEF_TTCR_2019.pdf

CHAPTER 10

FUTURE OF FOOD TOURISM IN INDIA: A PSYCHOGRAPHIC OVERVIEW

KHUSHBOO GUPTA[1*], and SARIKA MOHTA[2]

[1]Trilok Singh TT College, Sikar, Rajasthan, India

[2]OKIMR, University of Kota, Kota, Rajasthan, India

*Corresponding author. E-mail: drkhushboogupta2017@gmail.com

ABSTRACT

This chapter places specific focus on the future of food tourism in India. Theoretical understanding is offered related to different psychographic reasons that affect our food choice. Food choices largely depend on different physical, geographical, and cultural reasons with psychographic factors related to individuals as interest, attitudes, and beliefs, which motivates to eat a particular kind of food again and again. Further currently rampant practices in promoting food tourism are being discussed with further marketing tools for promoting food based tourism are suggested too.

10.1 INTRODUCTION

Food has an important place in human life. Ingestion of food is related to the psychography of the individual. Food preferences differ from person to person. Food has a great impact of the culture, tradition, art, places, and experiences of the people, thus each province of India has its exceptional food platter. Tourism and food cannot be separated from each other, as dining out is an integral part of tourism. Over the time tourists realize that experiencing a nation's food is essential to understand its culture because food manifests intangible heritage (Updhyay and Sharma, 2014). Ministry of Tourism (2008) envisaged in its annual report that "India's wide variety of customary cooking styles is a wellspring of vacation destinations that can be packaged and marketed by developing 'culinary tour routes' for special category of tourists keen on authentic tastes and cuisines." Eating food is related to relaxation, escapism, education status, and way of life that fill in as an inspiration factor for most of the tourists (Frochot, 2003). According to World Food Travel Association, the meaning of "Food Tourism" is travelling to look for pleasure by means of eating and drinking encounters at the destination. Food tourism has been addressed as a vehicle for territorial advancement reinforcing neighborhood creation through linkages in tourism supply chain partnership (Renko et al., 2010). Food tourism further categorized into culinary tourism, cuisine tourism, gourmet tourism, gastronomy tourism, farm tourism, and rural/urban tourism.

Food tourism is an interdisciplinary zone that incorporates various things, for example, centrality of food as indicated by culture, society, geography, and politics. Individuals see it from different perspectives:

1. *Activity-based perspective*: It defines the food-related experiences (sensory and cultural experiences) of the tourists in relation to a destination's culinary resources (Bjork and Kauppinen-Raisanen, 2016; Ellis et al., 2018; Presenza and Chiappa, 2013). This provides an opportunity to tourists to physically experience the food via visitation to food production sites, cooking classes, and food theme events (Ellis et al., 2018).

2. *Motivation-based perspective*: Tourist's desire to experience certain cuisines or food of a specific place is an important drive for destination choice (Lee et al., 2014). Presenza and Locca (2012) said that food tourism is a movement conduct of an individual propelled by a longing for experiencing certain food items. Evidences suggest that food tourism is a type of tourism in which food is one of the important motivating factors (Su, 2013; Bertella, 2011).

3. *Mixed perspective*: Explorers demonstrated that food tourism particularly decision of destination of tourism depends on both movement and inspiration (Adeyinka-Oji and Khoo-Lattimore, 2013; Hall, 2006). Ellis et al (2018) indicated that intersections between both perspectives cannot be denied as food consumption is not only a tourist activity but is an activity that is motivated by an interest in a particular food.

4. *Destination standpoint*: Food can be considered as a component of bigger ideas, that is, destination's proposal of a tourist experience

(Spilkova and Fialova, 2013; Wan and Chan, 2013). The selection of destinations on the basis of food might be used as a selling point of marketing and management of tourism strategies (du Rand and Heath, 2006).

10.2 THEMES/CONCEPTS OF FOOD TOURISM/DRIVING FORCES OF FUTURE FOOD TOURISM

The development of strong strategies is required for the growth of food tourism in future. Following themes or concepts might help to serve the purpose.

10.2.1 MOTIVATION

Motivation is the main factor of food tourism, as food tourism is more than just eating food. It relates to the authentic experiences, cultural learning, sensory appeal, interpersonal relations, and excitement and health concerns of an individual (Kim and Eves, 2012). This experience should be enjoyable and memorable (i.e., excitement, inspiration, and cultural exploration), which provide meaning (Scarpato and Daniele, 2003; Sharples, 2003). A study showed significant effect of various motivational dimensions (e.g., oddity and assortment, bona fide experience and renown, relational and culture, value/worth and affirmation, wellbeing concern, commonality and dietary patterns, tangible, and relevant delight) on food-related personality traits of tourists (Mak et al., 2017). Therefore the concept of motivation may work as a key element of design and creation of food tourism to fulfill different needs (i.e., physical, physiological, cultural, personal, and social and security) of the tourists.

10.2.2 CULTURE AND HERITAGE

Culture or legacy of a place assumes a significant job in plan of the tourism exercises. As indicated by Montanari (2009) food is a "cultural reference point" that, within it, contains altogether one of a kind information about the creation, culture, and topography of the destination from where it begins. Cianflone et al. (2013) considered food as a "statement of neighbourhood methods of utilization and of nearby developing or assembling praxis connected to the region and to its history." The plan of any food tourism offering will not be feasible if it does not take into account the social attributes (conduct, information, and customs of area) of the region. Gastronomy permits tourists to access the social and chronicled legacy of destinations through tasting, encountering, and buying (Ellis et al., 2018).

10.2.3 AUTHENTICITY

Food is known as a concept of place and culture linked with identity, destination, and icon dishes. Icon dishes are the yield of realness that be connected with inspiration, taste, culture, maintainable turn of events, neighborhood network, topography, food tourism. Food and authenticity are bound by cultural, historical, and locality aspects.

10.2.4 MANAGEMENT AND MARKETING

Management and marketing are very essential to popularize any place for tourism. This theme involves concepts of destination orientation, image creation, disciplinary approaches, motivations, satisfaction, consumer behavior, research themes, and the tourist (Lee and Arcodia, 2011).

Foods in this broadly links the network and district to tourism, and along these lines, inborn worth of the place (counting individuals) rather the area itself is a focal point of food tourism management and marketing. The marketing of food tourism creates a picture and feeling of place for a network. As food tourism is a catalyst for community engagement it thus has political capital driving rural and regional development (Ellis et al., 2018).

10.2.5 DESTINATION ORIENTATION

Research demonstrates that destination orientation has direct connections with types of tourism, place marketing, assets, items, and the management and marketing. Destination orientation overlaps with experiences, motivations and food, place, and culture. Thus what the heritage and culture of destination are equal to what food tourism is. The dish not just as a "social ancient rarity," conveying with its cultural knowledge and development of people groups, yet additionally as a national symbol replicated throughout the world. The food is without a doubt situated as an antiquity of culture that contains information of cultural heritage of destination (Metro-Roland, 2013) through consumption of the local cuisine tourist can get a truly authentic cultural experience. Orientation is the destination's history and culture, hence, food creates image, reputation, brand, and position (Banerjee, 2013). In this concept, food is used as the main attraction and will develop the market strategies that will focus on the food.

Knowledge of these five themes or concepts is essential while developing the strategies of promotion of food tourism, so that one can offer good tourism services to the visitors or tourists. India is a country that shows unity in diversity. It is a nation where wide variation is seen in food intake, cuisines, culture, tradition, and language of the people. Differences are seen in the Geography of the country also, which makes it an ideal destination for food tourism. The richness of ethnic cuisines of different states of India may enhance the visitors of tourists stay that positively enhance the culinary tourism in India, which can be a significant wellspring of employment for local people. Through proper management and marketing, India can be developed as a tourism hub especially in the sector of food tourism.

10.3 MARKETING TOOLS TO PROMOTE FOOD TOURISM IN INDIA

10.3.1 THE "INCREDIBLE TIFFIN" CAMPAIGN

Ab Karim and Chi (2010) recommended that cuisines that are distinctive and prestigious are appropriate to be created and promoted as a tourism product. In acknowledgment of culinary tourism's potential effect on the tourism economy, the Ministry of Tourism, India propelled the culinary branch of the Incredible India campaign, suitably dedicated "Incredible Tiffin" project in May, 2012. This initiative provides a tiffin packaged with local food for individuals outside the nation, to assist them with getting a thought of the choices of food accessible in India (Berry, 2014). In expansion to the tourism promotions, the initiative also expects to research and record regional cuisines (Budhraja, 2012).

10.3.2 CULINARY CLASSES

On the off chance that the world is tingling to gorge on exquisite Indian cuisine, the Indian kitchen is transforming into a hub for cuisine tourism over the subcontinent (Berry, 2014). Many of the tourists want to learn different cuisines of all over the world. Indian cuisine is very famous due to its flavor, richness, and diversity; thus it attracts a number of tourists who want to learn how to cook authentic desi khana (Indian food). Following points show why international tourists want to appreciate firsthand experience with Indian cooking.

1. *Flavors of Indian Cuisines*: Indian meals have various flavors in the form of curries, spices, and sweets; putting these flavors in food is always treated like an art. This art is the primary driver that draws in global visitors into the Indian kitchens. Sameer Gupta a specialist of Indian cuisine said that one of the principal purposes for the expanding ubiquity of the pattern is the craving to find out about Indian lifestyle, culture, and tradition. Also, food is without a doubt a significant element of the Indian lifestyle. In this manner, worldwide tourists need to learn Indian dishes in their accurate style without compromising its ingredients or flavor.
2. *Culinary heritage:* In search of real Indian cuisine, tourists go to simple households too. Indian kitchens are changing into ideal centers for cooking tourism, offering tourists with a choice to gain proficiency with the regional dishes while staying with locals. The tourists want to eat with family members of local households and relish the delicacies. Nowadays international explorers need those sorts of vacationer administrations that serve their palates as well as show them the genuine heritage of India (Indian values, culture, culinary legacy, and the Indian way of life). Different states of India can provide this type of services to enhance the culinary tourism.
3. *Flavor with nutraceutical value:* Prevention is always better than cure. Good food serves as one of the preventive measures of numerous acute and chronic diseases. Indian spices and ghee have nutraceutical potentials along with nutritional values. With the knowledge of these and their use in Indian delights one can cure many diseases. This part can be introduced in the tourism industry methodologies where tourists can know and get familiar with the marvel flavors of Indian spices and their uses.

10.3.2.1 INDIAN CULINARY CLASSES PLACES

Following are the places where the tourists can take Indian culinary classes:

1. The Pimenta-Spice Garden-Bungalows-Cooking Holidays, Kochi (Cochin)
2. Aakriti Eco Homestay, Nilgiri Mountains, Tamil Nadu
3. Silom House and Cooking School, North Goa
4. Bengali cooking classes, Kolkata, West Bengal
5. Private cooking class in an Indian home, Delhi
6. Spice Paradise cooking class, Rajasthan
7. Mercury Travels, Mumbai
8. Trans India Holidays, New Delhi

10.3.3 FOOD FESTIVALS

In India, food festivals or food fests have progressed significantly. They are a lively portrayal of the myriad tastes of the nation, complete with the elite delicacies and food-items of Indian states. Urban communities across the nation have become "foodie central" with an energizing arrangement of food festivals having a wide range of Indian cuisines. These festivals of the nation mirror the assorted societies and conventions prevalent in the country, which discover articulation through its huge assortment of regional cuisines of the country. Unique flavor of local cuisines of India crawls its way into these amazing and very enticing food festivals, convincing its guests to enjoy probably the most scrumptious food dishes.

Some famous food festivals of India are as follows:

1. *National Street Food Festival:* Every year in the month of December/January this food festival is organized in Jawaharlal Nehru Stadium, New Delhi. It is a fiesta of street food from various states of India. It is an ideal fest for passionate street sweethearts as they can get an assortment of much-adored street delights at one place. Street food is a fortune place of regional culinary conventions and is progressively assuming a significant job as an enhancer and power multiplier of the tourism industry. Asian street food is considered the best on the planet.
2. *Mei Ram-ew*: In the month of December, ethnic food festival of Meghalaya, Mei Ram-ew is organized at Sacred Grove, Mawphlang Meghalaya. It is an effort of North-East Slow Food and Agro Biodiversity Society to protect and advance the various forest foraged and locally developed foods that are cooked and served by indigenous inhabitants of the North East India.

3. *Great Indian Food Festival:* It is organized in the month of January at Dilli Haat, Delhi. The Great Indian Food Festival has 75 stalls from 12 states, has enough variety to send individuals straight into a culinary coma. Exciting competitions such as golgappa-gulping competitions and vadapav-eating competitions are also hosted in this festival.
4. *The Grub Fest:* The Grub Fest is organized in the month of March every year in New Delhi, Pune, and Mumbai. It is a perfectly enthralling collection of food, fun, and entertainment. It is a food carnival with culinary workshops, a natural food showcase, music exhibitions, and a large group of well-known restaurants. The celebration likewise has an exceptional field for mini food trucks called the Grub Mile. In this festival one can see the movies themed on food.
5. *International Mango Festival*: The International Mango Festival is organized in Dilli Haat, Delhi, It is a two days event organized during summer (July) that exhibits over 550 variations of mangoes. The Tourism and Transportation Development Corporation arranges this festival in collaboration with the National Horticultural Board, New Delhi Municipal Corporation and Agricultural and Processed Food Products Export Development Authority. Food dishes are readied using mangoes by acclaimed culinary experts. Social exhibitions and rivalries like mango slogan composing and mango eating challenges for women are basic pieces of the celebration.
6. *Goa Food and Cultural Festival*: In the month of April, this festival is organized in Panaji, Goa. It is an initiative of Goa Tourism Development Corporation. In this festival, much-cherished customary delights (approximately 70 food stalls of different recipes) are served to the tourists; thus the celebration emphasizes that Goan cuisine is much more than simply rice and fish curry.
7. *Gujarati Food Festival*: Consistently, an intricate food festival is organized in Gujarat, known as the Gujarati Food Festival that bears declaration to incredibly great delights, which are exclusive to this Indian state. Chefs of eminent lodgings and eateries of Gujarat participate in the festival with excitement and enthusiasm.
8. *Palate Fest*: It is organized in month of February at Nehru Park, Delhi. It is a three-day food and music festival that brings together some of the most loved and popular restaurants, food stalls, and even some embassy kitchens from across Delhi.

9. *Ahare Bangla*: It is a five-day-long food festival organized by the West Bengal government in the month of October at Milan Mela Grounds, Kolkata, which shows the extreme passion of Bengalis pertaining to food. Ahare Bangla is a great place for foodies to get a taste of classical Bengali dishes.

Some other names of food festivals are Bengaluru Food Fete, Sattvik Food Festival, Navi Mumbai Truck Festival, UpperCrust Food & Wine Show, and Horn OK Please, which depict the Indian culture and heritage through food.

10.4 INDIAN CUISINE IN INTERNATIONAL COOKERY SHOWS

Many Hollywood and Western television channels show Indian cuisine as a part of their popular culture. This is a time where Indian food is gaining momentum, with many international chefs trying to reinvent popular dishes and give them a makeover to cater to a wider audience of gourmands. This can be a good medium to spread the specialities of Indian cuisines which in turn enhances the culinary or food tourism in India.

10.5 ROLE OF RESTAURANTS IN FOOD TOURISM

Dining out is the most frequent leisure activity (Hall and Mitchell, 2005) and an integral part of tourism. Thus services provided in a restaurant play an important role in the success or failure of travel. Restaurants render a unique experience of eating (Josiam et al., 2004) and also provide key attributes to destination attractiveness as they serve as one of the key determinants of tourists' experience (Correia et al., 2007; Gross et al., 2008; Halland Sharples, 2003; Kivela and Crotts, 2006). Tourists' interest in culinary experiences has triggered enormous growth in the restaurant industry (Sparks et al., 2003); hence, today, tourists make up a significant part of the market for restaurants and cafes throughout the world (Hall and Sharples, 2003). Tourists have a significant contribution in the food and restaurant business; therefore understanding of tourists' culinary preferences is necessary for better product design, menu design, marketing campaigns, service quality, thematic ambience, food quality, and so on because poor quality and service failure can have negative outcomes, affecting health, trip disruption and ruining destination reputation (Pendergast, 2006). With the aim of giving normalized "world-class services" to the tourists, the Department of Tourism, Government of India has a willful plan for endorsement of cafés in the nation. Such autonomous eateries will be outside the inns and ought to have in excess of 30 seats.

Other activities or events such as day tours, old city food walks, cantonment food walks, food trails, farmers market, gourmet tours, food fairs that can showcase the real India by focusing on local Indian foods can be incorporated in tourism strategies to enhance the food or culinary tourism in India. The uniqueness of Indian cuisine is that cuisines of all states are equally enjoyed by the people of all over the country as well as outsiders also. Incorporation of these tools in tourism policy and strategies not only enhances the growth of food tourism in India but also improves the economy of the nation by providing employment.

10.6 CONCLUSION

Indian food has unique and fabulous flavors and offers a variety of dishes but, because of absence of facilities, till now it cannot be changed over into money. The Indian government is also taking initiatives to promote food tourism in country but some improvements are required in food sector, that is, hygiene and sanitation of food facilities, decorating and introduction of food, and delivering a quality experience to the tourists that can make their experience more memorable and unforgettable.

KEYWORDS

- food tourism
- psychographic segmentation
- Indian tourism
- marketing tools for food tourism

REFERENCES

Adeyinka-Oji, S.F., and Khoo-Lattimore, C. (2013). Slow food events as a high yield strategy for rural tourism destinations. *Worldwide Hospitality and Tourism Themes.* 5(4): 353–364.

Banerjee, M. (2013). Food tourism: An effective marketing tool for Indian tourism industry. *International Journal of Science and Research.* 4:795–800.

Berry, K. (2014). Progress and emerging issues in culinary tourism: A study with special reference to Punjab. *Journal of Hospitality Application and Research.* 9(1):28–46.

Bertella, G. (2011). Knowledge in food tourism: The case of Lofoten and Maremma Toscana. *Current Issues in Tourism.* 14(4): 355–371.

Bjork, P. and Kauppinen-Raisanen, H. (2016). Exploring the multi-dimensionality of travellers' culinary-gastronomic experiences. *Current Issues in Tourism.* 19(2):1260–1280.

Budhraja, S. (2012). Incredible Tiffin launch in Delhi. *The Times of India.* Retrieved from http://articles.timesofindia.indiatimes.com.

Cianflone, E., Bella, G.D. and Dugo, G. (2013). Preliminary insights on British travellers' accounts of Sicilian oranges. Tourismos: *An International Multidisciplinary Journal of Tourism.* 8(2):341–347.

Correia, A., DoValle, P.O. and Moc, C. (2007). Why people travel to exotic places. *International Journal of Culture, Tourism and Hospitality Research.* 1(1):45–61.

du Rand, G.E. and Heath, E. (2006). Towards a framework for food tourism as an element of destination marketing. *Current Issues in Tourism.* 9(3):206–234.

Ellis, A., Park, E., Kim, S. and Yeoman, I. (2018). What if food tourism? *Tourism Management.* 68:250–263.

Frochot, I. (2003). An analysis of regional positioning and its associated food images in French tourism regional brochures. *Journal of Travel and Tourism Marketing.* 14(3–4): 77–96.

Gross, M.J., Brien, C. and Brown, G. (2008). Examining the dimensions of a lifestyle tourism destination. *International Journal of Culture, Tourism and Hospitality Research.* 2(1):44–66.

Hall, C.M. and Mitchell, R. (2005). Gastronomic tourism: comparing food and wine tourism experiences. In: Novelli M (eds) Niche Tourism: Contemporary Issues, Trends and Cases. Oxford, UK: Butterworth- Heinemann, pp. 73–88.

Hall, C.M. and Sharples, L. (2003). The consumption of experience or the experience of consumption? An introduction to the tourism of taste. In: Hall CM, Sharples L, Mitchell R, Macionis N, and Cambourne B (eds) Food Tourism Around the World: Development, Management and Markets. Oxford, UK: Butterworth-Heinemann, pp. 314–335.

Hall, C. M. (2006). Introduction: Culinary tourism and regional development: From slow food to slow tourism? *Tourism Review International.* 9:303–305.

Josiam, B.M., Mattson, M. and Sullivan, P. (2004). The historaunt: heritage tourism at Mickey's dining car. *Tourism Management.* 25(4):453–461.

Kim, Y.G. and Eves, A. (2012). Construction and validation of a scale to measure tourist motivation to consume local food. *Tourism Management.* 33(6):1458–1467.

Kivela, J. and Crotts, J.C. (2006). Tourism and gastronomy: gastronomy's influence on how tourists experience a destination. *Journal of Hospitality and Tourism Research.* 30(3):354–377.

Lee, I. and Arcodia, C. (2011). The role of regional food and festivals for destination branding. *International Journal of Tourism Research.* 13(4): 355–367.

Lee, K., Alexander, A. C. and Kim, D. (2014). A study of geographical distance groups on length of visitors' stay at local food festival destinations. *Journal of Vacation Marketing.* 20(2):125–136.

Mak, A.H.N., Lumbers, M., Eves, A. and Chang, R.C.Y. (2017). The effects of food-related personality traits on tourist food consumption motivations. *Asia Pacific Journal of Tourism research.* 22(1):1–20.

Metro-Roland, M.M. (2013). Goulash nationalism: The culinary identity of a nation. *Journal of Heritage Tourism.* 8(2–3):172–181.

Ministry of Tourism. (2008). Annual Report 2007–08. Available at: http://tourism.gov.in/AnnualReport07-08.pdf (accessed 15 June 2012).

Montanari, A. (2009). Geography of taste and local development in Abruzzo (Italy): Project to establish a training and research centre for the promotion of enogastronomic culture and tourism. *Journal of Heritage Tourism.* 4(2):91–103.

Pendergast, D. (2006). Tourist gut reactions: food safety and hygiene issues. In: Wilks, J., Pendergast, D., and Leggat, P. (eds) Tourism in Turbulent Times: Towards Safe Experiences for Visitors. Amsterdam, The Netherlands: Elsevier, pp. 143–154.

Presenza, A. and Chiappa, G.D. (2013). Entrepreneurial strategies in leveraging food as a tourist resource: A cross-regional analysis in Italy? *Journal of Heritage Tourism.* 8(2–3):182–192.

Presenza, A. and Iocca, S. (2012). High cuisine restaurants: Empirical evidences from a research in Italy. *Journal of Tourism, Hospitality and Recreation.* 3(3):69–85.

Renko, S., Renco, N. and Polonijo, T. (2010). Understanding the role of food in rural tourism development in a recovering economy. *Journal of Food Products Marketing.* 16(3):309–324.

Scarpato, R. and Daniele, R. (2003). New global cuisine: tourism, authenticity and sense of place in postmodern gastronomy. In: Hall, C.M., Sharples, L., Mitchell, R., Macionis, N. and Cambourne, B. (eds) Food Tourism Around the World: Development, Management and Markets. Oxford, UK: Butterworth- Heinemann, pp. 298–313.

Sharples, L. (2003). Food tourism in the peak district national park, England. In: Hall, C.M., Sharples, L., Mitchell, R., Macionis, N., and Cambourne, B. (eds) Food Tourism Around the World: Development, Management and Markets. Oxford, UK: Butterworth-Heinemann.

Sparks, B., Bowen, J. and Klag, S. (2003). Restaurants and the tourist market. *International Journal of Contemporary Hospitality Management.* 15(1): 6–13.

Spilkova, J. and Fialova, D. (2013). Culinary tourism packages and regional brands in Czechia. *Tourism Geographies.* 15(2):177–197.

Su, C. (2013). An importance-performance analysis of dining attributes: A comparison of individual and packaged tourists in Taiwan. *Asia Pacific Journal of Tourism Research.* 18(6):573–597.

Updhyay, Y. and Sharma, D. (2014). Culinary preferences of foreign tourists in India. *Journal of Vacation marketing.* 20(1):29–39.

Wan, Y.K.P. and Chan, S.H.J. (2013). Factors that affect the levels of tourists' satisfaction and loyalty towards food festivals: A case study of Macau. *International Journal of Tourism Research.* 15(3): 226–240.

CHAPTER 11

SOCIAL MEDIA TRANSFORMING TOURIST BEHAVIOR

ASHMI CHHABRA

Department of Management and Commerce, IIS Deemed to University, Jaipur, India; E-mail: ashmichhabra06@gmail.com

ABSTRACT

The invention of Web 2.0 has brought major changes in the working of the online tourism industry in the last few decades. It has now become imperative for marketers to understand the A–Z aspect of the new and upgraded form of the world. This chapter consists of series of topics in order to acquaint the learners as how the online industry work starting from the trick of search and it is working to social media that is responsible for changing the way tourist extract information and perceive in accordance to their need and desire. The importance of various social media handles holds equal importance for both the tourists as well as the tourism industry. At last, an attempt has been made to associate the tourist behavior with that of the different consumer model and strategies have been suggested to the marketers.

11.1 TO INTRODUCE SEARCH AS A TRICK IN TOURISM

11.1.1 CONCEPT OF SEARCH

Human beings have evolved over time and so is the way they pursuit for their queries. This race has always been inquisitive about the things present around them. The advent of the World Wide Web, also known as Web 2.0, has provided a platform to quench there this nature of search. The late 1990s and early 2000s encountered a major change in terms of working of World Wide Web, the concept that was commenced with static HTML pages started shifting to responsive e-commerce opportunities involving two-way communication. Web 2.0 provided a platform that is more participative and has inclusive nature, as it allows not only to create but to cocreate, publish, and share your thoughts with the outside world. The technological tools have provided a medium to develop online communities, build up forums, and networks by the means of collaboration and distribution of content and application (Vicekry and Wunch-Vincent, 2007). The thought was further supported by Weinbery (2009), who supported that Web 2.0 is much more than just a medium for accessing information, it is a technology that cultivates, enhances, and modifies that interactions socially.

The key idea of search is to provide a platform for the basics of search engines to work. Organization can analyze what is trending and accordingly they construct content that is based on a certain explicit search query. In layman's language, Search acts as a filter to extract the right kind of information needed by the user from the web. The process of search is not only considered as swift but it affords an easy admittance to plethora of information. There exist various search engines such as Google, Yahoo, Bing, and AOL, while, various Users Generated Content (UGC) websites such as Facebook, Instagram, YouTube and LinkedIn, etc. Search engines have attained the top priority and the most valuable means for bridging the gap between the travelers and tourism businesses (Xiang, Wober, and Fesenmaier; 2000).

As of January 2020, as per a report by statista.com, *Google* leads the market with a share of 86.80% followed by *Bing* (5.87%), Yahoo (2.83%), Baidu (0.7%), and Yandex (0.76%). Also, the average monthly traffic on google. com is nearly 5170 million. While Facebook entails the highest number of active users amounting to 2449 million, are not these figures alarming enough to point out the growing importance of the concept of search?

Tourism is considered as an informative intensive industry, the tourism organization exchange the medium through various channels in order to build a relationship with the customers (Poon, 1993). Not only organizations, but even the customers are dependent on travel-related information to satisfy themselves (Vogt and Fesenmaier; 1998). This search of information within consumers has two components, internal search, which is done on scanning the long term memory for knowledge of the product, and external search, which is carried when an internal search is unable to provide enough information (Bettman, 1979; Engel et al., 1990).

On one side, where, it has brought unparalleled opportunities, on the other, it has added innumerable challenges and thereby, redefining the tourism industry in a number of ways (Werthner and Klein, 1999). Tourists, these days, continuously like to receive and share information online and to their virtual social network by the means of online social media software. Also, the hands-on web has led to the development of a new sort of interactions, which has resulted in an expansion of the experience of physical travel in multiple ways.

In simple words, Internet search not only aids the travelers in choosing various aspects related to their travel but also provides a platform to organizations to reach their target audience in real time. A study conducted by Hitwise, one of the leading Internet research firms, postulates that the generation of online traffic to websites (hospitality) has resulted in increase in the number of booking (Prescott; Hopkins, 2008).

The following section will help in critically analyzing the pros and cons of the power of search and its relative impact on consumer behavior as tourists. Also, how the tourism industry can strategically make use of the *search* aspects to win over the battle and why we have termed it as "Trick of trade."

In the following section, we will understand this notion.

11.1.1.1 IMPORTANCE OF SEARCH FOR CONSUMERS AND THEIR TOURIST BEHAVIOR

Have you ever pondered why the concept of search has gained such approval among the laypeople, that for every second feature of life we start Searching?

With no doubt, Internet search has provided a platform that can provide plethora of information at just one click. Most travelers these days are dependent on Internet searches to look for relevant information and has considered it as a part of the overall planning (TIA, 2005, 2008). Travelers are conducting research in order to find the most relevant information that is based on their travel knowledge, the destination and the search engines (Pan and Fesenmaier, 2006).

Surprisingly, the Internet acts as a major factor in the process of developing, learning, and growing at the neural level for human beings. It has just turned the way people interact with each other.

On one hand, where Web 2.0 have brought positive changes in terms of social nearness, collaboration, interaction and personalization, on the other, it is making us dependent on technology. The situation have arrived where we do not feel like applying brains, we do not want to think, and rather we believe in the power of a CLICK. Ask yourself, when was the last time you made use of Google Maps to look for directions. If your answer is very recent, then I am sure you must have understood by now, as how technologically dependent we have become. We, as a human race, strongly support the slang popularly known as Googling. To put it in simple manner, this all has impacted the attention span of human beings and has disrupted the power of memory. Companies have well understood the notion that the Internet acts as a quick and effective distraction and thus have integrated well in their overall marketing plans.

Apparently, *search* is turning into a powerful tool in the formation of tourist behavior. Websites like TripAdvisor, Lonely Planet, MySpace, Facebook, and YouTube that contain content from actual travelers (also known as user-generated content) is changing the way travel information is processed and evaluated. A process that starts from examining locations, deciding hotels, searching top-tourist spots, to whatnot, all is happening with a click. The trick of trade has become SEARCH now.

The travelers often involve themselves in intensive research using the web and other mobile platforms before getting on to the final conclusions. Each individual search query is found to be attached to a different user's goal: (1) Navigational goal: when users look for a specific web page like a home page. (2) Informational goals: when users want to obtain an informational piece, for example, location of a local restaurant. (3) Transactional goal: goals that are economic in nature, and are attached to an action, for example, flight bookings (Jansen and Molina, 2006). Jansen et al. (2008) further carried this study and found that most of the times users' queries are largely informational (81%), followed by navigational (10%) and transactional (9%). Further, Xiang et al. (2009) postulate that user queries are mostly related to the specific tourist destination and are short expressions of travelers'.

Also, it will be worthy to mention the increased power of bargaining that is adding heat to the overall competition of survival by the travel companies. To add to this, the comparative philosophies that the websites such as trivago.com, booking.com, tripadvisor.com are providing a podium to the users to instill their kitty with different itineraries offered at different platforms. *I Know all* kind of attitude has bought challenging and tough times for the dealing companies.

11.1.1.2 IMPORTANCE OF SEARCH TO THE ONLINE TOURISTS INDUSTRY

The power of search for the online tourists industry is equally important as it is for the individuals. Tourism business and organizations have made the Internet as an integral part of communication strategy as they consider it as one of primary communication channels for attracting and retaining customers (Buhalis and Law, 2008; Gretzel and Fesenmaier, 2000).

The intensity of new technological changes with which the industry has been coping with has already brought so many changes in the traditional working and structure of the industry. One such challenge that has become imperative for the online industry is to maintain a high rank on the Search Engine Results Pages to increase the chances of getting accessed by potential consumers. In order to compete with the tourism businesses and forums that attract the consumers by providing ample of information, it is important to contend with the modified and enhanced algorithms of the way pages are ranked by the search engines (Lawrence and Giles, 1998).

Interestingly, the past research shows a positive relationship between the search engine interface and rank of the pages. Majority of users do not look beyond the first three pages of search engines (Henzinger; 2007). Users put more trust in organic list, and such list are found to have more conversion rates (Marketing Sherpa, 2005; Jansen and Resnick, 2005). Henceforth, it is imperative for the firms to imply strategies that can be used to build up a high rank in google search and to win the battle of Internet SEARCH. Some of the strategies are as follows:

1. *Relevance:* This is one of the most important concepts to be considered while trying to form an image and attaining high rank in the searches. Factors included are significance of the given page, use of specific keywords, the title tag of the web page, presence of backlinks and forward linkages, and amount of time spent on a particular page decides the relevancy of the page. Not to forget, more relevancy increases the popularity in the search results.
2. *Popularity:* Another way to attract traffic to your website/page is to add current trending concepts or topics, it could be anything from a popular news, to the blog post or story in trend. This aids in increase number of social shares (sharing through social medium), which thereby increases the visibility of the website/page.
3. *Segmentation:* It is referred to as dividing the target on the basis of some common needs and wants. There are innumerable tools available in the market that can help in segregating the database such as Google analytics, google trend, PPC data, and Facebook analytics. With the help of these one can know what exactly the consumer wants and in that way they can promote the content that he/she likes. For example, if someone is searching for a trip in Switzerland, then they

can be captured by showing deals and sending repeated reminders through the use of various social media handles.
 4. *Diversity*: One should remember while trying to win this search battle that you need to be distinctive and be able to provide some unique concept. People do not want to read the same concept everywhere. For example, live interaction with the experts, past travel interviews, interactions with the regular customers are some of the innovative ways that can help in making a good rapport with the potential travelers and also makes the content looks different.
 5. *Quality:* It is highly suggestive that in the lieu of providing something unique and distinctive one should never forget the quality of the black and white. People read and they keep in mind whatever is written. Not to forget, one of the major factors while deciding your page rank on the search engines used by Google is quality. Add something that depicts quality and emotionally engages the reader.
 6. *Trust:* The Google Webmaster Guidelines suggest using valid practices and build a trustworthy website. This all increases the chance of upgrading algorithmically by the search engines. Keep improving should be the mantra for the online players to beat the completion of Search.

11.2 SOCIAL MEDIA AND TOURISM MARKETING

Which social strategy will work the best? What is the best channel to promote my offers? What people want to see and share? How to engage consumers by the means of unique customer advantage? What medium has the capacity to earn higher return on investment? (Stelzner, 2015)

11.2.1 SOCIAL MEDIA AND CONSUMERS

Social media marketing has become a modern and innovative way of doing business especially in tourism marketing. It has not only provided versatility but has also led to an expansion of the tourism industry by many folds. Modern day consumers use online tools to create and share their experiences to the online world. We, as humans, love to be socially accepted and appraised, and to do that, we adopt various methods to be a part of a social group.

Talking of consumer as a tourist, s/he loves to share and discuss their travel plans within and even outside their network. Thinking from a psychological aspect will take us way deeper to understand the urge that a human being feels behind sharing his/her travel-related stuffs. From economics perspective, this feeling could be as similar as what we discussed in our economics class about "Giffin goods." We develop a sense of accomplishment, and a sense of pride in discussing and showcasing our wealth through our travel. In my view, this topic also arranges for a big research to the fellow colleagues and students in discussing about the facets of conspicuous consumption in travel-related behavior. This term *conspicuous consumption* was coined by Norwegian–American economist and sociologist Thorstein Veblen in 1989 in his book "The Theory of the Leisure Class." He underlined the concept by explaining that sometimes the consumers are involved in buying expensive goods in order to display their wealth and income than to cover the real needs of the consumer.

People buy what they see, hear, and trust and social media provides a perfect display place for both the travelers as well as the online tourism industry. The most basic use of social media gets us linked with the higher order goals, collaborate, create, connect, collect, and consume (Hoffman and Novak, 1996). Each human is said to have their own level of engagements and needs in order to connect with that of the different mediums.

Hoffman and Novak (1996) proposed 4Cs—Connecting, Creating, Consuming, and Controlling, for evaluating the consumers motive to use social media.

- Connecting: Connecting is an intrusive motive of a human to evaluate the social media group that a consumer belongs to.
- Creating: A sense of autonomy and competence provides an outward locus of control that leads to higher social media involvement.
- Consume: It is a part of nonsocial goal and is intrusive in nature. It is negatively correlated with autonomy and competence.
- Control: It is directed to social media knowledge and acts as a positive link between autonomy and competence.

A peer recommendation, pictures posted by a dear friend, multiple social sharing, and check-ins all gears up the feeling of following footsteps and acting the same way. Social media has allowed to bypass the traditional way of doing things, people now have access to real information through the means to written testaments by actual travelers, or content shared by various websites relaxes a traveler in many ways.

11.2.2 MEDIA HABITS AMONG PEOPLE

As on January 2020, Facebook is the most popular and widely used social networking sites (SSNs), as per the statistics (statista.com). As per a survey in 2019, around 45% of the world's populations use social media, on an average of 144 min each day on social media. Philippines tops this list, with an average of 3 h and 53 min each day on social media. Around 40% of the population found that social media is a way to keep them updated with the current trends and events, while, around 30% believed that they use social media because their friends are using. Look at the statistics in Figure 11.1.

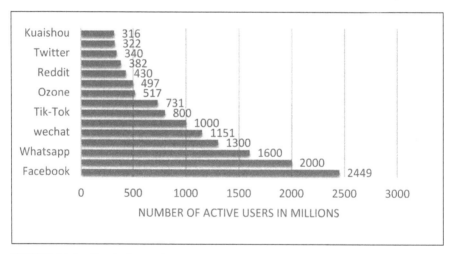

FIGURE 11.1 Graph showcasing most popular social networks worldwide as of January 2020, ranked by number of active users (in million).
Source: www.statista.com

As already been discussed in the previous sections that travelers are evolved as more informative and educated in terms of extracting information on social media. In 2019, people from Britain were asked to indicate as to what extent there travel are inspired by social media. While older generations believed that social media do not influence them, Facebook was found to more the most influential among youngsters. 50% of generation X and 51% of generation Y believed that their travel is influenced by Facebook. In 2019, 1,00,000 travel-related hashtags were searched on weekly basis in the United States. More than 46% of Indians confirmed that they post and upload their pics while on holidays, in comparison to 35% of US users.

The most popular travel booking brand in the United Kingdom is found to be booking.com, followed by STA travel. In 2014, the most popular online travel site in the Asia Pacific was found to Ctrip.com with a number of 68.66 million unique users in the month of October.

All the figures definitely take us to the fact that travel and social media usage have become an inseparable entity. There can be many factors as why travelers prefer to use social media before taking any decision. Trust has been found to the vital reason (Yoo et al., 2009). Also, it should be noted that the behavior of a traveler vary across the stages of traveling (before travel, during travel and after travel). It is important here for the travel marketers to alter their offerings in the same manner. Communicate in the way as travelers are looking for. Sometimes all they want is acknowledgement. For example, a positive review can be acknowledged by a Thank you note to the reviewer can rejoice and provoke his/her emotional attachment with that of the brand.

Why do you think people will be motivated to write about you? What are they going to get? The answer to this is simple, "GIVE THEM A REASON"! There exist various reasons of motivations among the user to share their experiences, it could be either simple desire to help others to simple desire of sharing experience.

All you have to do is strategize according to their needs. Search and recognize the target market diversity and try to find synergies.

11.2.3 UNDERSTANDING SOCIAL MEDIA IN TOURISM INDUSTRY

Social media and tourism marketing go hand in hand, informally they are like a match made in heaven. If we go by figures, then travel is the most talked about topic on social media. Travel services are viewed as experience products carrying intangible nature with the limitation of assessing quality before the actual travel. Social Media has profoundly changed the conception the technique travel and tourists use to pursue, read, examine, trust and evaluate the travel destinations. But what is social media? Social media are the websites that aid in facilitating information, content creation, discuss, share, modify, and networking with the help of Web 2.0 with the known and unknown individuals and societies. Chan and Guillet define social media as "a group of Internet based applications that exist on Web 2.0 platform and enable the users from all over the world to interact, communicate and share ideas, content, thoughts, experiences, perspectives, information and relationships." Travel and tourism Industry was fast enough to adopt the pace with which the technology is growing (Kanellopoulus, 2006).

Moreover, the advent of various collaborative trip planning tools have made it so easy and interesting for the individuals to be a part of the overall strategic planning. Travelers are now able to involve themselves in various business processes like marketing, development of new products, promotion, etc. All these strategic moves have enhanced the emotional connection with that of the travelers.

Increased exposure and traffic are the two main benefits that marketers realize in using social media (Analytics and business survey; 2015). With no doubt, social media has the power to multiply word-of-mouth effects, however, the major problem that comes is people really do not really know how to use it (Divol et al., 2012). Many researchers have argued that it is practically little difficult to gauge as which product or review has the capacity to blast and can go viral. Hence, it is suggestive for the companies to develop metrics to find out what works in this highly competitive world.

Prudent use of social media by the travel and tourism industry persuades a traveler to share his experiences and right positive reviews on various social media platforms or on websites. This creation of content that is published on the Internet directly by the users is known as UGC. UGC can be understood as a way of promoting content by real-life travelers. Here, it is imperative to understand that it is not necessary that user generated content needs to be published on a social medium. It can even be done on websites or on applications. Let us understand this with the help of an example, assume you have reviewed a hotel on a website called Trivago.com. This dot.com business is not a social medium, however, it is an online social travel agency. This hotel would now like to import your review from Trivago.com to its website. This can be done by the means of a program called *Application Program Interface*. This concept draws a clear distinction between social media platforms from that of websites or any other applications.

The global presence of Social media can be traced out from the following statistics. The graph clearly depicts the growing popularity of social media around the world. As per the reports presented by statista.com, the total number of users on social media around the world are estimated to be 3.43 billion by 2023.

Social Media Transforming Tourist Behavior

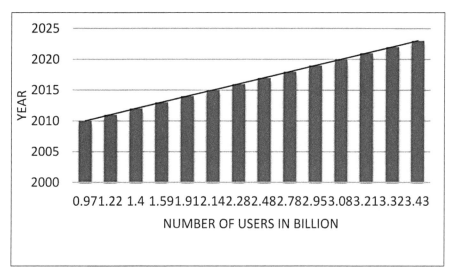

Source: www.statista.com

It is highly suggestive to the travel and tourism industry to comprehend the metamorphoses offered by the various platforms in order to reap the benefits. Past literature advocates that various attempts have been made to classify the types of social media. It is divided into subgroups according to empirical functionality: blogs, networking sites, virtual advertisements, collaborative projects, and sites dedicated to feedback (Chan and Guillet, 2011, pp. 347).

In order to be competitive, it is domineering to gain thorough knowledge about its usage, especially in tourism. According to Parra-Lopez et al. (2011, p 640), the subcategorization can happen on the basis of familiar websites. For example, Facebook is a web SSN, while, Twitter is an online service that allows its users tweet on various topics of their interest. On the other hand, Snapchat is a mobile-only platform that enables its users to share photos and videos. Pinterest, a web community has recently gained popularity that enables its users to pin the images and share their thoughts with others through images and videos. Microblogging, forums, blogs, social recreation, and social bookmarking are a few of the innovative methods of being in touch with the travelers. The crux is to understand as to when and how the travel community can reap the benefits by prudently using simple, yet complicated applications.

Understanding social media is a complex task, on the basis of its distinguished features identified (Constantinides and Fountain, 2008; Marigold and Faulds 2009; Kaplan and Haenlein 2010; Heinonen 2011) it is classified in the following types:

- Collaborative projects: edit ability of messages (status on Facebook can be edited by the one who published it, while, Wikipedia can be edited by anyone)
- Virtual communities: distinguished on the basis of areas that they cover (trivago.com is a travel website, while, Facebook can be used to recommend or share experiences. Twitter allows to tweet opinions or diaries (personal blogs)
- Content communities: enables the users to share various media contents like videos, text, pictures, etc. (YouTube, Flickr, Pinterest, and Facebook).
- SSNs: these are the websites that allow users to create their personal profiles, and let them share this content with known and unknown (e.g., Facebook, LinkedIn).
- Virtual games/social worlds: these offers an interactive platform for the users with the other users (online games, or websites like Second life).

Social media advertising is becoming talk of the town these days (Table 11.1). The further monetization of social networks has become of the main trends within Social Media Advertising. The amalgamation of shopping and payment methodology into social networks has increased the user engagement, conversion rates, and performance of progressive targeting.

11.2.4 SOCIAL MEDIA ADVERTISING

TABLE 11.1 Country-wise Spendings on Social Media Advertising in 2019

Country	US dollar (in million)
United States of America	38,393 m
China	16,167
United Kingdom	3,880
India	3,770
Germany	3416

Source: www.statista.com

Before we move into further discussion, let us first understand the social media trends revolving around tourism industry.

1. *Travel based on research:* The conventional way of planning a trip has changed and on top of everything presence of optimal social media platforms like TripAdvisor, Trivago, MakeMyTrip have provided a perfect solution to any and every travel-related problem. Travelers are

extensively involved in Internet research much prior to anything else. It is believed that extensive research prior to traveling can give a deep insight into the area, update us about various do's and don'ts, and endless amount of additional information that can aid their journey.

a) Bruised passport promoting Kerala tourism   b) Vik and Savi, Founder of Bruised Passport

c) Dan Flying Solos promoting Indonesia travel   d) Drew Binsky advising travel guide to Vietnam

Sources: a) https://www.youtube.com/watch?v=UK-ouZuKNV4; b) https://www.bruisedpassports.com/who-are-savi-vid; c) https://www.danflyingsolo.com/raja-ampat-indonesia-budget-diving/ ©Copyright 2014-2021 / Dan Flying Solo; d) https://www.youtube.com/watch?v=BwhjfrqpCEU

Blogs are becoming an important source of information for travelers for getting travel advice and suggestions. The Internet seems to be flooded with freelancers as travel bloggers, promoting their travel in the most picturesque manner. Moreover, reading and sharing travel experience creates an urge to travel and visit the place. Bruised Passport, Four Happy Feet, Dan Flying Solo, A broken Backpack, Drew Binsky, and The blonde Abroad, to name a few of the top travel bloggers. It is highly suggestive for the marketers to offer collaborations and make it a part of overall strategic marketing plans. One of the biggest advantages of using such collaborations is that the companies are often able to attract their earned and owned fan base.

Similarly, the power of so-called *hashtags* can also help the tourism industry to build a community and form an image among those who they want to attract.

2. *Online Recommendations:* With the help of various online communities users are asking for Facebook recommendations. They are gathering information and feedback related to their stay, food, and traveling.

Facebook has the highest number of active users as compared to any other social networking website, hence, making it one of the most trusted and surfed website. Companies can therefore use this technique to attract the users through the way recommendations.

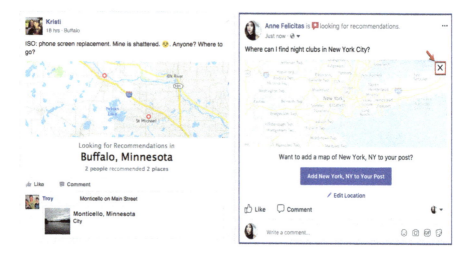

3. *Power of Social Sharing to acquire information:* Social media user wants content, a lot of it. Travelers are intentionally taking help from social media for planning their trips, and deciding various other factors. It is acting as a source of inspiration to future travelers. Users often caught themselves in a situation where they are not even sure about as to which destination they would like to hit. In such case, companies can put their foot forward and recommend places or put articles to plant a seed.

4. *Direct-to-consumer communication:* Consumers these days lack patience, they look for instant replies and quick support to their queries.

Social media has the capability of out beating the shortcomings of manual planning. Continuous touch with the users, providing instant solutions, rendering to their questions, keeping them posted

Social Media Transforming Tourist Behavior

is all helping the online tourism industry to grow. The idea is simple, people expect a reply, just do not make them wait.

5. *A paradigm shift in incentive schemes:* There is a conventional shift in the way companies have started providing incentives to their users. Maintaining the old customer is way more economic than acquiring a new customer in terms of cost and efforts involved. Social media has provided a superior way to track people who are posting good things or who are constantly involved in social sharing.

    But why do you think people will write good about you and especially when they are encountered with so many brands each day. The reason could be simply the added advantage that you can provide them. An incentive can simply be a compensation or any benefit that the user will see as an added advantage. As such initiatives can easily be tracked and thus, it is easy to incentivize people. If they do not have a reason, give them. Provide them with the incentives for discussing.

6. *Alterations to services:* With the ease of booking tickets people can now directly do booking from either their desktops or various mobile applications. It is here where these online tourism industries can play an important role. They have to design their promotional plans in such a way that seems promising to the users. It is highly advisable to the agents to segment the market and alter their offering only after careful consideration of their profile. Such segmentation will help in maintaining the trust of the users. Never forget, everyone likes personal touch!

11.2.5 SOCIAL MEDIA CAMPAIGNS

Social media campaigns are one of the innovative ways as they offer a low-cost yet impactful way to attract the attention of the target audience. A campaign usually consists of series of advertisements on a common theme presented on at least one social media platform for a stipulated amount of time. It serves many vital purposes like attracting new fresh traffic, creating brand loyalty, hitting the right nerve of the target audience, and a way to drive sales. To put this out it in a simple manner, it can be termed as a coordinated marketing method designed to emphasize information and builds emotions and sentiments. Time and again various initiatives have been taken by the travel and tourism industry to promote themselves through the way of innovative campaigns. Whether it is about promoting a country's tourism or their own travel agency, this industry has never taken aback. Wondering, what campaigns can do?

To make this topic more interesting, let's go through the following real-life examples.

11.2.5.1 SOME EXAMPLES OF FAMOUS SOCIAL MEDIA TRAVEL CAMPAIGNS:

1. *Jet Blue "Reach across the Aisle":* A campaign by Jet Blue airlines in 2006 was launched amidst the American elections. The idea of the campaign was to promote harmony, maintain peace, and bring unity in the citizens. The tagline "across the aisle" was a call out to the people to set the differences aside and an appeal to work in harmony.

A shot from Fox News channel showcasing advertisement

Snapshot of the advertisement that went viral

2. *Norway "Sheep with a View"*: The Norwegian tourist board came up with the campaign called "Sheep with a view" with an objective to promote its tourism. Through the series of advertisements, they showcased their lifestyle, culture, and its scenic beauty. The approach was simple yet mesmerizing by giving the viewers a sheep's view of the country. The campaign was highly appraised and was viewed by more than 8 million people.

A still from the Norway "Sheep With A View" campaign

Source: https://www.203challenges.com/sheep-with-a-view-the-cute-woolly-guides-of-norway/

3. *Airbnb's "Let's keep travelling forward"*: Campaign got aired after uplifting the ban on travel by America's president Donald Trump. The campaign rolled around the central idea "to limit travel is to turn back progress."

    The idea was considered to be melted well with the overall positioning of the brand.

Airbnb "Let's keep travelling forward" campaign

4. *Easyjet's "Imagine"*: In 2018, a campaign called Imagine was launched by EasyJet with a central theme on wonders of air travel. Through this campaign the airlines wanted to build an emotional connection with the flyers. The ad showcased a plane flying above the clouds, and conveys to life the several daydreams of a traveler on board.

11.2.5.2   OBJECTIVES OF SOCIAL MEDIA TRAVEL CAMPAIGNS

A travel campaign can help in many ways, whether it is about building an emotional connection with the destination, bringing out the memories, making visitors fall in love with the destination, or about increasing the travel bookings, campaigns can do it all. All you have to do is choose the right objective.

Each travel player holds its own objectives in terms of strategizing their marketing campaigns. Some of the common objectives behind creating social media travel campaigns are as follows:

- To create or increase awareness
- To target new segments
- To attain local and global publicity
- To encourage visitors to plan visits
- To change a particular prevailing perception
- To attain a distinctive image about the destination
- To create destination-specific buzz
- To increase database
- To increase likes/fanbase
- To Improve negative image of the destination

11.2.5.3   LET'S DO THIS

Pick and choose any travel campaign of your choice and analyze their different objectives behind their social media campaigns. List it down and discuss it in your group.

11.2.6   TRENDING WAYS OF ATTRACTING TRAVEL AND TOURISM

- *360 view of the hotel room or lobby:* Most of the hotels these days have introduced this concept of giving 360 view of their common areas so as to give a live feeling to the travelers. This helps the travelers to analyze the environment and the surroundings of the places around.
- *Create a Snapchat story/tweet on Twitter/engage LinkedIn groups/ Livestream on Facebook and Instagram:* Involve your future travelers by a means of interactive sessions, answer to their queries, reinforcing your message. Be in constant touch is the mantra

360 view of a room

- *Adding buy button along with ads:* It is considered to be a way to sell more with less efforts. A service recently offered by Facebook can let you grow your e-commerce business. Due to the highest amount of active users on Facebook, this provides a massive opportunity to the owners.
- *Introducing microblogging*: Microblogging is a web service that allows the subscriber to broadcast short messages to other subscribers of the service. Creativity is well received within social media and is likely to attract more attention. Twitter can be used by the travel and tourism companies in order to briefly describe about a place or an experience.
- *Introducing the concept of Bleisure (Business + leisure)*: Try to combine the components of both business and leisure. Offer extended holidays ranging from sightseeing to relaxation, or may be hiking or camping trip. Such trips have the tendency to appeal in the most effective manner. Businesses often find that their employee's productivity gets improved after such trips. According to SAP Concur Research, millennial's are found to be more excited and engaged in this sort of trips.

According to a Carlson Wagonlit Travel (CWT) Solutions Group survey, men take more business trips than women in total. In both gender groups, 20% of business travelers asked said they take one or more bleisure trips per year. This indicates that women have a slightly higher overall bleisure rate than men. Also, such trips epitomize an ideal way of saving on travel cost through personal holidays.

- *Wow customers before travelling*: The primitive step of the business should be restrained to not upsetting the customers in the first place. The best way to do this is to keep them informed on every step, without exception. Employ effective customer relationship management (CRM) processes, ensure deadlines and keep up to your promises. Another method to do this is giving them reminder calls before and generally calls during their travels. In the absence of calls, emails should be dropped. The idea is to give more than expected and cater to their latent demands (unaware needs). Express gratitude for providing them with small gifts, it can be the smallest like passport holders, a box of cookies, or selfie stands.
- *Highlight your Patron in distributing your social content, and reward loyalty:* Why will they write reviews? Then give them the reason!! Pay gratitude to the ones who are loyal toward your business. This will help in boosting your business. These accounts have their own friend circle and their own followers, who get attracted to what they write. Incentivize their loyalty with some rewards. For example, Hilton hotels offers Loyalty rewards programs to their agents located in the United States and Canada. They provide incentives directly into agent's accounts after successful completion of trips by their clients. This motivates the agents to refer more among their client list.

    Similarly, *Marriott Bonvoy*, a loyalty program designed by Marriott group. A loyalty program designed for their customers lets them earn while they travel. They offer points on every dollar spent while they travel, right from starting from hotel bookings, car rentals, flights, and not only this they have partnered with some exclusive travel partners that offer them incentives when they travel.

Good always goes a long way! Follow some basic rules and things will work in your way. Nobody remembers what happened yesterday, but they do dream of their travel.

11.3 UNDERSTANDING TOURISM BEHAVIOR THROUGH HOWARD SHETH MODEL

Howard Sheth model was developed in 1969 with the joint effort of John Howard and Jagdish Sheth and was published in their book *The Theory of Buyer Behaviour*. This model was conceptualized in order to understand as

Social Media Transforming Tourist Behavior   203

how information is processed by the consumers. It also emphasized on how social, psychological, and marketing factors can impact their buying behavior.

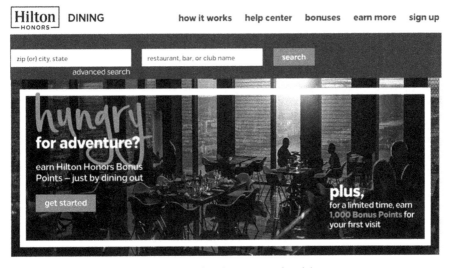

Hilton Honors, a loyalty program for visitors.

Marriott Bonvoy, a loyalty program.

The next question comes is, how behavioral model can help a marketer? Learning of various models benefit firms to understand the core concepts of consumer behavior: how they think, feel, react between different alternatives, what factors influence their purchase, why and they shift to other brands, and what strategies marketers should adopt in order to reach the customers effectively.

In tourism, consumer behavior can be understood as the way how travelers take decisions to spend their available resources on their travel plans. Evidently, if a travel agency is looking to optimize their marketing efforts then they are bound to understand consumer behavior in tourism.

This model highlights rational brand choice behavior of a consumer within:

- The limited individual capacities: Limited capacity a consumer possesses like income, price, and choices.
- Incomplete information: no/very little information available about a product.

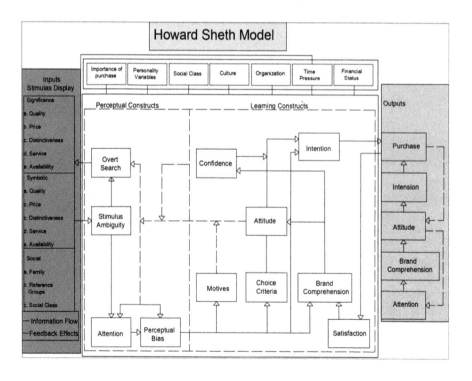

This model suggests three significant levels of decision-making in the selection of a particular service: *Extensive Problem solving, Limited Problem*

solving, and *Routinized Response Behavior*. Let us discuss these levels in detail with respect to tourists' behavior:

- *Extensive problem solving*: At this stage, a traveler is naïve and has no clue about the market. He is confused about the offerings and he has no fixed choice criteria or special preferences. It can be compared to a situation wherein you want to somewhere sneak out because of your boring schedule but you have no clue where to go, how much will it cost, where you will stay, etc.

    Information that is readily obtainable and can be assessed quickly will be preferred by the travelers. A travel agent can constructively build up strategies that can acquaint the customers, alongside helps in the formation of perception and preferences. This market can be segmented on the basis of their special needs.

- *Limited problem solving*: At this level, a consumer is in a better position, s/he has information about various choices available (destinations, hotels). The choice criteria is somewhat fixed, and s/he is well aware of the close competitors.

    It is suggestive to the travel firms to maintain rapport with these prospective segment as lesser time is required to form intensions of this cohort. It is a volatile situation, the online agents can use the power of *remarketing*. Google has explained remarketing, as a way to connect with people who previously interacted with the website or mobile app. It allows to strategically position the ads in front of these audiences as they browse Google or its partner websites, thus helps in increasing the brand awareness or remind those audiences to make a purchase. A simple text can help in reinforcing a message. Live online interactions, flash sales, communication on the last date of sale can be used efficiently. Just remember, be in *constant touch*, but don't overdo as you might irritate them.

- *Routinized response behavior*: A traveler, here, is fully aware of the options available. The choice criteria is well-defined, a customer knows what he wants. This behavior is a result of high experience due to consistent travel history. Hence, there is a strong disposition toward one particular brand. Consumers, here, are brand loyal because of the company's positive image and/or past experience, hence, it is very difficult for the other competitive firms to break through the walls. The best, companies can do here is, offering exclusivity. Try to find customer's latent demands, and try fulfilling them. New destinations, freebees, a little wow-ing to this segment can help the firms to cater to this segment too.

TABLE 11.2 Levels of Decision-making in the Selection of a Particular Service

Stage	Information	Choice criteria	Buyer	Competitor
Extensive Problem solving	No information	No particular choice criteria	No clue	No clue
Limited Problem solving:	Little information	Some-what defined	Undecided about some-what brand	High evaluation between competitors
Routinized Response Behavior:	More information	Choice criteria is well-defined	Strong Disposition about a brand	Little evaluation because of strong disposition

Source: Author's creation.

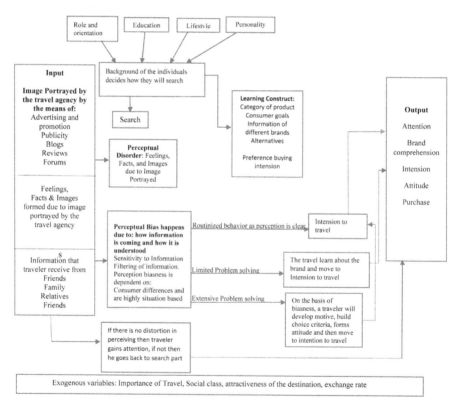

Author's creation, Modified from Howard Sheth Model.

11.3.1 VARIABLES/CONCEPTS/CONSTRUCTS

There are four important variables in this model:

- Inputs
- Hypothetical construct: perceptual and learning construct
- Exogenous variable (outside variables)
- Outputs

11.3.1.1 INPUTS

These are the variables that help in the formation of clues for a particular brand or a product.

These variables can take up three forms:

1. *Significant Stimuli:* These variables are significant in nature and generally refers to the product attributes that a brand claims. For example, quality, price, attributes, distinctiveness, service, and availability.
2. *Symbolic Stimuli*: This covers the psychological impact that a product characteristic is perceived by the consumers as a proclamation by the brand. In this view, the communication used by the company's should be in line with how they want their product to be perceived.

    To trigger such needs, a travel agent should employ a picturesque view of the destination, creative videos, recommendations from the previous travelers, shared pictures, etc. Such attempts aid in creating a positive perception about a particular destination.
3. *Social Stimuli*: This comprises the information that a traveler tries to possess from the social circle. For example, social shares from friends, family, relatives, social class, and various other reference groups.

11.3.1.2 OUTPUT

It is fundamentally the response that the consumer gives as an effect of internal processes. For example, decision of purchase, portrayal of interest, and other activities. To every organization, the most important output can be a purchase, a final purchase is an economic activity that aids in generating revenues. The hierarchy of output variables are:

- *Attention*: The level of concentration and consideration that a buyer possesses about a product after exposure of stimulus.
- *Brand Comprehension*: It signifies the level of awareness processed and stored in the minds of a consumer that a buyer retains regarding a particular product.

- *Intension*: It is the ultimate aim and objective that is created in the minds of the consumers. In tourism behavior this could be a sudden urge for planning a trip, or choosing a particular destination over others.
    - In routinized behavior consumer directly moves to purchase without much evaluation.
- *Attitude:* It is the evaluation of the brand on the basis of intention to buy (as a consumer is aware of various brands, but deciding between the alternatives is tough: limited problem solving stage). This is solely based on individual likes, dislikes, behavior, interest, and awareness toward a product.
- *Purchase:* The actual purchase of a product resulted from all the above steps.

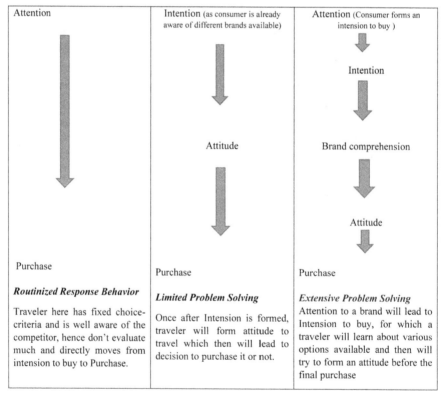

Perceptual and learning construct/hypothetical construct.

These constructs consist of the psychological variables that influence during consumer decision making process. They are often considered as abstract, undefined and indirect pieces of a human behavior. Actions are a result of such construction, and thus these aid in decision making. There are two main constructs:

- *Perceptual construct:* This includes information that is collected and perceived from the input stage.
- *Learning construct:* Every decision is dependent on how and what perception and opinions are formed by a buyer. This biasness can vary from person to person and can highly depend on various other external factors like past experiences, peer pressure, purchase motive, etc. Who knows, s/he may be biased about using a particular brand. It has three components:
  - Selective exposure: A consumer gets exposed only to those messages that he finds to be pleasant, and in conjunction to his own needs.
  - Selective attention: Consumers will pay attention only to those products who s/he thinks is aligned with the expectation.
  - Perceptual defense/perceptual blocking: These are those factors because of which consumers blocks or defense in perceiving.

11.3.2 EXOGENOUS VARIABLES

These are the factors that are not involved directly, however, can influence the buying behavior of an individual, in our case its tourists. Factors such as the importance of travel, exchange rate, safety of a country, individual's social status, the attractiveness of a country, prior knowledge, and experience of a place and a travel agent.

11.4 SOCIAL MEDIA STRATEGIES AND MODEL PROPOSED BY ENGEL, BLACKWELL, AND MINIARD

An old proverb "Those who fail to plan, plan to fail" indorse the importance of planning during traveling. It is the resourceful planning that can reduce the chances of risks associated with traveling to a foreign land (Engel et al., 1990). They have to accept poor quality services and products. Existing research proposes that selecting a travel destination follows a general decision-making model and comprises of five stages: need recognition, information search, evaluation of alternatives, purchase decisions, and postpurchase decisions (Kotler et al., 2010; Zeithaml et al., 2012).

An alternative view to this model proposes three stages: Pretrip phase, during-trip phase, and posttrip phase (Engel et al., 1990; the anticipatory phase), the experimental and the reflective phase (Craig Smith and French, 1994; Jennings, 1997, 2006). This prospective was found to be more complex in nature as compared to general decision-making model. As it requires critical analysis that aids in combining many services and at the same time aims toward achieving multiple goals.

The following section will concentrate on a detailed explanation of the tourist decision-making process along with suggestive social media strategies.

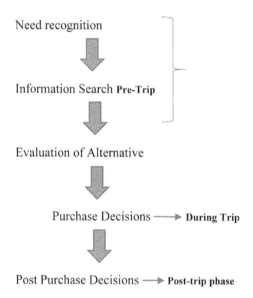

Source: Engel, Blackwell, and Miniard (1990).

11.4.1 PRETRIP PHASE

Any travel planning starts with general *recognition of need*. Needs could be of different classes or could be at different levels, need could be triggered by a problem which could be either problem solving or problem recognition. For example, you may simply feel a need for vacation out of boredom from a routine job or planning a travel for upcoming summer vacations.

Also, this need for stimulation can arouse due to external stimuli or internal stimuli. At this stage, a customer commonly contemplates about an explicit destination that he is aware of or have already voyaged. In order to quench his sudden need/problem solving, he will start looking for information from various sources. This being the first stage is the toughest to diagnose even by the traveler himself. For example, this need arousal can simply have originated as a way to peek out of the boredom or can be a need to spend next summers into the woods.

Once after realizing the need, a customer then moves on to the next step where he will try to find the information about various destinations, hotels and other activities. They may generally employ both personal (word of mouth by friends and family) and nonpersonal (websites, advertising, salespersons, etc.) sources for obtaining information (Zeithaml et al., 2012). According to a research by Google, carried among leisure travelers, 84% of the travelers use Web for planning their travel. Social media constitutes more than one-tenth of the search results (Xiang and Gretzel; 2010). Number of researchers have considered social media as one of the most important factors during travel planning process (Cox et al., 2009; Tussyadiah et al., 2011) because of the amount of information present on the web. This stage involves lesser time and cost as compared to any other stage. Pan and Fesenmaier; 2006, carried a study and illustrated on how information is accessed by the users using Internet. It was found that on an average, a user takes 36 min to collect information regarding potential accommodation, dining and tour options. The finest strategies that can be adopted at this hour be, appearing in the first few research results on Google (please refer above for details on strategies), engaging consumers through live interactions on their corporate pages and social media pages, promoting adding reviews by past travelers, adding blogs and news, various FAQs, offering bulletins, adding different types of content visual or textual, etc. At this time, the consumer is assumed to be forming perception about various things, hence, the travel agents should make judicious use to it toward the formation of a positive attitude. User-generated content like Travel blogs, communities, blogs, websites reviews, Meta-search can play a significant role here, as it helps them to reduce the risk associated with traveling. People trust what they see coming from the actual travelers, hence user-generated content generally works here.

Also, a helping hand can be taken from third-party organizations like travel clubs, tourists' guides, and various associations to furnish information through various means.

Until now, consumers have identified various alternatives: products that can be considered and products that are a big no. Here, different philosophies and different thought processes are employed in order to rule out the best out of all. This evaluation is done on different bases that are highly subjective. No two people and their needs can match with each other For instance, for you, budget might be the criteria to rule out expensive options, while for your neighbors,' number of extra services offered during travel is a deciding factor. Also, a travel agent can check who has a bigger role in play while deciding.

- The initiator: the person who initiated travel
- The influencer: the person who tries to influence the decisions like destination, hotels, or even can cancel the plan sometimes.
- The decider: the person who takes the final travel decision.
- The buyer: the person who pays for the travel.
- The user: people who are actually going to travel.

Each person has their role and status in this process, it is up to the travel agent to furnish details and target accordingly. Also, a personal touch with the customers can bring out a huge difference in the whole process. A customer here might be in a lot of confusion and is versatile about the whole decision process. A firm can take help from destination marketing organization (DMO). DMO is defined by Destination marketing Association International 2013, for being responsible for representing specific destinations and for helping the long-term development of communities in these destinations through travel and tourism policies. Li and Wang (2011, p 298) mention the "DMO" websites as the technology platform where potential visitors can access 'detailed product information, appealing promotional activities, effective communication, convenient transaction process and post-purchase services'. Over and done with this platform, the potential tourists can read the reviews from the actual tourists, about their experiences at the destination.

After critically evaluating various alternatives, it is the time to take a final decision about the purchase. It will be interesting to note here, that it is not necessary that purchase will happen here, a consumer may go back to the first stage, if he feels unsatisfied or in a confused state of mind. These purchase intention can also get affected by uncontrolled factors (losing job, sudden tragedy in the family, epidemic, national emergency).

11.4.2 DURING TRIP PHASE

Until here, the process was all about plannings and things were on black and white. This is the phase when a traveler is actually experiencing what s/he has paid for. Note, expectation and perception vary across people, and therefore cannot be linked to the temporal dimensions (Jennings, 2006). Everyone has a different set of expectations and outcomes at this stage which by no doubt is dependent on various fragments of supply provided by the travel operators (Uriely, 2005). A tourist interprets the destination subjectively also known as "tourism gaze," a term coined by Urry (1990).

After the final purchase at this stage, the consumer actually starts feeling. This feeling can be positive (state of satisfaction) or negative (a state of dissatisfaction, he might feel cheated). It is important for the travel agents to be in constant touch with their consumers. This phase can also be perceived as when the sharing starts happening by the actual travelers, on social networking sites. Friends and families will now become recipients and cocreators of the content shared by them on various platforms (Yoo and Gretzel, 2011).

A study reported that information shared on the social media platforms greatly influences the decision-making process (Tussyadiah and Fesenmaier, 2009). In another study conducted by Sparks and Browning (2011) exclaimed that the likeliness of booking is determined by valence, framing, and inclusion of ratings in reviews published online. A user-generated content can help in gaining information about a place by the amount of coherence in the story (Tussyadiah et al., 2011). During this phase, a firm can strategically ask the travelers to promote their travel by means of hashtags on Facebook and Instagram, pinning on Pinterest, tweets on Twitter, etc. Their travel story can be shared on their websites by the means of blogs. Make their story Instagramically sound and shoot out to the world.

11.4.3 POSTTRIP PHASE

This phase constitutes sharing experience on social media, consumers can be involved in actual generation or enriching the content (Kaplan and Haenlein, 2010). Fotis et al. (2011) supported the argument that social media are predominantly used after holidays for experience sharing. Participation across consumers varies according to their expected social benefits, hedonic benefits, and functional benefits (Parra-López et al., 2011). Fotis et al. (2011) found out that people usually use social media to share their experiences postholidays.

This urge of sharing can be well used by the agencies to disseminate information and promote their own brand. Sometimes, readers get infatuated just by reading.

As a marketer, there is a lot to understand and that can only be done by discovering the art of right set of strategies.

11.5 EXPECTATION VERSUS SOLUTION

Table 11.3 provides an author view on the various touch points, expectations of a user at each stage and solutions against it. Touch points can be explained as any contact point where a business encounter its customers for exchange of information, providing service or handles the transaction. Identifying various touch points will help in making sure that the users are satisfied at each step.

This comprehensive view will also help the industry by reflecting the pointers which the user demonstrates/expects from start to finish.

TABLE 11.3 Author View of Various Touch Points, Expectations of a User and Solutions

Phase	Touch Points	Expectation of a Customer	Solution
Pretrip	**For need arousal:** Blogs, articles, various social media handles, cold calling, Emails **For Information search:** Website, mobile applications, Third party websites, Tour booking page. **Explore Itineraries:** pre-sales support channels, Tour details page: inclusions and exclusions **Book a Tour**: Mobile Applications, website page, Tickets detail page	Sophisticated Tour searching	Find a way to support advanced searching with easy free flow website/apps.
		Printer-friendly brochure	Support printer friendly brochure along with support to print tickets
		Real-time support	Extend support through various means like customer service or dedicated agent
		Option to compare itinerary	Allow the website to support different itinerary. This allows them to feel confident about deal offered and accepted
		Easy booking process	Simplify the page flow of booking. Inefficient and Cumbersome flow are repelling for the users.
		Booking through multiple mediums but user friendly	Develop user friendly options like mobile applications or adding hints to various fields. The idea is make everything smooth.
During Trip	Tour guide, emails, WhatsApp, customer care Support, company's website	Easy communication	A Tour guide with vast local knowledge acts as a great help for the travelers.
		Informed decisions	Make them acquaint with solutions to any anticipated problems. A book of FAQs can be prepared.
Post-trip	Surveys, Feedbacks	A delighted welcome	Sometimes, a customer just look for a hearty welcome, make sure to gain from this.
		Photo album	A photo album makes them feel delighted and there, promotes word of mouth publicity.

Source: Author's creation.

KEYWORDS

- social media marketing
- Web 2.0
- tourists
- tourists behavior
- Howard Sheth Model
- Engel
- Blackwell
- Miniard

REFERENCES

Adapa, S. *Tourism Marketing. Hospitality, Travel, and Tourism*, 36–50.

Albarran, A. B. Social Media Marketing . In *The Social Media Industries*. Routledge: New York, NY, 2013; pp. 86–91.

Ansari, S.; Ansari, G.; Ghori, M. U.; Kazi, A. G. Impact of Brand Awareness and Social Media Content Marketing on Consumer Purchase Decision. *Journal of Public Value and Administration Insights* 2019, 2, 5–10.

Ayertey, S.; Howell, K. Service Failure and Recovery Strategy in Computer-Mediated Marketing Environments (CMMEs). Leveraging Computer-Mediated Marketing Environments Advances in Marketing, Customer Relationship Management, and E-Services 2019, 173–192.

Car, T.; Stifanich, L. P.; Šimunić, M. Internet Of Things (Iot) In *Tourism and Hospitality: Opportunities and Challenges*. 2019.

Centobelli, P.; Ndou, V. Managing Customer Knowledge through the Use of Big Data Analytics in Tourism Research. *Current Issues in Tourism* 2019, 22, 1862–1882.

Chapter 7. Tourists' Reflections on Experience. *Tourist Behaviour* 2005, 162–183.

Christou, E.; Sigala, M.; Gretzel, U. *Social Media in Travel, Tourism and Hospitality: Theory, Practice and Cases*. Routledge: London, 2016.

Constantinides, E. From Physical Marketing to Web Marketing: the Web-Marketing Mix. *Proceedings of the 35th Annual Hawaii International Conference on System Sciences*.

Constantinides, E.; Fountain, S. J. Web 2.0: Conceptual Foundations and Marketing Issues. *Journal of Direct, Data and Digital Marketing Practice* 2008, 9, 231–244.

Cross, M. Opportunities of Social Media. *Social Media Security* 2014, 21–43.

Fotis, J.; Buhalis, D.; Rossides, N. Social Media Impact on Holiday Travel Planning. *International Journal of Online Marketing* 2011, 1, 1–19.

Giglio, S.; Pantano, E.; Bilotta, E.; Melewar, T. Branding Luxury Hotels: Evidence from the Analysis of Consumers' "Big" Visual Data on TripAdvisor. *Journal of Business Research* 2020, 2019, pp. 495–501.

Gursoy, D.; Mccleary, K. W. An Integrative Model of Tourists' Information Search Behavior. *Annals of Tourism Research* 2004, 31, 353–373.

Hall, K. The New Community Rules: Marketing on the Social Web. *Journal of Applied Communications* 2012, 96.

Hoffman, D. L.; Novak, T. P. Marketing in Hypermedia Computer-Mediated Environments: Conceptual Foundations. *Journal of Marketing* 1996, 60, 50.

Jansen, B. J.; Molina, P. R. The Effectiveness of Web Search Engines for Retrieving Relevant Ecommerce Links. *Information Processing and Management* 2006, 42, 1075–1098.

Jansen, B. J.; Pooch, U. A Review of Web Searching Studies and a Framework for Future Research. *Journal of the American Society for Information Science and Technology* 2001, 52, 235–246.

Jennings, G. *Tourism Research*; Wiley Australia: Milton, Qld., 2001.

Kanellopoulos, D. N. Current and Future Directions of Multimedia Technology in Tourism. *International Journal of Virtual Technology and Multimedia* 2010, 1, 187.

Kaplan, A. M.; Haenlein, M. Users of the World, Unite! The Challenges and Opportunities of Social Media. *Business Horizons* 2010, 53, 59–68.

Lategan, G.; Williams, M. Student Learning and Employability: Immersion in Live Events. *The Study of Food, Tourism, Hospitality and Events. Tourism, Hospitality and Event Management* 2018, 133–142.

Padma, P.; Ramakrishna, S.; Rasoolimanesh, S. M. Nature-Based Solutions in Tourism: A Review of the Literature and Conceptualization. *Journal of Hospitality and Tourism Research* 2019, 109634801989005.

Parra-López, E.; Bulchand-Gidumal, J.; Gutiérrez-Taño, D.; Díaz-Armas, R. Intentions to Use Social Media in Organizing and Taking Vacation Trips. *Computers in Human Behavior* 2011, 27, 640–654.

Pearce, P. L. *Tourist Behaviour*, 1st edition. Channel View Publications, 2005.

Pearce, P. L. *Tourist Behaviour: Themes and Conceptual Schemes*. Channel View Publications: Clevedon, UK, 2010.

Poon, A. *Tourism, Technology and Competitive Strategies*. CAB International: Wallingford, 2006.

Predicting the Influence of Travel Web Site Effectiveness Characteristics on Technology Acceptance and Its Marketing Implications. *Jurnal Pengurusan* 2008, 27, 105–128.

Tourism Social Media: Transformations in Identity, Community and Culture. Tourism Social Science Series Tourism Social Media: Transformations in Identity, *Community and Culture* 2013, i.

Tussyadiah, I. P. A Concept of Location-Based Social Network Marketing. *Journal of Travel and Tourism Marketing* 2012, 29, 205–220.

Tussyadiah, I. P.; Fesenmaier, D. R. Mediating Tourist Experiences. *Annals of Tourism Research* 2009, 36, 24–40.

Tussyadiah, I. P.; Park, S.; Fesenmaier, D. R. Assessing the Effectiveness of Consumer Narratives for Destination Marketing. *Journal of Hospitality and Tourism Research* 2010, 35, 64–78.

Uriely, N.; Belhassen, Y. Drugs and Tourists' Experiences. *Journal of Travel Research* 2005, 43, 238–246.

Vermaat, M.; Sebok, S. L.; Freund, S. M.; Campbell, J. T.; Frydenberg, M. *Discovering Computers 2016: Tools, Apps, Devices, and the Impact of Technology*; Cengage Learning: Boston, MA, 2016.

Werthner, H.; Klein, S. *Information Technology and Tourism—A Challenging Relationship,* Springer-Verlag, Wien, 1999.

Xiang, Z.; Fesenmaier, D. R. Identifying the Online Tourism Domain: Implications for Search Engine Development for Tourism. *Information and Communication Technologies in Tourism* 2008, 486–496.

Xiang, Z.; Gretzel, U. Role of Social Media in Online Travel Information Search. *Tourism Management* 2010, 31, 179–188.

Xiang, Z.; Pan, B. Travel Queries on Cities in the United States: Implications for Search Engine Marketing for Tourist Destinations. *Tourism Management* 2011, 32, 88–97.

Xiang, Z.; Wöber, K.; Fesenmaier, D. R. Representation of the Online Tourism Domain in Search Engines. *Journal of Travel Research* 2008, 47, 137–150.

Yoo, K.-H.; Gretzel, U. Influence of Personality on Travel-Related Consumer-Generated Media Creation. *Computers in Human Behavior* 2011, 27, 609–621.

Yoo, K.-H.; Lee, Y.; Gretzel, U.; Fesenmaier, D. R. Trust in Travel-Related Consumer Generated Media. *Information and Communication Technologies in Tourism* 2009, 2009, 49–59.

CHAPTER 12

MEGA-EVENTS TOURISM AND SUSTAINABILITY: A CRITIQUE

PRIYAKRUSHNA MOHANTY[*], OSHI SINGHANIA, and USWATHUL HASANA

Department of Tourism Studies, School of Management, Pondicherry University, Puducherry, India

[*]Corresponding author. E-mail: pkmohanty90@gmail.com

ABSTRACT

Event tourism has emerged as one of the most influential and rapidly growing forms of international tourism in the face of its recent history. Considered as an intersection of event management and tourism management, event tourism has been applauded for influencing both tourism demand and supply. However, in the recent past, the concept of event tourism has seen its fair share of criticisms especially with regard to mega-events. While some of the scholars have criticized it for not addressing "difficult" questions like fiscal reforms, global power structures, injustice, inequality, and environmental degradation, others have accused it of providing shelter to crony capitalism. Issues like gender parity or equality remain big question marks in the study of event tourism. Furthermore, the recent outbreak of COVID-19 pandemic has exhibited the high vulnerability aspect of mega-events in general. It is argued that event tourism must be examined through the lens of critical inquiry for it to move forward while addressing its gray areas. Hence, attempts have been made in this current study to trace out the dark sides of event tourism which can challenge its sustainability. The work is based on a systematic desk-based review of secondary data. Thematic content analysis has been employed to analyze the data collected. The chapter concludes that despite its rising popularity, event tourism has many critical features and weak links that need to be addressed to ensure its sustainability.

12.1 INTRODUCTION

Events are an integral part of the tourism systems as they constitute major elements both at the origin point (events as push factors to travel) and at the destination point (event as a pull factor in marketing and development of the destination) (Getz and Page, 2016). Mega-events, in particular, have been recognized not only for their sizable contribution to the growing employment, tourist expenditure, government revenue, and income (Fourie and Santana-Gallego, 2011; Lee et al., 2013; Lee et al., 2017) but also for their ability to influence destination image and awareness which are critical factors in stimulating local tourism (Lee et al., 2005, 2017). Mega-events are defined as "ambulatory occasions of a fixed duration that attract a large number of visitors, have a large mediated reach, come with large costs and have large impacts on the built environment and the population" (Müller, 2015, p. 638). It is argued that effective hosting of mega-events can generate additional economic benefits to both host and neighboring regions in the form of additional investment and business (Magno and Dossena, 2020).

However, as postulated by Getz (2008) with the growth of mega-events, perceived negative impacts and criticisms across all spheres have gained momentum and have become widespread. While some of the scholars have criticized it for not addressing "difficult" questions like fiscal reforms, global power structures, injustice, inequality, and environmental degradation (Rojek, 2014), others have accused it of providing shelter to crony capitalism (Higgins-Desbiolles, 2018). Furthermore, the methodology for evaluating the economic impact of mega-events has been accused of being skewed toward the motive of overstating the benefits to the host community (Crompton, 2004; Matheson, 2002).

Safety and security of both tourists visiting the destination for a mega-event and event organizers mostly from the host community have constituted another area of criticism (Donaldson and Ferreira, 2009; Toohey and Taylor, 2014; Wylde and Page, 2014). Furthermore, the recent outbreak of COVID-19 has highlighted mega-events as one of the focal points that have the potential for mass transmission of infectious disease leading to their cancellations (Flaxman et al., 2020; Miles and Shipway, 2020). Incidents like COVID-19 also exhibit the high vulnerability aspect of mega-events in general. Therefore, it is argued that event tourism must be examined through the lens of critical inquiry for it to move forward while addressing its gray areas (Ziakas, 2015). Hence, attempts have been made in this current study to trace out the dark sides of event tourism which can challenge its sustainability. It must be noted that in the following sections that "mega-events" have been referred to as just "events" in most of the cases to ensure better readability and elimination of repetition.

The chapter has been drafted in three major sections. In the first section, the intrinsic elements of event tourism have been studied in detail to trace out the economic, social, and environmental (the three pillars of sustainability) criticisms concerning mega-events in general and event tourism in particular. Apart from economic impacts, mega-event management has been a subject of criticism for creating infrastructural hindrances and challenges. Hence, the second section of the chapter discusses about the infrastructural criticisms of mega-event tourism. The last section of the chapter provides general suggestions and recommendations to address the criticisms associated with event tourism.

12.2 METHODOLOGY ADOPTED

This chapter can be classified as a conceptual/review article in the doctrine of tourism (see Xin et al., 2013). The majority of the data in the chapter has been collected from the systematic review (Denyer and Tranfield, 2009) of peer-reviewed articles highlighting critical aspects in the context of event tourism management. The reviewed articles were collected from three major academic search engines (Google Search, Science Direct, and EBSCOhost) through advanced search with keywords "event tourism," "critique," "mega-event," and "criticism." After the collection of articles, the keywords and abstracts of each article were given a thorough read, and articles which were found to be out of context were omitted. The remaining articles were fed to the NVIVO 10 software for analysis of collected papers.

Three major "nodes" (*refer* Bazeley and Richards, 2000) namely economic, social, and environmental constraints based on the triple bottom line of sustainability in event tourism (Hede, 2007) were created in NVIVO 10. Also, the article references were collected at this stage by the reference management software EndNote X9. Then, full papers of the filtered articles were read and criticisms were categorized under the three created nodes in NVIVO. During the assigning of the criticisms to various nodes, a set of criticisms emerged that may not be classified into any of the three defined nodes. It was found that those criticisms associated with the infrastructural issues have not been discussed in detail in the previous studies. Therefore, another node called the "infrastructural" criticisms was created which served as one of the contributions to the event tourism scholarship. Then, the first draft of the paper was designed, and few modifications along with add-ons were made to the first draft after a brainstorming session among all the three authors. Upon consent from all the authors, the final version of the paper was drafted along with the references and submitted to the editors to be considered for publication.

12.3 ECONOMIC CRITICISMS

Any kind of tourism irrespective of its form and nature is mostly faced with criticism questioning its impacts and whether it is worth to do a significant investment in that form of tourism. Consequently, the success or failure of any form of tourism is measured by the impact it creates on the host community and the destination. Of all the criticisms which are discussed in the academic literature, the criticism in terms of its economic impacts holds a special place because it plays a critical role in deciding the future possibilities of the growth of that form of tourism (Baade and Matheson, 2004). Just like any other form of tourism, event tourism comprising of both mega- and micro-events has been criticized for its economic costs and imbalances in distribution. Often, these events are promoted by claiming that they contribute much to the economy by creating jobs, boosting the regional economy, and promoting tourism, thus encouraging countries to embrace event tourism (Daniels et al., 2004). However, many authors argue that contrary to the popular belief, event tourism also causes serious negative economic impacts which affect the economy of the host community both at macro- and micro-levels (Diedering and Kwiatkowski, 2015).

One of the important arguments to be taken into consideration before studying the economic criticisms on event tourism is that most of the literature which assesses these impacts highlight the positive aspect while purposefully ignoring the negative impacts to justify the taxpayer's money utilized for such events (Cibinskiene, 2012; Daniels et al., 2004; Higham, 1999). Such studies can be categorized into two types:

1. The reports about the impacts of those events which are biased to attract sponsors for future events and to gain public support (Tranter and Keefee, 2004);
2. The studies where there is a flaw in the methodologies which are used for the assessment (Crompton, 2004; Lee and Taylor, 2005; Morgan and Condliffe, 2007).

This section of the chapter deals with the various aspects of the economic impacts which are caused by event tourism.

For any type of tourism to be considered successful, the benefits received should be more than the costs associated with its operation (Cornelissen, 2004). Since Event Tourism demands for infrastructural facilities, the hosting country has to spend a lot on this area for constructing new stadiums, better road network, and other infrastructure (Short, 2008). These infrastructure requirements are fulfilled with the aid of public funds which are not returned to the local economy, because the expenditure spent by the hosting country is more than the benefits. The issue of costs outweighing the economic benefits received from hosting such events is more common especially in the case of developing nations where there is a lack of infrastructure and other facilities required to host such events (Cornelissen, 2004; Spilling, 1996). Even when this is the ground reality, most of the countries still show interest in hosting such events for the political gains irrespective of the economic or social impacts (Ritchie, 1984). As a result, these events end up using the taxpayer's money when the benefits are enjoyed by corporate sectors (Hall, 2012; Mules and Faulkner, 1996).

Event tourism indeed generates income as a result of increased tourist expenditure, but a major part of this expenditure does not go into the local economy. Hence, economic leakage is one of the major impacts when a country or region is hosting an international event (Diedering and Kwiatkowski, 2015). The majority of the tourist's expenditure is spent on hospitality establishments, restaurants, and car rentals which are not owned by local people and also revenues earned through entry tickets benefit the sports organizations and not the local government (Matheson, 2002). Hence, economic benefits generated are enjoyed by corporates, while the costs are incurred by the local community (Daniels et al., 2004; Diedering and Kwiatkowski, 2015; Mathieson and Wall, 1982).

Often local retailers or vendors suffer the most during these mega-events. This is caused because of the halt in daily business since locals do not prefer going out as a result of overcrowding, and the other main reason is the dominance of foreign vendors (Daniels et al., 2004). The massive amount of attention these events receive drastically increases the sponsorship rate which is difficult for the local businesses to afford. There is also inequality in the distribution of the economic benefits with the areas closer to the events receiving most of it (Daniels et al., 2004).

Spilling (1996) study on the impacts of the Lillehammer Olympics throws light on one of the serious drawbacks of the economic benefits acquired from hosting mega-events. He states that the economic benefits do not serve long-term goals, and even if there is a long-term economic benefit, it is at a very negligible rate when compared to the overall economy of the region. The economic benefits which result from the events are restricted to a temporary period resulting in enormous costs for organizing the events (Spilling, 1996). A case study on the economic impacts of Beijing Olympics disclosed that the economic benefits gained from hosting such events are inversely proportionate to the size of the country's economy. The total impact of the Olympics on the GDP of Beijing was only 0.1% which is not a significant amount considering the total expenditure spent on organizing the event (Li et al., 2013).

Hosting such mega-events boosts tourism which results in the increased inflow of tourists which leads to the rise in price for goods, making it difficult for the locals to afford. Local residents find it difficult to manage the sudden inflation in prices such as increased house rents and real estate (Moscardo, 2007; Ritchie, 1984).

12.4 SOCIOCULTURAL CRITICISMS

It has been highlighted that the sociocultural impacts of event tourism have drawn the attention of academic researchers, but studies have been relatively less compared to economic impacts (Getz, 2009; Ohmann et al., 2006; Smith, 2009). Social and cultural events include carnivals, festivals (musical events and food festivals), religious events, arts, and entertainment (Getz and Page, 2016). Duguma (2019) stated that these events are diverse in nature and change from one destination to another and in cultural contexts and may also vary from small events to mega ones. These events significantly affect the community or a region in both positive and negative ways. Sharpley and Stone (2014) pointed out that social impacts affect the lifestyle and quality of life of local residents. Balduck et al. (2011) argued that events are short term in nature and immediate changes are noticeable in their quality of life. In comparison, cultural impacts reflect norms, tradition, and changes in social relationships (Getz, 2008) and are long term in nature (Balduck et al., 2011). Events play a significant part in the life of residents by enhancing their sense of pride and cultural identity. Smith (2009) noted that events bring visitors in contact with the local communities which causes sociocultural change and these changes can be valuable or damaging to the host community depending on their cultural differences and nature of the contact. In this section, the negative impacts of sociocultural events have been discussed.

Balduck et al. (2011) pointed out that local authorities often neglect negative effects to get the support of the public in hosting the event. The following negative sociocultural impacts of an event are as follows: (1) *Commodification and staged authenticity:* Events contribute to the social and cultural development of the host community but commercialization or commodification of activities can destroy the sociocultural values and traditions. Staged authenticity refers to the modification of the nature of events to satisfy the needs of the visitors (Ritchie, 1984). Gursoy et al. (2004) showed concern that events may become *tourist trap* losing its authenticity and becoming just a commercial activity for generating revenue. For these issues of loss of authenticity and satisfying tourist demands, the term *festivalization* came into being explaining how cultural events are exploited (Getz and Page, 2016). (2) *Disruption of quality of life of residents:* Bagiran and Kurgun (2016) refer to an increase in noise, litter, overcrowding and traffic congestion that causes problems for the residents. They try to escape the impact of the events, changing communities' social and leisure habits. Due to events, the prices of goods and services inflate making it difficult for low-income groups (Getz, 2009). When preparing for mega-events, large-scale infrastructures are developed which increases the real estate value as well as house rents, consequential in the dislocation (Wilkinson, 1994). (3) *Health:* The global outbreaks (like COVID-19, Swine flu, etc.) and other communicable diseases can be a risk for event visitors and the host population. Preparing for mass gathering for an event also includes public health measures, because these kinds of events have the potential to import and export infectious diseases and put pressure on health resources (WHO, 2011). (4) *Prostitution and sexual assault:* Increase in demand of sexual encounters among the event attendees, many destinations have been actively promoting their sexual content. This has led to the risk of spreading HIV/AIDS and STDs (Cooper et al., 1993). Sexual and common assault during the event has also increased (Hall, 1992). Violence and harassment have become common issues suffered by event attendees. This can lead to the negative image of the destinations. (5) *Crime and Vandalism:* As visitors coming to events carry cash and valuables with them (Mathieson and Wall, 1982), it provides a source of crime and vandalism. It can cause an increase in theft, destruction of property, violence, drug trafficking and other petty crimes (Hall and Selwood, 1989).

The conflict between the community and the event organizers is one of the possible negative impacts of event tourism (Higgins-Desbiolles, 2018). This occurs due to the lack of proper consultation with the local community regarding the planning of the event and not considering their views. Lack of trust and protests are the possible outcomes of such conflicts. The reasons for many such events facing resistance from the local community are because they completely ignore the voices of the local community in the planning process (Jago et al., 2010). Thus, opting out for neo-liberalistic approaches while planning events would create a form of event imposition on the local community which may result in strong opposition toward hosting such events from the local members (Higgins-Desbiolles, 2018).

Events can augment the image of the destination, but if not properly managed can also diminish the image of the event as well as the destination (Jago et al., 2010). Examining the sociocultural impacts of events on host communities is important as they can have some serious negative effects which can disrupt the normal lives of residents and has the potential to diminish the image of the destination than does a normal tourism (Deery and Jago, 2010).

12.5 ENVIRONMENTAL CRITICISMS

The tourism industry and its allied segments are always criticized for being one of the largest contributors to environmental pollution. Event tourism emerging as the fastest growing sector over a decade has brought it in the notice as a potential contributor to this global issue (Dickson and Arcodia, 2010), but studies related to environmental impacts of events have not been as eminent as studies done on economic and sociocultural impacts (Getz, 2008). As this is a time of global climate change, scarcity of natural resources, and rising energy costs, environmental problems have lately come to the forefront in the event literature (Getz, 2009).

Andersson and Lundberg (2013) stated that events potentially impact ecosystems, natural, and man-made environments; contribute to carbon emissions; and create waste (Dickson and Arcodia, 2010). Therefore, it is important to pay greater attention to the environmental outcomes of event tourism. Tranter and Keefee (2004) examined a motor racing event in Australia and argued that its environmental cost has been more than the claimed benefits as it pollutes the environment and wastes fossil fuel (Smith, 2009). Social events such as festivals and special events preserve and promote the cultural identity of the host community but negatively affect the environment and natural resources. These negative impacts of event tourism occur when the number of visitors attending the event is more than its carrying capacity (Duguma, 2019; Smith, 2009). As these events mostly take place outdoors in a limited place and involve a considerable number of visitors, it causes overcrowding which leads to degradation of land, destruction of flora and fauna, and contaminate the area around by littering. These events can cause noise pollution also which in turn can disturb the living creatures. Furthermore, Deery and Jago (2010) examined that mega-events such as Olympics, Commonwealth Games, FIFA World Cup, etc., take place in a vast geographical area with a huge number of spectators creating more negative environmental consequences than smaller events in terms of transport, building infrastructure, excessive energy, and water usage. Fuelled by widespread negative publicity relating to pollution at these kinds of mega-events has raised interest in standards and practices for green events and venues, but many critics reject this idea completely that mega-events can ever be green or sustainable (Getz and Page, 2016).

Tranter and Keefee (2004) suggest that events companies compete for the opportunity to host grand and spectacular events to attract tourists. They emphasize on economic benefits overseeing the environmental measures. Until recently carbon footprints and energy cost of event tourism have mostly not been included in impact assessments. As long as the economic benefits of event tourism have an upper hand, environmental measures will remain unappreciated (Getz, 2009). On the contrary, Yuan (2013) noted that tourism cannot pursue without a healthy environment. Even the tourists attending events have high expectations on environmental quality, whereupon economic success depends. These negative environmental impacts can threaten the status of future events.

12.6 INFRASTRUCTURAL CRITICISMS: THE MISSING LINK

Apart from the above-discussed areas, there are other negative impacts which are caused because of event tourism. Among the various negative impacts which have been studied concerning the events and event tourism, the least studied area is the problems faced by the local residents in the form of displacement or evictions. A study on the evictions and housing issues in the Canadian perspective as a result of three mega-events disclosed that international events resulted in forced evictions irrespective of the resistance from the local community (Olds, 1998). *Exclusivity* or *Squeezing out* of locals is, thus, a common problem associated with event tourism (Daniels et al., 2004). The effect of exclusion is severe in the poorest sections of the community, especially where there is a lack of community groups which contradicts the claim that organizing mega-events boosts community spirit (Ritchie and Hall, 1999).

The mega-events which are promoted globally attract a large number of spectators, thereby placing a huge demand for infrastructure which cannot be fulfilled by the host destination (Short, 2008). When the host destination has less infrastructural capacities, problems such as chaos in public transport facilities and overcrowding at hospitality establishments are the common sight leading to crowding and congestion (Higham, 1999).

Even though it is claimed that events can boost the tourism market, it is also proved to have hindered its growth in a few cases. Domestic tourism of the host destination may suffer a major setback due to event tourism. Mostly, domestic tourists avoid traveling to places where events take place to avoid chaos (Higham, 1999). Also, international travelers resist to visit places hosting mega-events fearing price inflation and travel inconvenience (Liu and Wilson, 2014). Apart from these two factors, there is another major criticism for event tourism stating that it causes *crowding-out* effects, because it is argued that many events attract only a particular section of tourists (Preuss, 2011). Defined as "any reduction in private consumption that occurs because of an increased demand based on the staging of the event" (Preuss, 2011), *the* crowding-out effect is more common if the region is already a well establish tourist destination where the events just replaces the tourist economy rather the supplementing (Matheson, 2002). A study conducted on the crowding-out effect and travel intentions post-London 2012 Olympics strongly supports these arguments (Liu and Wilson, 2014).

Commuters are affected by the traffic caused by hallmark mega-events, and it is also reported that tourists who visit the region when the event is happening also suffer from these issues (Mules and Faulkner, 1996; Tranter and Keefee, 2004). A study conducted on the impact of motorcycle events in Canberra states that the roads and tracks for the race were closed for traffic resulting in disruption to the public and visitors. The region also faced serious issues regarding road safety (Tranter and Keefee, 2004).

The recent studies on event tourism also question its sustainability (Hall, 2012; Ziakas, 2015). These events are conducted in large scales appealing to a mass tourist market and also the large demand it places on the need for infrastructure such as new stadiums which makes its less sustainable (Hall, 2012; Tranter and Keefee, 2004).

12.7 RECOMMENDATIONS AND SUGGESTIONS

To attain sustainability, event tourism must address the economic, socio-cultural, environmental and infrastructural constraints mentioned in the preceding sections of this paper. In this section, major recommendations and suggestions have been mentioned that can contribute to addressing the challenges and issues faced by event tourism.

To ensure long-term effects, events, in general, should be economically, socially, and environmentally sustainable. This can be achieved by conducting events that are smaller in scale and organizing events with the use of existing infrastructure (Hall, 2012). There should be cooperation between the host and neighboring regions to ensure more number of night stays better tourist satisfaction and larger economic benefit in total (Lee et al., 2017). A proper framework should be established to assess the impacts of event tourism and also the assessments should be free from biases to have a clear picture of the costs and benefits of the event. This will help in organizing such events in the future successfully (Crompton, 2004; Lee and Taylor, 2005; Morgan and Condliffe, 2007; Tranter and Keefee, 2004). Proper guidelines must be placed to have a check on economic leakage, rising inflation, and unequal distribution of economic benefits (Crompton, 2004; Hodur and Leistritz, 2007; Li et al., 2013; Morgan and Condliffe, 2007).

To maximize the favorable social impacts of events, community involvement in decision-making and implementation of plans is necessary (Liu and Wilson, 2014). Event tourism planning should follow a *bottom-up* approach rather than a neo-liberalistic method in the planning process so that local community views can be included and also their support can be gained, thus avoiding community opposition and resistance. There should be stricter laws regarding forced evictions which are common during mega-events in the name of urban restricting (Olds, 1998). The main reason for the exclusion of the local community from the planning process is the limited timeframe in which the events are planned and organized. This issue can be avoided if an adequate amount of time is spent on the planning process with insights from the local community (Ritchie and Hall, 1999). To reduce negative sociocultural impacts, event managers organizing the event should have proper skills and knowledge about the culture, history, and worldview of participants and host communities (Duguma, 2019). One of the rising problems for the spread of infectious diseases like SARS or COVID-19 can be controlled by proper event planning, dissemination of information, taking precautionary measures and being ready with contingency plans before, during, and after the conduct of events (Ahmed and Memish, 2020; Gallego et al., 2020).

Events can reduce, reuse, and recycle in useful and meaningful ways. If properly managed, events can result in minimizing the impacts on the environment (Dickson and Arcodia, 2010). Dustbins should be placed at several places of events venues and even the nearby places to encourage the segregation of waste (Duguma, 2019). Event organizers should use recyclable things and should discourage plastics and other nonrecyclable products. Organizers should raise awareness and educate all the stakeholders about how they should behave while attending the event, keeping in mind the environmentally sustainable principles (Yuan, 2013).

When developing infrastructure for mega-events, environment-friendly building materials and methods should be used (Collins et al., 2009). Organizers should be encouraged to use natural lights and ventilation. If not possible, they should use energy-efficient or energy-star-rated products to reduce energy consumption. Encouraging the use of solar energy can also help in reducing energy costs (Ahmad et al., 2013).

To overcome the transport-related infrastructural issues, event organizers should encourage event attendees to use public transport while traveling, which can help in decreasing traffic congestion and minimizing pollution levels (Collins et al., 2009; Izawa, 2012). Overcrowding is one of the issues during an event. Therefore, a proper crowd management system must be implemented. The crowd should not be dispersed, rather a queuing system should be used. The use of crowd barrier control is also essential, and efficient communication should be there among staff. A detailed plan of emergency action drills for fire, bomb threat, crowd surge, and crowd collapse, and evacuation should also be laid out (Upton, 2008). Security at all places needs to be tightened to control criminal activities and assaults occurring during the time of events (Ohmann et al., 2006).

12.8 CONCLUSION

In the quest to achieve the sustainability objective for mega-event tourism, the authors of the paper have examined a deal of scientific literature about the management, marketing, and operationalization of mega-events. Since critical studies can provide insights into the challenges in the path of sustainability, major critical areas based on the triple bottom line of event tourism (economic, sociocultural, and environmental) have been discussed and outlined in the paper. An additional set of criticisms called the infrastructural criticisms has also been discussed as a contribution to the existing body of event tourism literature. In the final section of the paper, suggestions and recommendations that can assist in ensuring sustainability by addressing the major challenges have been discussed. The chapter concludes that despite its rising popularity, event tourism has many critical features and weak links that need to be addressed to ensure its sustainability.

KEYWORDS

- event tourism
- sustainability
- criticisms
- mega-events
- infrastructure

REFERENCES

Ahmad, N. L., Rashid, W. E. W., Razak, N. A., Yusof, A. N. M., and Shah, N. S. M. (2013). Green event management and initiatives for sustainable business growth. *International Journal of Trade, Economics, and Finance, 4*(5), p. 331.

Ahmed, Q. A., and Memish, Z. A. (2020). The cancellation of mass gatherings (MGs)? Decision making in the time of COVID-19. *Travel Medicine and Infectious Disease, 34,* p. 101631.

Andersson, T. D., and Lundberg, E. (2013). Commensurability and sustainability: Triple impact assessments of a tourism event. *Tourism Management, 37,* pp. 99–109.

Baade, R. A., and Matheson, V. A. (2004). The quest for the cup: Assessing the economic impact of the world cup. *Regional Studies, 38*(4), pp. 343–354.

Bagiran, D., and Kurgun, H. (2016). A research on social impacts of the Foça Rock Festival: The validity of the Festival Social Impact Attitude Scale. *Current Issues in Tourism, 19*(9), pp. 930–948.

Balduck, A.-L., Maes, M., and Buelens, M. (2011). The social impact of the Tour de France: Comparisons of residents' pre-and post-event perceptions. *European Sport Management Quarterly, 11*(2), pp. 91–113.

Bazeley, P., and Richards, L. (2000). *The NVivo qualitative project book*: SAGE Publications.

Cibinskiene, A. (2012). Impact evaluation of events as factors of city tourism competitiveness. *Economics and Management, 17*(4), pp. 1333–1339.

Collins, A., Jones, C., and Munday, M. (2009). Assessing the environmental impacts of mega sporting events: Two options? *Tourism Management, 30*(6), pp. 828–837.

Cooper, C. P., Fletcher, J. E., Gilbert, D. C., and Wanhill, S. (1993). *Tourism: principles and practice* London: Pitman Publishing Limited.

Cornelissen, S. (2004). Sport mega-events in Africa: Processes, impacts, and prospects. *Tourism and Hospitality Planning and Development, 1*(1), pp. 39–55.

Crompton, J. (2004). Beyond economic impact: An alternative rationale for the public subsidy of major league sports facilities. *Journal of Sport Management, 18*(1), pp. 40–58.

Daniels, M. J., Backman, K. F., and Backman, S. J. (2004). Supplementing event economic impact results with perspectives from host community business and opinion leaders. *Event Management, 8*(3), pp. 117–125.

Deery, M., and Jago, L. K. (2010). *Delivering innovation, knowledge, and performance: The role of business events.* Business Events Council of Australia, Australia.

Denyer, D., and Tranfield, D. (2009). Producing a systematic review. *The Sage handbook of organizational research methods.* (pp. 671–689). Thousand Oaks, CA: SAGE Publications, Ltd.

Dickson, C., and Arcodia, C. (2010). Promoting sustainable event practice: The role of professional associations. *International Journal of Hospitality Management, 29*(2), pp. 236–244.

Diedering, M., and Kwiatkowski, G. (2015). Economic impact of events and festivals on host regions-methods in practice and potential sources of bias. *Polish Journal of Sport and Tourism, 22*(4), pp. 247–252.

Donaldson, R., and Ferreira, S. (2009). *(Re-) creating urban destination image: Opinions of foreign visitors to South Africa on safety and security?* Urban Forum.

Duguma, W. H. (2019). Social Event and Environment: Impact Assessment and Its Management Practices among the Maccaa Oromo of Western Ethiopia. *Research and Science Today, 17*(1), pp. 168–177.

Flaxman, S., Mishra, S., Gandy, A., Unwin, H., Coupland, H., Mellan, T., . . . Perez Guzman, P. (2020). Report 13: Estimating the number of infections and the impact of non-pharmaceutical interventions on COVID-19 in 11 European countries. Imperial College London.

Fourie, J., and Santana-Gallego, M. (2011). The impact of mega-sport events on tourist arrivals. *Tourism Management, 32*(6), pp. 1364–1370.

Gallego, V., Nishiura, H., Sah, R., and Rodriguez-Morales, A. J. (2020). The COVID-19 outbreak and implications for the Tokyo 2020 Summer Olympic Games. *Travel Medicine and Infectious Disease, 34*.

Getz, D. (2008). Event tourism: Definition, evolution, and research. *Tourism Management, 29*(3), pp. 403–428.

Getz, D. (2009). Policy for sustainable and responsible festivals and events: Institutionalization of a new paradigm. *Journal of Policy Research in Tourism, Leisure and Events, 1*(1), pp. 61–78.

Getz, D., and Page, S. J. (2016). Progress and prospects for event tourism research. *Tourism Management, 52*, pp. 593–631.

Gursoy, D., Kim, K., and Uysal, M. (2004). Perceived impacts of festivals and special events by organizers: An extension and validation. *Tourism Management, 25*(2), pp. 171–181.

Hall, C. M. (1992). *Hallmark tourist events: Impacts, management and planning.* Chichester: Belhaven Press.

Hall, C. M. (2012). Sustainable mega-events: Beyond the myth of balanced approaches to mega-event sustainability. *Event Management, 16*(2), pp. 119–131.

Hall, C. M., and Selwood, H. J. (1989). America's Cup lost: Paradise retained? The dynamics of a hallmark tourist event. *The planning and evaluation of hallmark events*, pp. 103–118.

Hede, A.-M. (2007). Managing special events in the new era of the triple bottom line. *Event Management, 11*(1–2), pp. 13–22.

Higgins-Desbiolles, F. (2018). Event tourism and event imposition: A critical case study from Kangaroo Island, South Australia. *Tourism Management, 64*, pp. 73–86.

Higham, J. (1999). Commentary-sport as an avenue of tourism development: An analysis of the positive and negative impacts of sport tourism. *Current Issues in Tourism, 2*(1), pp. 82–90.

Hodur, N. M., and Leistritz, F. L. (2007). Estimating the economic impact of event tourism: A review of issues and methods. *Journal of Convention and Event Tourism, 8*(4), pp. 63-79.

Izawa, M. (2012). *Greening event goers at the 2010 FIFA World Cup: A user perspective assessment of sustainable transport strategies.* USA: Cornell University.

Jago, L., Dwyer, L., Lipman, G., van Lill, D., and Vorster, S. (2010). Optimising the potential of mega-events: An overview. *International Journal of Event and Festival Management, 1*(3), pp. 220–237.

Lee, C.-K., Kang, S. K., and Lee, Y.-K. (2013). Segmentation of mega-event motivation: The case of Expo 2010 Shanghai China. *Asia Pacific Journal of Tourism Research, 18*(6), pp. 637–660.

Lee, C.-K., Lee, Y.-K., and Lee, B. (2005). Korea's destination image formed by the 2002 World Cup. *Annals of Tourism Research, 32*(4), pp. 839–858.

Lee, C.-K., Mjelde, J. W., and Kwon, Y. J. (2017). Estimating the economic impact of a mega-event on host and neighbouring regions. *Leisure Studies, 36*(1), pp. 138–152.

Lee, C.-K., and Taylor, T. (2005). Critical reflections on the economic impact assessment of a mega-event: the case of 2002 FIFA World Cup. *Tourism management, 26*(4), pp. 595–603.

Li, S., Blake, A., and Thomas, R. (2013). Modelling the economic impact of sports events: The case of the Beijing Olympics. *Economic Modelling, 30*, pp. 235–244.

Liu, D., and Wilson, R. (2014). The negative impacts of hosting mega-sporting events and intention to travel: a test of the crowding-out effect using the London 2012 Games as an example. *International Journal of Sports Marketing and Sponsorship, 15*(3), 12–26.

Magno, F., and Dossena, G. (2020). Pride of being part of a host community? Medium-term effects of mega-events on citizen quality of life: The case of the World Expo 2015 in Milan. *Journal of Destination Marketing and Management, 15*, p 100410.

Matheson, V. A. (2002). Upon further review: An examination of sporting event economic impact studies. *The Sport Journal, 5*(1), pp. 1–4.

Mathieson, A., and Wall, G. (1982). *Tourism, economic, physical and social impacts.* London, UK: Longman.

Miles, L., and Shipway, R. (2020). Exploring the COVID-19 pandemic as a catalyst for stimulating future research agendas for managing crises and disasters at international sport events. *Event Management, 24*, pp. 537–552.

Morgan, A., and Condliffe, S. (2007). Measuring the economic impacts of convention centers and event tourism: A discussion of the key issues. *Journal of Convention and Event Tourism, 8*(4), pp. 81–100.

Moscardo, G. (2007). Analyzing the role of festivals and events in regional development. *Event Management, 11*(1–2), pp. 23–32.

Mules, T., and Faulkner, B. (1996). An economic perspective on special events. *Tourism economics, 2*(2), pp. 107–117.

Müller, M. (2015). What makes an event a mega-event? Definitions and sizes. *Leisure Studies, 34*(6), pp. 627–642.

Ohmann, S., Jones, I., and Wilkes, K. (2006). The perceived social impacts of the 2006 Football World Cup on Munich residents. *Journal of Sport and Tourism, 11*(2), pp. 129–152.

Olds, K. (1998). Urban mega-events, evictions and housing rights: The Canadian case. *Current Issues in Tourism, 1*(1), pp. 2–46.

Preuss, H. (2011). A method for calculating the crowding-out effect in sport mega-event impact studies: The 2010 FIFA World Cup. *Development Southern Africa, 28*(3), pp. 367–385.

Ritchie, B. (1984). Assessing the impact of hallmark events: Conceptual and research issues. *Journal of Travel Research, 23*(1), pp. 2–11.

Ritchie, B., and Hall, M. (1999). *Mega events and human rights.* The First International Conference on Sports and Human Rights, Sydney, Australia.

Rojek, C. (2014). Global event management: A critique. *Leisure Studies, 33*(1), pp. 32–47.

Sharpley, R., and Stone, P. R. (2014). Socio-cultural impacts of events: Meanings, authorized transgression and social capital. In S. J. Page and J. Connell (Eds.), *The Routledge handbook of events* (pp. 347–361). London and New York: Routledge.

Short, J. R. (2008). Globalization, cities and the Summer Olympics. *City, 12*(3), pp. 321–340.

Smith, A. (2009). Events and sustainable urban regeneration. In R. Raj and J. Musgrave (Eds.), *Event management and sustainability* (pp. 32–42). Oxfordshire, UK: CABI.

Spilling, O. R. (1996). Mega event as strategy for regional development: The case of the 1994 Lillehammer Winter Olympics. *Entrepreneurship and Regional Development, 8*(4), pp. 321–344.

Toohey, K., and Taylor, T. (2014). Managing Security at the World Cup *Managing the Football World Cup* (pp. 175–196): Springer.

Tranter, P. J., and Keefee, T. J. (2004). Motor racing in Australia's Parliamentary Zone: Successful event tourism or the Emperor's new clothes? *Urban Policy and Research, 22*(2), pp. 169–187.

Upton, M. (2008). *Safe Event Management.* Paper delivered to the Theatre Managers Association Conference, Birmingham.

WHO (2011). *Global mass gatherings: implications and opportunities for global health security Report by . 86 (November).* http://www.hajinformation.com/main/l.htm%0Ahttp://apps.who.int/gb/ebwha/pdf_files/EB130/B130_17-en.pdf

Wilkinson, J. B. (1994). *The Olympic Games: Past history and present expectations*: NSW, Australia: Parliamentary Library.

Wylde, A., and Page, S. J. (2014). Safety, security and event management: A case study of the London 2012 Olympics and the private security industry. In S. J. Page and J. Connell (Eds.), *The Routledge handbook of events* (pp. 444–462): Routledge.

Xin, S., Tribe, J., and Chambers, D. (2013). Conceptual research in tourism. *Annals of Tourism Research, 41*, pp. 66–88.

Yuan, Y. Y. (2013). Adding environmental sustainability to the management of event tourism. *International Journal of Culture, Tourism and Hospitality Research, 7*(2), pp. 175–183.

Ziakas, V. (2015). For the benefit of all? Developing a critical perspective in mega-event leverage. *Leisure Studies, 34*(6), pp. 689–702.

CHAPTER 13

LOCAL ECONOMIC INCENTIVES OF ART EVENTS: A CASE STUDY OF KOCHI–MUZIRIS BIENNALE

BIJU THOMAS[1] and A. VINODAN[2*]

[1]*RLGT – Regional Level Tourist guide, Ministry of Tourism, Government of India, Southern Region*

[2]*School of Commerce and Business Management, Central University of Tamil Nadu, Neelakudy, Tamil Nadu 610005, India*

[*]*Corresponding author. E-mail: vinodan_tt@yahoo.co.in*

ABSTRACT

The purpose of this chapter is to investigate the local economic incentives of one of Asia's mega-events: Kochi–Muziris Biennale. A review of the existing literature and the contextual observation was made to reach a meaningful conclusion of the study. The study examined the genesis of modern art events and their economic incentive possibilities to the local community in the initial sections. The subsequent sections discuss the local economic incentives of Kochi–Muziris Biennale under 10 different areas. The study assumes significance in the event studies in India as Kochi–Muziris Biennale is the only biggest modern art event in India in terms of local participation.

13.1 INTRODUCTION

The global spread of Biennale as an event is calling for a detailed multifaced study on its origin, its effects on art, the destination city, economic feasibility, etc.. According to Lim and Lee (2006, 408), biennale as a bi- annual mega-event that is listed as a "must- see" happening of that region or country and, by its existence, attracts global attention and has both short- and long-term effects on the host nation's economy. It is further explained as a large scale, international group exhibition that recurs every two to five years (Neill, 2012) or a large-scale, transnational exhibition (Niemojewski, 2010).

It is a fact that it would seem difficult to study the origin of Biennale as it takes new shapes and adds more to its character as it moves from one location to another. It would be much easier if we study the origin and history of Individual Biennales. Biennale is also considered as an alternative space to a museum providing a platform for artistic debate and discussion, experiments, periphery developments as in decentralization, and also as an extension of the global elitist appetite for contemporary art as well as a model to generate cultural tourism (Esche, 2011). The socioeconomic influence of art events is to be studied as it touches different aspects of contemporary human life. However, an event becomes more meaningful to an area only when it is directly connecting the local community concerned. More specifically, the event includes society more connected to what the respective society earns out of that. Economic benefit considered to be more important for the community concerned, who are not directly participating in the event either as an organizer or as a participant. The present study is an attempt to understand the economic incentives, not the impacts of art event, as impact measurement requires more objective evaluation tools, whereas incentives are more subjective measure and understand the contributions of the event. In this direction, the present study tried to understand the historical and contemporary understanding of modern art event while exploring its local economic incentive considering Kochi–Muziris Biennale (KMB) as a case study.

13.2 GENESIS AND CONTEMPORARY UNDERSTANDING ON BIENNALE

The history of Biennale can be traced to Venice, where it was started 125 years ago in 1895 as an Exhibition of Venetian art. Over a century, the event has assumed a mega status and has come to include other disciplines such as architecture and design, theatre, and cinema. Based on the period of recurrence, triennials, quadrennials, and quinquennials come under the broader umbrella of the Biennial, though sometimes the event becomes Perennial (Jones, 2010) as it represents productions from different disciplines recurring at different periods to the extent that some of the events are not repeated frequently.

While exploring the subsequent observations on Biennale, Jones (2010) had stated that their evolution can be traced to the Venice Biennale because they were established with similar intentions of modernization, utopian structure, urban regeneration and tourism, knowledge production, international capital investments, as well as the political aspirations of new economies of the world.

Biennale scholars such as Niemojewski and Hoskote (2010) have a different view of the Biennale of the 20th and 21st centuries, they argued that the history of the biennale should be revisited, as the emergence of new biennales in the Third World countries were established as a counter Venetian history.

The word peripheries has a new meaning in the twentieth century, where world is becoming a global village; it is not just about the peripheral nations but within a nation and a city. In the past, Biennale was known to have contributed to the creation and development of new cities and towns. Crystal Palace exhibition in the 19th century was established as an architectural wonder and a universal exhibition to create new industrial cities to become centers of the world and attract international investments and status (Roces, 2005).

The significance of Biennale often discoursed in the context of Biennial or not to Biennial conference that was conducted in the city of Bergen in Norway in 2009, where the supporters of Biennial got together to discuss the history, present, and future and formed the theoretical framework for the conduct of the Biennial. The participants were from the West, and the developing countries and the conference came to be known as the Bergen Conference.

Initially, many Biennales were organized based on the Venetian model of National Interest; the third edition of Havana Biennale of 2009 revolutionized the intent by organizing the event under the modern idea of considering art as a common universal theme and taking away the awards that were the pride of the Venetian Biennial. The Havana Biennale introduced the concept of the conference as a platform for sharing knowledge, discussion, and debate for the first time. Artistic discourses were encouraged from the peripheries (away from the mainstream city/country), and art production became more of site oriented than of a national theme stressing more on cultural exchange. The cultural exchange took place through workshops with free zones for experimentation and innovation in new mediums of artistic and creative expression (Niemojewski, 2010; Weiss, 2011).

The developing nations have used Biennale as a tool to attract the world's attention to itself when the rest of the world is technologically and economically progressing at a breakneck speed. The Sao Paolo Biennale of

Brazil, which was established in 1951, was very successful in achieving its objective. The Biennales of Africa, South America, Middle East, Asia, etc. opened up the concept of universal art, moving the focus of the art from West to global South and South–South development dialogues, encouraging the decentralization of creativity and development of the Peripheries (Weiss, 1995, 48).

Generally, it has been perceived that most of the decentralized Biennales have a context of resistance in their birth. The Colombo Art Biennale can be directly related to a form of resistance against the 26-year-long civil war. The Johannesburg Biennale was organized a year after their first civil election in 1994, which put an end to the Apartheid. Gwangju rose from the dreadful memories of the Tianmen massacre (Hoskote, 2012; Marchart, 2014).

Today, there are five mega-art events in South Asia. They are Asian Art Biennale in Dhaka (1981), Colombo Art Biennale (2009), Katmandu International Arts Festival (2009), Dhaka Art Summit (2012), and the KMB (2012). All of these have given a high focus on the region and good shares of artists who participate from the host country.

13.3 KOCHI–MUZIRIS BIENNALE

The Indian art scene was on the rise before the fall of Lehman Bros and the economic recession it triggered in 2009, in the years that followed the art world meltdown. India too was affected, and the recovery was slow when KMB announced its arrival in 2012. Kochi Biennale Foundation was started as a nonprofit public charitable trust with state government support. Considering the historic and social significance of Kochi, one of the main founders of the KBF, Bose Krishnamachari, has stated: "Nowhere else did we find the multiculturalism of Fort Kochi. More than 44 communities co-exist here. It's a secular world and was ideal for the Biennale." (Kuruvilla, 2019).

Kochi took a few centuries to develop after the land came up in the backwaters following a devastating flood in the state in the 14th century. The international travelers of the time, such as the Venetian Nicolo Conti and Chinese Ma Huan, have mentioned about the developing new town on the Malabar coast in their writing. It was the arrival of the Portuguese in the 1500s that changed the destiny of the Kochi kingdom and its port town. Very soon it came to be known as an international emporium of trade where the Arabs, Europeans, Chinese, and the other traders of the world sold and bought goods, and in the course of time, power changed hands from Portuguese to Dutch and to English till 1947.

The mythical Muziris (Muchiris meaning hare lip in the local language, Greek pronunciation Muziris) is believed to have gone down with the flood of 1341, the very flood that developed the Kochi Island. Muziris now is all but a mention in the books of Pliny the Elder, travel notes of Arabs, Chinese, etc. When the rest of the world has not even heard of Christianity, Apostle Thomas is believed to have come to Muziris port in a Roman trading ship and envoys from the land of prophet Mohammad has arrived in the 7th century during his lifetime. To back up this claim, both the first Christian church and Muslim Mosque of India were built in this land and remains.

13.4 ECONOMIC IMPACT OF ART EVENT

In general, art has immensely contributed toward cultural and folklore recognition and development of the different platforms for their presentation concerning contemporary social–cultural discourses. However, the economic contribution of an event is more reflective than the other impacts in a contemporary society. There will be direct, indirect, and induced effects of the event to the local community or economy (Rivera et al., 2008). More specifically, it is expected that there is an increase in private spending on cultural consumption, public or the government spending on the cultural programs, investment in new equipment and facilities related to events, and development of other infrastructure connected to events, resulting multiplier effect on the regional economies (Getz, 2017).

For the understanding of the impacts of events, generally, two types of impacts are identified. They are short- and long-term impacts. The short-term impact is an array of economic and intangible positive and negative effects on the area or the city and the local community, whereas long-term impacts are mainly focused on infrastructure development (Džupka and Šebová, 2014). Economic impact studies of events are in a nascent stage in India. Most of these impacts' studies are intended to understand the quantitative contribution of the event on the local economy.

It has also been observed that besides economic incentives, Biennale can support and promote tourism of the region by making the location or city itself as the artifact. For instance, Guggenheim Bilbao in Spain has listed the economic benefits to the local economy, and maintaining the cultural sector has the potential to impact the tourism industry and regeneration of a city through "the exploitation of the obsolete or abandoned industrial spaces" (Baniotopoulo, 2000).

In the present study, the attempt is being made to understate the local economic impact of KMB through secondary data verification and consolidation and to explore various segments that were hitherto unexplored in the context of India. Since the data available on KMB are scattered and there is less uniformity on the arguments put forth, it is essential to have a holistic understanding of the local economic incentives of KMB to strengthen the event and make it more meaningful in the years to come. In this direction, the study explored various decisions of local economic incentives of KMB based on a consensus of information available.

13.5 LOCAL ECONOMIC INCENTIVE KOCHI–MUZIRIS BIENNALE

Economic impact analysis focuses mainly on the improvement of the basic product/image of the area or city, where the events are being conducted while understanding the increase in consumption and length of stay of visitors and their satisfaction with the tourist product. In other cases, it may even go to explore the revisiting tendencies and attracting new visitors and it stimulates the local and regional service or product demand. The possibility of opening new market segments and exploring the additional source of income possibilities and the expansion of the market are such avenues to the locality (Snowball, 2008; Wood, 2005). Since the study is to understand the economic incentive of KMB, quantitative measures provided in the previous studies were considered as a means of substantiating the authors' arguments. Generally, construed visitors' spending and subsequent effects are not part of the study. More specifically, the local incentives of an event can encompass the following parameters.

1. *Increased visitation:* KMB falls in the top 10 art events of the world; it has a positive impact on the local economy, and the destination has gained prominence as a cultural destination along with its hugely popular historical tag. Most of the visitors to the KMB are first-time visitors to Kerala, which indicates that a large number of new visitors are attracted through KMB. For instance, in the second edition of the biennale in 2014, there were six lakh visitors and nearly 60% of them were new visitors to Kochi (Malayil, 2019).
2. *Increased transactions***:** Increased business transaction is considered as one important economic incentive to the local economy of hosting

destinations of events (Crompton, 2006). As KMB was able to keep Kochi in the cultural map of the world, that designated position was able to strengthen its economic base as the baseline survey of the MB indicated that KMB was able to improve the socioeconomic condition of Kochi (Sujit and John, 2019). The inferences can be made that KMB was able to support the reviving economy of Kochi after the outbreak of the Nipah virus and flood in the preceding year. As mentioned above, the Indian Chamber of Commerce, Kerala Round Table, had stated that 60% of the KMB visitors were first-time visitors to the state, and there was a 50% increase in sales for the local traders and the corresponding rise in the business of local inbound tour operators and hospitality sectors. The observations of other stakeholders in the tourism sector are praiseworthy to state here in this context; the hotel chain company CGH Earth director Sidharth Dominic said that their properties in Fort Kochi saw a growth of 50% in bookings, growth in longer duration of stay, and increase in food and beverage sales by 15%, during the Biennale period (Malayil, 2019). This is in tune with the observation of Sujit and John (2019) that there is a significant increase in service-based transactions in Kochi because of KMB.

3. *Employment generation*: Employment generation is considered as a major measurement rode for economic incentives to a locality (Kim and Miller, 2014). The possibility of creating an employment option needs to be examined for every event as it costs a lot for the society where it is organized; generating employment to the local community is an important economic incentive (Anderson and Lundberg, 2013). As a widely promoted destination of India, Kerala expects peripheral job creation while conducting a mega-event. Since the number of visitors are increasing year by year, it is imperative to have basic services to cater to these visitors apart from hardcore Biennale services such as volunteering and assisting the artist. The observation from the baseline study indicates that a significant number of jobs were created in connection with KMB particularly event-related operations. However, there is a need to explore job creation in hospitality, logistics, and small business sector as the study of KPMG indicates that there is a significant increase in visitation for KMB (Malayil, 2012).

4. *Space optimization*: Space is a major constraint in major event organizations. Exploring useful place and its optimization is the strategy to be followed by the organizers of the event to make it more visitor-friendly and art adaptive. The 500-year-old heritage town had become

a ghost town of memories and dilapidated old buildings when the KMB arrived with its convergence of modern ideologies. An event like KMB could give a jolt to a sleeping town like Fort Kochi, which is way past its glory days and made it aspire to turn its very ruins and forsaken memories to a hub of activities, which could have a positive impact on the presentation of its social and economic well-being. According to a report released by the KPMG, who are the knowledge partners for the KMB, through the celebration of international contemporary art, KMB invokes the historic cosmopolitan legacy of the modern metropolis of Kochi and its legendary predecessor, the ancient seaport of Muziris (Malayil, 2012). The intermittent study report (Sujit and John, 2019) also reflects that KMB has led to restoration of abandoned spaces in Kochi and used creating aesthetic ambiance to the artists as well as visitors.

13.6 DESTINATION IMAGE BUILDING

As a destination, Kochi was able to garner more attention among international travelers as a part of KMB. The state already had a tagline of God's own country, which is widely promoted among tourist-generating regions of the world. KMB is another feather to the brand Kerala effort to attract more number of tourists to the state and particularly to Kochi. The reflections from the stakeholders are worth stating here that KMB becomes a catalyst to attract a good number of visitors to Kochi. In the future, the possibility of exploring Kochi as a Biennale destination, as in the case of Manchester and Barcelona, known for its football, Thrissur for its Pooram, Alleppey for its Nehru Trophy Boat Race, etc., is becoming a reality (Malayil, 2019). Furthermore, it has been observed that KMB has become a major driver of art and culture in India and bolstered Kochi's global reputation as a vibrant place for cultural pluralism, as observed in the KPMG report submitted to the Government of Kerala (Malayil, 2012). Other Biennale of India, Pune Biennale, is yet to garner better mileage in projecting Pune as a destination (Kuruvilla, 2019). It has also been noted that the respondents of a baseline study agreed that Kochi can become a center of cultural excellence (Sujit and John, 2019). This indicates the credibility of Kochi to become a better tourist destination especially a cultural hotpot of Kerala in all respect, and thereby, destination Kochi can have a brand image of its own in the years to come in the tourism map of India.

13.6.1 PUBLIC INFRASTRUCTURE DEVELOPMENT

The development of public infrastructure is part and parcel of any event. The coordinated effort of the government department and the organizers KMB was able to showcase commendable public infrastructure especially public utility space in important areas of Kochi. This is made possible without leveraging the mega-event syndrome, which is generally overpromising and underdelivering of facilities, underestimating costs, using public properties for private vested interest, neglecting the concerns of the local population, and revisiting the existing urban priorities (Müller, 2015; Zimbalist, 2015).

13.6.2 INCLUSIVITY

The inclusion of the local community and local artists is imperative to garner success in events. The positive contribution in terms of their participation as visitors is found to be the popularity of the event. This, in turn, supports local happiness, and the organizers can have an inclusive event and thereby ensure the support for the upcoming events (Séraphin et al., 2018). Exposure to the local artist was quite encouraging as the study indicates that KMB was able to enhance exposure to local artists, and it was also able to showcase their talent on a larger platform (Sujit and John, 2019). As mentioned above, the increasing number of visitors year by year indicates the popularity of the program, which effectively removed the tag of an elitist program. As the footfall indicated, the domestic travelers as well as a large number of art enthusiasts from within Kerala were able to attend the program. The observations of the organizers also attest to the same as the most celebrated Venice Biennale, the oldest and one of the most prestigious events, was able to attract a far lower number of visitors than Kochi what Kochi gets (Kuruvilla, 2019).

13.6.3 TOURIST INFRA AND SUPERSTRUCTURE DEVELOPMENT

Muresan et al. (2016) observed that the development of tourist infrastructure and superstructure is part and parcel of event tourism, and thereby, it can support the local people's quality of life to a greater extent. The creation of new infrastructure and modernization or reorganization of existing infrastructure found to be an important attraction of art-based events everywhere. Since the observations supplement the fact that there is a good number of inbound tourists flow noticed during KMB, the development of related infrastructure was quite obvious. In general, Kerala has less than 10,000 rooms for a 125-day season compared to other leading state Goa, which has 35,000 rooms available for a 220-day season. Goa has 14 days of tourist retention as compared to seven days of Kerala (Malayil, 2019). This indicates the need for alternate accommodation facilities to cater to the seasonal demands owing to KMB. In this direction, the researchers were able to understand that most of the visitors were exploring homestay facilities in and around Kochi while attending KMB. The baseline study also attests that same and stated that KMB has a significant impact on homestay occupancy during the KMB season (Sujit and John, 2019). This infrastructure can, in turn, be used for the other tourism-related events, and also, it will have better occupancy if we effort to project Kerala as a 365-day destination.

13.6.4 SKILL DEVELOPMENT AMONG SERVICE PROVIDERS

Though the skill development is important for both demand and supply sides of operators of an event, it mainly depends on the kind of event. As far as an art-based event is concerned, the skill development or horning the skill among local artists become necessary, and thereby, they can explore further venues. The skill development among service providers is found to be a more important economic incentive as the event requires various services at a particular point of time to cater to a variety of demands. The visitors consider the biennale venue as the confluence of culture and social practices so the tendency to explore services and goods demands the assessment of skill gap among existing support service providers of the city and calls for appropriate skill development program. At Kochi, innovative tour operators have developed specialized heritage tours, which include walks to historical sites, visit to a cafe where the Colonial Dutch cake, Breudher, still gets made, a Gujarati sweetshop, and even through its music, from the home of a Carnatic vocalist to a concert by the Mehboob Memorial Orchestra, a group of ghazal and qawwali enthusiasts (the music arrived in the island with the Dakhni Muslims, a Sunni Islamic community from Hyderabad) with an interest in playback singers Mohammad Rafi and H. Mehboob (Kuruvilla, 2019). The new demands demand new ways of looking at opportunities and acquiring skills to deal with it.

13.6.5 CONSERVATION

Events promote cultural conservation and presentation as it promotes the local cultural vividness and encourages people to partake in entertainment events, visit the county's museum, and provide a platform for cultural exchange, in turn leading to cross-cultural understanding (Canfield Fair Organization, 2015). As a part of space optimization, KMB has led to the restoration of abandoned spaces in Kochi. Over three editions, KMB has established itself as one of the most important art exhibitions in the world; the old colonial buildings such as Aspinwall House, the mother venue, have become synonymous with Kochi Biennale, just as the Giardini and the Arsenale are with the Venice. The possibility of conserving and maintaining cultural properties both tangible and intangible should be one among many priorities of the program. In general, apart from the opportunity for the local artists to contemplate the works of their contemporaries from around the world, the biennale paves the way for newer experiences. There are different kinds of connections that are being built through the art exhibition (Kuruvilla, 2019).

13.6.6 TRANSPORTATION

Events have a significant impact on the local transportation (Thomas et al., 2015). There is a significant improvement in the transportation sector in Kochi after the KMB. The visible remarks of this were the introduction of a metro under the Cochin Metro Rail Corporation Limited and a proposed water metro. There is a substantial increase in the transport sector during the KMB season in all means. Air transport and road transport had a significant impact on the event. The contribution of the event to local transportation is one of the important areas which is to investigate; KMB significantly impacted traffic flow and transportation at Kochi and was able to project Kochi as a tourist destination.

13.7 CONCLUSION

While examining the economic incentives of the KMB, the authors tried to explore various economic and related dimensions and concluded with 10 aspects. This includes both general economic incentives and tourism bound incentives. However, it is pertinent to state that aspects such as visitor impact, spending pattern, earning generation possibilities among local people, and local spending are not considered as it requires quantitative measurement. The study significantly assists in understanding the basic contribution of an event to the local economy.

KEYWORDS

- local economic incentives
- Kochi–Muziris Biennale
- tourism
- destination
- India

REFERENCES

Anderson, T.D. and Lundberg, E. (2013). Commensurability and sustainability: Triple impact assessments of a tourism event, *Tourism Management, 27*, 99–109.

Arnegger, J., andHerz, M. (2016). Economic and destination image impacts of mega-events in emerging tourist destinations. *Journal of Destination Marketing & Management, 5*(2), 76–85.

Baniotopoulo, Evdoxia. 2000. "Art for whose sake? Modern art museums and their role in transforming societies: The case of the Guggenheim Bilbao". *Journal of Conservation and Museum Studies, 7*: 1–5 (published in 2001).

Canfield Fair Organization (2015). The canfield fair event. [Online]. Available: http://www.canfieldfair.com

Crompton, J. (2006). Economic impact studies, *Journal of Travel Research, 45*(1): 67–82.

Crompton, J. L., and Lee, S. (2000). The economic impact of 30 sports tournaments, festivals, and spectator events in seven U.S. cities. *Journal of Park and Recreation Administration, 18*(2): 107–126.

Crompton, J., Lee, S. and Shuster, T. (2001). A guide for undertaking economic impact studies: The Springfest example. *Journal of Travel Research, 40*(1): 79–87.

Esche, C. (2011). Making art global: A good place or a no place. In: Rachel, W. Ed., *Making Art Global (Part 1): The Third Havana Biennial 1989*. London: Afterall Books in association with Academy of Fine Arts & Van Abbemuseum.

Getz, D. (2017). Developing a framework for sustainable event cities. *Event Management*, 21(5), 575–591.

Getz, D., Pettersson, R., and Wallstam, M. (2015). Event evaluation: Definitions, concepts and a state of the art review. *International Journal of Event and Festival Management, 6*(2), 135–157.

Hoskote, R. (2012). A Biennale for India. *Domus 1*(3): 310.

[Online]. Available: https://www.newindianexpress.com/states/kerala/2019/mar/02/kochi-biennale-boosts-kerala-economy-local-traders-see-50-per-cent-rise-in-business-1945522.html

Hoskote, Ranjit. (2010) Biennials of Resistance: Reflections on the Seventh Gwangju Biennial. In *The Biennial Reader*, eds. Elena Filipovic, Marieke van Hal, and Solveig Øvstebø, pp. 306–321. Ostfildern: Hatje Cantz.

Online]. Available: https://www.thehindu.com/news/national/kerala/art-in-the-marketplace-how-the-kochi-muziris-biennaleis-driving-interests-worldwide/article26613334.ece

Jones, C. (2010). Biennial culture: A longer history. In: E. Filipovic, M. Van Hal, and S. Ovstebo, *The Biennial Reader*. Norway: Bergen Kunstall & Hatje Cantz, pp. 68–69.

Kim, S., and Miller, C. (2014). Impact study of the 34th Mistletoe Marketplace, Jackson: Publication.

Kuruvilla, E. (2019, March 23). Art in the marketplace: How the Kochi–Muziris Biennale is driving interest worldwide. *The Hindu*.

Lim, S T and Lee, J. (2006). Host population perceptions of the impact of mega events. *Asia Pacific Journalism of Tourism Research, 11*(4): 407–421.

Malayil, J. (2019, March 9). How Kochi biennale boosted Kerala; 50% rise in business, 60% visitors first timers. *The New Indian Express*.

Marchart, O. (2014). The globalization of art and the 'Biennials of Resistance': "A History of the Biennials from the Periphery." In Cumma Papers #7 published on Cummastudies Blog, edited by Nora Sternfeld and Henna Harri. Department of Art, Helsinki. http://cummastudies.files.wordpress.com/2013/08/cummapapers7.pdf

Martin W., Dimitri, L and Pettersson, R .(2020). Evaluating the social impacts of events: in search of unified indicators for effective policymaking. *Journal of Policy Research in Tourism, Leisure and Events, 12*(2), 122–141.

Müller, M. (2015). The mega-event syndrome: Why so much goes wrong in mega-event planning and what to do about it. *Journal of the American Planning Association, 81*(1): 6–17.

Muresan, I. Oroian, C. Harun, R. Arion, F. Porutiu, A. Chiciudean, G. Todea, A. and Lile, R. (2016). Local residents' attitude toward sustainable rural tourism development. *Sustainability, 8*, 100.

Niell, P. O. (2012). Biennial culture and the emergence of a globalized curatorial discourse. In *The Culture of Curating and the Curating of Cultures,* pp. 51–85. Cambridge, MA, and London MIT Press.

Niemojewski, R. (2010). Venice or havana: A polemic on the Genesis of the contemporary Biennial. In: E. Filipovic, M. Van Hal, and S. Ovstebo, *Biennial Reader*. Norway: Bergen Kunstall & Hatje Cantz, pp. 88–103.

Roces, M. P. (2005). Crystal Palace Exhibitions. In E. Filipovic, M. Van Hal, and S. Ovstebo, *The Biennial Reader*. Norway: Bergen Kunstall & Hatje Cantz, p. 51.

Séraphin, H., Platania, M., Spencer, P and Modica, G. (2018). Events and tourism development within a local community: The case of Winchester (UK). *Sustainability,10* (3): 728.

Snowball, J. J. (2008). *Measuring the value of culture: Methods and Examples in Cultural Economics*. London, UK: Springer.

Sujit, A.S. and John, A. (2019). Socio-cultural and economic impact of Kochi- Muziris Biennale. *International Journal of Recent Technology and Engineering, 8* (4): 573–577.

Weiss, R. (1995). The long process of getting to the edge of the world. *The Journal of Arts Management, Law and Society 25*(1): 39–56.

Weiss, R. (2011). A certain place and a certain time: The third bienal de la habana and the origins of the global exhibition. *In Making Art Global (Part 1): The Third Havana Biennial 1989,* 14. London: Afterall Books in association with Academy of Fine Arts & Van Abbemuseum.

Wood, E. (2005). Measuring the economic and social impacts of local authority events. *International Journal of Public Sector Management, 18*(1), 37–53.

Zimbalist, A. (2015). *Circus Maximus: The Economic Gamble Behind Hosting the Olympics and the World Cup.* Washington, DC: Brookings Institution Press.

CHAPTER 14

ROLE OF EVENT TOURISM IN ECONOMIC DEVELOPMENT

MELIKE SAK[1*], ASLI SULTAN EREN[1], and GÜL ERKOL BAYRAM[2]

[1]Department of Tourism Guidance, School of Tourism and Hotel Management, Sinop University, Sinop, Turkey

[2]School of Tourism and Hospitality Management, Department of Tour Guiding, Sinop University, Nasuhbeyoğlu District, Sinop, Turkey

*Corresponding author. E-mail: melikesak@windowslive.com

ABSTRACT

Event tourism has become a very effective type of tourism in the development of destinations where tourism activities are carried out intensively in recent years. Since it is one of the tourism types that people prefer extensively, event tourism provides many positive effects to the region. Especially, it has a great impact on the development of tourism in the region and economic development. Event tourism also affects the increase in income from tourism, as it is effective in the longer tourism season. At the same time, event tourism has an important role in improving the image of the region, increasing its attractiveness and ensuring its sustainability. Accordingly, event tourism has many positive effects both in the short and long term. Event tourism, which has very important economic and cultural effects, is a type of tourism that people prefer in regions where recreational activities are intense, to be motivated and have fun by moving away from their working life and negative situations. Due to the high interest of tourists today, event tourism, which provides economic income in many regions of the world, contributes greatly to the development of tourism. Today, many tourist destinations support the development of local and national image by focusing on event tourism, as well as contributing to the economic development of the region and local people, thus contributing to the development of tourism to a great extent.

14.1 INTRODUCTION

The tourism sector undergoes a great development and change after the Second World War and an important sectoral reason, especially the last features of which are for development for many countries (Kınacı et al., 2011: 1). When looking at regional development plans, it is possible to say that the agricultural sector was the sector with the biggest share in the economic development. It has been observed that, over time, the development of the industry and service sector left a greater share of the economic development than the agricultural sector. With the developing technology, it has started that you do not need your activity in the industrial sector and the agriculture sector, and it has been observed that it has a greater impact on the sectoral basis in the service sector (Bahar, 2007; Gülgeroğlu, 2000).

The tourism sector, also known as the chimneyless industry, provides positive dynamics in the development of countries through closing the current account deficit and the foreign currency it brings to the economy (Alpagu and Koç, 2016: 157). The tourism sector, which has diversified with the desire of people who are bored with the monotony of city life to go to different destinations and offers a wide range of services in line with their interests, has become a need today.

As a result of the changes in the tourism sector, the increase in the use of the resources at hand has led to a decrease in resources. The measures taken to ensure the continuity of the sector as a result of the economic income that people obtain from tourism are combined with the concept of development, and the concept of development in tourism has emerged. The concept of development is briefly defined as the development and change of the economic structure (Küçükoğlu et al., 2018: 2620). Along with the changes in the tourism sector, the concept of development has started to be mentioned with this sector and has a very important place. There are important criteria for development in the tourism sector. Sustainability of social life and environmental and cultural factors takes place, so it is thought that development in tourism will take place.

Event tourism, which has been on the rise in recent years, is very popular with its return to regional development and its role in promoting the country. Regional events have an important place in the social development of the region and the transfer of the culture to the world by making the destinations they organize as a brand because of the culture of a society and the spirit of the society (Altay and Altınışık, 2017: 112).

14.2 THE CONCEPT OF DEVELOPMENT

The concept of development is considered to have the same meaning as development and progress, but contrary to what is thought, the development concept has a broader and different meaning. Considering the meaning of the concept of development, it can be explained as positive changes and innovations in social, economic, and cultural aspects in the existing structures of developing countries. In addition to this, we can say that the development concept also includes developments in the concepts of production and industrialization in these countries (Küçükoğlu et al., 2018; Taban and Kar, 2014). In addition, with the development, an increase in the welfare level of the individuals is observed. Thus, the definition of the concept of development emerges.

When the concept of development is analyzed globally, it is also considered as an international political structure, and it is considered as an impressive element for societies (Brauch, 2008; 32). In a study in which Alkin made a different definition of the development concept in 2008, Alkin said, "It is the economic environment that creates improvements in the living standards of the society, the quality of the manufactured goods, or the organization of production." On the other hand, R.A. Flammang defined the concept of development in 1979 as "the situation that encompasses both more output and changes in technical and theoretical structure."

The concept of development has gained different dimensions from the past to the present with the history of humanity and has evolved over time in line with the changes in people's quality of life and life styles. The concept of development has acquired different names and meanings with the changes it has experienced over time. In addition to being named with different names, the concept was used instead of words that have close meanings. These concepts, that is, industrialization, growth, progress, modernization, and structural change, can be given as examples (Yavilioğlu, 2002: 60).

In addition to taking the concept of development with different names over time, when looking at the history of the concept, different definitions have been made for this concept. We can say that the reason for this is that the concept of development is a concept open to social changes and cannot be considered as a uniform concept. Therefore, each branch of science has brought a different explanation to the concept of development (Yavilioğlu, 2002: 60).

The concept of development has a different definition for each discipline. For example, while Marx stated the concept of development as a result of historical conditions, Milner defined development as state action. Another explanation stated that in addition to the definitions of Marks and Milner, Frederick Nixson should define the concept of development by isolating it from politics and its historical past (Yavilioğlu, 2002; Nixson, 1984). In the face of this new approach by Nixson, H.W. Arndt conducted a scientific study for the concept of development. Arndt started his work with Adam Smith for doing his job in economics. For this reason, he investigated how Smith defined the concept of development and stated that he defines it from the concept of development and industrialization. In this period, Smith defined the concept of industrialization as an improvement at an economic level and separated it from the concept of development (Yavilioğlu, 2002; Smith, 1985). The concept of economic development emerged during the period. Thus, the concept of development left being the equivalent of the word industrialization to the word economic development. Later, A. Marshall defines the concept of development as the development of ideas and thoughts and has moved away from the concept of economic development (Yavilioğlu, 2002; Arndt, 1981). Afterward, Schumpeter made the concept of development into two completely separate concepts with economic development with his work titled "Economic Development Theory." In the 1920s, the concept of development and the words of economic development were separated from each other, assuming to have separate meanings. Following the publication of the book entitled *Economic Development of the British Overseas Empire* by Lilian Knowks, an economist historian in 1924, Vera Anstey's book entitled *Economic Development of India* and R.H. He talked about the processes of development published by Tawney and in his books (Yavilioğlu, 2002; Arndt, 1981). The changes that the concept of development has experienced over the years continued to occur in the 1950s. As a result of this situation, the concepts of economic/economic development and development are handled differently. Thus, it is possible to say that the concept of development has become a concept, in which studies have been made by taking its place in the literature. At the same time, studies in the literature on the concept of development examined the relationship between development and different sectors.

The concept has had various types in itself since the development concept has been associated with different branches of science over time. These concepts have become important for development over time. The most important of the concepts is sustainable development, which is a very important concept in terms of both development and continuity. Sustainable development is the activities that countries carry out in order to be sustainable after meeting the requirements for development. Sustainable development, which will ensure the continuity of the welfare level gained by the society, has become more important due to the careless use of available resources, rapid growth of the population, and technological developments. As a result of the rapid depletion of available resources, people have become more in need of sustainable development. As a result of this situation, some measures have been taken.

According to Gladwin (1995), the basis of sustainable development is the use of society's life resources, social environment, and existing units with caution and avoidance. With the concept of sustainable development taking place in the literature, it has started to be mentioned in many areas. The concept of sustainable development, which is especially important for the protection of the resources that societies need for their future, is a system that includes the concepts of justice, rights, and law according to Wilson (2003). Güzel (2009) defined the concept as the aim of ensuring the continuity of the society and the environment without disrupting the balance of the society and the environment, leaving useful social and physical areas for future generations. The concept of sustainable development is based on three basic dimensions that include these definitions and many other definitions in the literature. These three basic dimensions can be listed as follows. It is the economic, social, and environmental dimension (Shaving, 2012; Haris, 2000; Demirayak, 2002; Ergün and Çobanoğlu, 2012; Gürlük, 2010).

The economic dimension includes items that are decreasing and running out. The economic dimension, which is an understanding that aims to create new production areas and to use the available resources in order to make the products at the economic level sustainable, is an understanding realized in the economic field. Continuity has spread to many areas such as education, political, and social equality and has given importance to the sustainability of these areas. Finally, the environmental dimension has been a concept targeting the environment and nature as well as the concept of sustainable development, and it has been an understanding aimed at the continuity of energy resources and all ecological systems smoothly.

The concept of development has many definitions in many respects over time and has become a frequently used concept in the literature. It is possible to say that this concept, which takes place in every field where people are involved, has become a very important factor for all societies that make progress, including underdeveloped countries. As a result, the concept of development is an indispensable concept that raises the standards of societies. As a result of this situation, it is possible to say that the concept of development is an indispensable factor for increasing the welfare level of the society.

14.3 CORRELATION BETWEEN DEVELOPMENT AND TOURISM

The World Tourism Organization (WTO) defines tourism as: "It is the activities that arise from the travels and accommodation that they make for holidays, business, and other purposes, provided that they do not exceed one year outside the places where people reside permanently." Another definition is: "In overnight stays away from home, meeting demands, providing accommodation, and supportive services and generating income related to these needs are employment (Kınacı et al., 2011; Ryan, 1991).

When we look at the definitions in the literature about tourism, we can say that not only to reach the touristic product but also to have economic inputs. The concept of development, which is mentioned with the concepts of growth and progress, has become a phenomenon experienced in the tourism sector. As the tourism industry is an international activity, it provides foreign exchange refund. As a result of this situation, tourism is an income increasing sector and provides positive input to the countries in terms of development.

Tourism has become an indispensable development factor for the economic advances of developing countries and developed countries, as it is among the rapidly growing sectors that bring economic income to countries. The tourism sector, which has gained diversity according to the interests of people over time, has moved away from the sea–sand–sun trio and has gained diversity in fields such as sports, congresses, events, nature, culture, and history. Thus, tourism has accelerated economic development. In addition, the tourism sector has become more associated with development with the creation of employment areas. The fact that the tourism sector gains diversity, is not limited to the summer months, and creates employment areas has become an important development area for the countries, and the fact that the tourism sector is growing rapidly affects this situation positively.

Considering the studies on the relationship between tourism and development, Aslan said in a study he conducted in 2003 that there were various relationships between tourism and development in the long term; then, Çeken stated in a study in 2008 that the imbalances experienced in the development with the tourism sector would be eliminated and an equal development could be achieved in the same year; Jimenez stated that tourism has positive effects for national and international development in his research. Considering tourism and development in the literature and other expressions, many dynamically express tourism and development together (Bozkurt and Topçuoğlu, 2013).

The tourism sector has been playing a role in the economic development of countries for the last two decades; therefore, tourism offers a wide range of products in terms of development. Countries have attached importance to the development of the tourism sector, which is such an important development tool. Tourism sector, which has contributed greatly to economic progress, is another area of development, and employment. Tourism is a labor-intensive sector, and as a result of this situation, it is possible to say that the service provider is more likely to provide employment because it is only human compared to other sectors (Kunu et al., 2015; Yıldız, 2011).

On the other hand, the tourism sector requires careful use of available resources to ensure continuity of development. The sustainable development approach should be adopted in order to prevent the income of countries from tourism. If tourism resources are used in a balanced way, an increase in development is expected to be expected (Çeken, 2008; Braden and Winer, 1980).

The effects of tourism on development and society are increasing day by day; this can be achieved by ensuring development. As long as each concept exists in both concepts, it will continue. The concept of tourism and development is associated in many ways, and when they become sustainable, they can continue to exist in a balanced way. This situation reveals the concept of sustainable development and tourism. In order to talk about the continuity of the development in the tourism sector, it is necessary to ensure its continuity in a continuous and balanced manner. Bulin et al. explained the qualities required for sustainable tourism development as follows in a study they conducted in 2012:

- *Quality:* The importance given to the social carrying capacity required to ensure the continuity of the tourism sector and the protection of the ecological environment should be taken into consideration more than the experiences of the visitors coming to the region.
- *Continuity:* The deterioration of the environmental, cultural, and social structures, which are described as tourism resources, affects sustainability in tourism development. Sustainability cannot be maintained without giving sufficient importance to these elements.
- *Balance:* Sustainable tourism development has to establish a balanced relationship between tourism stakeholders.

In the definition of Bulin, natural resources, cultural values, and people are at the center of the qualities required for tourism to continue sustainable development. According to the World Trade Organization (WTO, 1998: 21) in terms of sustainable tourism, tourism development "While the needs of the local people are met with the tourists who are served; Providing economic, social, and aesthetically satisfactory resources for future enterprises, provided that cultural integrity, sensitive ecological processes, biodiversity, and vital support systems are maintained and maintained." Both explanations argued that the values in the tourism sector should not be harmed in order to maintain sustainability. Sustainable tourism development draws attention to the continuity of tourism and aims to be a basis for continuity. Thus, development policies will be realized in tourism, and tourism will continue to exist by becoming sustainable.

14.4 EVENT TOURISM REGIONAL EFFECTS

Destinations all over the world develop themselves with tourism attractiveness and income from this attraction, namely, tourism (Kişioğlu and Selvi, 2013: 70). Over time, the culture of the local people, traditions, and customs of that culture started to attract attention. The effort of people to learn new culture has brought with them temporary travel from one place to another. Tourism has given the opportunity to promote their cultures to the world (Giritoğlu et al., 2015; Getz, 2008).

Following the intense and tiring life with the growth of the cities, the negative life standards and the lack of recreation areas lead people to participate in activities outside the city in their spare time (Akten and Akten, 2011; Can, 2015). In the developing and changing world, people need recreational activities to make their living standards healthier and more efficient (Can, 2015: 5). People living in big cities want to escape crowded and tiring city life. This motivation caused people to participate in tourism activities and recreational activities developing in the environment (Can, 2015; Şahin et al., 2009).

Event tourism has many positive and negative effects, and the effects differ according to the economy, tourism, and trade, and these ethics consist of positive effects in general. On the other hand, it can be said that it has effects such as becoming a global brand, promoting the region, sponsorships, spreading the earnings throughout the year, increasing the investments in the region, creating a new and strong image (Eryılmaz and Cengiz, 2012).

Tourism has subtitles that appeal to many different facts and various themes (Giritoğlu et al., 2015). Event tourism, which is also examined under cultural tourism, is among the tourism types that have developed and gained great importance in recent years (Kişioğlu and Selvi, 2013: 70). Researchers agree that event tourism plays a major role in branding destinations (Şengül and Genç, 2016; Lee and Arcodia, 2011; Chalip and Costa, 2005, Crockett and Wood, 1999). Branding a destination will accelerate the marketing of physical, cultural, and historical touristic attractions in that region and will help prolong the tourism season, create an alternative tourism product, and increase the number of tourists (Yıldırım et al., 2016; Tayfun and Arslan, 2013; Timur et al., 2014).

Nowadays, cities have a great importance in tourism marketing. Some cities generate larger tourism income and attract more tourists from the rest of their country. This situation reveals the importance of city branding in tourism (Yıldırım et al., 2016; Bilgili et al., 2012). It is known that there are benefits such as increasing economic income, providing new employment opportunities to the local people, recognition of the region, and creating a positive image about the region in the region, where the event tourism is held (Giritoğlu et al., 2015, Yoon et al., 2010; Kim et al., 2012; Prentice and Anderson, 2003; Huang et al., 2010; Kim et al., 2010; Gürsoy et al., 2004).

Today, activities have become an important phenomenon for tourism marketing strategies. Event tourism expression is defined as the type of tourism, where the activities organized to create a new tourist product or to make the existing tourist product more attractive are carried out systematically and in a planned manner (Can, 2015; Tassiopoulos, 2005). The primary intention of the tourists participating in event tourism is expected to be the desire to take part in an event organized in touristic destinations (Can, 2015: 7). Event tourism, which is considered among the subbranches of alternative tourism, is "to maximize the number of participants by using it as primary or secondary attraction. It is defined as the planning, development, and marketing of special events." (Can, 2015; Kozak and Bahçe, 2009). Recreational activities and various activities carried out in the destinations attract tourists to that region, causing the tourism season to extend and benefit from tourism income (Can, 2015: 7). In his study, Getz (1997) defined it as "planning, developing, and marketing activities as primary or secondary tourist attractions in order to maximize the number of tourists participating in the activities" (Can, 2015: 7).

It is very easy to reach information in the following days because we live in the information age. Countries also want to be more remarkable when marketing tourism products and they do some efforts for this (Tayfun and Aslan, 2013: 193). For this reason, some activities help create the brand image of countries or cities (Tayfun and Arslan, 2013: 194). Today, some cities are remembered with the events they organize. Events such as the Cannes Film Festival, the Rio Carnival, and the Berlin Film Festival are the events that have been organized, as well as the cities where they are organized, as well as the cities they have organized (Yıldırım et al., 2016: 51).

Event tourism has positive effects that they leave in the regions where they are organized, as well as negative effects. Levels of positive or negative effects of activities also vary according to the type, size, and destination of the organized activities (Can, 2015: 8).

People seek different activities in order to evaluate their leisure time outside their working life and other obligations. These activities are called recreational activities. Recreational activities carried out at home and recreational activities carried out far away from the house are divided into two activities: travel and tourism activities (Tribe, 2005; Metin et al., 2013).

Event tourism, as a great source of motivation to participate in tourism today, ensures that many tourism businesses are full at the end of the season or turns many destinations into tourism products. It not only provides economic benefits in the destinations, but also provides many environmental benefits such as infrastructure development (Can, 2015: 11).

14.5 ROLE OF EVENT TOURISM IN ECONOMIC DEVELOPMENT

The most important factor of the beginning, development, and spread of tourism activities is the formation of different cultures with civilizations (Alpagu and Koç, 2016: 157). To put it more simply, tourism is a civilization project that helps people develop culturally and raises people's level of welfare (Alpagu and Koç, 2016: 157). Migration from growing cities and villages to cities as a result of industrialization has formed today's metropolitan cities. People living in metropolitan cities want to get away from monotonous and boring city life and participate in relaxing and entertaining recreational activities (Can, 2015; Tel and Köksalan, 2008). It is known that tourism or recreational activities in which people participate or in different destinations increase the quality of life of people (Alpagu and Koç, 2016: 157). The technological and economic developments experienced in the last 50 and 60 years have created considerable changes in the development and implementation of the concept of tourism (Aydın, 2012; Emekli et al., 2006). Today, people have started to accept the idea of spending their free time in a different country or city (Alpagu and Koç, 2016: 157).

Event tourism attracts a great deal of attention by the tourists as it enables them to reach opportunities that they cannot encounter in their daily lives or experiences that are difficult to experience (Meydan Uğur and Çelik, 2010: 37). When tourists participate in an event tourism, they want to know the destination and its surroundings better and understand the philosophy underlying local activities (Meydan Uğur and Çelik, 2010: 37). Activities may differ in terms of the concepts they contain. In this case, the opportunity for people who have a special interest in the events organized is provided (Yıldırım et al., 2016: 52).

The concept of economic development has become a very important issue for developed or developing countries and has become an issue that all countries emphasize on (Ün et al., 2012: 345). The tourism sector has become the favorite sector of many countries due to its economic contribution to the countries. Tourism revenues help countries' economic development, development, and growth plans (Bahar, 2007: 2). When developing or underdeveloped countries are analyzed, the tourism sector, which is called flueless industry, is among the important development plans. When analyzed from this point of view, the economic effects of tourism in less developed agricultural countries can be observed more clearly than the effects in developed countries (Bahar, 2007: 3). The main reason for this is that, thanks to the tourism sector, the underdeveloped or developing countries facilitate reaching the conditions that will increase the level of welfare of the local people such as infrastructure development, employment opportunities, and foreign exchange (Gülbahar, 2009: 28).

Creating an image or creating a new brand is of great importance in terms of ensuring continuity in the marketing of goods and services. The concept of brand should not only be considered as reputation quality (Atay and Altınışık, 2017: 111). The concept of brand can be defined as all cases that evoke the motive of ownership in individuals (Altay and Altınışık, 2017; Ertuğrul and Demirkol, 2007). The concept of goods or services makes a difference by being an abstract concept in the tourism sector. For this reason, the brand understanding in the tourism sector also varies. Since the marketed services and goods are destinations and activities in the destinations, the phenomenon that needs to be branded must also be the destination (Atay and Altınışık, 2017: 111). Social, cultural, and economic factors are of great importance in the branding and growth of event tourism (Kişioğlu and Selvi, 2013: 73). In a study by Karagöz (2006), he pointed out that tourism, tourism created by event tourism, and the tourism activities remain alive outside the tourism season. Event tourism, which helps local people to raise their living standards by creating new income sources, contributes to the definition of the country due to its place in national and international media (Kişioğlu and Selvi, 2013: 73). Irshad (2011) pointed out that activity tourism and tourism can be kept alive for four seasons with the increase of tourists and thus the continuity of economic income. Looking across the world, the chimneyless industrial tourism sector, which corresponds to an average of 7.6% and provides job opportunities for over 210 million people in the world, is one of the largest and most important sectors in the world (Soyak, 2013: 2). According to the 2018 data of the WTO of the United Nations, world tourism revenues increased by 4% and reached $1.7 trillion.

There are three main reasons why job opportunities, which are the factors that affect the economic development positively or negatively, show rise or think (Beceren, 2003: 6):

- regional growth;
- a service that exists in one area develops faster in another area;
- tourist attractions are more diverse than other countries.

Based on the above reasons, it is possible to say that the activities organized in one destination are rapidly developing compared to other destinations, the image of the brand is formed, or the diversification of tourist attractions primarily contributes to the economy of the country with the foreign currency it has brought to the country in which it is included (Bahar, 2007: 6).

14.6 CONCLUSION

As it is known, the concept of development is a concept that increases the welfare levels of the societies. With this increase, countries act with the aim of increasing the economic inputs they obtain. Implemented in a planned manner, it has been an indispensable element for countries by applying it in many sectors. Development, which is a very important concept for the tourism sector, which is one of the most important income sources of the countries, has started to be mentioned together in line with the positive opportunities it creates and the economic income obtained by the country and its stakeholders. The concept of development is a phenomenon that emerged in order to ensure the development and progress of countries in economic, agricultural, social, and cultural sense (Adıgüzel, 2018: 35). As a result of this situation, the concept of development is of vital importance for the tourism sector. In addition to this, the tourism sector, which is called chimneyless industry, has become an inseparable whole for the development of countries.

With the growing competitive environment, development plans of the countries have started to be more comprehensive, different, and remarkable. Countries have created sustainable development plans to continue their development with the development. Thus, development has become a very important factor for a country's existing resources.

Event tourism is a type of tourism that has developed quite a lot in recent years. Many destinations have become an attractive element for tourists by using recreational activities in marketing strategies determined for differentiation and most importantly branding purposes (Can, 2015: 14). Event tourism, which has become a type of tourism chosen by many cities or countries thanks to its gains and positive perception, has enabled people to meet not only recreation but also the need to have fun in their spare time. The presence of many varieties of event tourism has given people the opportunity to choose, as well as the interest of tourists visiting the destination chosen with special attention, and their desire to leave more foreign currency.

It should not be forgotten that every individual has the freedom to travel. These travels benefit all tourism stakeholders, not only the tourists who travel. These benefits can be listed as rest and entertainment for tourists, development of infrastructure for local people, increased employment opportunities, promotion to the country, economic gain, and increased welfare of the society. As a result, more contribution should be made to the development of event tourism, which is included in the tourism sector, which plays a major role in the development of countries, and attention should be paid to the sustainability of the organized tourist activities.

KEYWORDS

- tourism
- event tourism
- economic development
- touristic development

REFERENCES

Adıgüzel, B. (2018). Sustainable tourism development, tourism stakeholders, Ayder. *Gazi University Journal of Tourism Faculty*, *1*, 34–54.

Akten, M., and Akten, S. (2011). A model approach to determination of recreational potentials: Gülez method: I. In: *National Sarigol District and Its Values Symposium*, Sarıgöl, Turkey, February 19, 2011.

Alkin, E. (2008). *Introduction to Economics, (11–20 Units)*, İ. Şıklar and T.C. Anadolu, (Eds.), 7th ed. University Publication No: 1472, Open Education Faculty Publication No: 785, Anatolian University Publications.

Alpagu, H., and Koç, E. (2016). The methods that measuring the economic impacts of tourism. *Journal of Information Economics and Management*, *6* (1), 157–164.

Arndt, H. W. (1981). Economic development: A semantic history. *Economic Development and Cultural Change*, 29, 3.

Aslan, A. (2008). An econometric analysis on economic growth and tourism. *Turkey Erciyes University Journal of Social Sciences*, 24, 1–11.

Atay, L. and Altınışık, Ö. (2017). The influence of events on destination branding: Çanakkale-Battles 100th Anniversary Events Case. *Journal of Social Sciences and Humanities Researches*, 19(40), 110–128.

Aydın, O. (2012). Top 5 countries in the eu's rural tourism and rural tourism in Turkey. *KMU Social and Economics Research Journal*, 14 (23), 39–46.

Bahar, O. (2007). The place and economic importance of tourism sector in regional development. *Journal of Muğla University Social Sciences Institute*, 19, 1–19.

Beceren, E. (2003). ShiftShare approach in regional development analysis. *Journal of Süleyman Demirel University Faculty of Economics and Administrative Sciences*, 8(3), 27–48.

Bilgili, B., Yağmur, Ö. and Yazarkan, H. (2012). A research on the efficiency and efficiency of festivals as touristic products (Example of Erzurum-Oltu Kırdağ Festival). *International Journal of Social and Economic Sciences*, 2(2), 117–124.

Bozkurt, E. and Topçuoğlu, Ö. (2013). Relationship Between economic growth and tourism in Turkey. *Gumushane University Electronic Journal of Social Sciences*, 7, 91–105.

Braden, P. V. and Louse W. (1980). *Bringing travel, tourism and culturel resource activities in harmony with regional economic development: Tourism marketing and management issues.* Washington, DC: George Washington Üniversity.

Brauch, H. G. (2008). Reconceptualizing security: Conceptual quartet of peace, security, development and environment. *Internationalrelations*, 5(18), 1–47.

Bulin, D., Stanciulescu G., and ve Calaretu B., (2012). Stakeholders engagement for sustainable tourism. In: *International Conference of Business Excellence*.

Can, E. (2015). The relation among leisure time, recreation and event tourism. *İstanbul Journal of Social Sciences*, 10, 1–17.

Chalip, L., and Costa, C. (2005). Sport event tourism and the destination brand: towards a general theory. *Sport in Society*, 8(2), 218–237.

Crockett, S. R., and Wood, L. J. (1999). Brand Western Australia: A totally integrated approach to destination branding. *Journal of Vacation Marketing*, 5, 276–289.

Çeken, H. (2008). A theoretical study into effect of tourism on regional development. *Afyon Kocatepe University Journal of Faculty of Economics and Administrative Sciences*, 10(2), 293–306.

Demirayak, F., (2002), Biodiversity-nature conservation and sustainable development, *Tübitak Vision 2023 Project Prepared for the Environment and Sustainable Development Panel*.

Emekli, G., İbrahimov, A., and Soykan, F. (2006). Geographical perspectives on globalization of tourism and the situation of Turkey. *Aegean Geographical Journal*, 15, 1–16.

Ergün, T., and Çobanoğlu, N. (2012). Sustainable development and environmental ethics. *Journal of Ankara University Institute of Social Sciences*, 3(1), 97–123.

Ertuğrul, S., and ve Demirkol, Ş. (2007). Branding and its importance in touristic product demand. *Journal of Social Sciences*, 2, 61–70.

Eryılmaz, S. S., and H. Cengiz, Mega (2012). The economic impacts of mega events upon the Host City, The Sample of Formula 1, *Sigma*, 4, 77–96.

Flammang, R. A. (1979). Economic growth and economic development: Counterparts or competitors? In: *Economic Development and Cultural Change*. Chicago, IL: University of Chicago Press, 28(1), 47–61.

Getz, D. (1997). *Event Management and Event Tourism*. New York: Cognizant Communication Corporation.
Getz, D. (2008). Event tourism: Definition, evolution and research. *Tourism Management, 29*(2), 403–428.
Giritoğlu, İ., Olcay, A., and Özekici, Y. K. (2015). Segmentation of festival events as a tourism diversity: A review on Turkey. *Ordu University Journal of Social Sciences Research, 5*(13), 306–323.
Gladwin, T. N., Kennelly, J. J., and Krause, T. S. (1995). Shgifting paradigms for sustainable development: Implications for management theory and research. *Academy of Management Review, 20*(4), 874–907.
Gülbahar, O. (2009). Troubleshooting role in regional disparities tourism (Turkey Case). *Journal of Economics and Administrative Sciences, 23*(1), 19–47.
Gürlük, S. (2010). Is sustainable development applicable in developing countries? *Journal of Eskişehir Osmangazi University Faculty of Economics and Administrative Sciences, 5*(2), 85–99.
Gürsoy, D., Kim, K., and Uysal, M. (2004). Perceived impacts of festivals and special events by organizers: An extension and validation. *Tourism Management, 25*(2), 171–181.
Güzel, P. Çoknaz, D., and Atalay, N. M. (2009). Environmental aspects of sustainable development under the International Olympic Committee (IOC) and Olympic organizations. *Hacettepe Journal of Sport Sciences, 20*(2), 59–69.
Haris, J. M. (2000). Basic principles of sustainable development: Global development and environment institute, Working Paper 00-04.
Holzner, M. (2011). Tourism and economic development: The beach disease? *Tourism Management, 32*, 922–933.
Huang, J. Z., Li, M., and Cai, L. A. (2010). A model of community based festival image. *International Journal of Hospitality Management, 29*(2), 254–260.
Irshad, H. (2011). Impacts of community events and festivals on rural places. Rural Development Division Alberta Agriculture and Rural Development.
Jımenez, I. C. (2008). Which type of tourism matters to the regional economic growth? The cases of Spain and Italy. *International Journal of Tourism Research, 10*, 127–139.
Karagöz, D. (2006). Events tourism and events tourism in the context of the economic impact of foreign visitor spending: 2005 Formula 1 Grand Prix of Turkey case. Unpublished master thesis. Anadolu University Institute of Social Sciences, Eskişehir, Turkey.
Kınacı, B., Albuz, P., N., and Seyhan, G. (2011). *Tourism and Environment (Environmental Protection)*. Ankara, Turkey: Pegem Academy.
Kim, K., and Uysal, M. (2012). Perceived socio-economic impacts of festivals and events among organizers. *Journal of Hospitality and Leisure Marketing, 10*(3–4), 159–171.
Kim, S. S., Prideaux, B., and Chon, K. (2010). A comparison of results of three statistical methods to understand determinants of festival participants' expenditures. *International Journal of Hospitality Management, 29*(2), 297–307.
Kişioğlu, E., and Selvi, M. S. (2013). The impact of local events on destınatıon ımage of Tekirdağ: An assessment ın terms of local shareholders. *IAAOJ, Social Science, 1*(1), 68–102.
Kozak, M. A., and Bahçe, S. (2009), *Special Interest Tourism*. Ankara, Turkey: Detay Publishing.
Kuş Şahin, C., Akten S., and Erol, U.E. (2009). A study to determine recreational participation tendency of the eğirdir vocational school students. *Artvin Çoruh University Faculty of Forestry Journal, 10*(1), 62–71.

Küçükoğlu, M., Taş, H. Y., and Ercan, H. (2018). The role and importance of transfer spendings in turkey within the understanding of social state. *International Journal of Community Research*, *9*(16), 2618–2653.

Künü, S., Hopoğlu, S., Sökmen Gürçam, Ö., and Güneş, Ç., (2015), Tourism-regional development relationship: A research on eastern black sea region. *Iğdır Universit Journal of Social Sciences*, *7*, 71–93.

Lee, I., and ve Arcodia, C. (2011). The role of regional food festivals for destination branding. *International Journal of Tourism Research*, *13*(4), 355–367.

Meydan Uğur, S., and Çelik, A. (2010). A research on determining perceived socioeconomic impacts of event tourism at destination of Istanbul. *Journal of Faculty of Business*, *11*(1), 35–50.

Nixson, F., (1984). Economic development: Utopian ideal or historical process. *METU Studies in Development*, *11*, 1–2.

Prentice, R., and Andersen, V. (2003). Festival as creative destination. *Annals of Tourism Research*, *30*(1), 7–30.

Ryan, C. (1991). *Recreational Tourism: A Social Science Perspective*. Newyork: Routledge.

Schubert, S. F., Brada J. G., and Risso, W. A. (2011). The impacts of international tourism demand on economic growth of small economies dependent on tourism. *Tourism Management*, *32*, 377–385.

Smith, A. (1985). *Wealth of Nations*, Translators Yunus, A. and Bakırcı, M. Istanbul, Turkey: Alan Publishing.

Soyak, M. (2013). The recent trends in the international tourism and the evolution of tourism policies in Turkey. *The Journal of Marmara Social Research*, *4*, 1–18.

Şengül, S., and Genç, K. (2016). Use of regional cuisine as a supportive product within the scope of festival tourism: A study on mudurnu silk road culture art and tourism festival. *Pamukkale University Journal of Social Sciences Institute*, *23*, 79–89.

Taban S., and Kar, M. (2014). *Development Economy*. Bursa, Turkey: Ekin Publishing.

Tassiopoulos, D. (2005). *Event Management: A Professional And Developmental Approach*, 2nd ed. Cape Town, South Africa: Juta Academic.

Tayfun, A., and Arslan, E. (2013). An investigation on satisfaction of domestic tourist from Ankara shopping fest under the tourism of festival. *Journal of Business Studies*, *5*(2), 191–206.

Tel, M., and Köksalan, B. (2008). Sociological investtigation of sport activities of lecturers (East Anatolian Sample). *Fırat University Journal of Social Science*, *18*(1) 261–278.

Tıraş, H. H. (2012). Sustainable development and environment: An Examine. *Theory Journal of Kahramanmaraş Sütçü İmam University Faculty of Economics and Administrative Sciences*, *2*, 57–73.

Ün, E., Tutar. F., Tutar. E., and Erkay. Ç, (2012). The role of rural tourism in economic development: Example of Turkey. In: *International Conference on Eurasian Economies*, *4*, 345–350.

Wilson, M. (2003). Corporate sustainability; What is it and where does it come from? *Ivey Business Journal*, 1–5.

World Tourism Organization (WTO) (1996). Agenda 21 for the Travel and Tourism Industry. Erişim: http://www.worldtourism.org/sustainable/doc/a21-def.pdf

World Tourism Organization (WTO) (1998). Guide For Local Authorities On Developing Sustainable Tourism. Madrid: World Tourism Organization.

World Tourism Organization (WTO) (2018). Erişim Tarihi: 14. 02. 2020 https://www.eunwto.org/doi/pdf/10.18111/9789284421152

Yavilioğlu, C. (2002). The semantic history of the concept of the development and its conceptual origins. *Cumhuriyet University Journal of Economics and Administrative Sciences*, *3*(1), 59–77.

Yıldırım, O., Karaca, O. B., and Çakıcı C. (2016). A research on the perceptions and satisfaction of local people on "Adana, International Orange Blossom Carnival." *Journal of Travel and Hospitality Management, 13*(2), 50–68.

Yıldız, Z. (2011). Development of tourism sector and its effects on employment. *Suleyman Demirel University The Journal of Visionary, 3*(5), 54–71.

Yoon, Y. S., Lee, J. S., and Lee, C. K. (2010). Measuring festival quality and value affecting visitor's satisfaction and loyalty using a structural approach. *International Journal of Hospitality Management, 29*, 335–342.

CHAPTER 15

ROLE OF HOST COMMUNITIES IN INDIGENOUS CULTURAL EVENTS AND TOURISM INTERACTIONS: CHALLENGES TOWARD IMAGING THE EVENT LOCATED AT LITTLE-KNOWN DESTINATIONS

SAMIK RAY

RLG, Department of Tourism (Government of India), Eastern Region, Kolkata 700071, India E-mail: samikray331@gmail.com

ABSTRACT

Indigenous cultural events are primordially rooted within the indigenous sociocultural fabric of community identity. In tourism, it is a niche attraction and often subsumed within the sets of niche tourism offers. Among 5As (attraction, accommodation, access, amenity, activity), attraction is the most crucial since it is the major motivator of present-day tourism and a significant driver for destination and tourism product imaging. Indigenous cultural event in a virgin and authentic format appears to be the most potential tourist attraction when contemporary holiday trend seeks an authentic experience in contact with locals at visitation state. It could maintain its authenticity and virginity when it is located at a little-known destination. Yet, it has not registered high demand as an attraction offer compared to other niche choices. Appropriate imaging is required to increase its attractiveness in the tourism market. As a natural inheritor and bearer of event, indigenous native hosts play a significant role in imaging. Neither industry nor academics pay much attention to those events, but its significance in tourism practice cannot be denied; thus, it demands attention. Consequently, indigenous cultural events' imaging and the role of indigenous natives toward imaging register only a little attention. Discourses over tourism-potentials of indigenous cultural events located at the little-known destination and its imaging are need of the hour. Thus, this chapter deals with the concept of indigenous cultural events, its interaction with tourism, its significance toward sustainable development of the little-known destination, the importance of imaging to establish its tourism potential, and the role of indigenous native hosts in this regard.

15.1 INTRODUCTION

Traveling is an ever-present phenomenon in civilization's timeline. The fact of traveling is the only substantial link between early migration for food gathering and contemporary tourism. A shift from those early impulses to the urge of exploring any cultural novelties, including indigenous events in the late pre-Christian era, could be the earliest connection between tourism and culture. Recently, cultural content has become a significant tourism driver. Experiencing indigenous culture and events on holiday is of late development too though indigenous locations experienced several imperialist encounters since the pre-Christian era, before and after Alexander III of Macedon, and also turned to be well-beaten locations with repeated expeditions and visits by traders, adventurers, missionaries, colonialists, and enthusiast scholars over the ages.

Since the 1980s, indigenous locations began to experience frequent interactions with strangers in hundreds or thousands. With the growing demand for "authentic" or "off-the-beaten" experience on holiday or travel, indigenous tourism practice set out to crawl utterly in sheer association with aboriginal/native/ethnic tourism, but gains a reputation as niche tourism practice quite lately, not before few decades. Trends to define principle, standard, promotional initiatives at indigenous destinations began only in the 21st century with Aboriginal Tourism Team Canada, Aboriginal Tourism Association of Canada, The World Indigenous Tourism Alliance, Indigenous Tourism of British Columbia, New Zealand's Maori Tourism Society, PATA, and others. The World Tourism Organization also has accepted its importance putting indigenous tourism promotion high on the international agenda (Favilla, 2017).

Neither indigenous tourism nor its offer, indigenous cultural event, has high appeal yet in the tourism market compared to other niche choices as indigenous destinations are mostly little known, isolated, remotely located, and hardly able to assure common holiday needs like relaxation and indulgence. Hence, most of the indigenous cultural events' destinations, particularly in Asia, are either denied to be a tourist location or have too low appeal in tourism.

15.2 A QUEST FOR A PRAGMATIC SENSE OF INDIGENOUS

Indigenous, as an idea, was known since the use of the classical Greek term "Pelasgians" for forerunner, ancient, original, primitive people. With the colonial ventures and interventions, it entered into a new semantic domain. Cultural and racial differences from the colonials led colonized described as native, aboriginals, wild, nomad, inferior, underdeveloped, uncivilized, and lately indigenous. Semantically indigenous overlaps "native" and "aboriginal" when perceived as original to the land, contrary to late settlers. Postcolonial outlook specifies indigenous as originally settled community at any destination having deep-rooted empathy and affinity to their land, culture, and nature and often affected or marginalized socioeconomically, culturally, and politically by colonials or mainstream societies who impose hegemony over them. The term is currently used to qualify and specify about 370 million populace belong to 5000 different groups, their culture, society, language, law, right, and, more recently, tourism at their destinations, but the description is loaded with variations due to the absence of a universally accepted parameter to define it.

This chapter will deal with both marginalized and nonmarginalized indigenous communities who either inhabit within an ancestral territory or resettle outside and managed to survive with some of their original sociocultural traits amid globalized or colonial cultural allures. This chapter also includes natives and aboriginals who survive with ethnocultural distinction to encompass a pragmatic and broader description of indigenous.

15.3 INDIGENOUS CULTURAL EVENTS

15.3.1 WHAT IT OUGHT TO BE

Indigenous cultural event enquiries are often subsumed either within cultural event study or under indigenous event research, hardly combined in one study. Interdisciplinary approaches toward "indigenous and culture" or "event and culture" were also evident but scarcely. Research on events and cultural issues is notably a post-colonial trend while over indigenous issues is a recent development, not more than few decades, although missionaries, civil servants, surveyors, scholars of the colonial period put effort to explore indigenous sociocultural, economic, political system (Haimendorf, 1943, 1945, 1947, 1948; Verrier 1944, 1947; Hunter, 1868, 1880; Mann, 1867; Scott, 1794) at the behest of colonial hegemony with strong colonially biased and subjective attitude describing indigenous populace and their system arbitrarily as native, ignorant, backward, and aboriginal. Recent studies of Finlayson (1991), Hinch and Butler (1996), Cohen (1996), Zeppel (1998, 2001), Aramberri (2002), Blundell (2002), Xie (2003), Small and Edwards (2003), Gursoy et al. (2004), Chang (2006), Kerber (2006), Fuller et al. (2007), and Phipps and Slater (2010) are relevant to contemporary perspective and, thus, quite significant.

When an event is shared and perceived as the unique communal and cultural identity by an indigenous community itself and performed within an ancestral territory, it can be mentioned as an indigenous cultural event. It is primordially rooted within the indigenous cultural behavior. Thus, the community sets to be distinguished and separated from other cultures (Weber, 1968). Indigenous event is a significant collective pleasurable cultural display (Quinn, 2009, Janiskee, 1980) toward communal creativity (Turner, 1982) or a creative spend of social space and time to become socialized (Ray, 2019). It encapsulates community identity (Matheson, 2005), and renews the community life-stream periodically (Falassi, 1987).

15.3.2 ASIAN PERCEPTION

Hosting indigenous cultural events such as festivals, fairs, and competitive games across Asia is evident through centuries thus are neither accidental nor an abrupt episode. Its significances lay together in trade, sociocultural, entertainment, and ethnic identity values. Those events emerged as an agent of creative socialization offering periodic opportunities to the indigenous multitude to show affinity with tradition or become socialized and precisely directed to focus over specific intangible cultural objective though overt intent is largely a social gathering for entertainment, trading, sociocultural events, and religious happenings. Participation in events then turns to be a necessity and glorious social act to Asian indigenous (Ray, 2019).

Asian indigenous events are organized to commemorate different occasions and needs of communal life. For example, some festivals mark the change of harvest season such as Gawai of Dayak community (Borneo and Sarawak of Malaysia), Tadau Ka'amatan of Kadazan-Dusuns (Sabah, Malaysia), Mizos' Pawl Kut (Mizoram, India), and Nongkrem of Khasis (Meghalaya, India). Similarly, Mopin and Solung (Arunachal Pradesh, India) are agriculture-oriented events. Mopin is a celebration of the harvesting season, indigenous to the Galo people, while Solung is for harvest in abundance, original to the Adi community. Religious rituals are the core part of those celebrations irrespective of motivations like commemorating successes at harvesting or seeking better produces. Cultural performances reflecting their unique ethnic identity are organized at the event for creative recreation and socialization. It appears strongly in Adis' Solung and Mizos' Pawl Kut. Moreover, Mizos involve in hunting and fishing during Pawl Kut. In Mooncake or Lantern festival, the indigenous Chinese peasant populace commemorates their historical victory over Mongolian warlords and celebrates the success in harvesting. Thus two diverse motives mingle together. Ka Shad Suk Mynsiem of Khasis, Sume Gerilak of Bondas (Odisha, India), and Thaipusam of Tamil indigenous (Malaysia) are primarily religious festivals, whereas Thai New Year and Bengalee New year of Bangladesh and West Bengal of India are overtly secular but somewhat linked to religious rituals. Male'an Sampi (Lombok, Indonesia), a cattle race event, and Kila Raipur Sports event (Punjab, India), known as rural Olympic, are examples of the sports competition event, while Tattooing Festival at Wat Bang Phra (Thailand), Bali Arts Festival (Indonesia), and Myoko Music Festival of Apatani community (Ziro, India) are typically indigenous art events. Bhutan's Tshechu is indigenous to the land of Dragon or National Happiness, apparently religious but functionally an event of local trading and socialization leading to create national bonding across the country. Livestock fairs are common in Asian indigenous culture, and its significance is located primarily in communities' economic subsistence linked to ethnic identity since the indigenous economy principally runs on agriculture and farming. Livestock fairs of Sonepur, Nagaur, Jhalawar, Pushkar, Kolayat, Agra, Gangapur, and Birur (India) offer scope for business socialization. Indeed, trading together with opportunities to enjoy folk music and dances, magic shows, races, jugglery, fire-eating, sword-swallowing, stilt-walkers, gambling, wrestling, animal fights, and pilgrimage to sacred lake or confluence push the buyers, sellers, and visitors to come to fairs with family, relatives, friends, and neighbors. Asian indigenous cultural events are periodical, occur at a traditional venue set aside, and, thus, get social sanctions. The length of events varies too. While Bengali New Year day is a daylong event, Sekrenyi festival of Angami community (Nagaland, India) lasts for 10 days and Bali Art Festival goes for a month.

15.3.3 TYPOLOGICAL FRAME: WHERE TO BE PLACED!

Event management, tourism, and cultural studies often delve into event typologies using varied parameters. Among widely accepted genres planned events receive substantial scholastic attention. Unplanned events do not get any attention, as they are not relevant to event management theory and practice. As per variation in magnitude, demand, value, size, scope, and tourism significance, planned events are categorized into Mega, Hallmark, Major, and Local types. Structuring events into cultural, political, art and entertainment, business, science and education, sporting, recreational, private categories based on form or content, purpose, and program parameters divulge a new dimension in categorization spectrum (Getz, 2000, 2005, 2008; Oklobdžija et al., 2015). The geopolitical parameter is also used to divide events into international, national, regional, provincial, and local types. The portfolio approach (Getz, 2008) classifies events vertically based on principles of hierarchy in events' value, demand, economic implication, and credential for destination image building.

Since categorization approaches focus only on mainstream or upper-crust events, defining indigenous cultural events is very difficult. It becomes critical when happenings are traditionally periodic, indigenous calendar oriented, destination and community specific, and emblematic to their affinity toward land and culture. Thereby, indigenous events neither are unplanned nor match the planned events' perception found in those approaches. Indigenous cultural events are usually described as the local with low demand, low market value (Ruhanen et al., 2013), and yet economically least beneficial since those events are community-directed, small by magnitude and size, located mostly at little-known destinations and not yet placed in existing world tourism maps.

Pride for community tradition makes the events available as virgin and authentic that set forth enormous tourism potential and a huge impact on destination's image and attractiveness in the growing contemporary trend of seeking authentic experience on travel or holiday. Further, indigenous cultural events cannot be placed at a lower level of event class hierarchy as they geopolitically belong to the local type. Since overlapping with conventional event categories by nature, theme, focus, participants' character, and value is common, placing indigenous cultural event within the above said typological formats would be difficult.

15.4 INDIGENOUS CULTURAL EVENTS AND TOURISM INTERACTION

15.4.1 AN IMPRESSION

Tourism's interactions with culture, event, and indigenous contents are interdependent for mutual sustenance and subsistence, which is a historical fact too. Those contents, in disjunction or conjunction, attract and motivate travelers and play the role of the destination imaging agent over the ages but, importance of indigenous cultural events is yet to be understood by industries and academics.

Variations within indigenous cultural events are apparent but never exist in absolute terms. Program blending and overlapping are thereby frequent. Hence, indigenous religious ceremonies often appear with fair and artistic expressions such as in Thaipusam and Tshechu, sports competitions with fairs such as in Kila Raipur, and fairs with sports and performing arts such as in Puskar. The growth of tourism primarily depends on attraction potentials. The indigenous cultural event could be the best offer for any niche tourism varieties when seeking specialized services and activities with authentic and creative socialization experience on holiday is the trend. The niche features and uniqueness of those events could become a strong tourism motivation amid new trends. When attraction choices or offers in some measure converge, distinguishing niche varieties cannot be validated. It becomes apparent when at indigenous destinations event tourism focuses on all sorts of indigenous cultural events, cultural tourism on all tangible and intangible indigenous cultural contents including events, indigenous tourism on indigenous events, culture, people including natives and aboriginals as a center of attraction. Most varieties of indigenous events are perceived as cultural when organized, accumulated, learned, and shared through community experience traditionally (Davies, 1976; Giner, 1972) and communal interrelationships (Ray, 2008, 2017a, 2017b). Therefore, tourism ventures at indigenous destinations could be named after any niche variety or as indigenous-cultural-event-based tourism. The second nomenclature is more precise as indigenous cultural events are the principal attraction offer, a tourist motivator, and an opportunity for high tourist spends at an indigenous destination.

15.4.2 DEMAND–SUPPLY PERSPECTIVE

Interaction between indigenous cultural events and tourism is the demand–supply perspective dependent. These events do not yet register high demand as the major tourism attraction or offer (Ryan and Huyton, 2000a, 2000b, 2002), but as a subset of varied niche tourism attractions generate some demand. Event locations and motivations have a direct bearing on demand generations. Events located at remote and little-known destinations register either at very low or zero demand, while it would be a bit higher if its location is a known place or near to that. Motivations like keen interest in indigenous life and culture or off-the-beaten cultural experience, are open to creating demand for indigenous cultural event experiences. Only cultural adventurists and researchers take tours with those motivations. Demand and scopes of interaction are directly proportional to each other.

The travelers prefer visiting known destinations where supplies against holiday demands like relaxation and indulgence, facilities to contact home, trouble-free access, tourist-friendly environment, competence to understand and reciprocate verbal commands, and any other professional requirements are unchallenged. Experiences of visiting those events in little-known destinations are extremely seasonal, strange, and crude because events are cyclic and periodical, host communities are still virgin, and space for an overnight stay near to event site is barely basic. All those supply-side constraints limit the scope of interaction.

15.4.3 GUEST–HOST PERSPECTIVE

Guests neither are residents nor tourism entrepreneurs. They visit an unknown, strange, sometimes mystic land and culture for a temporary period, return to home with memories and mementoes, and left behind a cultural shock, a surprise for the indigenous hosts. Hence, both guests and the majority of indigenous hosts perceive each other as strange. Interaction between indigenous cultural events and tourism occurs within the context of such bizarre gazing.

Most visitors of indigenous cultural event seek unique, off-the-wall, and authentic experience. One could get this experience while interacting in contact with the community or connecting the traditional bearers of the event. Nature of experiences gained out of interaction at visitation is conditioned to travel intention, travel span, and type and volume of contacts and connects. When intentions are just casual curiosities and the travel span is short, interaction turns to be brief and casual based on temporary contact with hosts and their culture. Experiences thereby become highly superficial and caged in casual photographs, subjective to guests' preconceived notions or information gathered while gazing at an event at a distance. It would be less superficial when the intention is gathering knowledge and experiencing off-the-beaten events. The impression about event and community are gathered at brief interactions with selective locals while gazing at the event and staying overnights in a friendly and admiring atmosphere. If visitors come for benevolence or economic contribution to community-causes interaction turns to be sympathetic, and experiences obtained from the above with a superiority feeling highlighting socioeconomic inconveniences of the community. If purposes are 'learning and discovery,' research or study, and adventure or volunteering, overnight stay will be longer and interaction turns to be emotive, affinitive, supportive, and participatory directing to connect the community by heart. Experience and impression of visit taken back become more authentic and balanced tilting to objective interpretation.

15.4.4 HOSTS' ROLE IN INTERACTION

Precisely, hosts are destinations' indigenous residents, inheritors, and traditional bearers of all communal cultural traits, including events. The existence of the nonindigenous population at locations is usual as exclusively indigenous destinations such as the land of Jarawas (Andaman Islands, India) are rare. The opportunity to interact with visitors is open to both groups. Interaction usually begins with the arrival of visitors, continues all through the visitation while experiencing the event; using facilities or amenities; consumption of services in need or on demand, and ends with their departure. Indigenous cultural events at remote and little-known locations are usually impeded by infrastructural constraints, thus makes the guest experience unpleasant. In this perspective, hosts' friendly attitude and satisfactory interpretation about any limitations that a place bears can turn guests' unpleasant experience into memorable ones. Thus, friendly service inputs and substantial interpretation about anything and everything of the community from local hosts together can portray a strong image of destination, community, and event within the mind of visitors. It may ensure repeat visits and better image creation. Thus it promotes the place among infinite numbers of potential consumers. The habit of experience sharing in the post-consumption stage also creates an enormous visiting urge among the people with whom experiences are shared. Images formed by hosts play a crucial role in pulling the tourists, destination positioning (Kotler, et al, 1993), events' promotion, and strengthening the interaction between tourism and indigenous cultural event.

15.5 IMAGING

15.5.1 TOURISM PERSPECTIVE

Imaging a destination and its attractions is a portrayal process or psychological construct (Reynolds, 1965). Images are constructed based on information and impression (Echtner and Ritchie, 1991, 2003) stimuli or inputs received from varied sources. It becomes crucial in the tourism perspective as portrayals reveal the potentials of the destination, its people, culture, and other attractions as tourism commodity and create demand within the potential market or among curious and interested to visit and experience events (Ray, 2018). Imaging is a dynamic process, takes place in pre-visit, visitation, and post-visit state, and continues perpetually till the destination and its attractions could pull tourists toward sustainable economic regeneration.

Imaging, not as a term, but as a process, was prevalent even in the ancient military or trading strategies. Attractions such as fairs, festivals, and sports competitions as is found in Olympic also contributed to creating images of events and locations since the early days. Records of expeditions, voyages, adventure, and missionary or emissary experiences too contributed significantly toward imaging a destination and its attraction since the 4th or 5th century BCE. Writing of Xenophon, Lucian of Samosata, Pausanias, Faxian, Xuanzang, Itzing, Ibn Jubayr, Ibn Battuta, Coryat, and Cook are notable in this regard. Colonialists too involve in mapping the image of colonized destinations to establish their hegemony over the colonies' resource potentials. Indeed, all those early efforts are external stimuli (Dann, 1977; Kotler, 1982) to the cognition process of acquiring information and impressions toward destination imaging (Ray, 2018). Destinations' images received from those earlier inputs may contradict or barely corroborate the contemporary portrayal. Thus they are dynamic. Impression or perceptions of contemporary visitor, host, and travel trade personnel thereby turn to be crucial in imaging (Ferrario, 1979; Ritchie and Zins, 1978; Wee et al. 1985; Phelps, 1986; Embacher and Buttle, 1989; Gartner and Shen, 1992; Illum and Schaefer, 1995; Bramwell and Rawding, 1996; Baloglu, 1997; Chaudhary, 2000).

15.5.2 AGENTS OF DESTINATION IMAGING

Imaging agents play the role of image construction (Alhemoud and Armstrong, 1996; Bramwell and Rawding, 1996; Court and Lupton, 1997; Gartner, 1993; Gunn, 1972; Murphy, 1999; Selby and Morgan, 1996; Young, 1999). Tourism connection or residential status is not a prerequisite (Ray, 2018) for it. At the pre-visit stage, visitors initially get acquainted with indigenous cultural events and their location from earlier records, previous visitors' experiences, and tour companies' promotions which are secondary agents and secondary inputs. Those inputs or facts often mingle with agents' subjective impressions and interpretations. Sometimes, it turns into a touristic-fact by purposeful edit and modification to suit the intention of making attraction or destination a commodity. Hence, the authenticities of secondary images raise debate. It could be best tested only at the visitation to reveal contradictions between those inputs and impressions created at visit through senses of the visitor or out of inputs transmitted by the locals. Images obtained at visitation are thereby primary (Phelps, 1986) and usually constructed by creator senders (Ray, 2018) or generator transmitters. At the post-visit stage, images are recreated by visitors based on inputs received in interaction with the hosts and subjective interpretation of what visitors sensed while gazing. Recreated images are transmitted to the rest of the world through different modes of sharing.

So, agents are either primary or secondary image formation agents. As the authentic impression of communities, events, and destinations' 5As is the desired goal of visits the role of primary image formation agents turns crucial. Principally, local hosts and visitors can form it. Secondary agents can do the same if their portrayals become objective and authentic. Previous visitors, irrespective of their profession or amateur activities and tourism agents neither acquainted with indigenous culture nor native, belong to the secondary image formation agent category. Locals who are primary imaging agents and belong to the destination side did not receive much attention in typology studies (Gartner,1993), although their role in authentic imaging is crucial.

15.5.3 ROLE OF HOST COMMUNITY

An entire lot of residents at any little-known indigenous cultural event destination is considered to be the host and primary imaging agent since destinations are scarcely populated in small areas and lacking professionalism. The significance of hosts' image-building role by qualitative and quantitative magnitude is precisely hierarchical (Ray, 2018). It is missing in the little-known destinations as the economy of those locations is not yet tourism-dependent and professionally organized guest services are hardly available there. Roles of all the hosts (indigenous natives, non-indigenous native, nonnative, and nonresident indigenous native), then, turn to be vital in image-building, then.

Hosts' involvement in imaging indigenous events and its locations spreads principally over three stages, from selection to post-visit state and contributions are restricted within the impacts over visitors at the visitation. Nonresident indigenous natives' role in imaging can be proactive at the selection state due to their strong geo-cultural attachment to the place but spatial alienation from homeland restricts their role within secondary image formation activity. Impressions conveyed by them about events, community, and home are either as reliable as the image portrayed by indigenous native residents or overrated and exaggerated. Hosting Chinese New Year and lantern festivals abroad by Chinese indigenous immigrants are examples of indirect proactive imaging as it could prompt potential visitors to decide to visit those events at its original locations. In the case of cultural genocide, underrating in their portrayal is natural. Cognitive distortion syndrome also led the portrayal to become unusual.

At visitation state, almost all the residents play somewhat role in imaging. Nonnatives and nonindigenous natives are culturally stranger to indigenous natives. The same feeling about indigenous natives is available among those two groups. Cultural difference makes nonnative and nonindigenous ardently curious and keen observers of indigenous life and events. They gaze the events from proximity for a considerable period. Consequently, portrayals made by them become more objective, unbiased, and authentic compared to habitual bearers. Indigenous communities of Austro-Asiatic origin inhabit with mainstream Odiyas in different parts of Orissa (India). Odiya inhabitants observed indigenous cultural events such as Chhow, Sume-Gelirak, Bija, Uli, or mango festivals for years from nearest vicinity and portrayed those events in different national and international media in the last few decades. Thus, many visitors from the country and abroad had visited those events in recent years. Sometimes, portrayal becomes biased and subjective when nonnatives and nonindigenous natives hold superiority feeling about their own culture. Despite contradictions over portrayal, act their role in primary image formation at the visitation state is undeniably crucial.

Indigenous native community is the most important among the hosts inhabit at destinations since they are the only authentic interpreters and bearers of indigenous traditions. Thus, inputs supplied by them become highly decisive in primary image construction and also to imaging indigenous destination and its cultural attractions. Variation in nature of participation divides indigenous native resident hosts into nonparticipant and direct and indirect participant groups. Nonparticipants are not linked to tourism benefits, either socially or economically. Yet, they convey varied information about their life and issues while coming across the guests expecting to get some way to resolve their issues or to raise it at an appropriate forum through visitors. In little-known indigenous destinations, such happenings are natural and frequent. Received information could be subjective or objective but not conditioned to vested concerns of tourism, thereby contribute to authentic image formation little by little. Indirect participants are not overtly linked to tourism, but they get somewhat benefited, maybe indirectly, when visitors come and generate additional income and revenue while using and buying artistic and nonartistic produces of the communities, spending for stay at indigenous native-run accommodations and transportation by locally used vehicles, and watching the indigenous cultural novelties including events. Indeed local art, craft, and produces certainly contribute to image differentiation and then positioning. In this regard, the roles of indirect participants such as artisans and farmers are vital in image formation.

Volumes of direct participation in tourism activity are typically low when the destination and its attractions are not well known, and organized tourism venture is hardly available. Experiences of visits to indigenous cultural events are highly intangible. Thus, visitors acquired it through interactions with locals and by gazing or self-sensing the events at the visitation. In addition, cognition is well dependent on interpretations of direct participants about indigenous cultural contents and codes of events as they bear it through generations. Direct participants construct or shape visitors' primary experience at the visit and eradicate contradictions between primary and secondary images. When the focus of the visit is an indigenous cultural event, comprehensive imaging of the event and its destination is conditioned to periodicity, frequency, and total temporal length of contacts with direct participants and depth of connects to them. In little-known indigenous event destinations, visitors establish frequent contacts with the service providers of food outlets and accommodations, local assistants, guide interpreters of indigenous origin, and key performers at events. Actually, during stay and visit to events, only those direct participants came to be known to visitors. Hence, their role in shaping the impression and image is most crucial.

15.6 CHALLENGES

Imaging indigenous cultural event poses a challenge because event experience is highly intangible, destinations are little known, organized tourism services are barely present, and hosts are principally innocent and professionally ignorant. Hosting indigenous cultural events across Asia is common for centuries. Most events are organized, performed, participated in, observed, and experienced by the community themselves. Footfalls of the outer world at the events are hardly evident, thus not located in tourism maps but sometimes are placed as a little-known destination in demographic, cultural, population, and general-purpose maps. Contrarily, all those events have enormous tourism potentials when demand for an authentic experience in contact with hosts on tour grows fast.

Tourism within the carrying capacity limit is a sustainable developmental tool. Bhutan is one among few destinations, which have promoted sustainable indigenous Tshechu event in the tourism market with success controlling visitors flow within carrying capacity limit. On the contrary, increasing footfalls of tourists at the Puskar fair or uncontrolled tourism at Kumbha or Gangasagar fair becomes a concern in sustainability respect. It is not yet an issue for indigenous cultural events at little-known destinations with limited or rare tourist footfalls. In the context of high tourism growth and development, the potential transformation of a little-known destination to a known tourism location counts only upon a time. The indigenous community is the year-round users of destination resources. So, sustainable tourism practice at little-known destination would be best understood by the community. Appropriate imaging of indigenous cultural event and control over tourist footfalls ensuring a balance between promotion and sustainable practices is a challenge to them.

Appropriate imaging is primarily conditioned to authentic and in-depth cognition of event and 5As of destination. Imaging agents have to form such images as they transfer the same to the outer world. At little-known indigenous destinations, cognition becomes difficult due to local hosts' ignorance of tourism knowledge and prejudices or myths about events that hosts obtained through locally developed common beliefs. It also happens due to inferiority or superiority feelings about self-culture. Visitors' impression, thus, becomes pseudo, inaccurate, fallacious, and imprecise. Eventually, it would affect the image of the destination and its event. Lack of general education and tourism service perception creates a pseudo image.

Most indigenous people are usually a bit suspicious about tourism since they perceived the tourists as intruders. Thus they fail to understand tourism's development potentials. Lack of education and little exposure to the outer world are other constraints in this regard. Once they felt that tourism is an additional income tool, the entire indigenous community wished to be involved in guests' services, irrespective of their competence. Visitors then become confused and develop polar opposite impressions out of contradictory service and knowledge inputs. Altogether, it affects proactive imaging. The absence of enough education, tourism training, and organized tourism activity make this happen.

It is believed that understandings which come from indigenous hosts are authentic since they are the traditional bearers of community culture but contribute either little or zero value toward proactive imaging if service inputs and messages conveyed to visitors are unorganized and placed with subjective interpretations. Usually, objective portrayal becomes a challenge to them as they are neither experts in the subjects nor keen observers of self-culture.

Above all, visitors' impressions grow of interactions with the hosts through a common language known to both. Inability to communicate in the local language bars the visitors to interact with a whole lot of locals. Hence, visitors try to communicate with local hosts who only can convey all the messages through a common language distinctly. Thus, visitors during visit spend most of the time with those faces to form and shape images about the event and its location that they take back. Indeed, discovering such a person at a little-known indigenous destination is a big challenge. Moreover, imaging is also challenged by seasonal occurrences of events, visitors concerns over digesting crude realities and the supply of basic tourism facilities.

15.7 CONCLUSIONS

About 5000 distinct indigenous groups inhabit around the world. Over half of those communities settled in Asia. An indigenous cultural event is a distinguishing trait that separates the community from the rest. Most of those located at a remote and little-known destination, where the economy runs mainly on limited agriculture and farming and other needs such as infrastructure, education, and health are ignored. Sometimes, natural calamities caused their economic distress.

Tourism now emerges as a crucial tool of sustainable development; specifically, its practice at little-known indigenous destinations is quite pragmatic. Moreover, culture, event, and indigenous contents either together or separately act as critical tourism motivators. Most new-generation travelers want to discover destinations in contact with its inhabitants and their culture in an authentic manner. Indigenous cultural events of little-known destinations could be the best possible offer in this regard. Appropriate imaging is a prerequisite to indigenous events' shift from creative cultural socialization to a potential tourism offer. Indigenous native hosts play a crucial role in imaging offers and its attractiveness but is challenged by several factors. Lack of tourism perceptions among the inhabitants, suspicious attitude toward guests, and a dearth of organized tourism service primarily impede the portrayal process. Again communicative incompetence, unprofessional services, myth-based knowledge input, subjective interpretation and inherent seasonality also obstruct destination image formation. In this regard, a separate study to challenge the challenges is the need of the hour.

KEYWORDS

- challenges
- little-known destination
- imaging
- indigenous cultural event
- interaction

REFERENCES

Alhemoud, A., and Armstrong, E. (1996). Image of tourism attractions in Kuwait. *Journal of Travel Research*, 34, 76–80.

Aramberri, J. (2002). The commercialized crafts of Thailand: Hill tribes and lowland villages. *Annals of Tourism Research, 29*(4), 1194–1196.

Baloglu, S.(1997).The relationship between destination images and sociodemographic and trip characteristics of international travellers. *Journal of Vacation Marketing,* 3(3), 221–233.

Blundell, V. (2002). Aboriginal cultural tourism in Canada. In *Slippery Pastimes: Reading the Popular in Canadian Culture*; Nicks J., and Sloniowski, J., Eds. Waterloo: Wilfrid Laurier University Press, 37–60.

Bramwell, B., and Rawding, L. (1996). Tourism marketing images of industrial cities. *Annals of Tourism Research,* 23(1), 201–221.

Chaudhary, M. (2000). India's image as a tourist destination—A perspective of foreign tourists. *Tourism Management,* 21, 293–297.

Chang, J. (2006). Segmenting tourists to Aboriginal cultural festivals: an example in the Rukai tribal area, Taiwan. *Tourism Management,* 27, 1224–1234.

Cohen, E. (1996). Hunter-gatherer tourism in Thailand. In *Tourism and Indigenous Peoples*; Butler, R., and Hinch, T. Eds. London; Boston: International Thompson Business Press, 227–254.

Court, B., and Lupton, R. A. (1997). Customer portfolio development: Modeling destination adapters, inactives, and rejecters. *Journal of Travel Research,* 36 (1), 35–43.

Dann, G. (1977). Anomie, ego-enhancement and tourism. *Annals of Tourism Research,* 4(4), 184–194.

Davies, B. (1976). *Social Control and Education.* London: Mthuen.

Echtner, C. M., and Ritchie, J. R. B. (1991). The meaning and measurement of destination image. *The Journal of Tourism Studies,* 2 (2), 2–12.

Echtner, C. M., and Ritchie, J. R. B. (2003).The meaning and measurement of destination image. Reprint of original article published (1991). The meaning and measurement of destination image. *The Journal of Tourism Studies,* 2 (2), 2–12. *The Journal of Tourism Studies,* 14 (1), 37–48. Retrieved on April 6, 2018 from https://www.jcu.edu.au/__data/assets/pdf_file/0006/122487/jcudev_012328.pdf

Embacher, J., and Buttle, F. (1989). A repertory grid analysis of Austria's image as a summer vacation destination. *Journal of Travel Research,* 27, 3–7.

Falassi, A. (1987). *Time out of Time: Essays on the Festival.* Albuquerque: University of New Mexico.

Favilla, M. (2017). Report of the UNWTO panel on indigenous tourism: Promoting equitable partnerships ITB Berlin, Germany, March 9, 2017, (cf.cdn.unwto.org/.../report_of_the_unwto_panel_on_indigenous_tourism_promoting...) accessed on May 15, 2019.

Ferrario, F. F. (1979). The evaluation of tourist resources: An applied methodology. *Journal of Travel Research,* 17, 18–22.

Finlayson, J. (1991). *Australian Aborigines and Cultural Tourism: Case Studies of Aboriginal Involvement in the Tourist Industry.* Wollongong, Australia: University of Wollongong.

Fuller, D., Caldicott, J., Cairncross, G., and Wilde, S. (2007). Poverty, indigenous culture and ecotourism in remote Australia. *Development,* 50(2), 141–148.

Gartner, W. C., and Shen, J. (1992). The impact of Tiananmen Square on China's tourism image. *Journal of Travel Research,* 3, 47–52.

Gartner, W. (1993). Image formation process. *Journal of Travel and Tourism Marketing,* 2(2/3), 191–215.

Getz, D. (2000). Festivals and special events: Life cycle and saturation issues. In *Trends in Outdoor Recreation, Leisure and Tourism*; Garter, W., and Lime, D., Eds. Wallingford: CABI, 175–185.

Getz, D. (2005). *Event Management and Event Tourism,* 2nd ed. New York: Cognizant.

Getz, D. (2008). Event tourism: Definition, evolution, and research. *Tourism Management,* 29 (3), 403–428.

Giner, S. (1972). *Sociology.* London, UK: Martin Robert.

Gunn, C. (1972). *Vacationscape: Designing Tourist Regions.* Austin, TX: Bureau of Business Research, University of Texas.

Gursoy, D., Kim, K., and Uysal, M. (2004). Perceived impacts of festivals and special events by organizers: An extension and validation. *Tourism Management*, 25, 171–182.

Haimendorf, C. (1943). The Chenchus–Jungle folk of the Deccan. In: *Vol. 1. The Aboriginal Tribes of Hyderabad*. London, UK: Macmillan.

Haimendorf, C. (1945). The Reddis of the Bison hills–A study in acculturation. In: *The Aboriginal Tribes of Hyderabad*, vol. 2. London, UK: Macmillan.

Haimendorf, C. (1947). *Ethnographic notes on the tribes of the Subansiri region*. Shillong, India: Assam Govt. Press.

Haimendorf, C. (1948). The Raj Gonds of Adilabad. In: *The Aboriginal Tribes of Hyderabad*, vol. 3. London, UK: Macmillan.

Hinch, T. and R. Butler. (1996). Indigenous tourism: A common ground for discussion. In *Tourism and Indigenous Peoples*; Butler, R., and Hinch, T. Eds. London; Boston: International Thompson Business Press, 1–11.

Hunter, W. W. (*1880). A Brief History of the Indian Peoples. Oxford: Clarendon Press.*

Hunter, W. W. (1868). *The Annals of Rural Bengal*. London, UK: Smith Elder and Co.

Janiskee, R. (1980). South Carolina's harvest festivals: Rural delights for day tripping urbanites. *Journal of Cultural Geography*, 1, 96–104.

Illum, S., and Schaefer, A. (1995). Destination attributes: Perspectives of tour operators and destination marketers. *Journal of Travel and Tourism Marketing*, 4(4), 1–14.

Kerber, J. E., Ed. (2006). *Cross-cultural Collaboration: Native Peoples and Archaeology in the Northeastern United States*. Lincoln, UK: University of Nebraska Press.

Kotler, P., Haider, D. H., and Rein, I. (1993). *Marketing Places*. New York: The Free Press.

Oklobdžija, S. et al. (2015). The role of events in tourism development. *BizInfo Journal*, 6 (2), 83–97.

Matheson, C. M. (2005). Festivity and sociability: A study of a Celtic music festival. *Tourism Culture and Communication*, 5, 149–163.

Mann, E. G. (1867). *Sonthalia and the Sonthals*. London, UK: Tinsley and Co.

Murphy, L. (1999). Australia's image as a holiday destination—Perceptions of Backpacker visitors. *Journal of Travel and Tourism Marketing*, 8(3), 21–45.

Phelps, A. (1986). Holiday destination image—The problem of assessment. *Tourism Management*, 7, 168–180.

Phipps, P. and Slater, L.(2010). *Indigenous Cultural Festivals: Evaluating Impact on Community Health and Wellbeing*. Melbourne: Globalism Research Centre, Royal Melbourne Institute of Technology.

Quinn, B. Eds. (2009). *Festivals, Events and Tourism in the SAGE Handbook of Tourism Studies*. London, UK: SAGE Publications.

Ray, S. (2008). Cultural tourism or culture based tourism: An analytical view. *Tourism: Theory and Practice*, 6(1), 7–21.

Ray, S. (2017a). Approaches towards ethno-cultural contents of the hosts and socially responsible tourism. *Tourism: Theory and Practice*, 15(1/2), 28–58.

Ray, S. (2017b). Challenges towards integration process of tourism and culture in the Indian perspective. *International Journal of Economics and Management Science, 3*(2), 23–30.

Ray, S. (2018). Changes in the role of local or host community in destination imaging. *Journal of Tourism*, 19 (1) 71–85.

Ray, S. (2019). Event tourism in Asian context. In: *Tourism Events in Asia*, A. Hassan and A. Sharma, Eds. London, UK: Routledge, 4–19.

Reynolds, W. H. (1965). The role of the consumer in image building. *California Management Review*, 7, 69–76.
Ritchie, J. R. B., and Zins, M. (1978). Culture as determinant of the attractiveness of a tourism region. *Annals of Tourism Research*, 5(2), 252–267.
Ruhanen, L., Whitford, M. and McLennan, C. (2013). *Demand and Supply Issues in Indigenous Tourism: A Gap Analysis Final Report*. Brisbane, Australia: University of Queensland.
Ryan,C., and Huyton, J. (2000a). Aboriginal tourism—A linear structural relations analysis of domestic and international tourism demand. *International Journal of Tourism Research*, 2 (1), 1–15.
Ryan, C., and Huyton, J. (2000b). Who is interested in aboriginal tourism in the northern territory, Australia? A cluster analysis. *Journal of Sustainable Tourism*, 8 (1), 53–88.
Ryan, C., and Huyton, J. (2002). Tourists and aboriginal people. *Annals of Tourism Research*, 29(3), 631–647.
Scott, J. (1794). *Ferishta's History of Dekkan*. London, UK: Shrewsbury.
Selby, M., and Morgan, N. J. (1996). Reconstruing place image: A case study of its role in destination market research. *Tourism Management*, 17(4), 287–294.
Small, K., and Edwards, D. (2003). Evaluating the socio-cultural impacts of a festival on a host community: A case study of the Australian festival of the book. In: *Proceedings of the 9th Annual Conference of the Asia Pacific Tourism Association*, pp. 580–593.
Turner, V. (1982). Introduction. In: *Celebration: Studies in Festivity and Ritual*, V. Turner, Ed., Washington, DC: Smithsonian Institution Press, pp. 11–29.
Verrier, E. (1944). *The Aboriginals*. Oxford, UK: Oxford University Press.
Verrier, E. (1947). *The Muria and their Ghotul*. Oxford, UK: Oxford University Press.
Weber, M. (1968). *Economy and Society* (translated by G. Roth and C. Wittich, Eds.). New York: Bedminister Press (Original work published 1922), pp. 341–342.
Wee, C. H., Hakam, A. N., and Ong, E. (1985). Temporal and regional differences in image of a tourist destination: Implications for promoters of tourism. *Service Industries Journal*, 5, 104–114.
Xie, P. F. (2003). The Bamboo-beating dance in Hainan, China: Authenticity and commodification. *Journal of Sustainable Tourism*, 11(1), 5–16.
Young, M. (1999). The relationship between tourist motivations and the interpretation of place meanings. *Tourism Geographies*, 1(4), 387–405.
Zeppel, H. (1998). Indigenous cultural tourism: 1997 fulbright symposium. *Tourism Management*, 19(1), 243–244.
Zeppel, H. (2001). Aboriginal cultures and indigenous tourism. In *Special Interest Tourism, Australia*, R. Derrett and N. Douglas, Eds. Milton, Australia: Wiley, pp. 232–259.

CHAPTER 16

WORLD NOMAD GAMES AS AN EMERGING LARGE-SCALE EVENT AND ITS ROLE FOR TOURISM DEVELOPMENT IN KYRGYZSTAN

AZAMAT MAKSÜDÜNOV[1*] and KYIALBEK DYIKANOV[2]

[1]*Department of Management, Faculty of Economics and Administrative Sciences, Kyrgyz-Turkish Manas University, Bishkek, Kyrgyzstan*

[2]*Department of Management, Social Sciences Institute, Kyrgyz-Turkish Manas University, Bishkek, Kyrgyzstan*

*Corresponding author. E-mail: azamat.maksudunov@manas.edu.kg

ABSTRACT

The World Nomad Games (WNG) is a new emerging large-scale event in the world, where ethnic sports can be exhibited. It was started in 2014 and until today WNG has been organized three times (2014, 2016, and 2018) in Kyrgyz Republic. Actually, these kinds of events have economic and noneconomic impacts on the destinations. In this chapter, the WNG role for tourism development in Kyrgyz Republic will be investigated. Kyrgyz Republic as a tourism destination was opened in 1991 after the collapse of the USSR. Today, tourism is identified among the priority sectors in the country. However, our country does not use its full potential in tourism industry and the WNG can play crucial role to rise to a new level of development.

16.1 INTRODUCTION

Thinking a common understanding makes it easier to analyze about the same subject when talking about large-scale events. By supporting it, we can range large-scale events as Football World Cup, Olympic Games, Asia

Games, Festivals, World Nomad Games (WNG), and others. As a concept, large-scale organization is defined as cultural, commercial, and sports organizations with a striking character, mass popularity, and international importance (Roche, 2000, p. 11). The distinction between an event and a large-scale event is essentially one of size. Large-scale events are larger than regular events (Martin, 2015). Such events create significant economic, cultural, and social impacts for the host country or city. Because large-scale organizations demand great attention and effort, both positive and negative effects occur inevitably. For example, researchers have suggested that host regions can witness positive economic and social benefits through hosting large-scale sport tourism events (Chalip, 2006; O'Brien, 2006). According to Konstantaki and Wickens (2010), large-scale events are generally as leveraging opportunities for economic growth, also urban and rural development. Increasing income, job opportunities, minimizing inflation, increasing interest of tourists, worldwide recognition of the host country, and foreign exchange entries can be the best examples for positive impact (Homafar et al., 2011). On the other hand, some negative impacts such as economic costs (taxes, real estate) and socio-psychological impacts (disorder, security issues, traffic congestion) can also be significant reason. In addition, in countries where large-scale organizations are held, a number of sectors such as construction, services, and tourism should revitalize a flow of resources to the country, as well as the lack of infrastructure in the country, quality of life and social–cultural improvements should be provided (Karaca, 2012).

In general, large-scale events directly affect economic and social life of host communities. If large-scale events are organized correctly, it can offer different expansions for the economy, culture, and tourism development. Hosting mega sport and culture events are important in contributing national economy, providing experiences, and establishing diplomatic communications at the international level and for being part of the global powers (Terekli and Çobanoğlu, 2018).

The positive and negative effects mentioned above are important for the cost analysis of hosting large-scale organizations for countries such as Kyrgyzstan with limited opportunities as a country that is still in first stages of development. This is because many social and economic problems are awaiting immediate solutions in such countries. Therefore, it is important to evaluate the importance and positive and negative effects of WNG for Kyrgyzstan (Maksudunov et al., 2018). The WNG is a new emerging large-scale event in the world, where ethnic sports can be exhibited. It was started in 2014 and until today WNG has been organized three times (2014, 2016, and 2018) in Kyrgyz Republic. The next WNG is being planned to be held in Turkey this year.

In this chapter, WNG role for tourism development in Kyrgyz Republic will be investigated. Kyrgyz Republic as a tourism destination was opened in 1991 after the collapse of the USSR. Today, tourism is identified among the priority sectors in the country. However, our country doesn't use its full potential in tourism industry and the WNG can play crucial role to rise to a new level of development.

16.2 KYRGYZ REPUBLIC AS A TOURISM DESTINATION IN CENTRAL ASIA

Tourism is one of the fastest growing sectors of the global economy. Tourism plays an important economic role in many countries of the world, replenishing budgets, promoting regional development, and improving the socio-economic conditions. According to the assessment given by the UN General Assembly, the UN Economic and Social Council, and the WTO, "By the end of our century, tourism will become a leading sector of the global economy, being an extremely important tool in improving the economic and social situation of many states, in particular developing countries, it has become an important factor development of national economies of states" (Сариева, 2013). Worldwide Tourism Organization identifies tourist destinations as a central element in the process of formation and delivery of tourism products. A key element of tourism as a system is the territory that attracts tourists, where they make their trip and where they spend some time—tourist destination. Tourism destination as a complex phenomenon includes tourist attractions, tourist infrastructure, and related services (Кирьянова, 2011). While the whole world develops its own tourism potential in the developing period, they make big profits from tourism sector.

If we follow the Central Asian (CA) countries, they are located in the center of the Asia and contain large and untapped tourism resources to serve world tourism market. After the independence in 1991, the CA countries have sharply started to develop tourism infrastructures and superstructures (Kantarci et al., 2015). In addition, this region is located in Silk-Road and well-known trade route in the history, which connected Europe and Asia. One of the main destinations in this region is Kyrgyzstan.

16.3 KYRGYZ REPUBLIC

The Kyrgyz Republic is located in the Central Asia between 39 and 43 degrees of northern breadth. Territory of the Kyrgyz republic makes 198,500 square km., 925 km from the west on the east, and 454 km from the north on the South. The general length of border is 4508 km and the highest point is 7439 m (Jenish peak), the lowest point is 394 m (area Lejleksky). As seen in the Figure 16.1. It has borders with the Chinese National Republic, Uzbekistan, Tajikistan, and Kazakhstan. Kyrgyz Republic is a mountainous country, 90% of territory located above 1500 m, the average height makes 2750 m. The mountains covered about 90% of the country territory. It is said that there are many mountain peaks, valleys, lakes, rivers, waterfalls, and others. In addition, fauna and flora of the country are rich and attractive. Therefore, Kyrgyzstan is known as "Switzerland of Central Asia." One of the most incredible points about the country is that one can find all climates and all seasons there, and that often at the same time.

Since Kyrgyzstan has its own history and culture, it is the most suitable place for tourists who want to spend their holidays as a nomad. In fact, local people still use these features in their daily lives in order to not forget history and culture and pass it from generation to generation. At the same time, these features are exhibited as the most important tourism product for tourists.

FIGURE 16.1 Map of Kyrgyzstan.

Source: https://www.nationsonline.org/oneworld/map/kyrgyzstan-administrative-map.htm, 05.02.2020.

According to National Statistic Committee (NSCKR, 2019), population of the country is 6,389,500 with 1.8% annual growth rate in 2018. The Gross Domestic Product (GDP, PPP current international) per capita in Kyrgyzstan is 3884$ by the end of the 2018. Service industry is important field of local economy. Service industry has been increasing its impact on the economy last two decades. Share of services on GDP is around 50% in 2018, the same indicator was around 30% in 2000. Unemployment rate (2018) is around 6%.

TABLE 16.1 Selected Social and Economic Indicators of Kyrgyz Republic

Series Name	2000	2005	2010	2015	2016	2017	2018
Population, total (million)	4.8	5.1	5.4	5.9	6.0	6.1	6.3
Population growth (annual %)	1.2	1.13	1.20	2.06	2.04	1.93	1.88
Population density (people per sq. km of land area)	25.51	26.91	28.40	31.05	31.69	32.31	32.92
Life expectancy at birth, total (years)	68.5	67.9	69.3	70.6	70.9	71	–
GDP per capita, PPP (current international thousand $)	1.6	2.1	2.7	3.4	3.5	3.7	3.8
Services, value added (% of GDP)	29.9	42.4	49.3	52.1	50.1	49.9	49.7
Unemployment, total (% of total labor force) (national estimate)	7.54	8.11	8.64	7.56	7.21	6.89	5.96

Source: https://databank.worldbank.org/home.aspx, 05.02.2020.

Although tourism is considered one of the main sectors of the economy in state programs, it is not at a sufficient level. According to the Report of Travel and Tourism Competitiveness Index (2007–2019), Kyrgyzstan has being ranked on the bottom level (Figure 16.2). In 2019, Kyrgyzstan is 110th place among 140 countries.

16.4 THE KYRGYZ TOURISM INDUSTRY

After independence, as other post-soviet countries in Central Asia, there were good opportunities to focus on tourism sector for Kyrgyzstan as well. Tourism is considered one of the priority and dynamically developing sectors of the economy, since the country has a huge natural, tourism potential, as well as cultural and socio-historical heritage, which contribute to the development of various types of tourism in the Kyrgyz Republic (Москаленко, 2016). As mentioned above, Kyrgyzstan is an idyllic country

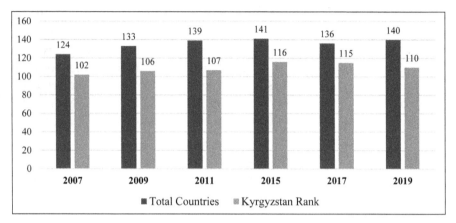

FIGURE 16.2 The Travel and Tourism Competitiveness Index of Kyrgyz Republic. *Source*: https://www.weforum.org/, 05.02.2020.

with a high enough mountainous nature. In fact, it continues to impress visitors by being among the few countries in the world in terms of nature. Therefore, recently awareness of the importance and positive effects of the tourism sector has begun to emerge. We can even highlight the fact that the tourism sector is at the forefront of the country's economic, social, and promotional impacts. Kyrgyzstan has an important tourism potential, but it has great opportunities for both domestic and foreign tourism development. Since the country is mountainous, some of the highest peaks in the world are located in Kyrgyzstan and have an undiscovered and intact environment at the same time. The mountains, rivers, lakes, plateaus, valleys, and waterfalls of the country make the Kyrgyz Republic the Swiss of Central Asia. Some important beauties are illustrated in Figure 16.3. As Sarieva stated in her work, most of the different basic tourism types are available in Kyrgyzstan (2015). For example, medical, recreational, sports, cognitive, eco, business, adventure, climbing, trekking, skiing, event tourism, and others. However, we mentioned about the types of tourism above, but in general, we can divide the tourism sector of Kyrgyzstan into three dimensions such as Issyk-Kul lake beach tourism, cultural, and soft adventure tourism including eco-tourism, and extreme sports and hard adventure tourism. Tourists are attracted to the country through this type of tourism. Tour operators also carry out their promotional activities in this area.

Kyrgyzstan has great potential to expand the range of tourism services, thereby artificially extending the tourist season up to year-round. Ecotourism is gaining momentum in Kyrgyzstan today. Recently, Kymyz treatment

World Nomad Games as an Emerging Large-Scale Event   293

FIGURE 16.3 Some beauties of the Kyrgyz Republic.
Source: https://www.facebook.com/VladUshakovkg/photos/pcb.1379196402257257/137919
6272257270/?type=3&theater, 10.02.2020.

(horse milk), which has become widely popular among the local population, has begun to attract tourists both from the Commonwealth of Independent States (CIS) countries and from far abroad. There are special Kymyz treatment procedures that last for several days and benefit your health. Since Kyrgyzstan is a mountainous country, it also attracts mountaineering enthusiasts. A large number of tourists from foreign countries prefer this extreme sport. By the way, mountaineering is not the only extreme sport popular in Kyrgyzstan. There are also skiing, rafting, rock climbing, etc. In summer, hiking tours to the mountains, bike rides, etc., are popular. As mentioned above, Kyrgyzstan has a great role in tourism in terms of culture and history recognition as it is the country settled on the Silk Road and has a unique history. One of historical places is Sulayman-Too Sacred Mountain which is another entry of the UNESCO World Heritage Sites in Kyrgyzstan. The mountain is located in the city of Osh, which used to be a site for Muslim pilgrimage. Today, the rock formations of the Sulayman Mountain are a popular tourist attraction because of its splendid view. The mountain forms over the plains surrounding the Fergana Valley (www.everything-everywhere.com, 05.02.2020). Also, Burana and Uzgen Towers are part of the Kyrgyz archaeological-architectural places and are protected by the state as a monument of cultural heritages.

Positive information about Kyrgyzstan is published in the world press in terms of the attractiveness of all tourism, its suitability for tourists, and its importance. Even CNtraveller (https://www.cntraveller.com/topic/destinations, 05.02.2020) and CNN (www.edition.cnn.com, 05.02.2020) showed Kyrgyzstan as the top 20 countries to visit in 2020, while TurStat (www.turstat.com/topskiresortcis, 05.02.2020) chose Karakol Ski area in Kyrgyzstan as the best skiing place among the CIS countries. These indicators and interests prove that Kyrgyzstan has an important place in the world tourism market and is seen as a country with famous tourism destinations.

The tourism industry of the republic should become a priority in the development of the country, contributing to the improvement of the image of Kyrgyzstan as a country of tourism. The tourism industry must comply with international standards of service and carefully use the existing natural potential of the country. While the representatives of the private sector carry out various activities for the development of the tourism sector, the state also plans and works on important forward-looking decisions and programs. As an example, the program of the Government of the Kyrgyz Republic for the development of the tourism sector for 2019–2023 reflects current world trends in the field of tourism and the current situation in the tourism industry of the republic. The program on a systematic basis defines goals, objectives, activities with specific deadlines, responsible performers, and financial resources to achieve effective results in the tourism sector.

Finally, we can specify that tourism opens up new opportunities not only for tourists but also for the local population, it greatly contributes to the socio-economic development of the destination. Tourism has a huge impact on transport and communications, the construction and production of consumer goods, the hotel business, and restaurant spheres. All of these support the development of the country from all sides and increase its importance. Considering the dynamic growth of tourism in the modern world, its tangible multiplicative impact on other sectors of the economy, the well-being of society and the environment, the tourism industry of the Kyrgyz Republic in the future should become one of the priority areas for the development of the country's economy. However, we cannot say that Kyrgyzstan has developed the tourism sector at a sufficient level, but new research and efforts are underway. Among the many development projects, we can state that the WNG is an important contributing effort in the tourism sector.

16.5 OVERVIEW OF THE WNG AS A LARGE-SCALE EVENT

In developing world competition, it has become important to recognize the country as a destination in order to have important points in the field of international tourism. One of the results of the active development of tourism in the world is an increasing number of destinations available for tourists. Based on this, World Tourism Organization (WTO) highlights tourist destinations as central element in the formation process and tour product delivery. As a tourism destination, we can take Central Asia or Kyrgyzstan as the only country. If we look even further, mountain lakes, regions, plateaus, and canyons located in Kyrgyzstan are all considered tourist destinations.

As Turdumambetov (2019) stated that the beautiful nature, history, and culture destinations of the country are of course not sufficient in world tourism competition. In fact, some important factors such as infrastructure, level of service, ease of transportation, and food and beverage establishments are also insufficient. In addition, the opportunities of tourists to participate in interesting and important events specific to the country come to the fore during travel. If we look at this way, the WNG can be shown as a large-scale event that can attract tourists and move our country forward as an important destination in Central Asia.

The WNG is a grandiose country project, which as a national brand is very dynamically gaining a strong position in the international arena. The main idea of the Nomad Games is the idea of rapprochement of peoples and cultures. For us, nomads, this is a holiday of returning to our origins, an opportunity to show our children and the whole world the wealth of the nomadic culture. The WNG are aimed at developing the ethnosport and ethnoculture movement in the world, as this is the heritage of human civilization. The mission of the WNG covers the revival, development, and preservation of the ethnoculture, diversity, and originality of the people of the world in order to foster a more tolerant and open relationship between people (WNG, 2018). In addition, it is obvious that goals of the WNG include popularizing, developing, and promoting ethnosports at the world level, including traditional games and competitions from around the world. Also, supporting for the scientific and methodological foundation of the ethnosport movement, including ethnosports, traditional games, and traditional competitions are main objectives, as well. The other important intentions of the organizers WNG are strengthening and further developing interfaith and intercultural dialogue, understanding, friendship, harmony, and cooperation between the people of the world, and demonstrating the cultural diversity of the world.

According to the information of the organizing committee of the World Nomads Games, the WNG is the largest international project of the Kyrgyz Republic, initiated by the Government of Kyrgyzstan in 2012 to revive and preserve the culture of nomadic civilization. Some facts about results of the previous WNG are given in Figure 16.4. If we look at the chronology dates of the World Nomads Games, they are listed as follows.

- The First WNG were held from September 9th through 14th, 2014, in Cholpon-Ata, in the Issyk-Kul Province of Kyrgyzstan. A total of 583 athletes from 19 countries participated in competitions held in 10 types of sports, plus an additional 1200 participants in the cultural program.
- The Second WNG were held from September 3rd to 8th, 2016, in Cholpon-Ata, in the Issyk-Kul Province of Kyrgyzstan. A total of 1200 athletes from 62 countries participated in competitions in 26 types of ethno sports
- The opening ceremony of the Third WNG is planned for September 2nd, 2018, in Cholpon-Ata, in the Issyk-Kul Province of Kyrgyzstan. A total of 1976 athletes from 74 countries participated in competitions in 37 types of ethnic sports.

By organizing three times, the WNG have had the opportunity to be recognized as a large-scale organization like European Olympic Games or other large-scale sport events in the world. In fact, WNG are modern international sports competitions of nomadic peoples, in the past, in ethnic and ethnocultural sports. The WNG competitions were based on folk games of historically nomadic peoples, not only in the CA region but in other regions and continents of the world (Абытов, 2017).

World Nomad Games as an Emerging Large-Scale Event   297

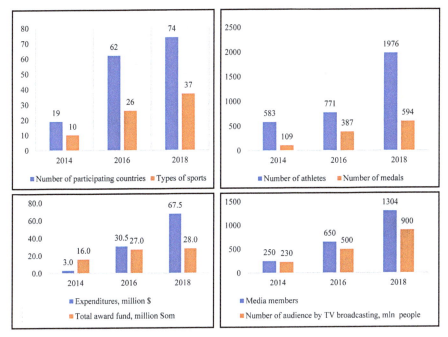

FIGURE 16.4 World Nomad Games' results.
Source: Retrieved from World Nomad Games Organizing Committee Reports.

As stated above, for the first time, while the number of participating countries and athletes is low, it is seen that the numbers and interests increase in the next ones. This means that the World Nomads Games have increased their worldwide prestige. However, it can compare the differences and developments in the games organized three times.

The idea of reviving and preserving the historical and cultural heritage of nomadic peoples; civilization was supported by many states, bringing together various countries in the first and second WNG and attracted the attention of other countries. In total, about 2000 participants from 79 countries of the world took part in the Third WNG in sports, cultural, and scientific events. Unlike the second games, the number of competitions in national sports has been increased. Representatives from different countries competed in 37 sports, while 26 in second, and 10 in first time.

Organizers of WNG noted that for viewers, this is a way to learn new things, to touch the pristine nature and ancient traditions, to see the hospitality and sincerity of nomads. Therefore, the program of the event includes not only sports but also acquaintance with the life, lifestyle, traditions, art, and philosophy of nomads. As seen in Figure 16.5, the third WNG successfully completed with a closing ceremony with wide participation. All this suggests that the WNG is important and necessary not only for the Kyrgyz people but also for many nomadic peoples whose ancestors were nomads in the recent past historical period. Of course, many people care about what it benefited WNG, to us—the Kyrgyz Republic. This is, above all, an additional, and very useful image for our country as a tourist product or activities in the international arena.

FIGURE 16.5 The closing ceremony of 3th WNG in Cholpon-Ata city, Kyrgyzstan.
Source: http://worldnomadgames.com/en/galleries/?gallery=The-closing-ceremony, 30.01.2020.

16.6 IMPACT OF THE WNG ON TOURISM DEVELOPMENT IN THE COUNTRY

Any country hosting large-scale organizations should pay attention to preliminary preparation, suitability, and some standards. Certain changes, either forward or backward, occur, depending on the situation before and after the event in some sectors in the country. Therefore, the effects of the World Nomads Games held in our country on the infrastructure, tourism, economy, country image, and socio-cultural values of our country are not ignored. According to recent study conducted by Maksudunov (2017), local residents believe that the WNG created significant socio-economic impact in the country. In this chapter, impact of the WNG is evaluated under two headings: direct and indirect impacts.

16.6.1 DIRECT IMPACT OF THE WNG

In order to evaluate the direct impact of the WNG, it is necessary to look at number of foreign visitors, tourism income, and tourism infrastructure for the relevant period of time.

Normally, most of tourists come to Kyrgyzstan from CIS for beach tourism in Issik-Kul. Lake Issyk-Kul is one of the largest fresh water lakes in the world and it is the world's second largest alpine lake, after Lake Titicaca in South America. According to National Statistic Committee of Kyrgyz Republic (2019) in 2018, 1.4 million tourists visited Kyrgyzstan. A significant part of them fell in the Issyk-Kul region, where the number of vacationers amounted to more than 9,00,000 people. According to the State Border Service of the Kyrgyz Republic, the number of foreign citizens crossing the border in 2014 amounted to more than 4 million people and unfortunately, we cannot see that this indicator has more changed level until 2018. As you see in 2018, it exceeds 7 million. In other words, it is almost 1.5 times more than other years (Figure 16.6). On the other hand, we cannot see that the number of visitors coming to rest has changed a lot. As you see in Figure 16.7, their number is 1132.2 million in 2013, 1245 in 2014, 1265.1 in 2015, 1273.2 in 2016, 1375.10 in 2017, and 1380.40 million in 2018.

According to sources of the National Statistic Committee of Kyrgyz Republic, the largest number of foreign citizens crossing the border of the Kyrgyz Republic are citizens of Uzbekistan and Kazakhstan, Russia, and Tajikistan. The number of Uzbek citizens who crossed the border with Kyrgyzstan in 2018 increased sharply. This fact is associated with the agreement on the removal of restrictions at border points with Kyrgyzstan and the full-format functioning at the borders with Uzbekistan. With Kazakhstan this trend is associated with a limitation of the period of compulsory registration, which was 5 days. But from July 15, 2017 in Kyrgyzstan and Kazakhstan, new rules for the stay of citizens in the territory of two countries have been launched. Mandatory registration period extended to 30 days. Of the countries outside the CIS, the largest number of citizens crossing the Kyrgyz border are Turkey, China, India, and Germany.

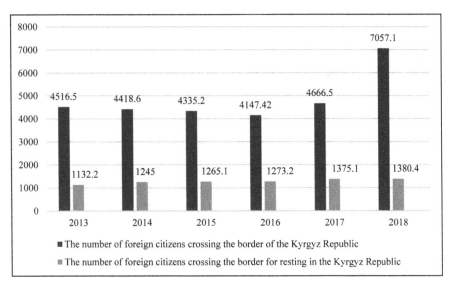

FIGURE 16.6 The number of foreign citizens crossing the border and the number of visitors who had a rest in the Kyrgyz Republic in 2014–2018 (thousand people, %).

Source: National Statistic Committee of Kyrgyz Republic. Retrieved 10.02.2020.

If we look at the result because of what we have mentioned, can we state that the WNG contributed to the country's tourism? One of the aims of the World Nomads Games was to develop this large-scale organization as a brand, to create more attention to the country and to increase the number of tourists. So, did these thoughts achieve their purpose? We do not point that it has not reached completely. It can be stated that it has a direct effect even if it is low. It would not be right to ignore the great efforts and goals of both the states, the private sector and the public. The WNG, of course, contributed to the increase in the number of tourists coming to the country between 2014 and 2018 (Figure 16.6). It can be said that the result of border, customs and other positive agreements with neighboring Kazakhstan and Uzbekistan in 2017 caused them to participate in the 3rd WNG. Games provided the attraction of 60,000 tourists in 2nd WNG. Kyrgyzstan was included in the top 10 countries recommended by the WTO for visiting by tourists. The previous head of the Department of Tourism of Kyrgyzstan, and present Minister of Culture, Information and Tourism Azamat Zhamankulov, told one of the media about the increase in the number of tourists after the Games of nomads from Europe, Arab countries. According to him, it was after the Nomad Games that the ranks of those interested in seeking to see Kyrgyzstan increased. "The influence of the Nomad Games is very great. We conducted a survey of tourists coming to us, most of them said that they recognized Kyrgyzstan through the Nomad Games, saw the tourism potential, and then arrived. The number of tourists coming from Europe, Arab countries has increased," said Zhamankulov. Of course, the effect of these activities may not be obvious at first, but it is no doubt that they will have a great effect over time with the development of brand.

As mentioned the number of visitors coming to the country above, we tried to show them according to the income level below as well (Figure 16.7).

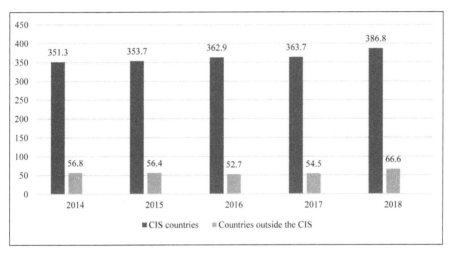

FIGURE 16.7 Dynamics of the export of tourist services of the Kyrgyz Republic in 2014–2018 (million dollars).

Source: National Statistic Committee of Kyrgyz Republic. Retrieved 10.02.2020.

Moskalenko clarified that tourism industry is one of the few sectors of the economy that has the most powerful multiplier effect and has a direct impact on more than 30 related industries (2015). In terms of employment, tourism holds a leading position in the Kyrgyz Republic but despite this, according to official data of the National Statistical Committee of the Kyrgyz Republic, the share of tourism in GDP over the past 5 years has been insignificant, in 2014 the share in GDP was 4.3% in 2015, 4.7% in 2016, 4.6 in 2017, 5% and in 2018 also 5% (Figure 16.8).

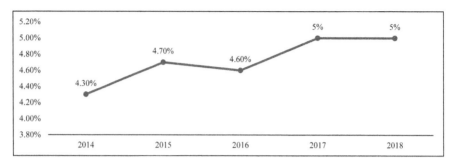

FIGURE 16.8 Gross value added in the tourism sector of the Kyrgyz Republic (as a percentage of GDP).
Source: National Statistical Committee of the Kyrgyz Republic 2019.

As indicated, the gross value added in the tourism sector in 2018, according to preliminary estimates, amounted to more than 27 billion Soms, or 5% of GDP, maintaining the level of the previous year (Figure 16.8).

Although the number of tourists mentioned above and the level of income do not have a very explosive effect, it can be said that World Nomadic Games contributed to a certain level along with other reasons. However, the expectation was greater. Large events require more attention and demand, and with this in mind, it is a great success compared to the country whose economy is not very good but has the potential to carry out such activities.

In terms of infrastructure impact of WNG, there are some important projects had built before the event. One of them is Horse-racing hippodrome in the city of Cholpon-Ata is located 270 kilometers from the city of Bishkek and covers an area of 25 hectares (Figure 16.9). The arena is the only one in Central Asia located on the lake. The total capacity of the hippodrome is 10 thousand people. According to official website of the WNG Committee (www.worldnomadgames.com), this project is unique, since for the first time in such a short time, construction of not only national but also international significance was carried out in Kyrgyzstan, in compliance with all relevant norms and standards. Another important project is a Gazprom sport complex, which was built before WNG and most of the games took place there. In addition, Tamchy airport was also commissioned in the Issik-Kul region. It was good opportunity for neighbor countries to fly directly to the Issik-Kul region where WNG organized.

In addition, even with some deficiencies, it is true that before the beginning of the 3rd World Nomadic Games, the main route between Balykchy and Korumdu was actively put forward and the construction of the roads directing

World Nomad Games as an Emerging Large-Scale Event

to Kırçın and Grigorevka valleys and plateaus is also took important place. Kyrchyn is a famous gorge, which was considered as the most important place during the WNG (Figure 16.10). Thousands of yurts (boz üy) were set there, and traditional shows and games that demonstrated the nomadic history and culture for guests from all over Kyrgyzstan and the world took place. Therefore, before this large-scale event, on the roads leading to the Kyrchyn gorge, signs were put up warning of dangerous bends and narrowing of the road. There were set also public toilets, police stations. All of these above, remained as the contribution of WNG to tourism of the country.

FIGURE 16.9 Horseracing hippodrome in the city of Cholpon-Ata.
Source: http://worldnomadgames.com/ru/galleries/?gallery=Finalnyi-match-po-kok-boru-mezh-du-komandami-Kazakhstana-i-Kyrgyzstana-foto-R-Iliasov

16.6.2 INDIRECT IMPACT OF THE WNG

Abytov (2017) in his recent research focused on importance of WNG, which strived to preserve and revive the culture of the nomadic peoples of the world, through the strengthening of cultural ties between the participating countries. In addition, through WNG, showed not only the participants in the games but also through the media all over the world provided an opportunity to see all the beauty and wealth, entertainment, the triumph of life, and life of all the nomadic peoples in the world. All of these can be concluded as important influences in the continuation of culture and hand on the history to the generation.

FIGURE 16.10 Kyrchyn during the WNG.
Source: http://worldnomadgames.com/ru/galleries/?page=3&gallery=Foto-galereia-V-ushchele-Kyrchyn-otkrylsia-etnogorodok-Kyrgyz-aiyly-iz-288-iurt

According to Mambetaliev (2017), this event led to the reincarnation of ethnic sports in the contemporary world and is of great socio-cultural importance. The WNG became a great event for Kyrgyz people and foreign guests. They had the opportunity to see the identity, culture and sports and life of the nomads. This event is considered one of the largest projects for the development of the country's tourism potential over the years of independence. An equally important goal of the WNG is to increase the tourism potential of the country, not only in Kyrgyzstan but also in the future, in other countries, the heirs of nomadic civilizations, cultures, and peoples.

In addition, it should be emphasized on the importance of the scientific-practical conference, which was held as part of the WNG. At scientific forums of the WNG, 244 scientists from more than ten countries of the world representing such specialties as history, ethnography, pedagogy, physical culture and sports, folklore, art, and music and other famous specialists and organizers of science, presented scientific reports and discussed issues history and philosophy, art and literature, pedagogy, tourism, and architecture of ethnoculture and ethnosports movement. All of them were aimed at determining current trends and development directions traditionally ethnosport, identifying the role and place of the nomadic civilization in the course of human evolution (Азизбаев и Тагаев, 2018).

Another important effect of WNG was manifested in the unity of the people, in the formation of tolerance and patriotism. Prof. Dr. Kadyraly Konkobaev explained the WNG's cultural and historical influences as follows: "Turkic origin people have been living from Central Asia to Anatolia by dispersing from the Altai region. So all Turkic people have a nomadic life. By developing events like WNG, the culture and history of nomadic peoples can be introduced to the world. As a result, we can get to the world and attract more attention" (Maksudunov et al., 2018, pp. 818–819).

The promotion and announcement of the country's history, culture, customs, and other characteristics that belong to the country play an important role in the tourism sector. Therefore, the indirect effects of the WNG on the country and people will definitely benefit in the future and will cause both economic and social development. Because, through large-scale events such as WNG, the opportunity to promote the world mass is obtained and the interest in the country and the public starts to increase. As a result, the number of visitors to the country increases and the country reaches both economic and other developments.

16.7 CONCLUSION

Large-scale events give both positive and negative effects for the host country. However, it is without doubt that organizing correctly and planned will have an important role such as the image of the country, its recognition, and the development of important areas such as the tourism sector.

The WNG went down in history not only for Kyrgyzstan but also as a large-scale event that led to the recognition of the nomadic peoples' games, culture, history, and lives around the world. Of course, Kyrgyzstan is the owner of this great project. For this, it was the first time in 2014, the second time in 2016 and the third time in 2018 in the region of Ysyk-Kol in Kyrgyzstan. The data mentioned above can show as evidence that this world-wide event has been getting more popular. In addition, this event has emerged as a tourism brand for Kyrgyzstan. Even if it is at a low level, while contributing directly to the tourism of the country, its indirect effects have shown great importance. Because, in the first WNG, 250 media members joined in 2014, 230 million TV audiences, 650 media members, and 500 million audiences in 2016, and 1304 media members and 900 million audiences in 2018 were reached. These indicators are proof that the Kyrgyz Republic is recognized worldwide and attracts positive attention.

The question of what kind of WNG provided for the development of country tourism can be viewed positively in general. For the country whose economy is not very good, having such an important and big event three times is a success. However, some deficiencies should be mentioned, such as costs, the number of tourists not increasing at the desired level.

Fourth WNG were given to Turkey. The continuation of this activity from now on belongs to republics with a nomadic history. Since the economies, locations, and perspectives of each country are different, the level of effectiveness of the event may be reflected differently on the benefit and tourism of the country. Finally, we can express the following; Even if large-scale events are costly or difficult, their direct and indirect positive effects will be prominent if organized correctly and planned. WNG has also been an experience for Kyrgyzstan. Even if we get positive or negative effects from this, it is a great success to reach this decision and organize it successfully in the eyes of the world.

KEYWORDS

- **large-scale event**
- **World Nomad Games**
- **tourism**
- **tourism development**
- **Kyrgyzstan**

REFERENCES

Chalip, L. Towards social leverage of sport events, *Journal of Sport & Tourism*, 2006. 11(2), 109–127, DOI: 10.1080/14775080601155126.

CNN Travel. CNN Travel's 20 best places to visit in 2020. https://edition.cnn.com/travel/article/places-to-visit-2020/index.html (Accessed on 05.02.2020)

Conde Nast Traveler. Destinations. https://www.cntraveller.com/topic/destinations (Accessed on 05.02.2020)

Facebook.https://www.facebook.com/VladUshakovkg/photos/pcb.1379196402257257/1379196272257270/?type=3&theater (Accessed on 10.02.2020)

Homafar,F., Honari, H., Heidary, A., Heidary,T., & Emami, A. The role of sport tourism in employment, income and economic development. *Journal of Hospitality Management and Tourism*, 2011. 2(3), 34–37.

Kantarci. K., Basaran. M.A., & Ozyurt. M.P. Comparative analysis of Central Asian tourism product from point of view of Turkish travelers: A case of Kyrgyzstan, Kazakhstan, Tajikistan, Uzbekistan and Turkmenista. *International Conference on Eurasian Economies*, 9–11 September 2015, Kazan, Russia.

Karaca, S. Culture-Based Urban Development and Cultural Planning Approach. Master Thesis, Mersin University Institute of Science and Technology, Mersin, 2012.

Konstantaki, M., & Wickens, E. Residents' perception of environmental and security issues at the 2012 London Olympic Games. *Journal of Sport and Tourism*. 2010. 15(4), 337–357.

Maksüdünov. A., Dyikanov. K., & Unal. A. Dünya Göçebe Oyunlarının Kırgızistan Açısından Önemi: Uzman Görüşlerine Dayalı Bir Araştırma International. *Central Asia Symposium in Kyrgyz*, Turkish Manas University, Kyrgyzstan, April 17–20, 2018.

Maksüdünov. A. Yerel Halkın Büyük Çaplı Spor Organizasyonlarının Etkilerine Yönelik Algıları: Dünya Göçebe Oyunları Örneği. 3ncü Uluslararası Türk Dünyası Turizm Sempozyumu. 20–22 Nisan 2017 Bişkek / Kırgızistan.

Martin. M. What makes an event a mega-event? Definitions and sizes. *Leisure Studies*, 2015. 34(6), 627–642.

Nations Online. Administrative Map of Kyrgyzstan. https://www.nationsonline.org/oneworld/map/kyrgyzstan-administrative-map.htm (Accessed on 05.02.2020)

National Statistic Committee of Kyrgyz Republic. Tourism in Kyrgyzstan, Annual Publication. (2019)

O'Brien, D. Strategic business leveraging and the Sydney 2000 Olympic Games. *Annals of Tourism Research*. 2006. 33, 240–261.

Roche, M. *Mega-Events and Modernity: Olympics and Expos in the Growth of Global Culture*, Routledge, London. 2000.

Terekli, S. & Çobanoğlu, H. Developing economic values in football: Example of Turkish Football Federation. *Open Access Library Journal*. 2018. 5, 1–14.

The World Bank Data Bank. Indicators. https://databank.worldbank.org/home.aspx (Accessed on 05.02.2020).

Turdumambetov, B. (2019). World Nomad Games as a Tourism Brand of Kyrgyzstan: (Based on Survey of Local Communities). Reforma, 3(83), 70–80.

TurStat, 2019. http://turstat.com/worldsnowday2019cisskiresorts (Accessed on: 05.02.2020)

World Economic Forum. The travel and tourism competitiveness index (05.02.2020).

World Nomad Games Official Website. www.worldnomadgames.com (Accessed on 08.02.2020)

World Nomad Games Official Website. The closing ceremony. http://worldnomadgames.com/en/galleries/?gallery=The-closing-ceremony (Accessed on 30.01.2020).

Абытов. Б. К., Всемирные Игры Кочевников как важный этап развития аналогов олимпийских игр, Известия вузов Кыргызстана. 2017. 12, 134–138. (Abytov, B. World Nomad Games as an important stage in the development of analogues of the Olympic Games, *Izvestiya vuzov Kyrgyzstana*, 2017. 12, 134–138.)

Азизбаев, С. С., и Тагаев, М. И. Всемирные игры кочевников: хроника событий и перспективы развития. Web of Scholar. 2018. 8(26), 34-38. doi: 10.31435/rsglobal_wos/30082018/6099. (Azizbayev, C, & Tagayev, M. World Nomad Games: A Chronicle of Events and Development Prospects, *Web of Scholar*. 2018. 8(26), 34–38.)

Кирьянова Л.Г. (2011). Маркетинг и брендинг туристских дестинаций. Учебное пособие. - Томский политехнический университет, 264 с., ISBN 978-5-98298-957-4)

Мамбеталиев, К.У. Демонстрационная сущность спорта как системообразующий фактор Всемирных Игр Кочевников. Исторические науки и археология, 2017. 12(86),

122–125. (Mambetaliev, K. The Demonstration Essence of Sport as a System-Forming Factor of the World Nomad Games, Istoricheskiye nauki i arheologii, 2017. 12(86), 122–125.)

Москаленко.О. А. Особенности и оценка развития туристского бизнеса в Кыргызстане, Наука, Новые технологии и инновации Кыргызстана, 2016. 1, 124-128. (Moskalenko, O. Features and an Assessment of Development of Tourist Business in Kyrgyzstan, Nauka, Noviye Tehnologii i Innovatcii Kyrgyzstana, 2016. 1, 124–128.)

Сариева. Ш. К. Основные направления туризма в Кыргызстане. Наука и новые Технологии. 2013. 7, 109-111. (Sarieva, Sh. Basic Types of the Tourism in Kyrgyzstan, Nauka, Noviye Tehnologii, 2013. 7, 109–111.)

Турдумамбетов.Б. Дүйнөлүк көчмөндөр оюндары Кыргызстандын туристтик бренди (жергиликтүү калкты сурамжылоонун негизинде). Реформа. 2019. 3(83), 70–80. (Turdumambetov, B. World Nomad Games as a Tourism Brand of Kyrgyzstan: (Based on Survey of Local Communities). Reforma. 2019. 3(83), 70–80.)

CHAPTER 17

PARTICIPATION AND ROLE OF WOMEN IN EVENTS AND FESTIVALS: A STUDY ON THE CONTRIBUTIONS OF WOMEN IN REVITALIZING AND SUSTAINING THE FOLK POTENTIAL OF FAIRS AND FESTIVALS IN INDIA

ANILA THOMAS

Department of Tourism and Travel Management,
Jyoti Nivas College Autonomous, Bangalore 560095, Karnataka.
E-mail: toms.anila@gmail.com

ABSTRACT

Fairs and festivals, kind of unmistakable occasions, are a fundamental piece of our life and regularly show the social capability of a network. India, prevalently known as the place that is known for captivating festivals, offers an assortment of reasonable celebrations, notable with cheerful mood and a plenitude of eagerness. Community-based events and celebrations improve the social and conventional inference of the destinations and strengthen the additional infrastructure advancement in neighborhoods. Events and festivals may not only be a force for fortifying existing agencies and organizations, but also for starting new ventures. The culture and customs of the community are supported and strengthened by most regional events. New sites and events are relived and recognized at old settings. Local festivals are available for anyone and throughout the community they are diverse and colourful. These community networks systems ensure an elevated level of societal connectivity by re-acquainting a sound social estimation with social orders. This chapter is an endeavor to examine the role of women in sustaining the cultural and financial assets, thereby distinguishing the uniqueness to help the folk potential of fairs and festivals of India on a global, national, and local level alongside the imperative key parameters of the tourism industry to attract more tourists towards the country. The study also recognizes appropriate guidelines for local people in sustaining the Folk potential of Fairs and Festivals in India.

17.1 INTRODUCTION

Cultural Tourism, a means for financial stabilization (Richards, 2007), has boosted the monetary growth of a nation by pulling in visitors from different parts of the world who are inspired by a passion for the historical, creative, logical, or connected with way of life and traditions and realities of a community, region, group, or institution. Such a movement is centered around the sentiment of the social conditions of the community, including sites, visual and performing arts, lifestyles, religious beliefs and values, traditions, fairs, festivals, and various societal events. Cultural insightfulness provides an interaction between cultural, folkloric, and historical segments of the society or of the destination to be utilized as assets and resources to draw in more vacationers and thereby boost the tourism and hospitality industry development (Borowiecki, 2016). The fundamental principle of cultural tourism is centered on the fact that there are a lot of elements and prodigies whose psychological and enthusiastic impacts are expected to fulfil the traveler's social needs.

India, a nation with diversified social and cultural ethnicity and traditional milieu, enthralls numerous explorers from various parts of the world. The traditions and customs of the nation urge the local community to live cordially in the society. With various dialects, different attires, distinctive religious practices and with various food habits, the Indian culture fluctuates radically, however, are of a similar disposition. It represents different frameworks of religious thoughts. The socio-cultural diversities are found in the form of folks, religion, dialects, various traditions, conventional and ethnic practices, indigenous celebrations, and fairs.

17.2 LOCAL AND REGIONAL FESTIVALS—A CELEBRATION OF ETHNICITY

India, the land well known for its incredible ethnic diversities, is copious with social and cultural fairs, festivals, and celebrations and all holistic seasonal congregations. The nation performs with devotion a wide range of alluring festivals and religious occasions energetically and profoundly as a tribute to the Rishis, Gurus Gods, and Goddesses and the triumph of good over treason since down the ages. These festivals and celebrations help to fortify the social and cultural roots and qualities, empower communities to save and sustain their customs and traditions, and bring financial values. Every one of these celebrations identifies with achievement of financial desires, for example, agricultural ecstasy, thriving in trade, innovative entrepreneurial growth, and social and communal advancement.

Local and regional celebrations are progressively being utilized as a means for advancing the tourism industry and the development of regional economy. The celebrations and festivals can be a main impetus for the advancement and improvement of cottage industries, utilization of rural culture, traditions and beliefs, ethnic mores, and so on. The events and celebrations give unique and rare chances to the rural folks to exhibit their traditional skills in creating ethnic commodities and furthermore help for its promotion. Rural religious celebrations and fairs provide opportunities to enhance social, financial, and cultural trade (Hu, 2007). They help in transforming human societies by encouraging group cohesion and knowledge transmission. Community-based events and festivals give a chance to celebrate the rural distinctiveness of the local community in strengthening the tourism industry of the region. The events and celebrations can be a stimulus to supplement required infrastructure for the region. Events and celebrations open doors for the rural communities to exhibit their ability, workmanship, craft skill, dance, cuisines, and different types of societal landscape and promote noteworthy livelihood through enterprising and entrepreneurial exercises (Edensor, 2016). A large number of business people, who live on temporary trade, explore new markets during these festival times.

17.3 PARTICIPATION AND ROLE OF WOMEN IN EVENTS AND FESTIVALS

Since ancient times, Indian women have relished a respectable place in the society and religious ceremonies. The term "Patni" consistently applied to the wife in the Brahmanas is demonstrative of her equivalent share in the social and religious side of the husband's life (Ghosh, 2005). Whenever man makes contributions to the Gods, as indicated by the ritualistic form of worship, the wife needs to take part in the ritual with him. Any oblation or offering to be made must be offered mutually and together. Accordingly, in every rite, sacrifices, festivals or celebrations, women's role was prevailing and even now it is continuing.

Fairs and Festivals are a fundamental part of our life and regularly show the social competence of a community. India, prevalently known as the place that is known for captivating festivals, offers an assortment of reasonable celebrations, notable with cheerful mood and a plenitude of eagerness. Community-based events and celebrations improve the social and conventional inference of the destinations and strengthen the additional infrastructure development in neighborhoods. Events and festivals may not only be a force for fortifying existing agencies and organizations but also for starting new ventures. For instance, those festivals and event celebrations, which involve agencies and voluntary organizations, offer more chances for improvement in a wide range of skills and thereby motivate for progressive and determined utilization of local instructive, commercial, and community spaces. These community networks systems ensure an elevated level of societal connectivity by re-acquainting a sound social estimation with social orders.

We have different annual religious festivals and celebrations wherein women acclaim to take a significant part in performing rites. Be it any celebration, such as Janmashtami, Ganapati Utsav, Navaratri, Diwali or Raksha Bandhan, women are the focal point of functions. During Diwali, according to the primeval custom of gathering excrement pile and expelling it away from the house, for an ethical and hygienic indicate, the custom of clearing the residue and washing the house prevails even today. Arranging the old and unwanted substances and reordering the house, redesign and renovation of infrastructure, decoration of the home premises, obviously, the entire brunt of the tiring work falls on the women. During festival time and other communal and religious celebrations, when everyone celebrates with mirth and rejoicing, relishing of flavorful dishes and desserts, the lady of the house, many a time, needs to observe strict fasting (Vrata) and keep vigil (Gupte, 1994). There are different sorts of "Vratas" as part of Hindu religious festivals, such as, Shivaratri, Janmashtami, Gauri puja or Satyanarayana puja, placating various manifestations of Gods when women need to observe Vrata.

During various events, festivals and communal celebrations, all culinary and aesthetic expressions come to spotlight. Celebrations are usually occasions to pay tribute to a specific god or goddess and every Deity is propitiated with the specific dish particularly most favorite of Him or Her. It is the woman again who rises to meet the high expectations and notwithstanding all troubles surpasses in setting up the innumerable sweet dishes vital for the event.

Further, events, festival, and celebrations imply chance to show all types of social and cultural artistic skills ranging from Rangoli, home decorations, music, dance and dramatization, all of which are given a religious implication. Moreover, the scrumptious dishes are to be prepared and first offered to the deity. Through these kinds of practices, women of the household get a chance to uncover their concealed resourceful and culinary talents and skills. Hostess of the house, the Grihini, who at this point plays the ideal host who receives and takes care of the guests and does not escape to engage the whole family's chain of visitors who will be streaming in as it is a celebration time for everyone (Dasgupta, 2007).

Women, to a great extent, remained as apathetic receivers of knowledge and enthusiastic experts of religious rituals. Attitudes and outlooks, created around patriarchal interpretations of religious conviction, have characterized and formed the social and cultural ambience of Indian women. Religious diversity has been a designating characteristic for India's populace for quite a long time. Religion assumes a pivotal role in the everyday life of Indians (Hecht, 2010). The pilgrimages to sacred shrines, various familial rituals, and customs, all are indicating the stimulating association of society to their religious responsibility. India has given more attention to all religions than it regularly is in the west and by the entire world.

As the religion and culture of a community is interrelated, religious structures are locked in a hover of mutual impact with social standards and patterns of social organization (Sinclair, 1986). In the chronicles of religion, the voice of women is hardly heard, because of the patriarchal aura of communities where these regions emerged, and which in the long run controlled a portion of the adjustments in the status of women activated by these new religions. The status of women in the public arena is a result of the transformation of religious texts and writings and of the social and institutional set-up of religious communities (Klingorova, 2015). The role of religion is, apparently, intricate and it diverges across time and destinations.

The influence of women in establishing religious norms and standards is trivial, even though in certain doctrines, we can see women who have thrived in partaking their normative views recognized, or men who advocated equal incorporation of women into religious ceremonies. It needs to be stated that there exists a certain disparity between standardizing contingency, which alludes to what the given religion proclaims (men and women as equal before God) and realistic constraints, which includes the participation of women in religious groups and social frameworks in terms of day-to-day affairs (Holm, 1994).

Development activities of contemporary India have generally ignored to support women in view of the patriarchal religious beliefs and ideologies. The perspective on women by the Hindu religion has changed through the span of history several times. In the ancient Upanishad period, women appeared to have been given more repute and appreciation than in later ages. According to the Hindu mythology, woman is the embodiment of liveliness and energy or in other words, a part of Shakti. High respect is particularly given to women who are mothers and disregard of her is considered unpardonable. One Hindu sacred writing state, "Various sins of people are expiable, but he who is reviled his mother, is never emancipated" (Verma, 2018).

The exposition of religiosity is a significant parameter of reputable and idiosyncratic womanhood in India. Loaded up with virtues and integrity, for example, impeccability, sacrifice and care, women have been considered responsible as a source for the satisfaction and affluence to the family. Indigenous social segmentations and practices are still dynamic in Indian society, and the Hindu perception on a typical woman is sustained both at the normative and functional level consistently in day to day survival (Bagchi, 2014). Better access to learning, employment, healthcare, and so on has created many changes to female lives inside the home and familial life. In the midst of various challenges faced due to social norms and standards, religion assumes a significant role in molding gender perceptions inside families and society.

17.4 CONTRIBUTION OF WOMEN IN SUSTAINING FOLK POTENTIAL OF INDIA

In India, it is just a century since women were acknowledged as undeniable experts on equal lines with their partners. Since independence, government strategic plans and policies, which guaranteed comparable chances for women to work, have acted as a driving force to women participation in each profession (Bhattarai, 2018). The escalation in the facilities for proficient and skilled knowledge and training as well as socio-cultural variables has intensified a substantial growth in the quantity of women experts. Since women bore the prime responsibility regarding kids' wellbeing, it was appraised that their empowerment would be related to the constructive triumphs as far as the wellbeing and endurance of their families concerned.

An experienced and learned inhabitants can easily get closer to and explore the potential of the emerging opportunities for progression and economic advancement in the globalized environment. Women constitute and represent a major part of the religious community involved in organizing various events as part of the rituals and traditional practices. The observations and inferences of the study have helped in identifying the set of roles played by women in sustaining the folk potential of India, namely,

- women as religious specialists with sacred devotion,
- women as facilitators in organizing traditional events and festivities, and finally,
- women as entrepreneurs who are playing a major role in sustaining the traditional products which depict the local folk culture.

17.4.1 WOMEN AS RELIGIOUS SPECIALISTS WITH SACRED DEVOTION

India, being a solid strict nation, there are not many sanctuaries where men are not permitted during the customs and functions. There are places of worship where men are barred from entering the premises on the day of the ceremonies or on selected days and events. Traditional ritualistic practices are not only events in which sacred performances happen but also incredible creators of one's reflective and spiritual life. One of the most intense life-changing ritual observances are "the Vratas," which are firmly identified with the reverential acts of a general public, particularly the womenfolk. By doing "Vratas" and "Upavaas," the spiritual intensity of devotees deepen, their endeavors are hallowed and afresh their mind, soul and body in an amicable way (Leslie, 1992).

Another solemn ritual, where women must be a vital participant, is "Srauta ritual," a solemn Vedic observance (Heesterman, 1993). Women have a structural role in the sacred rites with specific obligations and exercises that cannot customarily be performed by any other person. The holy instructional texts explicitly alluded the status of women in a divine occasion as "a religious practice that happened without the presence of a wife is no ritual at all" (Mullatti, 1989).

"Dasara," a festival intended to celebrate the women power, has drawn attention to the endurance, strength and insight of elderly women in the arena of religiosity (Obeng, 2014). The festival also divulges the fact that women get opportunities to act like guardians of trustworthiness, integrity, and ethics of the society. There are numerous events which exemplify the Gowli women as religious specialists who have affirmed their kind of sanctified power in a setting that would somehow be subjugated by the menfolk. Dussehra is the religious festivity that gives chance for the Gowli community of Battigeri, Godnal, Mainalli, and Basnal to exhibit the courage, strength and wisdom of elderly women (Chaudhuri, 2005). The affection and reverence toward the womenfolk during the festivity reflect that the women can errand and bestow all the divine qualities with utmost fortitude and power with the other members of the family. The festival also projects a fair image of the women as the transmitters and guardians of the integrity, reliability, and ethics of the society.

The *Attukal Pongala* a unique temple festival of Kerala representing the power of womanhood, is celebrated annually at the Attukal Bhagavathi temple, one of the most ancient and noticeable Hindu religious shrine in Kerala (Madhava Menon, 2002). Goddess Bhadrakali, the goddess of affluence and redemption, is the main deity of the Attukal Temple. The Attukal Bhagavathi temple is popularly described as *Sabarimala of Women* (Sengupta, 2018) as women form the major portion of the devotees during the annual festival, *Attukal Pongala Mahotsav*. During the celebration, only women devotees, from all over the country and abroad, are allowed to participate and offer "Pongala." The festival comprises of different rituals going on for 10 days and the most significant sacrament is on the ninth day of the festival, the world renowned "Attukal Pongala" (Sreedhara Menon, 2008). An ambience of conviction and festivity is evident throughout the festival and there are many celestial performances such as regular invocation of Bhajans, musical recitals, ballets depicting folk and temple arts, etc., in the temple premise. Attukal Pongala is supposed to be the largest religious gathering of women in the world *(Brockman, 2011)*. The number of women devotees upsurges each year. In 2009, the Guinness Book of World Records has certified Attukal Bhagavathi Temple as the event organizers of the largest religious gathering of women on a single day. Approximately 2.5 million women devotees participated to offer rituals (Tharoor, S., 2018). In 2018, around 4.7 million offer Pongala to the Goddess Attukal Bhagavathi. The mass gathering of women that congregated in the temple premise on this propitious day remind us of the famous Kumbh Mela festival of North India (https://www.religionworld.in/attukal-pongala-kerala-celebration-women-power/).

"Chakkulathu Kavu Sree Bhagavathi Temple" is a Hindu temple, located in Alappuzha District, Kerala, dedicated to goddess Durga. Situated on the banks of the holy Pampa River, this temple has fascinated many pilgrims, particularly women devotees, making it as one of the most renowned pilgrim destinations of the state. The noteworthy celebration of the temple is Pongala which happens during the period of Vrischikam, that is, during the month of November/December (Srikumaran, 2005). The temple premises will be crowded with lakhs of women devotees during the festival time and the devotees arrange places for offering the "Pongala" in the main streets adjacent to the temple. The temple has been revering women with religious enthusiasm and devotion for several centuries through a sacred ritual named as *Naari Puja*, where the priest of the temple washes the feet of female devotees, regardless of their caste or creed (Srikumaran, 2005). Perhaps, this is the only temple that practices such a unique custom. Innumerable devotees stand as witness to the very rare and special ritual that proclaim the glory of a woman. This ritual leads to a remarkable implication across the world that if a woman is demeaned, it results in misfortune.

Though priesthood of women is a very uncommon phenomenon among the Malayali Brahmins, the head priestess of Sree Nagaraja Temple, Mannarasala is an exception. Mannarasala, a prominent center of pilgrimage famed as an abode of serpent Gods, is the largest snake temple in Kerala (Mathew, 2013). The convictions and rituals associated with the Mannarasala temple are not the same as in most other temples due to the rare practice that is followed in the temple; the sacred puja is supervised by a Brahmin lady. On certain special days men might be allowed to venerate. The temple belongs to the Brahmin family of Mannarasala Illam and by tradition all main religious rituals are performed by the oldest lady in the family addressed as *Valia Amma*, is the most revered person of Mannarasala temple (Nair, 2017). From the time she assumes this high position as Amma, she should live as a Brahmacharini and observe penance. The remarkable gracefulness of Valia Amma who has transformed into an image of Naga divinities through fasting and different austerities has not darkened at all at this point because of the performance of religious practices and pujas. It has been the presence and the connection with the Mother, who has assumed a divine role and reached the heights of spirituality that has been the sole foundation for a prosperous and successful life for the devotees.

17.4.2 WOMEN AS RITUAL AND SPIRITUAL FACILITATORS

The facilitator needs to see how dissimilarities in strategic maneuver play out in the group. He/she should call attention to when individuals do not follow the understandings about group demeanor that folks have made. Tremendous facilitators remind societies that everybody's thoughts and ideas are significant, appreciated and worth sharing, regardless of whether they have had the chance to gain education, or feel like they have less supremacy than others.

In rural areas, the male folks from the local castes of woodworkers, blacksmiths, potters, and so on assumed a significant part in the manufacturing and promotion of their products. However, the women of these communities involved with helping the creation of different indigenous specialty items, their genuine role really taking shape of craftsmanship and art items were limited to articles and adornments identified with traditional and ritualistic practices. Women used to enliven the premises with auspicious edifices, decorated the walls with sanctified motifs for worship during the hour of fairs and festivities. Spiritual and traditional ritualistic practices can mold cultural outlook of communities and strengthen and reinforce strategic approaches needed to meddle with authoritative diplomacies and resistance (Bell, 1992). Divine and conventional practices of societies punctuate the periodicity of social recreation and the initiative of profound facilitators and it is pivotal to the welfare of the community (Rowlands, 1993).

Women face difficulty in terms of admittance to occupational education training because most skills training programs require basic education and most women are unlikely to get basic level of education in India, especially in the rural regions and therefore will not be able to benefit from the entrepreneurship training. Many agencies and associations are offering training programs to prepare women to partake and play their role in organizing exchange fairs.

17.4.3 WOMEN AS ENTREPRENEURS

Women are considered as a major portion of the human resource potential available in India for economic activities concerning all sectors. With the rapidity of economic progression, there is an upsurge in the number of manufacturing units and this has enhanced the prospects available for women as employee, business pursuers, and entrepreneurs. As Pandit Nehru, the first prime minister of India said, "in order to awaken the people, it is the woman who has to be awakened. Once she is progressing, the household moves, the village moves, the country moves and accordingly, we built the India of tomorrow" (Kumar, 2009). Entrepreneurial opportunities have opened new ways and avenues for women in their journey out of poverty towards equality and value. Most fundamentally, their expedition reflects the transformation of country's economic status from an insignificant underdeveloped to a developed one.

Women entrepreneurs have contributed immensely for the growth of Indian economy and their role differ widely from region to region. Rural women entrepreneurs in the south Indian regions predominantly engaged in readymade garment manufacturing, food processing, making pickles, bakery, handicrafts, printing and book binding etc. (D'Cruz, 2003). Most of the women in the northern part of India are interested in the light-manufacturing sector like leather, garments, beauty products etc., (Thank, 2009). However, to earn quick income was the fundamental reason behind the entry of women entrepreneurs in the social strata. These women do not have education or any formal training in management but they have developed practical skills required for running the small-scale sectors.

Together with contribution to the GDP, women entrepreneurs have also played a key role in addressing societal challenges. According to a report by the McKinsey Global Institute (April 23, 2018) estimates that a higher participation of women in the workforce, increasing the number of hours spent by them on the trade and other occupations, and involving them in higher-productivity sectors, will help to encourage such economic growth. However, the number of women entrepreneurs in India remains comparatively low. In India, a large percentage of women initiatives are in the micro enterprises and to a great extent, such initiatives start as a forced economic activity. These small-scale ventures can be categorized into agrarian and off-farm livelihood enterprises. They rarely achieve to a great extent and serve only to hardly sustain the women entrepreneurs and their families. The rural regions of India, traditionally, provide opportunities for a lot of women manufacturers and essential makers as potential entrepreneurs (Neogi, 2018). For instance, a dairy farmer who supplies dairy products to a nearby dealer or a neighborhood household is an entrepreneur. In any case, family obligations, traditional social norms and standards and the established man-centric structure imply that these women entrepreneurs have limited exposure to the outside world. This limits their versatility and makes them subject to intermediaries to reach the market or accomplish their target.

17.5 SPIRITUAL AND RITUAL KNOWLEDGE OF WOMEN IN SUSTAINING THE FOLK CULTURE—A STUDY ON LOCAL FAIRS AND FESTIVALS OF INDIA

The vigorous foundation of folk women and the substantial values of the folk culture make their role notable amidst the challenges instigated by globalization (Pande, 1990). Women's spiritual and ritual acquaintance and practices are indispensable features of the religious life followed in various cultures. The skilled male craft workers relished a conspicuous place until the independence of India and they enjoy an easy access to the public platforms including administrative and supervisory bodies. The Hindu sacred texts do not refer women as makers of cultic images (Ray, 2005). The circumstance was somewhat changed after independence of the nation. Along with their counterparts, women were also acknowledged. Though, there are social and religious restrictions for both on Hindu and Muslim women participation in various fairs, craft bazaars and local melas, many women have come forward to exhibit their skills and potentialities in craftsmanship. The outcome of their contributions has resulted in increasing the number of women achievers. Almost 80 women have received the President's national awards for Excellence in Craftmanship between 1965 and 1993 (Ray, 2005). To encourage more women to participate in the folk art/craft exhibitions held in various cities of the country as well as foreign destinations, the Government has provided necessary measures such as various schemes, financial aids, and so forth. Widespread acquaintance, perceivability and institutionalized patronage and promotion of rustic women' craft practices have given an innovative creative outlook to their skills and abilities. This impetuses to women's group identity in the rural regions.

The well-known "Ravechi fair," celebrated during the month of September, draws in an enormous number of visitors to the diverse, white salt desert of Kutch district of Gujarat. The fair comprises of an array of events such as varied and vivid cultural dances, folk songs and other art forms that represent the traditional life of Gujarat. The fair showcases a rustic and indigenous life of Gujarat rural folk through the display of artifacts representing the traditional rural folk culture of the region (Ray, 2005). The peculiar geographical surrounding, with sea on one end and dessert on the other, gives the Kutch an explicit identity that has enhanced by a rich tradition of the rural folklore and folktales of the region. Kutch propagates the most wonderful craft traditions in the country. Local women of the region utilized a few hours every day in making the most vivacious, finest and diverse collection of embroidery in the country. Women of certain regions of Kutch, Gujarat, have been traditionally practicing embroidery as domestic craft for home consumption for a considerable length of time. But the circumstances are changed recently. Due to its rising demand and acceptance in the urban markets, these women have become instrumental in bringing about an economic revolution and insurgency in many parts of the Kutch region (Naik, 1996). The Kutch women's economic transition, gained through their artistic capabilities, remarkably affects their societal and personal development.

"Mithila painting" (prevalently known as Madhubani Painting), was an incredible workmanship practiced predominantly by the women folk of various communities in the Mithila region of Bihar (Thakur, 2009). The works of art were traditionally canvassed by the local women on newly put mud walls and floors of their home. Currently, with the exposure to latest technical assistance, the practice is more advanced with the introduction of painting on fabric, handmade papers, and so forth. This type of painting is one of the most expressive and vigorous folk arts sketched by women artists predominantly on festivals and communal events of Mithila. Normally a wide range of ritualistic paintings are drawn on the walls of each home to make a perfect and divine ambience during the various religious festivals and communal celebrations of the region. Traditionally, the painting was one of the skills that was passed down from generation to generation in the families of the Mithila region, mainly by women (Thakur, 2009). For a considerable length of time, the women of the Mithila region of Northern Bihar have played a significant role through the wall and floor paintings as part of the occasion of their ritualistic traditions. These paintings inside their homes, on the walls of their compounds, create a sacred, divine and auspicious ambience for the ritualistic practices.

During the 1950s and mid-1960s, a few Indian researchers and craftsmen visited the region and engrossed by the paintings. Be that as it may, the official move to carry the paintings to the spotlight was done in the year 1966, when the All India Handicraft Board send a craftsman Mr. Bhaskar Kulkarni to Mithila to proliferate the women to make the paintings on paper (Thakur, 2003). He also elucidated the possibility of recognizing a new source of family income through the sale of these paintings. Despite the fact that Mr. Kulkarni discovered women of a few networks enjoyed the craft of painting, he had the option to persuade just a little gathering of Mahapatra Brahmin and Kayastha women to paint on paper (Thakur, 2003). By the late 1960s and early 1970s, two prominent women, Sita Devi and Ganga Devi were recognized as a great proponents of this great art form and represented the country in various international, cultural fairs and exhibitions organized by Japan, Russia, USA and many European countries (Thakur, 2003). Their achievement, affluence, and contributions enthused many women to begin painting on papers.

Madhubani painting got an official appreciation in 1969 when Sita Devi got the state award by Government of Bihar. Another legendary female personality is Jagdamba Devi, the first artist from Mithila who received a national award in Mithila paintings. In 1975, President of India gave the Padma Shri award to Jagdamba Devi and National award to Dita Devi of Jitwarpur village near Madhubani (Mahtab, 2017). Jagdamba's foster son,

Satya Narayan Lal Karn and his wife Moti Karn are also well-known Mithila artists and received the national award jointly in the year 2003. Another eminent personality was Sita Devi, who has also received the Padma Shri in the year 1981 and in the year 1984, the government of Bihar awarded her with Bihar Ratna (Mahtab, 2017). There are different estimates taken recently to commercialize the Mithila paintings comprehensively. The first Exhibition of Mithila paintings was organized in the year 1948 in London (*Thakur, 2009*). The initial strategies to market the paintings couldn't bring a lot of progress.

17.6 CONCLUSION

From the Vedic period to the periods of Mauryas, Cholas, Mughals, and British Rules, India has consistently been notable for its socio-cultural traditions and hospitality. "Unity in diversity" is exceptionally showing its prominence its inconceivable rich culture and legacy. There are numerous attractions that fascinate a large number of worldwide explorers to India and generate monetary benefits out of using the most of its dynamic and varied culture which is a mix of ethnicity, religious traditions and practices, fairs and festivals, culinary varieties, arts, crafts, dance, music, and many other subtle assets. India has such a remarkable extent of Indian culture and rich heritage when contrasted with the rest of the global terrains. In those times, many people have acclaimed for their yields in molding quite a bit of Indian philosophy, literature, architecture, art, and music. India is the origin place of several religious sects, for example, Hinduism, Buddhism, Islam, Christianity, Jainism, and Sikhism and they revered their religious Gods and Goddess and alongside, they have a good time with various festivals, giving opportunities to appreciate their spiritual delights.

Festivals and celebrations help to live with respectful likeness and concordance and motivate to be joined together in the various perceptions of society, like, numerous vernaculars, various religious philosophies, castes, and traditions. They furthermore convey the message of fraternity, goodness, behavior and ethical quality. In this way, people welcome festivals to act as mood elevators and to bring happiness and enthusiasm in their life. The pleasure of festivals equally touches the heart of all people without having any discrimination on the basis of gender, caste, creed, religion, and geographical distribution. Moreover, celebrations and festivals replicate social and cultural activities of various communities and thereby, renew many internal matters by collective observations and mutual considerations.

Surroundings for social understanding are furthermore developed through the festivals of different time of the year. Such kinds of social understanding provoke all the individuals to disregard their nastiness. Indeed, even they discard of their vicious disrespect for concerning to the intensity of that attentive social understanding. Be that as it may, festivities and celebrations intend to project the message of entertainment, fellowship, goodness, decorum, devotion, better understanding, disorderliness in the assorted idea of society and support for keeping up harmony and agreement which help to teach them oral instructive worth.

Women had a vital role in folk culture and enhance vibrancy and vitality to its traditional richness. Folk literature depicts the position and importance of women in folk culture and essence of the concept of the family. The social structure in today's globalized scenario has become complex beyond our perceptions. Though there are various social, economic and political factors contribute in capsizing women's position in the male-dominated social system, the unyielding spirit of women is effectively reflecting in every sphere of life. Women sustain their traditional religious practices mostly within their limited realms and these practices are often closely cohesive with knowledge and traditions of ethics, behavioral patterns, illustrations and lifecycle patterns appropriate to their association with their social ethos.

KEYWORDS

- event tourism
- role of women in events
- cultural potential of a community
- the folk potential of fairs and festivals

REFERENCES

Bhattarai, Madhusudan, et al., Employment Guarantee Program and Dynamics of Rural Transformation in India: Challenges and Opportunities, Ed.; Springer: Singapore, 2018.

Bochinger, Christoph, Dynamics of Religion: Past and Present; Rüpke, Jörg, Ed.; Walter de Gruyter GmbH & Co KG: Berlin, 2016.

Borowiecki, Karol Jan, et al., Cultural Heritage in a Changing World, Ed.; Springer: Switzerland, 2016.

Brockman, Norbert C. Encyclopedia of Sacred Places, 2nd Ed.; ABC-CLIO LLC: California, 2011; Vol. 1; p. 22.

Chaudhuri, Sarit K. Primitive Tribes in Contemporary India: Concept, Ethnography and Demography; Chaudhuri, Sucheta Sen; Ed.; Mittal Publications: New Delhi, 2005, Vol. 1; pp. 311–318.

Dasgupta, Sanjukta The Indian Family in Transition: Reading Literary and Cultural Texts; Lal, Malashri, Ed.; SAGE Publications India Pvt Ltd: New Delhi, 2007.

Edensor, Tim. National Identity, Popular Culture and Everyday Life, Bloomsbury Publishing: New York, 2016.

Ghadially, Rehana. Urban Women in Contemporary India: A Reader, Ed.; SAGE Publications India Pvt Ltd: New Delhi, 2007.

Ghosh, Raghunath. Facets of Feminism: Studies on the Concept of Woman in Indian Tradition, Northern Book Centre: New Delhi, 2005, p. 21.

Gupte, B. A., Hindu Holidays and Ceremonials: With Dissertations on Origin, Folklore and Symbols, Reprint; Asian Educational Services: New Delhi, 1994.

Heesterman, J. C. The Broken World of Sacrifice: An Essay in Ancient Indian Ritual, University of Chicago Press: Chicago, 1993, p. 106.

Henderson, Carol E. Culture and Customs of India, Greenwood Publishing Group: Westport, 2002.

Hecht, Richard D. Religion and Everyday Life and Culture; Biondo, Vincent F., Ed.; PRAEGER - ABC-CLIO: California, 2010.

Hirst, Jacqueline Suthren and Zavos, John. Religious Traditions in Modern South Asia, Routledge: New York, 2011.

Hu, Biliang. Informal Institutions and Rural Development in China, Routledge: London, 2007, p. 275.

Jain, Simmi. Encyclopedia of Indian Women through the ages: Ancient India, Kalpaz Publications: New Delhi, 2003; Vol. I; p. 84.

Kumar, R. and Kumar, Meenal. Women Health, Empowerment and Economic Development: Their Contribution to National Economy, Deep and Deep Publications: New Delhi, 2009, pp. 2 – 49.

Leslie, Julia. Roles and Rituals for Hindu Women, Ed.; Motilal Banarsidass Publishers Pvt Ltd: New Delhi, 1992.

Madhava Menon, T. A Handbook of Kerala, The International School of Dravidian Linguistics: Thiruvananthapuram, 2002; Vol. 2; p. 423.

Mahtab, Nazmunnessa, et al., Handbook of Research on Women's Issues and Rights in the Developing World, Ed.; IGI Global: Hershey (PA, USA), 2017, p. 375

Mathew, Biju, Pilgrimage to Temple Heritage, 8th ed.; Info Kerala Communications Pvt Ltd: Kochi, 2013, p. 147.

McKinsey Global Institute, The future of women at work: Transitions in the Age of Automation; McKinsey & Company: Washington, DC, June, 2019, https://www.mckinsey.com/featured-insights/gender-equality/the-future-of-women-at-work-transitions-in-the-age-of-automation.

Mullatti, Leela, The Bhakti Movement and the Status of Women: A Case Study of Virasaivism, Abhinav Publications: New Delhi, 1989, p. 94.

Naik, Shailaja D. Traditional Embroideries of India, APH Publishing: New Delhi, 1996, p. 23.

Nair, G. Ravindran, Snake Worship in India, Publications Division, Ministry of Information & Broadcasting: New Delhi, 2017.

Naples, Nancy A. Women's Activism and Globalization: Linking Local Struggles and Transnational Politics; Desai, Manisha, Ed.; Routledge: New York, 2002.

Neogi, Chiranjib, et.al., Women's Entrepreneurship and Microfinance, Ed.; Springer Nature: Singapore, 2018, p. 192.

Obeng, P. Rural Women's Power in South Asia: Understanding Shakti, Palgrave Macmillan: London, 2014.

O'Toole, William. Events Feasibility and Development: From Strategy to Operations, Butterworth-Heinemann, Elsevier, 2011.

Pande, G. C. Foundations of Indian Culture: Dimensions of Ancient Indian Social History, Motilal Banarsidass Publishers Pvt Ltd: New Delhi, 1990; Vol. II.

Picard, David, Festivals, Tourism and Social Change: Remaking Worlds; Robinson, Mike, Ed.; Channel View Publications: Clevedon, 2006.

Ray, Bharati. Women of India: Colonial and Post-colonial Periods; Ed.; Centre for Studies in Civilizations: New Delhi, 2005, pp. 501–523.

Religion World. Attukal Pongala in Kerala is the Celebration of Women Power. https://www.religionworld.in/attukal-pongala-kerala-celebration-women-power/ (accessed April 28, 2020).

Richards, Greg. Cultural Tourism: Global and Local Perspectives, Ed.; Routledge: New York, 2007.

Sengupta, Nirmal. Traditional Knowledge in Modern India: Preservation, Promotion, Ethical Access and Benefit Sharing Mechanisms, Springer Nature India Private Limited: New Delhi, 2018, p. 115.

Sharma, S. P. and Gupta, Seema. Fairs and Festivals of India: Unfolding the Colorful Cultural Heritage of India, Pustak Mahal: New Delhi, 2006.

Sreedhara Menon, A., Cultural Heritage of Kerala, D.C. Books: Kottayam, 2008.

Srikumaran, K., Theerthayathra: A Pilgrimage Through Various Temples, Bharatiya Vidya Bhavan: Mumbai, 2005, pp. 215–221.

Rahman, R. Women Entrepreneurship; Thakur, A.K., Ed.; Deep and Deep Publications: New Delhi, 2009, pp. 174–176.

Thakur, Upendra, Madhubani Painting, Abhinav Publications: New Delhi, 2003, pp. 51–59.

Tharoor, Shashi. Why I Am a Hindu, C. Hurst & Co. (Publishers) Ltd: London, 2018, p. 19.

Verma, Anjali. Women and Society in Early Medieval India: Re-interpreting Epigraphs, Routledge: New York, 2018.

CHAPTER 18

PROSPECTS AND CHALLENGES OF EVENT TOURISM IN BANGLADESH: POST-COVID-19

MD. WASIUL ISLAM[1*] and DABABRATA CHOWDHURY[2]

[1]Forestry and Wood Technology, Discipline of Khulna University, Bangladesh

[2]Suffolk Business School, University of Suffolk (UoS), Ipswich, United Kingdom

ABSTRACT

Events are recognized as one of the most important parts of tourism industry which are also crucial part of human society due to their diversified functions. The demand of event tourism has recently been increased remarkably. Therefore, the type and nature of event tourism has been changed over time. Event tourism can create considerable economic and touristic impacts on the hosting destination. Bangladesh has good potentials in event tourism. However, the onset of recent COVID-19 pandemic has created a huge barrier in such growth and development of event tourism which has been recognized as an emerging issue of academic discussions and research agenda. This chapter focuses on such event tourism in the perspective of Bangladesh and the impacts (sociocultural, economic, and environmental impacts) of COVID-19 pandemic on event tourism. The event tourism of Bangladesh is currently facing several challenges which warrant coordinated planning and actions to address these challenges considering new normal situation after the pandemic.

18.1 INTRODUCTION

The event industry is a dynamic and fast-growing sector which can be collaborated with tourism sector (Eck, 2018) to form event tourism. Event tourism is a subfield has been emerged at the nexus between tourism studies and event studies (Getz and Page, 2016). It is known as both professional practice, that is, industry and a field of academic study and research (Getz, 2008).

The existence of events is evident from the ancient period which have been changed and developed over time. Various factors like increased discretionary income, increased purchasing power, and better standards of consumers have changed the focus from fundamental to additional needs which created completely new consumers' demands. Demands increased the demand for a specific range of events which also motivated the development of various modern-day events. However, it was during the 20th century when the development of all the different types of events peaked and they came close to what we nowadays consider events (Oklobdžija, 2015).

Important events are recognized as change and image makers for the purpose of business and leisure travel. Therefore, these events are treated as high-value tourism attractions (Eck, 2018). Due to globalization event, tourism plays a significant role in tourism destination development as well as destination competitiveness or attractiveness (Eck, 2018; Hernández-Mogollón et al., 2014; Zima, 2011). Events can be analysed from a range of lenses like theoretical, managerial, sociological, economic, socio-psychological, or anthropological perspective, among others (Krajnović and Gortan-Carlin, 2018).

Event tourism can create considerable economic and touristic impacts on the hosting destination. Planned events facilitate to bring new market segments to a hosting destination that invite people of same interests to gather that promote various outcomes and impacts (Higgins-Desbiolles, 2018; Zima, 2011). If an event is staged and hosted appropriately then it has a great potential to provide media exposure, enlarge the visitor economy, promote development, and stimulate infrastructure improvement along with the development of new partnerships with aligned stakeholders (Eck, 2018).

Event management is part and parcel of event tourism to plan and manage various tourism activities. Event management can be described as the applied field of study and an area of professional practice mainly focused on the design, production, and management of planned events (Getz, 2008). Therefore, event management is considered as an emerging field of study as well as empirical and conceptual research (Higgins-Desbiolles, 2018).

Though the roles and impacts of planned tourism events are well discussed in the literature (Getz, 2008) but event tourism and other event-related research are still considered as insufficient. Here, events are basically compelled by economic benefits which have been heavily emphasized in research. However, other outcomes of events like social, cultural, and personal development have been ignored (Oklobdžija, 2015). However, recently the research on various aspects of event tourism has been magnified indicates the importance of such type of tourism (Getz, 2008).

Events are recognized as one of the most important parts of tourism industry which are also crucial part of human society. These are known as global phenomenon which importance and popularity is gaining greater day by day through the event industry (Oklobdžija, 2015). However, the onset of recent COVID-19 (SARS-CoV-2) pandemic has created a huge barrier in such growth and development of event tourism which has been recognized as an emerging issue of academic discussions and research agenda. This chapter focuses on such event tourism in the perspective of Bangladesh and the impacts of COVID-19 pandemic on such tourism.

This chapter consists of the following sections: classification of events and event tourism, various types and status of event tourism in Bangladesh, contributions of event tourism, community engagement in event tourism, present situation of COVID-19 pandemic in Bangladesh, impacts of COVID-19 pandemic on event tourism in Bangladesh, challenges of event tourism in Bangladesh, prospects of event tourism in post COVID-19 in Bangladesh, and conclusion.

18.2 CLASSIFICATION OF EVENTS AND EVENT TOURISM

Event tourism has been classified in various ways depending on the objectives. According to Getz and Page (2016), event tourism has been classified as: (1) business (e.g., meetings, conventions, corporate marketing events, government/political, fairs and exhibitions, markets, incentives, private parties which take place at convention and exhibition centres, hotels and resorts, and other marketplaces), (2) festivals and culture (e.g., festivals, carnivals, commemorations, parades, religious rites/events, pilgrimage, art exhibits and installations which take place at various festival places, art centres, shrines, museums and galleries), (3) entertainments (e.g., concerts, shows, award ceremonies, street performances which take place at concert halls, theatres, outdoor venues, parts and streets), (4) sports (e.g., professional leagues, participatory, recreational, fun, one-off tours and tournaments which take place at stadia and arenas, special-purpose outdoor facilities centres). Getz (2005) also added another type of event tourism, that is, educational and scientific (e.g., conferences, seminars, training which take place at universities, college, various other institutions, venues, and clinics).

Events are also classified according to their size and scopes which also categorize event tourism. These types of event are (Getz, 2008; Oklobdžija, 2015):

1. *Mega events:* generally associated to sports events which have impacts on the overall economic activity of the host country and is globally covered by various media (e.g., Olympic games, Paralympic games, FIFA World Cup, ICC World Cup, IAAF World Championships, etc.).
2. *Hallmark events:* distinctive quality of events of special importance and attractiveness both for participants and visitors. Events are identified with the spirit and soul of a host community that they become synonymous with the name of the place, and gain widespread recognition and awareness (e.g., Carnival in Rio, the Tour de France, Wimbledon, etc.).
3. *Major events:* often sports-oriented large-scale events with strong public interest and media coverage help to generate good economic results (e.g., Formula One Grand Prix).
4. *Local events:* focused mainly for local audiences and basically organized for their social, fun, and entertainment value.

Additionally, Eck (2018) classified events in four major groups which drive large-scale international tourism. These are:

1. *Niche events:* events that are closely related to the host destination (e.g., sports, arts, food, and drink).
2. *Participatory sports events:* these events attract a significant number of competitors from outside the host country/destination where these competitors also accompany several people (e.g., spouses, friends, family members) and often extend their staying.
3. *Signature cultural events:* internationally reputed as a "must see" (e.g., Sonar festival in Barcelona, White Nights in Melbourne, Edinburgh Fringe festival and Hogmanay in Scotland).
4. *International sports events:* these events bring large numbers of participants and spectators with worldwide media coverage which improves the profile of that destination.

Moreover, events can be categorized as planned and unplanned. Planned events are considered as the subject of study for event management (Oklobdžija,

2015). These events are phenomena with the spatial–temporal interactions particularly among the setting, people, time frame, and management systems (Getz, 2008). On the other hand, unplanned events take place as accidents, natural disasters, and other uncertain ways (Oklobdžija, 2015).

According to Getz (2008), "virtual events" communicated through various media (various digital media, e.g., online like various social media and platforms; and offline media) which are different kinds of event experiences offer something of interest and value to the consumers and tourism industry. These virtual events have been popular nowadays particularly with the advancement of technologies and digital platforms like social media-based online platforms. Such events have been even more popular during the current COVID-19 pandemic situation when almost all types of physical events with mass gathering have been cancelled due to health and safety reasons. The later part of this chapter discusses more elaborately about the impacts of COVID-19 pandemic on event tourism with reference to a developing economy. Bangladesh has been chosen deliberately as the context of such discussions. The following section basically focuses an overview of event tourism in Bangladesh.

18.2.1 VARIOUS TYPES AND STATUS OF EVENT TOURISM IN BANGLADESH

18.2.1.1 BUSINESS-BASED EVENTS

It is well known that the exhibitions and trade events were held in the ancient period (Oklobdžija, 2015). Till today, such events are globally very powerful and popular which also shape tourism industry. Bangladesh is well-known as a historically important business hub in South Asia where merchants from all over the world used to come for their trade and business purpose. Till today, Bangladesh is considered as a crucial business point of this region particularly for her readymade garments, jute, tea, leather, ceramic, pharmaceutical, and ICT sector.

Meetings, incentives, conferences, and exhibitions (MICE) tourism is one of such examples. MICE tourism is becoming popular in Bangladesh and influencing its economic development and growth, health development, and infrastructural development. Examples: meetings, conventions, corporate marketing events, government/political, fairs and exhibitions, markets, incentives, private parties which take place at convention and exhibition centres, hotels and resorts, and other marketplaces.

There are numerous examples of such business-based events which take place at various venues of Bangladesh. Some of the examples of such business events which often take place in Bangladesh are: Dhaka International Trade Fair; Bangladesh Denim Expo; Bangladesh Fashion Summit; Dhaka International Textile and Garment Machinery Exhibition; Dhaka International Yarn and Fabric Show; Bangladesh International Plastics, Printing and Packaging Industrial Fair; National Book Fair (*Ekushey* book fair); National Tree Fair; National Fisheries Fair; National Fruits Fair; Bangladesh Cultural Festival; Asian Tourism Fair; Bangladesh Travel and Tourism Fair; Dhaka Travel Mart; Garmentech Bangladesh; Asia Pharma Expo; Food Bangladesh International Expo; Dhaka Motor Show; Bangladesh Buildcon International Expo; Real Estate Expo Bangladesh; International Poultry and Livestock Bangladesh Expo; Bangladesh International Tea and Coffee Expo; Bangladesh International Trade Fair; Power Bangladesh; Agro Machinery Fertilizer and Seeds Expo; Bangladesh Water Expo; Ceramic Expo Bangladesh; Leather Expo; Dhaka Art Summit; Dhaka International Film Festival; Hay Festival Dhaka; Chobi Mela; International Photography Festival; CRACK International Art Camp; International Children's Film Festival; Bioscope Children's Photography Festival; among many others. A significant number of visitors gather at these events to fulfil their objectives.

18.2.1.2 FESTIVALS AND CULTURE-BASED EVENTS

Cultural tourism is a kind of tourism that is stimulated by culture. Such tourism is one of the oldest forms of tourism which is recognized as one of the most noteworthy and fastest growing components (Krajnović and Gortan-Carlin, 2018). Festival event is culture-based event which is known to have existed since the middle ages when they were financed by the church, although some types of similar events date back to the Roman times (Oklobdžija, 2015). Various types of festivals and culture-based events of Bangladesh are described below.

18.2.1.2.1 Religious Events and Festivals

Though religious or faith-based tourism is perhaps the least pronounced and emphasized tourism type but this is becoming a flourishing business as evident in the case of Mecca and Jerusalem (Kasim, 2011). Various religious events and festivals of Bangladesh are: Eid-ul Fitr (1st day of Shawwal month of the lunar Islamic calendar), Eid-ul Azha (10th day of Dhu al-Hijjah month of the Islamic calendar), *Chaand Rat* (the night before Eid-ul Fitr), Eid-e-Miladunnabi (12th day of Rabi-ul Awal month in the Islamic calendar as the birth of the Prophet), Ashura (10th day of Muharram month in the Islamic calendar), Shab-e-Qadr (odd nights of the last 10 days of Ramadan month of the Islamic calendar), Shab-e-Baraat (15th night of Shaban month of the Islamic calendar), *Bishwa Ijtema* (held in two stages during winter at Tongi very close to Dhaka: known as second biggest Muslims' gathering after the Hajj), Islamic conferences (also locally known as jalsa, mahfil), *Urosh* (birth and death anniversary of local Islamic leaders), among others from Muslim faith based.

Durga puja (2nd to 7th day of Kartik month of the Bengali calendar), Kali puja, Saraswati puja, Krishna Janmashtami (celebration of the birth of the Hindu deity Krishna), Dolyatra, Ratha Yatra (Dhamrai Ratha Yatraas the most popular one), Rash mela, and so on from Sanatoni (Hindu) faith-based; Buddha Purnima (Bengali word *purnima* means full-moon) (Buddha's birthday), Modhu Purnima (honey full-moon celebrated by the Barua and Chakma people of Chittagong), Kathin Chibardan (offering of woven robe made of cotton to monks and nuns) for Buddhists; *Boro Din* or Christmas day (25th of December of the Gregorian calendar), Easter Sunday (commemorating the resurrection of Jesus from the dead) for Christians are popular in Bangladesh when millions of visitors gather together to celebrate their special and auspicious events and festival. People used to greet, visit, and meet their family members, relatives and friends and also organize various formal and informal events to get together. They also like to visit various tourist destinations at home and abroad at these occasions.

18.2.1.2.2 *Cultural Events and Festivals*

Cultural events can reinforce the local identity and to improve the distinctive tangible and intangible resources of a destination (Simeon and Buonincontri, 2011). There are many cultural events and festivals in Bangladesh which have enriched and diversified the country from cultural perspectives. The most important and attractive is the celebration of Bengali new year festival, that is, *Pahela Baishakh* (*Boishakh* is the first month of Bengali calendar which starts on 14 April). This is a national festival and declared as public holiday. Various colourful processions with thousands of people; *Baishakhi* fairs with traditional and local items (foods, drinks, toys, etc.); kite festivals; cultural activities (led by Ramna *Botomul* at Dhaka); etc., are organized to celebrate this day.

Moreover, there are many other folk-based cultural events and festivals in Bangladesh. There is a saying "baro mase tero parban" (13 festivals in 12 months) which indicates the frequency of such festivals in this land. Some of these are: *Boshonto utshob* (spring festival also known as *Pohela Falgun*), *Nabanna Utshob* (winter and harvest festival celebrated with food, dance and music), *Borsha utshob* (monsoon celebration festival), *Nouka Baich* (boat racing festival during rainy season) are remarkable where thousands of people participate to these event destinations for their pleasure.

There are some other cultural festivals mostly celebrated by the tribal people of Bangladesh. Some of these remarkable festivals are marriage ceremony, biju festival, pani (water) festival, etc., for which tourists like to visit these areas. Gregorian new year (1 January), New Year's Eve (31st December), etc., are some other examples of cultural events and festivals celebrated all over the country. Moreover, there are many more national and local cultural shows and competitions took place regularly in Bangladesh.

18.2.1.2.3 National Day Observance-based Events and Festivals

In addition to above events, there are a number of national days in Bangladesh which are commemorated and recognized as important events and festivals like Language Movement Day (celebrated on 21st February which is recognized by UNESCO known as "International Mother Language Day"), Independence Day (26 March); Martyred Intellectuals Day (14 December), Victory Day (16 December);Genocide Remembrance Day (25 March), Armed Forces Day (21 November), National mourning day (15 August: death anniversary of the founder of the nation Bangabondhu Sheikh Mozibur Rahman), Birthday of Bangabondhu Sheikh Mozibur Rahman (17 March, 2020 is known as Mujib year to commemorate the 100th birth anniversary), National flag day (2 March); among others.

There are some other national events and festivals like Begum Rokeya day (9 December, a Bengali writer, educationist, social activist, and advocate of women's rights), Rabindra Jayanti (25 Baishakh of Bengali calendar as the birth anniversary of Rabindranath Tagore, the Noble laureate Bengali poet, writer, composer, and painter), Nazrul Jayanti (24 May as the birth anniversary of Kazi Nazrul Islam, the national poet of Bangladesh), National children day (17 March), etc.

18.2.1.2.4 International Day Observances-based Events

In addition to the abovementioned national days observances, there are many international days recognized by various organizations which are celebrated in Bangladesh both centrally and locally at various corners of the country. Some of these events are International mother language day (21 February), International Labour Day (1 May), Mothers' day, Fathers' day, World environment day (5 June), International women's day (8 March), International day of forests (21 March), World water day (22 March), World wildlife day (3 March), World tourism day (27 September), International day for biological diversity (22 May), International anti-corruption day (9 December), World no-tobacco day (31 May), International youth day (12 August), International literacy day (8 September), World AIDS day(1 December), Valentine's day (14 February), and so on.

18.2.1.2.5 Local Events and Festivals

There are some local events which take place all over the country like Shakrain kite festival, Pitha utshob (cake festival), Joy Bangla Concert (an annual concert to commemorate the 7 March speech of Bangabandhu Sheikh Mujibur Rahman), *Nouka Baich* (boat racing), so on are also popular events to the visitors.

18.2.1.3 ENTERTAINMENT-BASED EVENTS

There are various venues for the enjoyment of local and international culture-based entertainment in Bangladesh. Some of these are: Jatra Biroti, Alliance Française de Dhaka, US Embassy Dhaka, EMK Center, Bangladesh Shilpakala Academy, Satori Meditations, TSC of University of Dhaka, Jamuna Future Park, Star Cineplex, etc.

18.2.1.3.1 Music

Musicevent is recognized as one of the popular tourist products of a tourist destination (Krajnović and Gortan-Carlin, 2018). Bangladesh is very rich in musical heritage and diversity. Musichas always played an important role in the cultural, political arenas of the people of Bangladesh. There are various types of music festival like classical music festivals, jazz festivals, pop festivals, rock festivals, electronic music festivals, and folk festivals, among others. The main genres of music are classical music, Rabindra Sangeet/ Songs, Nazrul geeti, folk songs, adhunik/modern songs, and modern music with western and globalization influences.

There are various forms of dance in Bangladesh which is also very rich in their heritage and diversity. However, the main style is folk dance which is popular as Bangladeshi regional dance. There are mainly three types of folk dance: religious, social, and cultural. Some popular classic dances practised in Bangladesh are Kathak, Bharatanatyam, Odissi, and Manipuri. Some of the examples of folk dance are Baul dance, Chhokra dance, Fakir dance, Gambhira dance, Jari dance, Lathi dance, Dhali dance, Dak dance, Ghatu dance, Puppet dance, among others (Banglapedia, 2015a; Manga, 2018).

Various concerts, shows, award ceremonies, street performances take place regularly all over the country at various destinations like concert halls, theatres, outdoor venues, parks, streets, and any open spaces. Some of the examples: Bengal-ITC SRA Classical Music Festival, Dhaka World Music Festival, International Folk Festival, RockNation, Ocean Dance Festival, among many more.

18.2.1.3.2 Jatra and Circus

Jatra and circus are very ancient entertainment event in Bangladesh. Jatra is one type of folk drama combining with acting, songs, music, dance, and characterised by stylised delivery and exaggerated gestures and orations of the actors and actresses (Banglapedia, 2015b). The dictionary meaning of circus is "a traveling company of acrobats, clowns, and other entertainers which gives performances, typically in a large tent, in a series of different places." Big circus troupes generally have trained animals including Bengal tiger, elephants, horse, dog, goat, monkey, porcupine, etc., most of the circus troupe has at least one male dwarf who used to play the key role of a joker to entertain audience by his circustic and amusing performances (Banglapedia, 2014).

Earlier the jatra and circus were very popular in Bangladesh. However, due to the influence of modern and Western culture these are undermined items of entertainment. Nowadays, there are only limited number of jatra and circus performing cultural troupes which are mostly located and performed in the rural areas.

18.2.1.3.3 Others

Other types of entertainment like staged drama, presenting jokes, solo/group acting, miming, poem recitation, storytelling, are some forms that are popular in Bangladesh. Beside this, watching/listening movies, documentaries, dramas, other live or recorded events telecasted in television and radio/online/ social media platforms are sources of entertainment used in Bangladesh. However, nowadays, the use of online platforms particularly social media for entertainment has increased dramatically.

18.2.1.4 SPORTS-BASED EVENTS

Ancient historians noted sport events as significant and prestigious form of social activities, which reached its peak with the organization of the ancient Olympic Games (Oklobdžija, 2015). Some of the examples of such sports are professional leagues, participatory, recreational, fun, one-off tours, and tournaments which take place at stadia and arenas, special-purpose outdoor facilities centres. Sport-based events are very popular form of entertainment in Bangladesh. Nowadays, cricket is the most popular sport in Bangladesh. Besides, football, hockey, kabaddi (national sports), athletics, volleyball, handball, basketball, archery, swimming, badminton, lone tennis, Golf, etc., with many indoor games and sports are popular in Bangladesh.

Some of the examples of popular sports organized in Bangladesh are: South Asian Games (1985, 1993, and 2010); Bangladesh Games (largest domestic multisport tournament in Bangladesh); various important football tournaments are Bangabandhu Cup, Bangladesh Federation Cup, Bangladesh President's Gold Cup, Bangladesh Super Cup, BFF U-18 Tournament, Independence Cup, AFC Challenge Cup, SAFF Championship, Bangladesh Football Premier League, Bangladesh Championship League, Dhaka League, Bangladesh Super League, National Football Championship, Sheikh Kamal International Club Cup, etc.; various important cricket tournaments are ICC Knock Out World Cup, ICC Under-19 Cricket World Cup, ICC Cricket World Cup, Asia Cup, Women's Twenty-20 Asia Cup, ICRC International T20 Cricket Tournament for people with physical disabilities, etc.; various important cricket tournaments are Men's Hockey Asia Cup, Men's FIH Hockey World League, Men's Hockey Junior Asia Cup, etc.; other sports like Asian Women's Junior Handball Championship, Asian Archery Championships, Roll Ball World Cup, Chalanbeel Horse Race, etc.

18.2.1.5 EDUCATIONAL AND SCIENTIFIC EVENTS

Bangladesh regularly host different educational and scientific events particularly at the higher educational institutes (mainly universities), research institutes and organizations. Numerous international, regional, national, and local conferences, seminars, symposium, congress, training at different levels and stages take place every year where people from home and abroad participate to share and learn new science, technology, arts, business, etc. There is a new trend of organizing various subject-specific academic Olympiad for school, college and university going students (e.g., Bengali Olympiad, Mathematics Olympiad, English Olympiad, Physics Olympiad, etc.).

18.3 CONTRIBUTIONS OF EVENT TOURISM

Due to the close link between events and tourism industry, many destinations (cities, regions and countries) have recognized event tourism as a priority within the framework of sustainable tourism strategies (Eck, 2018). However, event tourism has both positive and negative impacts on a society and its environment (Getz, 2008). When appropriately hosted, events and event tourism have the potential to expand the visitor economy, develop local economy by creating new jobs, provide media exposure of the destination, revitalize local crafts and traditions, stimulate improved infrastructure, local access to outside goods and services, improve interactions between hosts and guests, which include the emergence of new partnerships (Eck, 2018; Kasim, 2011; Simeon and Buonincontri, 2011).

According to Getz and Page (2016), event tourism can (1) attract tourists/visitors and other stakeholders (like sponsors and media) which facilitate them to spend money which generates economic benefits, spread tourism geographically, assist urban and regional development (2) build positive image and facilitate branding of destinations (3) influence place marketing by making cities more liveable and attractive (4) animate destinations (like cities, urban spaces, resorts, parks, etc.) making them more attractive to visit and re-visit, and (5) function as a catalyst for other forms of expected development (like community capacity building, voluntarism, improved marketing, etc.). However, the concept of sustainability is important in case of event tourism like other forms of tourism even for mega events. It is recognized that events should be more than a "greening of events." Events need to be worth in evaluation and justified for public-sector intervention, portfolios, and populations (Getz and Page, 2016).

18.3.1 SOCIOCULTURAL IMPACTS

Event tourism specially when hosted at rural areas significantly affects the daily life of local population which has been ignored by many event managers to consider. Most of the event managers basically focus on the economic impacts and the ways to increase revenues from the events. Therefore, positive social impacts by minimizing negative social impacts should be at the center of the initial goal for a successful event management (Skoultsos and Tsartas, 2009).

Rural events influence host communities basically by building destination image and community commitment. The beneficiaries are the hotels, restaurants, shopping malls, transport companies, and the artisans. These events also facilitate to improve international exposure of their area, community involvement, cultural exchange between hosts and guests (Skoultsos and Tsartas, 2009).

There is a relationship between event perceptions and local residents' as well as tourists' happiness of the concerned destination. If the benefits provided by tourism and events are perceived as higher than the cost then local residents are supposed to be compassionate to participate in event/tourism activities as well as it is expected that they will positively interact with their guests (Séraphin et al., 2018). Therefore, these events increase awareness of the host destinations as well as the country (The Bangladesh Monitor, 2017a).

Many governments as well as industries use event tourism for implementing neoliberal agendas (Higgins-Desbiolles, 2018). The hosting of significant events in a destination facilitates a great opportunity to reconsideror reposition that destination. This promotes many destinations and countries to host such significant events successfully to enhance the growth of the destination. Therefore, tourism authorities deploy their resources to attract and support these events as a catalyst of a broader strategy (Eck, 2018).

18.3.2 ECONOMIC IMPACTS

Various research findings assure that the income of local people of both cities and rural areas increase when tourists visit the event tourism focused destinations which ultimately facilitate to improve the standard of living of the local population (Shamsuddoha and Nasir, 2010; Skoultsos and Tsartas, 2009) by creating job opportunities and income generation, support the development of local and national industries which facilitate to expand export markets (The Bangladesh Monitor, 2017a). MICE tourism is a strong revenue earner and foreign exchange generator. Earned revenues enter straight to the core of the country's economy which ultimately generate income for other sectors of the country (The Bangladesh Monitor, 2017a).

Though rural destinations organize various events as part of the economic development strategy of these areas but there are limited possible sources of gross regional productsin comparison to urban areas. Therefore, generally events are organized at the busy points on the annual calendar which has several positive and negative economic, social, environmental impacts on host communities (Skoultsos and Tsartas, 2009). However, Skoultsos and Tsartas (2009) argue that cash injection through event tourism in rural areas is significant but not at a level that can promote toward the entire rural economic development.

Destination marketing organizations are increasingly use various events due to increased expenditure by the increasing number of tourists at the destination. Therefore, nowadays events are treated as one of the crucial tourism attractions and resources (Higgins-Desbiolles, 2018). As an example, the festival is treated as one of the focal components of tourism development for many destinations like Amalfi Coast and Ravello in Italy, Batu Caves in Malaysia which are known as the key instrument of territorial marketing (Higgins-Desbiolles, 2018; Kasim, 2011; Simeon and Buonincontri, 2011).

18.3.3 ENVIRONMENTAL IMPACTS

Event tourism has both positive and negative environmental impacts depending on how that particular event is hosted. As event tourism grows rapidly, the impacts which are created by the event can influence the overall environment of that event. Therefore, it is crucial to understand not only the economic impacts of these events but also the environmental impacts especially considering its management perspective (Rich et al., 2016). Such understanding and assessment of environmental impacts are useful in evaluating the performance of the event in an unbiased way. The performance assists the organizers to plan the event accordingly to maximize its environmental benefits and minimize its negative impacts on the environment.

Rashmela is a (Hindu) religious annual event takes place at the southern part of the Bangladesh Sundarbans. This event is considered as a controversial event due to its occurrence in a sensitive mangrove ecosystem. Huge number of pilgrims and visitors of various religions like to go there during the three-day long event. However, many of them used to stay longer in the forest. It is claimed that there are lot of negative environmental impacts due to the event.

Many reports claim that though these pilgrims and visitors pay the revenue to the government, but they used to pollute the environment at that time and damage the forest by illicit felling and poaching of wildlife (mainly spotted deer). Such negative environmental impacts are not expected from any type of event hosted in either a natural or man-made destination. Likewise, the natural resources and physical resources may be negatively affected by an event (like picnic and mass tourism events in a natural destination). Therefore, environmental education and environmental awareness are important for the participants of the event so that they be environmentally responsible and accountable to take care of the destination environment. There are also many examples where events in natural destination can facilitate conservation and management efforts of that area. This warrants strong monitoring system to assess the impacts of events on their venues. It is suggested that events should follow "go green" approach to reduce their impacts on the environment.

18.4 COMMUNITY ENGAGEMENT IN EVENT TOURISM

Planned and systematic community engagement in organizing an event is considered as one of the important factors of successes of the event. It is evident in many research projects that an event can be unsuccessful due to poor or no community engagement in event planning, implementation, management, monitoring, and evaluation processes. In other word, event tourism can significantly influence the local community in various ways. Therefore, destination managers should properly understand primary stakeholders' (including local communities) roles in event tourism (Higgins-Desbiolles, 2018; Todd, Leask, and Ensor, 2017). Therefore, it is suggested that a successful and effective implementation of event tourism should focus on the local community by their active involvement. Moreover, they suggested that event tourism should warrant increased social capital through enhancing social resources, cooperation, sharing common goals, social cohesiveness, and community spirit among different local groups within a community (Skoultsos and Tsartas, 2009).

Researchers suggest that the impacts of event tourism should be focused on local population of the destination and event management should also be designed considering local population to achieve the development at destination level. Therefore, event tourism researchers need to apprehend the contributions of events to overall rural development, mainly by focusing social impacts and community at the centre of event management. Further research should focus on the effective ways of event management, how to minimize the negative social impacts and maximize positive impacts of event tourism to achieve rural development (Skoultsos and Tsartas, 2009).

More attention should be paid to the cumulative potential of small and medium tour operators as they can play an important role in pro-poor tourism. It is evident that small tour operators can play a substantial role in reducing poverty through paying mutual benefit of both tour operators and local communities (Briedenhann, 2011).

18.5 PRESENT SITUATION OF COVID-19 PANDEMIC IN BANGLADESH

The review of literature suggests that Bangladesh has repeatedly been affected by various natural and anthropogenic disasters or major humanitarian crises due to her geographic position as well as poor infrastructures. Impacts of climate change and the world's largest refugee camps along her southern border may be treated as most important existing crises. However, on top of these crises, the existing COVID-19 pandemic is the latest one which is significantly affecting the country from various perspectives.

Bangladesh detected her first confirmed COVID-19 case on March 8, 2020. Till today (August 16, 2020), the official number of confirmed cases in Bangladesh claims as 276,549 with 3657 deaths and 158,950 recovered from the virus (total test: 1351666) (DGHS, 2020). However, various research organizations and media claim that the number of confirmed cases and death are several times than the official recorded data. Still there are insufficient medical and health facilities for testing and getting treatment.

Within a week after the first case was detected, the government of Bangladesh took various steps to control the virus. They closed all education institutions on 18 March which are still that status quo. The government requested all nonessential businesses to move their normal activities online to reduce the outbreak. Nationwide public holidays (except the emergency services) were declared since 27 March until April 4 which was subsequently extended to several times and continued till 30 May. There were limited transections in Banks and other financial institutes at that time.

Additionally, the government has prohibited all type of mass gatherings. Therefore, any type of physical meetings, discussions, and all types of events including tourism events have been strictly prohibited. All the businesses were also restricted during this so called "lockdown" situation. However, nowadays such restrictions are much relaxed, and everything is going slowly toward normal though the pandemic is still continuing and considered as the pick stage of outbreak. But tourism destinations, related accommodations, attractions, and facilities are yet to be reopened in Bangladesh.

18.6 IMPACTS OF COVID-19 PANDEMIC ON EVENT TOURISM IN BANGLADESH

COVID-19 pandemic has affected almost all the business sectors of the world including tourism sector. Tourism is one of the sectors of Bangladesh that has been seriously affected by this pandemic. Though systematic research yet to be carried out to measure the impacts of this pandemic on overall tourism sector and its various subsectors like event tourism however, this section has been crafted relying various data and information published in various newspapers, documents, and reports (both online and offline).

The suspension and cancelation of enormous events, conferences, conventions, and sports leagues directly affect travel and tourism sector of Bangladesh (Ahammad, 2020). The pick season of traveling Bangladesh is during the winter (November–February). Consequently, the number of foreign tourists has dropped down drastically this current year just due to the coronavirus pandemic. According to World Travel and Tourism Council (WTTC), 49% foreign tourists in Bangladesh are from India followed by 19% from China. Besides these, a good number of tourists come from Malaysia, Pakistan, and the United States (Mia, 2020).

The government of Bangladesh suspended on-arrival visas for Chinese tourists on February 2, 2020 (The New Age, 2020). Moreover, on-arrival visas were suspended for all countries on 14 March and flights from all European countries except the United Kingdom were cancelled (Nooruddin and Shahid, 2020). Tourists from these countries cancelled their advance bookings and hardly there is any new bookings which incurred various types of losses due to the pandemic (Mia, 2020). Likewise, the number of outbound and domestic tourists have also fallen significantly which impacted tourism industry. However, international flights began to resume from Dhaka airport on June 16, 2020 with only Qatar Airways and Biman Bangladesh Airlines initially permitted to fly. Emirates airlines resumed their limited number of flights to Dhaka from June 24, 2020 (Star, 2020). Nevertheless, it seems that still it will take time for the foreigners to visit Bangladesh for tourism purpose. Moreover, the COVID-19 crisis will have massive impacts on the tourism industry of Bangladesh which will reshape the industry's future landscape (Ahammad, 2020).

18.6.1 SOCIOCULTURAL IMPACTS

Many employees involved in tourism sector have already lost their jobs due to COVID-19 pandemic. Report says tourism business has dropped significantly and people who are directly or indirectly employed in tourism sector are in a vulnerable stage to lose their jobs and livelihoods (Hasan, 2020). Such unemployment situation has profound sociocultural impacts to discuss.

The next subsection, that is, economic impacts of COVID-19 pandemic on event tourism directly influence sociocultural dimension of the destination. During the pandemic, people of Bangladesh have celebrated their two Eid festivals, one month fasting during the Ramadan, and Bengali New Year. The family life, social life, and cultural life of the unemployed (or less salary paid) people were severely affected. Many of them could not buy new cloths and foods for their family members on occasion to these religious and cultural festivals. Many owners of tour operators, travel agents, and other concerned organizations had to face the same consequences. During this pandemic, staff salaries and other ancillary expenses are there. Therefore, these businessmen are drowning in bank loans and the small businesses are facing extreme losses amid the pandemic.

Moreover, poverty due to unemployment may be harmful for the peace and harmony of a society. It may affect the law and order situation of an area. Illegal and antisocial activities may be increased at that pandemic period which may lead unrest situation for an area. Education of the children of affected families is hampered. Some of the reports already made such claims which seem very alarming in near future.

18.6.2 ECONOMIC IMPACTS

The economic disruption due to the outbreak of COVID-19 has severely threatened millions of livelihoods in Bangladesh. It has taken a heavy toll on almost all sectors of the economy of Bangladesh. There are more than 50 million workers in the informal sector of Bangladesh who are most vulnerable to the impact of the COVID-19 on their livelihood (Islam and Divadkar, 2020). It is estimated that 13% of people have become unemployed. Lower and middle-income classes have been experiencing a substantial reduction in income for the last few months since the pandemic started in March 2020. Therefore, the disposable income of the country people has been reduced which leads to forecast increased (25.13%) national poverty reported by Bangladesh Institute of Development Studies (BIDS) (Latifee and Hossian, 2020).

The pandemic has caused a reduction of exports and imports byaround 17% each and, also a decline of average revenue for all small and medium enterprises (SMEs) by 66% in 2020 compared to 2019 which also directly affected MICE events. Exceptionally, only foreign remittance inflow has been increased 11% in this period (Latifee and Hossian, 2020). Though readymade garment factories were allowed to continue their operations under the lockdown situation, an estimated one million garment workers (or one-quarter of total workforce) were laid off due to declining orders for export (Frayer, 2020).

Though many countries took remarkable steps in stimulus packages however, Bangladesh was bit slower to respond. The Prime Minister initially declared an emergency stimulus package of US$600 million (equivalent to 0.2% of GDP) on 25 March which was significantly extended on 4 April to US$8.5 billion (equivalent to 2.5% of GDP) (Islam and Divadkar, 2020). However, there is no stimulus package yet for tourism sector which has frustrated the tour operators and other concerned industry people. Therefore, the war against COVID-19 cannot be carried out solely by the government, it requires unparalleled level of support between the public and private sectors at both the local and international level.

Currently, only a very limited number of international flights are operating in Bangladesh which caused a sharp fall in the influx of inbound as well as outbound tourists. Domestic flights resumed their operations in a limited scale. As a result travel and tour operators, airline travel agencies, tourism service providers including accommodation, transportation, and hospitality are facing serious financial crises (Mia, 2020). Many employees involved in tourism sector have already lost their jobs. Report says tourism business has dropped significantly and people who are directly or indirectly employed in tourism sector are in a vulnerable stage to lose their jobs. It is estimated that Bangladesh may have to face economic loss of more than Tk. 3 billion (Hasan, 2020).

According to the Association of Travel Agents of Bangladesh (ATAB), aviation and tourism sector is largest service industry in Bangladesh must incur more than US$ 12 million daily losses due to COVID-19 pandemic. Moreover, according to the estimates done by Tour Operator Association of Bangladesh (TOAB), the tour operators may loss nearly US$ 708 millionin 2020 due to COVID-19 pandemic. Moreover, the Pacific Asia Travel Association (PATA)—Bangladesh chapter has predicted that the overall loss for tourism sector of Bangladesh may incur approximately US$ 1145 million till June 2020 due to the pandemic (Dhaka Tribune, 2020). According to the another report, Bangladesh Tourism Board claims so far there is US$ 1651 losses in tourism sector of Bangladesh and 4 million employees (70% of the total workforce) involved in this sector have been affected by losing their jobs due to such corona pandemic. Moreover, 15 million people dependable to these 4 million employees have been severely affected for the same (Chowdhury, 2020).

Meetings, incentives, conferences and exhibitions (MICE) tourism of Bangladesh has been affected seriously due to the global spread of COVID-19 which is assumed to be one of the last items to fully recover as international business arrivals are estimated to drop by 35% in 2020. Nowadays, MICE events are organized through online without the involvement of either any travel agent or event management agency. Nowadays business travel has been more expansive for all companies. On the other hand, with the rise of use of virtual conferencing software such as Zoom, Google Meet, Facebook, Stream yard, and so on many have started to realize that this type of ongoing expenses issuperfluous. Due to such virtual facilities with very low cost has undermined the necessities of organizing MICE events as prepandemic situation to lower the cost as well as to reduce the health risk due to the contamination of coronavirus. This is a frustrating situation for all stakeholders involved in travel and tourism industry (The Bangladesh Monitor, 2020b).

After the terrible Holy Artisan incident in 2016, tourism in Bangladesh is experiencing a deadlock condition for both domestic and international tourists. Bangladesh was successful to undergo an impressive recovery since the last four years. Tourists form home and abroad once again moved to the popular destinations (Sarkar, 2020).

Most of the accommodation providers, restaurants, tourists destinations are still closed (if not fully closed having limited operations and demands) which aggravated not only unemployment situation and their financial losses but created various social and cultural problems for the affected people. Especially the small- and middle-tourism-related businessmen of these destinations are drowning in bank loans and facing extreme losses amid the pandemic (Aziz, 2020).

Tourism industry of the country's largest tourist destination Cox's Bazar has been closed off for last four and a half months due to the pandemic. There are more than 470 hotels and motels, 2000+ eateries, Burmese markets, and 5000+ tourism-dependent businesses which are shut down over this pandemic period which claim to incur losses of US$ 118 million and forced some 150,000 people (including 150 tour operators) into unemployment which created lot of problems for these people and their dependent family members. The report adds that the loss will be further increased if the accommodations are not opened as well as tourism restrictions are not released soon (Aziz, 2020).

Rangamati Parjatan Complex was opened during the last Eid holidays (1st week of August) considering strict health guidelines and social distancing to recover the losses incurred (US$ 177K) during its last 137 days closure due to coronavirus pandemic. Some other tourist destinations in Cox's Bazar, Sylhet, Chittagong, and Chittagong Hill Tracts were also opened during the holidays. However, report said it failed to attract the tourists due to health risks. The report mentioned the government has lost considerably its revenue from the complex, the local people depended on this complex for their livelihood were living in a dire condition (Dhar, 2020). Nevertheless, another report mentioned local visitors thronged most of the tourist destinations (e.g., Jaflong, Lalakhal, Ratargul, Bichnakandi, Pantumai, Bholaganj Zero Line, and Bangabandhu Hi-Tech Park) of Sylhet region during this holiday amidst the pandemic though the local administration discouraged people to travel and crowding (S. Islam, 2020).

Event management companies involved in logistics support for event management to organise and operate mass gathering events (like corporate-funded concerts, exhibitions or large meetings like product launching and media events) for their clients are been among those worst affected by the current pandemic. The pandemic could force at least 50% of event management firms in Bangladesh to close (Shawki and Mamun, 2020).

These data simply indicate the extent of negative impacts on tourism industry caused by such current pandemic. As mentioned earlier, there is no separate data regarding the losses for only event tourism due the pandemic. However, we can assume the negative impacts from the list of the above-mentioned various event-based tourisms as well as the table of postponed events which has not only the economic impacts but also other impacts (Table 18.1).

TABLE 18.1 List of Some Important Events Postponed Due to COVID-19 Pandemic in Bangladesh

Name of the Event	Brief Description of the Event	Date	Venues
17th Dhaka International Yarn and Fabric Show 2020	Enable the Textile/Apparel Industry buyers to meet local and overseas textile and yarn manufacturers for excellent qualities and reasonable prices	February 26–29, 2020	International Convention City Bashundhara (ICCB), Dhaka
17th Dhaka International Textile and Garment Machinery Exhibition (DTG 2020)	In conjunction with the 17th Dhaka Int'l Textile and Apparel Accessories Exhibition (DitaTex), Dhaka Int'l Dyeing and Chemical Industry Exhibition (DYECHEM) and Bangladesh Int'l Sewing Machinery and Accessories Fair (BISMA)	February 20–23, 2020 (rescheduled: January 28–31, 2021)	International Convention City Bashundhara (ICCB), Dhaka
17th Dhaka Travel Mart 2020	A platform to promote inbound, outbound, and domestic travel in Bangladesh	March 12–14, 2020	Pan Pacific Sonargaon Dhaka Hotel
Birth centenary of the country's founder Sheikh Mujibur Rahman	2020 has been declared as "Mujib Year"	Round the year various events. Inaugural: March 17, 2020	All over the country
10th Bangladesh Travel and Tourism Fair 2020	The largest international travel event of Bangladesh	April 3–5, 2020 (rescheduled October 29–31, 2020)	Bangabandhu International Conference Centre (BICC), Dhaka
12th Bangladesh Denim Expo and Bangladesh Fashion Summit	Expected to attract 100 domestic and international vendors	April 6–7, 2020	Dhaka
Eid-ul-Fitr	Muslims' religious festival	May 25, 2020	All over the country
43rd Session of the D-8 Commission meeting, 19th Session of the Council of Ministers and 10th D-8 Summit	Developing-8 (D-8) is an organization for development cooperation among the following countries: Bangladesh, Egypt, Indonesia, Iran, Malaysia, Nigeria, Pakistan, and Turkey.	May 26–31, 2020	Dhaka
International Conference on Cultural Conservation through Tourism 2020	International conference participant country: India, Sri Lanka, Nepal, Bhutan, Thailand, and Bangladesh	June 24–25, 2020	Asiatic Society, Dhaka

TABLE 18.1 *(Continued)*

Name of the Event	Brief Description of the Event	Date	Venues
Eid-ul-Azha	Muslims' religious festival	August 1, 2020	All over the country
Asian Tourism Fair 2020	An exceptional platform for connecting Asian source markets	September 24–26, 2020	Bangabandhu International Conference Centre (BICC), Dhaka
Various day (national and int'l) observances	For example, Independence day, National flag day, National mourning day, Birthday of Sheikh Mozibur Rahman, Begum Rokeya day, Int'l Labour Day, World environment day, Int'l day of forests, Int'l day for biodiversity, etc.	Various dates	All over the country
National and international sports events	For example, New Zealand's (cricket) tour to Bangladesh, Bangladesh Premier League (Football), Women's Football League, Dhaka Premier League (Cricket), 9th 2020 Men's Hockey Junior Asia Cup, Premier Hockey League, ISSF International Solidarity Championships (Archery), etc.	Various dates	Dhaka
Cultural events	Celebration of Bengali New Year 1427, Rabindra Joyonti, Nazrul Joyonti along with numerous national and int'l cultural events	Various dates	All over the country

18.6.3 ENVIRONMENTAL IMPACTS

The lockdown has helped the nature to restore its resources by which many destinations recovered its natural beauty and attractions due to reduced environmental pollution. The biodiversity conservation efforts were advanced during the pandemic which created a proper time to shoot the destination for their promotional campaigns with the brand message (The Bangladesh Monitor, 2020a). However, various reports also claimed that illicit felling and poaching has been increased during the pandemic as many people lost their jobs or reduced their salaries. Moreover, due to health restrictions natural resource protection staff were unable to patrol their area.

Bangladesh Tourism Board has prepared a standard operating procedure (SOP) to reopen the tourism and hospitality sector. This SOP describes the detailed procedures for the entire journey of a visitor or tourist which includes various guidelines focusing pretours, on-going tour, and post-tour stages deal with the tour guides, availing transportation, accommodations, meals in restaurants, and other facilities.

18.7 CHALLENGES OF EVENT TOURISM IN BANGLADESH

The event tourism of Bangladesh is currently facing several challenges which are briefly mentioned below.

- There is either any separate policy document or specific to promote event tourism in Bangladesh.
- Shortage of skilled manpower in tourism especially in event tourism.
- Lack of infrastructure for good transportation and communication system, big venues for arranging mega events. Currently, MICE venues of Bangladesh cannot accommodate more than 1500 participants in one sitting. Therefore, hosting an event with 2000 or more participants becomes a serious problem. Moreover, there are also not enough breakout rooms adjacent to the main conference venues (The Bangladesh Monitor, 2017a).
- Lack of well-planned accommodation, food, entertainment, and other services to satisfy different types of tourists.
- The health safety, hygiene, and security system for both domestic and international tourists are not developed which is considered very important for event tourism especially considering post-corona pandemic era.

- Less research on event tourism leads slow development in event tourism.
- Not exploring the untapped potentials of event tourism in Bangladesh.
- The high price accommodation for price-sensitive travellers. The rent for convention centres is also treated high in Bangladesh.
- Complex visa processing system for many countries to visit Bangladesh.
- Less efficient airport staff and hassles at the airports may discourage foreigners to travel Bangladesh.
- Less active private actors in tourism sector.
- Less environmental education and awareness of domestic visitors.
- Law and order situation, political unrest situation, traffic jam in Dhaka and Chttogram cities, corruptions of the country.
- Lack of marketing initiatives for event tourism.
- Weak monitoring and evaluation system at the event tourism destinations lead to poor performance of event tourism.
- Less annual budget allocation to tourism sector.
- Barriers for foreign investment on tourism.
- Lack of coordination among concerned ministries to promote event tourism.
- Weak implementation of Public–Private Partnership (PPP) strategy in event tourism.

18.8 PROSPECTS OF EVENT TOURISM IN POST COVID-19 IN BANGLADESH

Bangladesh has tremendous natural beauties, historical and religious heritage, cultural diversity, archaeological, and historic heritage (Fahim and Dooty, 2014), which can be considered as potential resource of event tourism.

Though the GDP grew by only 5.24% in the FY 2019–2020 in comparison to 8.15% in 2018–2019 which was lowest in 12 years (5.05% in FY 2008–2009) due to mainly severe impacts of COVID-19 pandemic. However, the per capita income of Bangladesh has been increased to US$2064 in FY2019–2020 from US$1909 recorded in FY 2018–2019. The government as well as economists have blamed the ongoing corona virus pandemic for such contraction in GDP particularly in the last quarter (Ovi, 2020). The increased per capita income is one of the indicators of increased expenditure capacity of the local tourists for their recreational activities including event tourism. However, the low GDP growth will have a negative impact on overall advancement and hosting event tourism activities in coming years.

MICE sector has recorded a fast growth since 2009 which is even faster than traditional business travel. Currently MICE sector shares 54% of the total business travel market in the world. Though MICE tourism in Bangladesh is still at its infancy but there are immense potentials of this sector in this country (The Bangladesh Monitor, 2017b). Therefore, the tourism sector of Bangladesh should have special focus on untapped market of MICE to link and boost up the tourism industry. People who travel to a destination to attend a trade show, meeting or conference generally spend more time and money than other type of travellers.

Bangladesh is the second largest exporter of readymade garments and other exportable items are also growing up. Therefore, these exports-oriented organisations must organize various MICE events (focusing buyer–seller meets) for their international clienteles. These organizations have shown their capability and efficiency of organizing such MICE events of various sizes and nature. Given the existing and upcoming facilities, the country has all the potentials of hosting such MICE events. Moreover, Bangladesh has already very successfully hosted a number of international standard MICE events (The Bangladesh Monitor, 2017b) such as 136th Inter-Parliamentary Union Assembly, Buddhist conference, Business Process Outsourcing summit, PATA conference, mainly held in Dhaka, Chottogram and Cox's Bazar (Husain, 2017). These events are evident to host more such MICE events and activities to promote Bangladesh as a potential MICE destination (The Bangladesh Monitor, 2017b). There are a number of international branded hotels and five-star standard hospitality facilities not only in the capital city Dhaka but also in Chittagong, Cox's Bazar and Sylhet which can host large MICE events (The Bangladesh Monitor, 2017a).

Bangladesh has the infrastructure and capacity to organize MICE tourism. There are more than 80 convention centres of different sizes in Dhaka most of them are suitable for hosting international events. There are experienced event organisers who are efficient in handling and organizing events irrespective of their nature and size (Husain, 2017).

MICE tourism plays an important role in shaping various branches of economy, such as trade, transport, communication, financial services, health, culture, and sport-related services. On the other hand, such tourism indirectly creates demands products and services of other sectors like agriculture, industry, construction, and environmental protection (Husain, 2017). The government and the private sector should start working toward MICE. MICE can help Bangladesh to grow its tourism sector exponentially by creating more job opportunities, increasing tourist facilities, and infrastructural development (eTurboNews, 2016; Husain, 2017; The Bangladesh Monitor, 2017b).

MICE will help Bangladesh to further step forward into tourism industry and thus contribute to the country's economy. The more people will come to Bangladesh, the more they will get to know about the country (The Bangladesh Monitor, 2017a). The country would be able to earn substantial amount of foreign exchange if we can hold at least 10–12 such events each year, as a MICE delegate spends at least six times the amount of money, than that of an ordinary tourists (The Bangladesh Monitor, 2017a). MICE tourism can make various benefits to the hotels, restaurants, shopping malls, transport companies, and the artisans.

The Government of Bangladesh has taken an initiative to prepare a tourism masterplan (expected to be prepared by June 30, 2021) to transform the overall situation of tourism industry of the country (UNB News, 2020b). Ministry of Civil Aviation and Tourism has taken an initiative to declare 2021 as the "Tourism Year" to commemorate the golden jubilee of the country's independence (UNB News, 2020a).

Bangladesh is known as a secular country where people of various religions irrespective of their majority and minority are free to follow their faiths. Therefore, various religious institutions and infrastructures have been constructed here. Many of these infrastructures are ancient and have their special identity due to their architectural design and perspectives, religious, historical, and phenomenal importance. These are recognized as tourism products and attractions.

There are good opportunities to develop faith or religious events-based tourism in Bangladesh. The country is rich in religious heritage of Muslims, Hindus, and Buddhas along with other religions of tribal people and minorities (Fahim and Dooty, 2014; Uchinlayen and Suchana, 2018). Therefore, there are good potentials of faith tourism, that is, Islamic tourism, Hindus tourism, and Buddha tourism-based event tourism in Bangladesh.

Being a Muslim majority (90% of the total population) country there are thousands of mosques and shrines in Bangladesh. Hundreds of them are old (built several hundred years back), historical and culturally very important where thousands of visitors like to visit for spiritual purity. Some of these are: National mosque Baitul Mukarram mosque, Star mosque, Shat Gumbaz mosque, Chhota Sona mosque, Kushumba mosque, Baba Adam mosque, Hazrat Shah Jalal (R) shrine, Shah Mukhdum (R) shrine, Bayazid Bostami (R) shrine, Shah Amant shrine, among many of these. Millions of people visit these holly places round the year especially during some specific religious events.

Moreover, around 9% people of Bangladesh are Hindus. Dhakeshwari National temple, Bhabanipur temple, Chandranath temple, Kal Bhairab temple, Puthia temple, Kantajee temple, Ramakrishna math, and Ramakrishna mission, among others are recognized as significant holy places of worship for Hindus. These are not only the worship places for the Hindus but also recognized as religious and cultural tourist destinations for people of all religions. Various events (like pujas and other religious events) take place at these temples round the year.

In addition, Sompur Buddha Bihar at Paharpur is recognized as a UNESCO World Heritage Site (cultural) where thousands of visitors visit round the year. It is known as once Lord Buddha visited Bangladesh and stayed here for few dayswhich increased the importance of this destination to the Buddhist people. Therefore, some attractive and historical religious infrastructures like Golden temple, Ramu Buddha Bihar, Dharmarajika Buddha Bihar, Kuakata Buddha temple, etc., have been built several years back which attract not only considerable number of Buddhist visitors but also other believers. Many visitors also used to visit Holly Rosary Church and Armenian Church.

The concept of cultural tourism is noble in Bangladesh. Though Bangladesh is a small country in terms of its size however, due to rich and diversified cultural heritage there are significant potentials of event-based cultural tourism. There are different ethnic groups particularly in the Hill Tracts of Bangladesh (Chottogram and Sylhet) with different religions, subcultures, rituals, and festivals. Research shows that some of their festivals and rituals are treated as interesting to both the domestic and international tourists (Shamsuddoha and Nasir, 2010). Bangladesh has unique in cultural richness and diversity due to her spatial, temporal, and demographic diversity. Both the mainstream and tribal/indigenous population have their own rich culture, which are considered as important tourism resources and attractions.

Though it seems that event-based tourism particularly meeting and conference tourism demand may not be recovered as pre-pandemic era due to the benefits received through the virtual platforms that already discussed above however, exhibitions and trade fairs are still considered as effective if these are physically organized where participants can be motivated to build their network and experience products and services meeting face-to-face. Nevertheless, considering the nature of mass gatherings of participants of these types of events allow, it is still not clear when it will be considered as safe and secured to resume these events in new normal situation (The Bangladesh Monitor, 2020b).

It is claimed that there will be an emerging demand of travel and tourism particularly among the youth in the post-pandemic period due to be relaxed with fresh air after experiencing such a long and boring lockdown period. Domestic tourism is the entry point at this case which warrants to take necessary preparations and actions accordingly (M. W. Islam, 2020; The

Bangladesh Monitor, 2020a). Moreover, there is a good prospect of adventure tourism in Bangladesh considering its natural resources (Aiman, 2020).

18.9 CONCLUSION

Tourism is considered as a thrust and potential sector of Bangladesh. Event tourism is the bridge to link tourism and event activities. It is noticed since couple of years that the tourism sector of Bangladesh has gained some capabilities to be considered as a potential promoter to the national economic growth. However, the coronavirus pandemic has paled such advancement as this pandemic has created unprecedented challenges in such efforts like other countries. It requires more coordinated planning and actions to face various challenges which will be raised at most of the tourism destinations considering new normal situation.

Considering event tourism potentials, the government, private, academic, research institutions, and local community require to work hard to develop and promote this sector. The government should take proper actions for the development of event tourism particularly by formulating proper policies and financial support (Shamsuddoha and Nasir, 2010). Travel and tourism service providers should be provided with a specific incentive guidelines to support the industry (Dhaka Tribune, 2020). Development strategy of an area should be integrated and coordinated with event tourism planning.

Concerned local and international organisations, corporate business organisations, service clubs, tour operators should come forward to patronise event tourism facilities which will give MICE sector growth in Bangladesh. They should also enlighten their counterparts across the world that the country has such facilities and entice them, so that they hold their important meetings, conventions, and exhibitions in Bangladesh at ease.

KEYWORDS

- events
- event tourism
- COVID-19 pandemic
- sustainability
- Bangladesh

REFERENCES

Ahammad, T. (2020, May 22). Tourism industry potential in the post COVID-19 world. *The Daily New Nation*. Retrieved from http://m.thedailynewnation.com/news/253903/tourism-industry-potential-in-the-post-covid-19-world.

Aiman, S. (2020, February 14). Adventure travel in Bangladesh *The Daily Star*. Retrieved from https://www.thedailystar.net/lifestyle/news/adventure-travel-bangladesh-1867627.

Aziz, A. (2020, July 28). Covid-19 fallout: Cox's Bazar tourism industry sees Tk. 1,000cr in losses. *The Daily Dhaka Tribune*. Retrieved from https://www.dhakatribune.com/business/economy/2020/07/28/covid-19-fallout-cox-s-bazar-tourism-industry-sees-tk1-000cr-in-losses.

Banglapedia. (2014). Circus. Retrieved from Asiatic Society of Bangladesh http://en.banglapedia.org/index.php?title=Circus.

Banglapedia. (2015a). Folk dances. Retrieved from Asiatic Society of Bangladesh http://en.banglapedia.org/index.php?title=Folk_Dances.

Banglapedia. (2015b). Jatra. Retrieved from Asiatic Society of Bangladesh http://en.banglapedia.org/index.php?title=Jatra.

Briedenhann, J. (2011). The potential of small tourism operators in the promotion of pro-poor tourism. *Journal of Hospitality Marketing and Management, 20*(3-4), 484-500. doi:10.1080/19368623.2011.562439.

Chowdhury, S. (2020, July 18). Corona virus: Tk. 14 crore losses in tourism sector, claims the government is not taking care. *BBC*.

DGHS. (2020). Corona info: Directorate General of Health Services. Retrieved from https://corona.gov.bd/

Dhaka Tribune. (2020, April 22). Tourism sector for specific incentive combating coronavirus crisis. *The Daily Dhaka Tribune*. Retrieved from https://www.dhakatribune.com/business/2020/04/22/tourism-sector-for-specific-incentive-combating-covid-19-situation.

Dhar, B. (2020, August 6). Rangamati Parjatan Complex fails to attract tourists on Eid holidays. *The Daily Dhaka Tribune*. Retrieved from https://www.dhakatribune.com/bangladesh/nation/2020/08/06/rangamati-parjatan-complex-fails-to-attract-tourists-during-eid-holidays.

Eck, G. V. (2018). The role of events on tourism. Retrieved https://www.bizcommunity.com/Article/1/595/185051.html

eTurboNews. (2016, April 10). Bangladesh: tourism sector must focus on MICE market. *eTurboNews*. Retrieved from https://www.eturbonews.com/138497/bangladesh-tourism-sector-must-focus-mice-market/

Fahim, S. T., and Dooty, E. N. (2014). Islamic tourism: in the perspective of Bangladesh. *Global Journal of Management And Business Research*.

Frayer, L. (2020). The coronavirus crisis: 1 million Bangladeshi garment workers lose jobs amid COVID-19 economic fallout. Retrieved from NPR https://www.npr.org/sections/coronavirus-live-updates/2020/04/03/826617334/1-million-bangladeshi-garment-workers-lose-jobs-amid-covid-19-economic-fallout.

Getz, D. (2005). *Event management and event tourism (2nd Edition)*. New York: Cognizant.

Getz, D. (2008). Event tourism: definition, evolution, and research. *Tourism Management, 29*(3), 403–428. doi:https://doi.org/10.1016/j.tourman.2007.07.017.

Getz, D., and Page, S. J. (2016). Progress and prospects for event tourism research. *Tourism Management, 52*, 593–631.

Hasan, A. (2020, May 13). The impact of COVID-19 in tourism and hospitality industry of Bangladesh. *The New Age*. Retrieved from https://www.newagebd.net/article/106347/the-impact-of-covid-19-in-tourism-and-hospitality-industry-of-bangladesh.

Hernández-Mogollón, J. M., Folgado-Fernández, J. A., and Duarte, P. A. O. (2014). Event tourism analysis and state of the art. *European Journal of Tourism, Hospitality and Recreation*, 5(2), 83–102.

Higgins-Desbiolles, F. (2018). Event tourism and event imposition: a critical case study from Kangaroo Island, South Australia. *Tourism Management*, 64, 73–86.

Husain, I. (2017, July 16). Tourism industry thrives on seminars, conventions. *The Daily Dhaka Tribune*. Retrieved from https://www.dhakatribune.com/bangladesh/2017/07/16/tourism-industry-thrives-seminars-conventions.

Islam, M. W. (2020, June 7). Post COVID-19 domestic tourism scenarios in Bangladesh. *The Daily New Nation*. Retrieved from http://m.thedailynewnation.com/news/254610/post-covid-19.

Islam, S. (2020, August 5). Eid in pandemic: locals throng tourist spots during holidays in Sylhet. *The Daily Dhaka Tribune*. Retrieved from https://www.dhakatribune.com/bangladesh/nation/2020/08/05/eid-in-pandemic-locals-throng-tourist-spots-during-holidays-in-sylhet.

Islam, S. T., and Divadkar, Y. N. (2020). How Bangladesh's leaders should respond to the economic threats of COVID-19. Retrieved from https://www.weforum.org/agenda/2020/04/covid-19-coronavirus-bangladesh/

Kasim, A. (2011). Balancing tourism and religious experience: understanding devotees' perspectives on Thaipusam in Batu Caves, Selangor, Malaysia. *Journal of Hospitality Marketing and Management*, 20(3-4), 441–456. doi:10.1080/19368623.2011.562437.

Krajnović, A., and Gortan-Carlin, I. P. (2018). Music event as a tourist product: specifics, issues, challenges. *Mobilities, Tourism and Travel Behavior: Contexts and Boundaries*, 17. DOI: 10.5772/intechopen.71338.

Latifee, E. H., and Hossian, M. S. (2020, August 10). Corona crisis can be a best opportunity to start own business. *The Daile Observer*. Retrieved from https://www.observerbd.com/news.php?id=269275.

Manga, D. (2018). Popular folk dances of Bangladesh. Retrieved from https://www.desiblitz.com/content/popular-folk-dances-of-bangladesh.

Mia, S. (2020, February 27). Coronavirus hits tourism too. *The Daily Pothom Alo*. Retrieved from https://en.prothomalo.com/business/Coronavirus-hits-tourism-too.

Nooruddin, I., and Shahid, R. (2020). Defusing Bangladesh's COVID-19 time bomb. Retrieved from Atlantic Council https://www.atlanticcouncil.org/blogs/new-atlanticist/defusing-bangladeshs-covid-19-timebomb/

Oklobdžija, S. (2015). The role of events in tourism development. *Bizinfo (Blace)*, 6(2), 83–97.

Ovi, I. H. (2020, August 11). Bangladesh's per capita income rises to $2,064. *The Daily Dhaka Tribune*. Retrieved from https://www.dhakatribune.com/business/economy/2020/08/11/bangladesh-s-per-capita-income-at-2-064-for-fy20.

Rich, S. R., Tomas, S. R., Canberg, A. S., and Smith, W. W. (2016). Measuring the economic, social, and environmental impacts of special events a mixed methods approach. *Travel and Tourism Research Association: Advancing Tourism Research Globally*, 59. Retrieved from https://scholarworks.umass.edu/cgi/viewcontent.cgi?article=1684andcontext=ttra.

Sarkar, S. (2020, March 23). Bangladesh tourism and COVID-19. *The Financial Express*. Retrieved from https://thefinancialexpress.com.bd/views/bangladesh-tourism-and-covid-19-1584979385

Séraphin, H., Platania, M., Spencer, P., and Modica, G. (2018). Events and tourism development within a local community: The case of winchester (UK). *Sustainability*, 10(10), 3728.

Shamsuddoha, M., and Nasir, T. (2010). Cultural tourism: Bangladesh tribal areas perspective. *Revista de turism/Journal of tourism, 12*, 28–32.

Shawki, A., and Mamun, A. A. (2020, May 16). Future of event management business uncertain due to Covid-19. *The Business Standard*. Retrieved from https://tbsnews.net/economy/future-event-management-business-uncertain-due-covid-19-81949.

Simeon, M. I., and Buonincontri, P. (2011). Cultural event as a territorial marketing tool: the case of the Ravello Festival on the Italian Amalfi Coast. *Journal of Hospitality Marketing and Management, 20*(3–4), 385–406. doi:10.1080/19368623.2011.562425.

Skoultsos, S., and Tsartas, P. (2009). Event tourism: statements and questions about its impacts on rural areas. *Tourismos, 4*, 293–310.

Star, T. D. (2020, 16 June 2020). International flights from Dhaka resume. Retrieved from https://www.thedailystar.net/supplements/aviation-and-tourism/news/international-flights-dhaka-resume-1915373.

The Bangladesh Monitor. (2017a, August 16). Form body to promote Bangladesh as MICE tourism destination. *The Bangladesh Monitor, XXIX: 17.*

The Bangladesh Monitor. (2017b, October 1). MICE tourism may never fully recover from COVID-19. *The Bangladesh Monitor, XXIX: 17.*

The Bangladesh Monitor. (2020a, April 21). Bangladesh needs communication master plan for tourism branding. *The Bangladesh Monitor, XXIX: 17.*

The Bangladesh Monitor. (2020b, July 25). MICE tourism may never fully recover from COVID-19. *The Bangladesh Monitor, XXIX: 17.*

The New Age. (2020, February 2). No on-arrival visa for Chinese visitors: Bangladesh. Retrieved from https://www.newagebd.net/article/98400/no-on-arrival-visa-for-chinese-visitors-bangladesh

Todd, L., Leask, A., and Ensor, J. (2017). Understanding primary stakeholders' multiple roles in hallmark event tourism management. *Tourism Management, 59*, 494–509.

Uchinlayen, and Suchana, J. J. (2018). The scope for religious tourism: An overview of Bangladesh. *Journal of Business Studies, XXXIX*(2), 193–207.

UNB News. (2020a, February 22). 2021 to be declared as 'Tourism Year': Mahbub. Retrieved from https://unb.com.bd/category/Bangladesh/2021-to-be-declared-as-tourism-year-mahbub/45029.

UNB News. (2020b, January 19). Work commences on masterplan to boost tourism. Retrieved from https://unb.com.bd/category/bangladesh/work-commences-on-masterplan-to-boost-tourism/41764.

Zima, K. (2011). *Event tourism economical and tourstic impacts on regional economy: a study of Polish regions preparations for UEFA EURO 2012.* (Mater's), Södertörn University College, Retrieved from https://www.diva-portal.org/smash/record.jsf?pid=diva2%3A444721anddswid=4703.

CHAPTER 19

CHALLENGES FOR COMMUNITY ENGAGEMENT IN EVENT TOURISM: A CASE STUDY OF BUNDI UTSAV OF RAJASTHAN, INDIA

ANURODH GODHA

*Vardhman Mahaveer Open University, Kota, Rajasthan, 324021, India,
E-mail: anurodhgodha@gmail.com, anurodhgodha@vmou.ac.in*

ABSTRACT

Celebrations are part of everyone's life and symbolize joy. Tourism was a crucial factor in festival development and expansion. Towns, villages, and cities are increasingly involved in sharing their history, climate, and resources with tourists by supporting festivals. A massive carnival with spectacular performing arts, authentic crafts, Rajasthani royalty, and customs is Rajasthan's rich cultural extravaganza. The purpose of this chapter will be to identify the issues of community participation in event tourism in Rajasthan, India. There are two main reasons. First, the tourist influences in the local destination were also begun to feel most often, and, second, local people are identified as an important element in a destination's hospitality atmosphere. The topic scope is about the challenges of community engagement in event tourism to maintain sustainable events within communities with the aim of improving the economy. Results suggest that while festivals can offer opportunities for sustainable local economic development, these opportunities often remain untapped. This is why the conversation of tourism festivals in Rajasthan would have to be managed properly, in the interests of both maintaining festivals and promoting sustainable approaches to tourism growth by transforming challenges into opportunities. Cultural festivals have emerged as a resource for increasing tourism, extending tourism seasonality, enhancing city image, and boosting regional economies. The negative effects will indeed be to invest in festival growth and social involvement and to provide tourists genuine thoughts and feelings. This chapter is useful to the tourism sector to increase the value of local festivals to improve the economies of local communities and foster connections between tourism, festivals, and events.

19.1 INTRODUCTION

In several developing countries, tourism has become the prevailing sector speeding development. Tourist industry contributes greatly to the overall economic growth—as an industry that is the single largest economy to international GDP. Tourist numbers are increasing at a reasonable pace that shows continuing opportunities in the future. "As of 2019, 4.2 crore jobs were created in the tourism sector in India, which was 8.1% of the total employment in the country. International tourist arrival is expected to reach 30.5 billion by 2028. Tourist industry is not only a motor of development but also a power source of jobs. India ranked 34 in the Travel and Tourism Competitiveness Report 2019 published by the World Economic Forum. Total contribution by travel and tourism sector to India's GDP is expected to increase from Rs 15.24 lakh crore (US$ 234.03 billion) in 2017 to Rs 32.05 lakh crore (US$ 492.21 billion) in 2028. Total earning from the sector in India is targeted to reach US$ 50 billion by 2022 (George, 2019). Tourist investment in a variety of industries can increase the supply chain, including, but are not restricted to, housing, hospitality, agriculture, aviation, entertainment, and public transport (Endo, 2006). Over the past few decades, tourism industry has developed over time. Presently, the tourism industry is booming and acting as a leading sector of economic and social development. It activates jobs and investment, changes the economic structure, leads to foreign exchange income, and keeps a strong balance of pay. The tourist's money in a country is spent so many times in the process; tourism's total income numerous times exceeds actual expenditure. It is when double of tourism receipts is fully recognized as being extended to secondary and third sectors of the economy. Tourism develops the economic, social, cultural, educational, and political sectors to rise exponentially. Marketing strategies are essential in tourist industry due to fierce competition within and throughout tourist-industry-generating nations (Dayananda and Leelavathi, 2016).

19.2 THE EVENT TOURISM

The event industry rapidly has become one of the global economy's critically significant areas, which can have a significant impact on the environment and community groups. Easily controlled events could only be a feasible alternative if the short- and long-term environmental aspirations are taken into consideration (Dávid, 2009). The event industry is under intensive scrutiny of its arguments that community members benefited economically. Globally, local, regional, and national governments have strategically developed portfolios of events to boost tourism. Government expenditure in events is generally explained by the significant financial advantages that the host group is expected to achieve. Such reasoning also demonstrate noneconomic advantages, but economic effects stay a most accessible of all (Getz, 2008). The increasing importance of events in tourist offers is a consequence of the growing attention in travel associated with engagement in a particular event. Engagement in the event, thus, would become one of the primary reasons for tourism to the country. Assessment of the effectiveness of the sociocultural impact and influence of major festivals and events have a direct effect, but in small measure, on the growth of infrastructure in the regions in that they are arranged. They help to satisfy the government and lead marginally to revenue growth in the area because of direct expenditure. Tourism development, personalized services, to encourage similar groups of travelers or recurrent long-term events, mentioned on the visitor calendar of events, must be recommended. A detailed monitoring of the needs of the international visitors, the evaluation of certain needs and wants, and also the level of the confidence and enjoyment behaviors (Panfiluk, 2015) are also recommended.

19.3 COMMUNITY TOURISM

Community-related definitions exist, but these words are often ambiguous. A common definition of community is taken into account as a group of people with different features connected by communitarian ties, finding similar points of view, and engaging in prevalent acts in a specific geographical area or setting. Respondents differ in their increasing focus on specific description components. Community is similarly defined, but continuously modified by people from different backgrounds depending on geographical viewpoints; this study describes "local culture" as individuals living in Rajasthan (Wang et al., 2002). Community tourism is tourism wherein regional members of the society are actively involved and estate supervisors/customers, business people, employees, decision-makers, and conservators. Local host people also have perspective on actions undertaken regarding development of tourism within the area, in this tourism destination, and tend to work with several other potential companies to develop career opportunities, trade, skill building, and other local livelihood improvements. Collaborating communities can achieve certain facets, such as empowerment, and several conduct local individuals and small families (Beeton, 2006).

In recent years, communities also have endured growing difficulties. Changing agricultural practices contributed to unemployment, resulting in outward migration, reduced services, and many communities' marginal economic viability. The commercialization of agriculture as well as the effects of emerging technologies, including such Transportation infrastructure, automatization of farming equipment, heating systems, and industrial chemicals, all played a significant part in changing communal spaces throughout the time.

Consequently, decreasing trade deals, annual average agricultural productivity, and debt servicing ratios are also determinants of declining agricultural significance in economic sectors. Many Pacific Island Countries, largely dependent on agriculture and tourism, tend to give the two highly leading industries the greatest opportunity for successful economic progress. The advancement of links among tourist and agriculture will also strive to design business potential and to grow stronger in rural villages and to promote stable growth in both the tourism and agriculture sectors. Agriculture (including forestry and fishing) continues a means of livelihood for the bulk of the population for the large percentage of the region's nations. Nevertheless, its influence on the increased economic rewards has also been declining over the last couple of years, whereas the tourism sector has seen tremendous development in the very same time span and is now the "lifeline" in many of the volatile smaller areas. The problem for political decision-makers is to guarantee that tourism growth is financially viable and also that the advantages resulting from increasing visitors are greatly increased by adding nation significance, and any economic power increasing trend is fairly exchanged with weaker rural communities. The reinforcement of the links among tourism and agriculture and the creation of efficiencies must assist to use the tourist currency to accomplish inclusive and balanced growth.

It is vitally valuable that interactions among tourist industry and farming lead to efficiencies that strengthen one another and do not compete for key economic resources (Rogers, 2012). The responsibility of shifting climate conditions in several rural communities is introduced, for water shortage sincerely hampering the economic health and achievement of agricultural activities (Reid, 2003). Community participation is encouraged in the tourism sector as its representatives can be regarded one of the tourism products, and one's feedback in tourism development decision-making processes should be a priority in tourism development. Community engagement was a popular model for tourism growth in developing countries (Tosun, 2000). Tourist industry is regarded as one of the world's largest and most profitable industries in terms of employment, contributing to gross national product (Chili and Ngxongo, 2017). Local engagement is a prerequisite often taken as just an essential component for the growth and development of the tourism sector. The connection between the two terms regional and involvement, moreover, inevitably means that the region is still placed beyond tourism planning, decision-making, and strategic planning. Clearly, the ultimate goal would have been for groups to make a decision on the design, function, and regulation of the tourist system at their site. Area citizens also lack expertise, support, and even enthusiasm in effective tourism initiatives (Thetsane, 2019).

19.4 CASE STUDY AREA PROFILE

This section discusses topics of community participation in tourism events and festivals. Rajasthan, also widely recognized as "Land of Maharajas," is India's largest state. The state prominence retains its magnificent palaces, forts, and monuments. This royal state's vibrant culture and rich heritage bring countless visitors and tourists. Rajasthan is still the most visited place for domestic and international tourists. Rajasthan has a fascinating culture and traditions and colorful festivities, such as camel safaris, Pushkar fair, desert festivals, and so on, and has become one of the world's favorite destinations (Rathore et al., 2017). Tourism in Rajasthan is among the rapid developing industries that contribute to just the state through "generating profits, increasing living standards, providing platforms for local artisans and culture, and developing infrastructure." The state has several tourism products to attract visitors such as "forts and palaces, shopping, safari tours, wildlife sanctuary parks, heritage and pilgrimage sites, Rajasthan lakes, and many more." Rajasthan is renowned for its culture, heritage, a unique culture history, or one such festival or commemoration that supports and represents. The festival is held in Rajasthan's Hadoti area. This is a venue mostly on the list of every traveler and culture enthusiast, owing to its magnificent and different Bundi festival held every year around November (Lunar Kartik's Hindu Calendar). Bundi event explores the history, decorative arts, and traditions of Rajasthan. Implemented by the Department of Tourism of Rajasthan, the Bundi fair encapsulates tourist attention immediately with its traditional charm as well as ethnic background. This attracts the highest visitor footfall, from all over the country and abroad, during this festival season. Huge numbers of locals and visitors accepted the flowering delegation as participants displayed the glorious history of community culture. Enthusiastic visitors participated in numerous activities involving horse racing, turban tying, war tug, and a battle on Police Parade Ground using full of water reservoirs.

19.5 MAJOR ATTRACTIONS OF BUNDI FESTIVAL

Shobha yatra: Shobha yatra is a ceremony in Bundi's narrow streets during much of the festival celebration. The huge crowd is performed out through females that, attired in racial, stroll to the nearest water body or river to say prayers and light diyas mostly on riverbanks. This diyas lighting is known as Deepdaan, performed for peace and success of the family. A further common religious connotation would be that lighting diyas eliminates blackness from human livelihoods.

Festivities: Rajasthan is naturally derived and a person can experience the cultural difference, traditions, live performances, cuisine, the handicrafts, etc., which enhance the state's incredible beauty.

Handmade artifacts: There are several pieces exhibited for sale at the Bundi fair, designed solely by Rajasthan's skilled craftsmen. The pieces are distinctive and vibrant, mixing easily for any home-furnishing concept. The fair is filled with foreign visitors who enjoy discovering and purchasing these objects.

Deepdan ceremony: People lighten diyas and transfer them over to the females, who then let them flow into the river to become a member of the family.

Moustache competition and turban tying: At the competition, the participant only with the strongest moustache is rewarded, and the one who ties a lovely turban on his head in much less period seems to be the victor of the turban tying competition.

Folk music and dance performances: You can really see the cultural street dancing and songs of the groups that have not been at the center of Indian culture. The complexities of performances and entertainment can expose you to Indian music and architecture, especially Rajasthan. This is a vivid mix of dancing and song, very much like adoration for divine beings.

Camel/horse racing competitions: This is the reason, which makes people participate in various events. Citizens of Bundi participate and win with enormous admiration.

Live programs: For tourist entertainment, there are live programs. Therefore, if tourists are music or dance lovers, then folk performances will mesmerize them. These live shows by popular artists will surely attract many tourists over there.

A significant number of groups are actively interested in tourism. A tourism company seldom creates skilled employment for almost a small segment of the population. Craftsmen, temporary workers, as well as others offer their products or workers to tourism destination and tourism companies (and to neighbors who pay income from employment in tourism). Investigators needed to ask the viewpoint of the population about the growth of tourism sector. The researcher said that "Do you like tourists in your area?" All the participants answered "yes" and listed the reasons. As per the responses, tourism gives several social and economic benefits to villages. The study demonstrated the impacts of tourism for the community members. Many people in the community replied: "We could simply sell our goods, improve infrastructure, improve the schools, build roads in the town, and receive good revenue from tourism, such as souvenir shops." This chapter aims to define the key socioeconomic impacts of tourism on the region.

19.6 RESEARCH METHODOLOGY

For this analysis, primary information was gathered via a primary investigator survey, interviews and focus group discussions, and secondary data are gathered from appropriate published library/search engine research. The questionnaire was structured to include both closed- and open-ended questions and addressed topics such as demographics, socioeconomic statistics, festival advantages, local festival organizers' challenges, and suggestions for improvements. Fifty respondents responded to the questionnaire. Meetings were conducted with groups of 5–10 participants. Focus group discussions have been used to gather in-depth relevant data from festival artists, festival organizers, and locals. Issues addressed involved benefits from local festivals, obstacles to obtaining event benefits, and recommendations to improve festival benefits. Different event participants such as festival organizers, festival artists, tourism businesspersons, and local communities were interviewed. These participants were deemed significant due to their immense community knowledge, experience, expertise, and involvement with the study area festivals. Eventually, a visit to certain festival-related sites in the studied area was performed to know and communicate with participants. Visits also enabled the author to view various socioeconomic activities personally and provide better understanding of what is happening on the ground in relation to festival investment and benefit flow. While event tourism via Bundi Festival is growing community and economic system, the community and the society are continuously experiencing challenges.

19.7 IMPORTANT CHALLENGES

1. **Resistance of community engagement toward event tourism:** In Bundi festival, many different events are organized every year for the growth of event tourism in India, but still the tourism sector is facing different challenges, and one of them is resistance of community engagement toward event tourism; community resist in engaging in the event tourism because of multifaceted reasons as some of them do not have proper availability of resources. In addition, there are several other issues due to which participation of community is limited. Such challenges become the hurdle in becoming a successful event, because when local community is not serving well to the local event such as Bundi festival at an international level, then the tourism sector is not able to make it effective and is also lessen the economic benefits of tourism industry, which is going to serve directly to the Nation's economy and people.
2. **Part-time, seasonal, or small-scale employment areas:** Another challenge faced by community working in the Bundi festival event tourism is that the local people do not have full-time employment opportunity as the employment period is for short duration; employment opportunity arises only at the time of Bundi festival.
3. **Labor quality unsuitable for production system:** Bundi festival is an international-level tourism event, which is organized every year in Rajasthan, and it is very important that the workers doing job in this should be qualitative. But employees who work are simply not quite as perfect as that of the prerequisite of this global tourist event

festival. There is great demand of Bundi painting from international tourists as well as tourists search for more creations of art, but the quality is unsuitable as per the demand because of the poor production system due to lack of technology and other resources.
4. **Inadequate tourism education, training, information, and awareness:** People associated with Bundi festival are not properly educated, trained, and knowledgeable as the tourism industry wants; this is another challenge by which the community is not engaged in event tourism in the perspective of Bundi festival in Rajasthan.
5. **Damaging cultural heritage:** Hardly, monuments and wonderful artworks included the purpose of a culture and heritage. The cultural legacy tells the story of a nation's traditions, beliefs, and accomplishments, as well as of a certain collective's history, art, divine practices, and social principles. In attempting to tell us more about the history and showing us the progress and greatness of previous generations, cultural landscape symbolizes our vision to help everyone recognize humanity's diverse cultures more. However, the issue starts as local residents are not very well educated as they should be for a global tourist occasion such as Bundi festival, and therefore, the obstacle of destructive heritage and culture emerges.
6. **Changing social structure:** The social structure is changing due to innovation. The social structure effects of tourism are the ways in which tourism contributes to modifying values, attitudes, relationships, communal way of living, moral practices, and cultural celebrations. Some of the mentioned changes are becoming challenges for the community though they are not able to cope up with these social structure changes, and hence, it decreases the participation level of communities.
7. **Changing lifestyles and local values:** As the people's lifestyle is now changing continuously, they are now upgraded in their taste, preferences, values, and beliefs; this also brings some changes in the working pattern, and the local community is not in comfort zone, and hence, they are not participating well in the tourism events, which is also one of the reasons that become a challenge for the tourism industry.
8. **Losing comfort**: People confront the given hurdles and face many problems, because of that they are losing their comfort zone, and community engagement level becomes stiff, and they try to resist as well as will not able to work for the event that directly affects the tourism event.

9. **Insufficient funds**: The society, operating underneath the tourist destination of the Bundi festival, is not very well financed; those who have financial difficulties and cannot take part in these kinds of festivals also impact businesses of the state in a bad way.
10. **Nonadoption of technology:** Technology acts like the blood, and if it is circulate (use) throughout the event, then it will serve in better ways for the development, but unfortunately some of the people in the community are not adopting technology because they are not well aware of it, and some of them are not able to afford it; that is why, this point has become an important challenge.

These barriers hamper community participation throughout the travel and tourism industry. However, public participation in the tourism industry may play a significant contribution to the financial development and household income, while also continuing to improve the quality of life of the local community throughout the study area. Community participation in industrialized nations has become a sensible choice for tourism development; however, there are some challenges in developing economies. These barriers have had to be represented and reduced in order to encourage community participation in tourist industry strategic planning at any location. Constraints on community participation in the development phase in developed nations highlighted the significance of involving communities in the promotion of economy.

Among the most prominent national industries in Rajasthan, tourist industry has acknowledged itself as a driving force of growth, job creation, poverty alleviation, and hospitality as a company of tourism, one being the Bundi festival.

In order to recognize their "strengths and weaknesses, opportunities, and threats," the author performs a SWOT analysis.

Rajasthan has a wide variety of different ethnic, environmentally friendly, and human-created tourist attractions resources and products, which are mostly of world-class quality, as well as most of them are usually found in rural communities. It has the outstanding ability to inspire and motivate increased levels of national and export markets if sustainable project management techniques and concepts are implemented and adapted in true spirit, as well as other limits imposed/vulnerabilities are properly controlled and overcome.

Financial accounting of projects with a view to achieving the advantages of interested parties and performing them in a "transparent, fair, and responsible way, with proper consideration to environmental, economic, and social aspects of project resource, process, delivery and effects life cycle, project management" conservation generates a society perspective that appreciates resources prudently in order to accomplish an elevated level of economic security for current generation and to accomplish a democracy and public participation in influence of the society while preserving the integrity of the ecological and life systems (Armenia et al., 2019). In order to improve the level of festival celebration by implementing this project to sustainable activities, this method makes it much more profitable and can facilitate the prospect through the cautious use of natural surroundings and the strategic training, coordinating, and managing of the event for tourists.

TABLE 19.1 SWOT Analysis of Community Engaged Events Like Bundi Festival

Strength	Weakness
• Committed leadership	• Insufficient financial resources
• Improved communities economic structure	• Lack of proper planning, implementation and monitoring
• Community development	• Insufficient marketing
• Integrated development	• Limited community participation
• Fairs and festivals	• Poor availability of skilled and trained human resources
• Unique art and culture	• Inadequate service providers
Opportunities	**Threats**
• Growth of event tourism	• Failing to involve the communities
• Building Nation's image	• Failure to adopt and implement sustainable development
• Huge potential of urban/rural domestic populations	• Increasing competition in the region
	• Adverse cultural and environmental impacts
• Develop culture and civilization	• Conflicts/disturbances
• Wellness tourism	
• Strong private sector.	

Source: Author's compilation.

Provided that the defined weak points/constrictions and potential are adequately identified and effective plans planned, monitored, and reviewed, Rajasthan tourism must concentrate on the following (Brown et al., 2005).

1. Increase the tourist industry volume, length of service, and expenditures in all things considerably.
2. Raise the frequency of high-yielding domestic and international tourists (Becken and Simmons, 2008).

3. Furthermore, it promotes engagement of regional communities because it is highly relevant to sustainable tourism. Thus, it enables local communities to engage and take an active part in planning the entire tourism development process or even earning their livelihoods to safeguard one's existence.

19.8 CONCLUSION

The whole research reviewed and analyzed the challenges of community involvement in Rajasthan's Bundi Tourism Festival Case. This chapter discovered that the challenges rose by the lack of tourism knowledge and awareness among community members was found to be the core limitation in the Rajasthan region. Failure to learn that area citizens should participate in tourist activities seems to hinder community support for tourism ventures. Additionally, the local public do not understand tourist industry benefit, since they see tourism as an activity for society's wealthy and elites. Community leaders could also play a significant role in promoting awareness of tourism development in their relevant cities and towns through community meetings and workshops. In addition, NGOs could also play a significant role in informing locals about its great significance of tourism growth in their specific locations.

The communities where tourism projects are accessible must be prioritized when improvements are made, so that they can engage in cultural tourism in their societies. Such views are endorsed by Curry (2000), who argues that communities are holders of tourist destinations, so they must be involved in material benefits. This could encourage higher engagement in tourism growth.

To encourage more tourists and communities, people could use mouth publicity. Words are strong; just once they pass through one mind to the next and can change millions. Inform yourself or via social media and become a hand helping, text passing, clearly implying, and encouraging regional tourist industry. Then, go the extra mile. Let people support one another to develop beautifully.

Today in the era of technology, people have technology in their hands called smartphones. The whole method can also be used by communities participating in their pre/post-event. Societies are using information and communications technology (ICT) in an appropriate method for advertising and sales and other reasons such as photographers, contest videoing, traveler conversation, tourist interviewing, and so on. ICT not only benefited to community, but also benefited toward the tourist development as it gives proper information to the existing and potential tourist.

International tourists should provide ample funding for profitable growth through entrepreneurial education, offer additional local residents with training to learn the skilled information, and expertise educational programs across all abilities and genders. The assistance of local residents with awareness will also be used to make choices on tourist industry and will be much more knowledgeable and encouraged to participate in decision-making. In addition, the company should be able to evaluate whether certain great product share the profits from tourist destinations. Related tasks will also assess the impact on tourist industry and the community members in favor of their economic growth.

KEYWORDS

- event
- festival
- tourism
- challenges
- Bundi festival
- sustaining festival

REFERENCES

Armenia, S., Dangelico, R. M., Nonino, F., and Pompei, A. (2019). Sustainable project management: A conceptualization-oriented review and a framework proposal for future studies. *Sustainability, 11*(9), 2664.

Becken, S., and Simmons, D. (2008). Using the concept of yield to assess the sustainability of different tourist types. *Ecological Economics, 67*(3), 420–429.

Beeton, S. (2006). *Community Development Through Tourism*. Collingwood, Australia: Landlinks Press.

Brown, J., Mitchell, N. J., and Beresford, M. (Eds.). (2005). *The Protected Landscape Approach: Linking Nature, Culture and Community*. Gland, Switzerland: International Union for Conservation of Nature.

Chili, N. S., and Ngxongo, N. A. (2017). Challenges to active community involvement in tourism development at Didima Resort—a case study of Umhlwazini community in Bergville. *African Journal of Hospitality, Tourism and Leisure, 6*(2), 1–15.

Dávid, L. (2009). Events and tourism: an environmental approach and impact assessment. *Journal of Tourism Challenges and Trends*, *2*(2), 101–113.

Dayananda, K. C., and Leelavathi, D. S. (2016). Tourism development and economic growth in India. *IOSR Journal of Humanities and Social Science*, *21*(11), 43–39.

Endo, K. (2006). Foreign direct investment in tourism—flows and volumes. *Tourism Management*, *27*(4), 600–614.

George, A. (2019). Status, role and contribution of hospitality in select defense organizations of Government of India. *Journal of the Gujarat Research Society*, *21*(11), 673–686.

Getz, D. (2008). Event tourism: Definition, evolution, and research. *Tourism Management*, *29*(3), 403–428.

https://www.zostel.com/blog/vocal-for-local-in-travel-tourism/

Panfiluk, E. (2015). Impact of a tourist event of a regional range on the development of tourism. *Procedia Social and Behavioural Sciences*, *213*, 1020–1027.

Rathore, A. K., Joshi, U. C., and Ilavarasan, P. V. (2017). Social media usage for tourism: A case of Rajasthan tourism. *Procedia Computer Science*, *122*, 751–758.

Reid, S. (2003). Community participation in rural events: The potential to develop and utilize social capital. In *Advances in Convention, Exhibition and Event Research*. Hong Kong: Hong Kong Polytechnic University, pp. 42–51.

Rogers Tuifa'asisina Steve (2012). Agriculture and Tourism Linkages in Pacific Island countries. Food and Agriculture Organization of the United Nations http://www.fao.org/3/a-an476e.pdf

Thetsane, M. (2019). Local community participation in tourism development: The case of Katse villages in Lesotho. *Athens Journal of Tourism*, *6*(2), 123–140.

Tosun, C. (2000). Limits to community participation in the tourism development process in developing countries. *Tourism Management*, *21*(6), 613–633.

Wang, Y., Yu, Q., and Fesenmaier, D. R. (2002). Defining the virtual tourist community: Implications for tourism marketing. *Tourism Management*, *23*(4), 407–417.

CHAPTER 20

DIGITAL PLATFORMS AND FUTURE CHALLENGES OF TOURISM IN ASIAN COUNTRIES

JYOTI CHAUDHERY and JATIN MANIKTALA

Department of Commerce and Management, University of Kota, Kota, Rajasthan, India

ABSTRACT

Tourism is one among the highest growing and most vital economic sectors within the Asian countries. It is providing profit to both host communities also as destination areas. Recent technological advances offer considerable potential for the travel and tourism industry, and knowing the way to navigate this new landscape is crucial as consumers find innovative avenues online to be inspired and plan their trips. Additionally, the ever-increasing usage and accessibility of smartphones apps, wearable, and payment platforms also as new software only adds to the various challenges ahead of Asian countries. These all digital platforms are changing the travel landscape and giving new opportunities to enhance operational efficiency and customer experience. They can also provide new opportunities for rural entrepreneurs to enhance their market access and financial inclusion. However, many developing destinations have limited knowledge on the way to cash in of digital platforms and diminish the risks. Sometimes, thanks to lack of digital literacy and resources tourism that affected tons in rural areas. Digital technologies and platforms are troublemaking for tourism sector that operates from end to finish. Many low-income countries in Asia have potentially benefited from this digital transformation and so forth are in danger of being left at the rear if they fail to embrace this moment. Digital technologies and platforms can help develop economies by destination management and boost their competitiveness. This chapter gives the outline of digital platform and challenges faced by Asian countries in tourism sector and opportunities existing in tourism sector by using digital platforms.

20.1 INTRODUCTION

The digitalization of the tourism sector began as early the 1970s when it became possible to get flight tickets by electronic means. At first, development went slowly and only little steps toward digitalization were taken. Within the 1990s, it became possible to book trips by Internet but still most of the knowledge about the destination was to be found within the important destination. In Asian giants like India, China, and Japan, tourism is speedy becoming more popular and a neighborhood of lifestyle. Although one might not see it directly during the vacation season, tourism is flourishing and on weekends or working days people are traveling for work relaxation or fun. There are many mobile apps that are dedicated to tourism. Tourism prospers from the utilization of recent technology and advances within the digital world. The tourism sector has skilled a fantastic change thanks to advances in digitization processes and transformation. If we specialize in the buyer, it is clear that the way during which they approach the method of designing a visit has skilled a serious digital evolution from start to end and these players benefited economy from this evolution in terms of opportunities and access to provide knowledge.

20.2 TOURISM SECTOR

Tourism may be a powerful tool for development. It shows 10% of the world's gross domestic product (GDP) and provides 10% of jobs within the whole world. The industry is additionally connected with every other sector within the economy. Its ability to work in various locations and therefore the wide area of opportunities it offers from entry-level jobs and beyond means it's the power that would help connection and minimize development and income gaps. For years, growth during this sector has been invariable and studies forecast that it will still be. The International Air Transportation Association (IATA) estimates that the amount of travelers in 2035 are going to be 7.2 billion, almost double the 3.8 billion registered in 2016 and over the next 20 years the IATA forecast that the annual growth rate of travelers will attain 3.7%. Meanwhile, worldwide online travel sales are anticipated to peak $817 billion in three years' time compared to $564 billion in 2016 according to the Statista. Companies are therefore faced with a future full of opportunities to grow if they are able to adjust and evolve to answer the wants and demands of a consumer who has access to information again and again and is more connected than ever.

20.3 DIGITAL PLATFORMS

Digital platforms in the tourism industry are increasingly used both by the travelers and the businesses engaged in this industry. In developing countries, tourism service providers are using digital platforms both across traditional and nontraditional establishments. At the same time, foreign travelers are increasingly depending on digital platforms to plan their travel. The evolution of digital platforms and tools has a noticeable impact on tourism. A growing number of travelers plan their trips by online travel agencies (OTAs), digitally user-generated content (UGC), and other digital tools of tourism related.

Digital platforms are collectively understood as multilateral marketplaces designed to supply an interface for participants, like producers, users (customers), and other third-party service providers to network and make collaborative outcomes.

1. They have these basic characteristics: Operate a double-sided effect, that is, every party is often both a provider and a customer. This suggests that the user of the digital platform can either provide a service. For instance, a smartphone user might get to travel from India to Japan. They choose a route from India to Japan and as a customer they use one among the digital platforms which is out there in both the countries. The user enters the beginning and exits of the journey into the mobile application and therefore the mobile application looks for the closest ride at the time required by the user to visit their destination. Another user of the app at an equivalent time could be driving a free place in their vehicle and as a provider they offer to require the primary user to their destination for a selected payment. Next time, users change their roles within the process. The user who looked for a ride before can provide a ride for users and therefore the user who provided the ride before can look for ride.
2. Offer interaction between stakeholders with regulations/standard.
3. Reduce users search cost and easily produce value concerning digital platforms; the question of modularity arises where it is possible in digital content applications also as in their distribution. By making the digital platforms easy to urge, they are going to be a neighborhood of multiple mobile devices, networks, and a neighborhood of

the OS platforms. A digital platform creates value when producers interact with consumers. The platform provides open, participatory infrastructure for these interactions and sets out the conditions for his or her management. The foremost purpose of a platform is to allow trade between users and to facilitate the exchange of products, services, or social value, allowing value creation for all participants. The digital platforms create value within the community and thus people use it. Platforms can circumvent business rules, soften firm business boundaries, and transform the business of internal processes

Participants of digital platforms:

1. The owner of the platform—usually companies within the private sector. The owner of the platform is responsible for developing and managing the platform.
2. Users and consumers—individuals, communities, or business entities that use the price provided by the platform. The highest user will download the mobile app using the particular app store which uses its platform to provide developer services.
3. Manufacturer and producers—create offers that they sell employing a chosen platform.
4. Provider—role is to supply a platform interface.

Although Asia records for the very best number of worldwide Internet users, this varies by counting on the country. Countries like China and India have large populations that are now accessing the web mostly through mobile phones. Generally, the continent is witnessing strong economic process affluence and therefore the need for information which is acting as catalysts for the high users.

Digital platforms would be expected to extend the demand for tourism services through their impact on the financial and nonfinancial cost of travel: the worth of airfare and accommodations, expanding the selection of other destinations, the time spent making travel plans, or maybe reducing uncertainty about the standard of a future trip among others.

20.4 FUTURE CHALLENGES IN TOURISM

These are some of the mainly valued points of a tourism sector:

- **Changing structures of work:** Automation, freelance working, and therefore the sharing economy are all impacting how people work and are employed in tourism sector. Tourism is going to be experiencing a highest growth when it involves providing quality jobs, flexible work, and defining new relationships with employees.

- **Better communication in social media:** Social media has a basic pillar for brand spanking new generations and thus the very vital mean to hold out successful marketing campaigns that attain the specified effect and impact. The essential grounds is that the free-time user not only consumes tourism but also produces valuable information, writing comments, and making assessments about their experiences and about the services known in social media. These opinions are going to be consulted and brought under consideration by potential/future clients being then essential to require care of online communication.
- **24/7 Client service:** To provide its customer an instant, constant, efficient attention, and most prominently resolution of problems, the 24/7 chat box and the valuable artificial intelligence is very significant. Furthermore, it not only allows this much but also to its clients but it is foreseen that the programmable and flexible automation of services in the new model of tourism is the future trend in this industry.
- **Tailored made clients services:** The data collected from customers becomes primary factor when it involves knowing the tastes of our client and his actions. Altogether with the digital trail, it becomes valuable to analysis user's conversations about the service or brand in social networks of their purchases on the web, the areas where they stay, nearby areas and places, of their stay duration, etc., as it allows a predictive analysis of their behavior and details an exact profile of him. A necessary element to create valued offers customized knowledge and adapted to his requirements accordingly.
- **Harness technology for safe and secure facilitation:** The achievement and completion of technologies are fast weight. To ensure clearness in the opinion of tourists or to access too simple and safe payments, it has been understood that in the near future it will be tremendously useful for the identification of travelers at the airport. Currently, it is being used in hotels to administer claims or other services through smart contracts.
- **Multichannel options to be finer informed:** The fresh digital tourist may be a much additional informed person. He/she searches all sort of information and opinions on websites, forums, Referral Rewards Systems Shape (RRSS), blogs, and about the destination of his vacations, hotels, restaurants, etc., and he/she does so through multiple channels and devices before making a choice.

- **Ask to personalize experience:** Previous life experiences are which the emotional consumers believe and are literally called digital clients. Further, we will conclude that the purchasing decisions we usually make are associated with the sensation or emotion that a service or product produces us. It is something unconscious. When formulating effectual commercial strategies, it must be essential to require under consideration the client (tourist) experiences. It must be correct to analysis that the info through tools of predictive and advanced analytics is everything.
- **Tools and applications to access to shared information:** To improve the experience of the customer digitalization services such as Uber, Ola cabs, BlaBlaCar, and operators such as Airbnb is very vital nowadays. Its strategies, implications, and functionalities have become an indication for learning and decision-making for companies that belong to tourism sector.
- **Investment in infrastructure:** Investment in infrastructure was an important theme particularly when watching the ASEAN perspective. Arief Yahya (Minister of Tourism, Indonesia) highlighted the importance of foreign investment within the region, since government funding can only cover a part of the investment that is required within the case of Indonesia about 30% of the entire requirement.
- **Nimble management tools:** Especially in those applications that provide rapidity and efficiency when making the online reservations and when access hotel administrative/front office services. To realize this, it is necessary to choose an answer within the cloud with the power to place alongside other external applications like for instance the websites of wholesalers or tourist portals.
- **Unique experiences of clients:** The number of tourists growing all over the world and also demanding a lot that give them eye-catching experiences. For that, sole reason is that a tourist does not desire to consume the usual and similar kind of experiences every time but it wants to find fresh and extra personalized incentives in clients. Reality technologies and virtual experiences are services that are increasingly used in museums, famous places, hotels, and restaurants to live a fresh and memorable experience.

20.5 TOURISM OPPORTUNITIES BY DIGITAL TRANSFORMATION

1. Cashless society
2. Global leader in smart cities
3. 100% financial inclusion

Digital Platforms and Future Challenges of Tourism

4. ASEAN firms compete with the world
5. 100% digital literacy
6. Digitalization ID for all countries
7. Borderless digital service
8. All old world firms are digitalized
9. Among the global leaders in smart manufacturing
10. Seamless cross-border public services

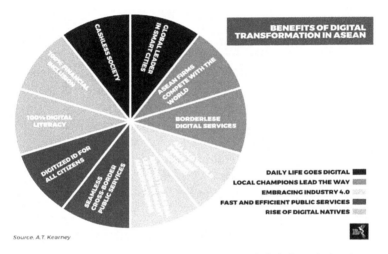

Source: https://theaseanpost.com/article/asean-truly-prepared-digital-revolution-0

20.6 DIGITAL TRANSFORMATION OF TOURISM SERVICES IN SOME ASIAN COUNTRIES

Asian economies are digitally engaged to support the economic growth and development path of emerging economies.

1. **India**—All the travel companies in India offer online services. Furthermore, as per reports 35%–40% of travelers prefer online bookings for planning their holiday. For these tech-savvy people, where to travel, how to go, and what's required to travel is not anymore a tedious task as online travel platforms outfits to each need of a traveler which incorporates from accommodation to adventure sports, to restaurants, to street food. To satisfy the changing needs of smart travelers, travel companies are rendering smart solutions within the sort of exciting packages on digital/online marketplaces with discounting prices.

2. **China**—Travel blogs and various traveling websites still are the most-used resource for Chinese tourists to plan their trips for overseas as they find it very easy for them to find the places to plan for (51% of FGRT respondents used this source in 2017 followed by 21% usage of social media).
3. **Malaysia**—Malaysia embarks on a comprehensive digitalization journey to use initiatives which will help in developing its tourism industry through education because of the creation of smart eco-management of destinations. Malaysia Prime Minister also supports digitalization in tourism. He promotes the investment in infrastructure and promotes incentives for content creation, data acquisition, and online platform presence. As per reports of the new National Tourism Policy (2021 to 2030), Malaysia in future also will be designating Special Tourism Investment Zones throughout the country, emphasis to draw in both hardware and technology-based investment within the tourism sector. Additionally, as a part of the country's National Ecotourism Plan 2016–2025, cluster-based ecotourism destinations with special concession packages are developed in Malaysia that inculcate the utilization of technology and smart eco-management of the destinations.
4. **Thailand**—Thailand is the fast and affordable overseas beach holiday for travelers data pegs January, May, and December to be the popular travel months for Indian tourists to Thailand. The country's tourism authority has also engaged with Mastercard to enable digital payments for a more experiential visit for Indian tourists. Further, it's noted a 20% increase within the quantity of spends done via cashless transactions in Thailand in 2018–2019. Manasi Narasimhan (Vice President, Marketing and Communications, South Asia, Mastercard) said that during a piece of writing "Over 1,000,000 acceptance points for digital payments make Thailand even friendlier for tourists trying to seek out safe, secure, and convenient cashless tourism. Mastercard is committed to work with local merchants, large and tiny alike, and Tourism Authority of Thailand to form more distinguished cashless experiences in Thailand and encourage tourists to travel to the present beautiful country."
5. **Indonesia**—Digital transformation will determine future and future viability of every tourism destination. The Ministry of Tourism of Indonesia has determined three focus strategies to develop its tourism: digitalization, home stay development, and connectivity,

then the event of marine tourism destination should suit the direction. Solutions to the initial digitalization transformation of Indonesia marine tourism destination as follows-Develop national digitalization movement, Appoint seaports because the leader to make value platform, Encourage collaboration with intra- and inter-destination stakeholders, and Intensive digitalization socialization and training.

20.6 CONCLUSION

This chapter tries to offer a thought that how digitalization in tourism offers support to the opinion that an acceptance of digital platforms within the tourism industry has facilitated and boosted international travel in Asian countries. Digitalization is useful in reducing the value of search and providing travelers with more information on a few given destination. The adoption of digital tools increases, less traditional destinations may beat the shortage of data and interest from foreign travelers and abate traveling costs thereby attracting more visitors. Digitalization in tourism will help in increasing sort of employment. Positively we will conclude that the adoption of digital tools, by inducing a greater demand for tourism services, will help in creating various jobs.

ASEAN policymakers are with some key messages on the digital transformation. We therefore take into discussion other aspects of the digital transformation that ought to be in argument at this stage. First, the digital transformation will work for some time and thus still disrupt the economy, society, and government policy. Prudence practices can bring development in themselves, like strengthened stakeholder networks. Practical thinking is just too very essential in responding to the continued transformation. Professional in business, unions, civil society, and government must be able to examine the implications within the policy thanks to transformation and also steel oneself against developments beyond typical election cycles.

Second, formulating better policies for a digital economy and society not only requires fruitful knowledge about the technological changes that are ongoing but also further efforts to enhance measurement, evidence, and analysis. New areas, like trust, data flows, the Internet of Things (IoT), and Artificial Intelligence, are at subsequent frontier for measurement. All countries got to work together to fill the info gaps, and in doing so enable better evidence building, policy development, the identification with prioritization of policy review, and action. Simultaneously, new opportunities are emerging for every one because of digital technologies, for example, by the utilization of nonofficial data sources and data analytics, statistics might be enriched with timelier, more granular, and fewer costly data.

KEYWORDS

- digital transformation
- digital platforms
- future challenges in tourism
- tourism opportunities

BIBLIOGRAPHY

Alstyne, M. W. (2016). In pipelines, platforms and the new ules of strategy. *Harvard Business Review*. https://hbr.org/2016/04/pipelines-platforms-and-the-new-rules-of-strategy.

Alvaez, M. A. (n.d.). *Challenges on tourism sector. how to satisfy the new digital client?* Retrieved April 2020, from izertis: https://www.izertis.com/en/-/blog/challenges-on-tourism-sector-how-to-satisfy-the-new-digital-client.

Bechte, A. (2018, June 6). *Top digital platforms to reach chinese tourists (expert tips)*. Retrieved April 2020, from https://pro.regiondo.com/digital-platforms-chinese-tourists/

Brysch, A. (2017). *Digital transformation in the tourism sector-copportunities*. Conference: International Conference on Tourism Dynamics and Trends, Seville.

Čorejová, T. G. (n.d.). Digital platform in tourism. In: *Proceedings of the marketing identity online rules -part II*. Smolenice, Slovak Republic, pp. 41–49.

Deloitte. (2017, May). Economic growth and development in Asia: What is thrrole of digital? Retrieved April 2020, from https://www2.deloitte.com/us/en/insights/economy/voice-of-asia/may-2017/digital-role-economic-growth.html

Internet World Stats. (2020). *Internet 2021 usage in Asia*. Retrieved May 2020, from https://www.internetworldstats.com/stats3.htm

Jain, N. (2019, April 20). *Digital platforms boosting the tourism sector*. Retrieved April 2020, from www.entrepreneur.com/amphtml/332133

Lopez-Cordova, E. (2020). Difital platforms and the demand for international tourism services. *World Bank Group*, 36.

Martec Series. (2020, March 31). *Asia accounts for over 30% of all Internet users worldwide*. Retrieved April 2020, from https://martechseries.com/analytics/asia-accounts-50-internet-users-worldwide/

McKinsey. (2016, October). *Digital innovation in Asia: What the world can learn*. Retrieved 2020, https://www.mckinsey.com/business-functions/mckinsey-digital/our-insights/digital-innovation-in-asia-what-the-world-can-learn digital platforms in asian countires-to find the topics

OECD. (n.d.). *To seize the opportunities of digitalisation, Southeast Asia needs to close the gap between technology 4.0 and policy 1.0*. Retrieved April 2020, http://www.eabc-thailand.org/news/advocacy/to-seize-the-opportunities-of-digitalisation-southeast-asia-needs-to-close-the-gap-between-technology-4-0-and-policy-1-0/

Pilat, D. (2017). *Digital transformation in the tourism sector- challenges and opportunities*. Bangkok,Thailand: OECD Southeast Asia Regional Forum.

Pranita, D. (2018). *Digitalization: the way to tourism destination's compititive advantage(case study of indonesia matine tourism)*. 2nd International Conference on Vocational Higher Education (ICVHE) (p. 11). Indonesia: KnE Social Science.

Puvaneswary, S. (2019, August 27). *Malaysia puses for digitlisation in its tourism industry*. Retrieved April 2020, https://www.ttgasia.com/2019/08/27/malaysia-pushes-for-digitalisation-in-its-tourism-industry/

Rasul, G. (2009). Prospects and problems in promoting tourism in south Asia a regional perspective. *South Asia Economic Journal*. https://doi.org/10.1177/139156140901000108

Ratnakumar, E. (2019, December 6). *Yourstory*. Retrieved May 2020, from https://yourstory.com/2019/12/mastercard-tourism-authority-thailand-tat-indian-tourists.

The World Bank. (2018, September 25). *Digital platforms and the future of tourism*. Retrieved April 2020, ttps://www.worldbank.org/en/news/feature/2018/09/25/digital-platforms-and-the-future-of-tourism-a-world-tourism-celebration.

Victor, P. (2018, February). *Is ASEAN truly prepared for a digital revolution?* Retrieved April 2020, from https://theaseanpost.com/article/asean-truly-prepared-digital-revolution-0

CHAPTER 21

THE FUTURE OF EVENT TOURISM: PATH FOR SUSTAINABLE GROWTH TOWARD 2030

SHRUTI ARORA and ANUKRATI SHARMA

Department of Commerce and Management, University of Kota, Kota, Rajasthan, India

ABSTRACT

Event and tourism as an industry had an impact on destinations and on the local community. Tourism is the act of traveling to different places to satisfy their preferred hobby, satisfaction, and excursion. As the number of visitors overall is expanding, so their desires and requirements for unique experiences is also increasing. And there comes the role of events and its significance in modern tourism. Events are one of the most imperative parts of tourism. In fact, the presence of event tourism could create an economic development and may even deliver constructive outcome in the general public. There are different sorts of events in the Asia composed particularly for engaging and pulling in vacationer, and there are all the more emerging each year. This chapter focuses on the significance and role of events in present tourism industry and development of event tourism in coming future. In the momentum section, a few cases, articles, and research papers from the event tourism literature and their outcomes are considered.

21.1 INTRODUCTION

Asia is a mix of varied cultures, nationalities, and traditions, full of exhilarating events going on consistently, including religious, traditional, and cultural festivals and events. These events may differ from one place to another, yet share something in common, that is, they are extremely memorable and entertaining! In today's competing world, each industry is expected to find a growth path for sustainability in its own field. As tourism is regarded as an important industry having positive effect on employment, revenue, and production, and proves beneficial for both economic and social development, events can play a significant role. On the other hand, if tourism is not designed and managed properly, it may cause harm to the physical, social, cultural, and financial environment of a tourist destination (Dwyer and Edwards, 2010). Asian countries are interesting, both in terms of its cultural and historical heritage. The consideration of potential tourists is pulled in by the chance to see history through various kinds of events, as well as to relax with exotic and traditional cuisine and other kinds of interesting pastimes. Various kinds of advertising and Internet allow experiencing visually what a particular country is offering. For example, a few tourists are becoming very challenging. They are not, at this point, inspired by straightforward outings, or just to see a specific landmark. They prefer extreme, interacting, as well as learning and enjoyable tours. Therefore, in this case, the more noteworthy impact is brought about by publicizing, which shows the events organized particularly for the tourist to encounters something new in various nations.

21.2 EVENTS AND TOURISM

Before starting the study of the event tourism sector, it is necessary to understand what is an event and tourism separately. The study of events is now a productive area in tourism industry. Events can create a center of attention for tourists, sponsors, or the media who in any case probably will not visit a specific destination. Events are the programs or the celebrations that are planned and organized at various places by different event planners or public or private organizations and may include a number of activities. Furthermore, tourism is a social, cultural, and economic experience which incorporates development of individuals from one place to another within or outside the nation varied from their normal environment for individual or specialized purposes. These people are called tourists. There are various types of events that are especially planned for these tourists and are created for a specific purpose that has become the power for an individual, community, as well as for the professionals and entrepreneurs. Likewise:

1. Business events like corporate meetings, conferences, incentives, product launch.

2. Celebrations and other social festivals like religious rites, art exhibition, festivals, fairs.
3. Entertainment events like concerts, award functions, road shows.
4. Sports event like World Cup, professional leagues

21.3 INITIAL BACKGROUND STUDY

Allied Market Research: Jan 2019—Asia-Pacific MICE Industry and Country (Indonesia, Australia, Singapore, Thailand, China, India, New Zealand, South Korea, Vietnam, Hong Kong, Japan, Malaysia, and rest of Asia-Pacific) created income of $229.0 billion out of 2017, and is relied upon to expand at a compound yearly growth rate of 8.6% to achieve $441.1 billion by 2025 (Sable, 2019). It speaks to the tourism industry that incorporates company events and activities. According to India News on 18th Dec. 2019 (The Weather Channel (TWC) India Edit Team, 18th December, 2019), India to turn out to be first Asian nation to Host International Geological Congress event twice, 1st time it was in 1964 and now during March 2–8, 2020. Also published in China daily by Jianna L. on 17th January 2019 (Jianna, 2019), international sports events have the possibility to support the nation's economy, basically the sports industry in developing nations. The way that Beijing was picked to have the 2008 Summer Olympics acted as a mechanism for China's games and related businesses to develop 35.43% every year from 2004 to 2008, far higher than the development paces of GDP and further industries. Seraphin et al. (2018) on the whole concluded that there is an association among the residents' happiness and tourism/event awareness and when the advantages of tourism and events are elevated than the price, local people are likely to be cheering the activity and they are probably going to communicate with visitors. Zlatanov (2015) concludes with the aim that every destination needs to develop its tourist magnetism and should make comprehensive plans for the enlargement of tourism. These plans should be incorporated, but also focusing on strategic planning of events if they want to grasp the full potential of event tourism. The events that take place in a particular destination should be logically planned and developed, and should be established as tourist attractions, a vehicle for more expansion, image builders, and animators of the destination. Getz and Page (2016) speak to create and market the events as vacation spots, or as an image makers and catalysts, it requires a showcasing direction and a promise to customer service. Especially, destination events which are deliberately organized to attract tourists must be positioned and branded in a way as to be attractive both to those seeking broad benefits such as entertainment, socializing, and as a relaxation activity and those with exceptional interests who inquire about very specific benefits. To develop sustainable tourism, it is important to recognize and evaluate the thoughts of residents toward tourism (Lee, 2013). If stakeholders are permitted to actively contribute in the event planning process, it is more expected that such initiatives would thrive in the long-term (Byrd et al., 2009). The host community is the main stakeholder for any tourism event and should be the essential point in tourism planning processes. The community perceptions of tourism can influence the local residents' behavior toward guests to their area and the events organized locally. As a result, investigating these perceptions is very important (Getz and Page, 2016).

21.4 IMPACT OF EVENT TOURISM

The chuck of modern tourists is now shifted with the ever-growing need for a wider range of offers that provide a wider choice of events (Mihajlović and Vidak, 2017). The 21st century witnesses tourism as the revolution or makeover of positive experiences in terms of satisfaction expressed by number, frequency, or continuity of visits to the particular destination. The event industry is a vibrant and fast-growing sector with clear synergies with tourism. When suitably hosted, events can possibly amplify the visitor economy, give media exposure, promote development, and persuade infrastructure redesigns which incorporate the development of new associations (Eck, 2018), therefore many countries observe the successful hosting of events as a vehicle for escalation, and that tourism bodies are dedicating assets to attracting and supporting significant events as a component of an extensive technique.

21.5 EVENTS AND FESTIVALS IN ASIAN COUNTRIES

Asia's rising economy is optimistically affecting the business travel showcase. Since January to August 2019, 17% of Asians voyaging overseas were on company/MICE trips, which contrasted that the earlier year was a better than expected increment of 8%. The MICE sector, with enticement travel and trips to job fairs, was to a huge extent accountable for this development, while conventional business trips were in decline (Press Release on 17th October 2019).

1. Thailand (2nd Asia Destination Film Forum and 2nd Mekong Mini Movie Festival): Today's tourists are more competent and are looking for new places to visit and gain new experiences, therefore the main focus is to commemorate sustainable tourism advertising and marketing via encouraging visual storytelling. There has been an occurrence in the recent times that tourists visit destinations that are more likely to be seen in films. A movie encloses a powerful influence on tourist destination choice and can build long-lasting prosperity in a destination. Many nations and destinations speedily comprehended these favorable circumstances and have effectively expanded the amount of tourists all the way through the enchantment of films.
2. India (Jaipur International Art and Calligraphy Festival): It's a worldwide stage to feature various types of art under one rooftop. Artists from various countries participate in this program. The foremost reason of the event is to persuade arts and acts as a platform to display the skills and ability of artists.

FIGURE 21.1 Sharma and Arora S (2020) (Compiled by Authors—Impact of event tourism)
Source: Impact of event tourism, Sharma and Arora (2020) (Compiled by Authors)

3. South Korea (Boryeong Mud Festival): A two-week event that has become popular among Koreans and visitors alike for its fun activities, skin-friendly activities. Alongside the many mud-related events, including mud wrestling, mud massage and mud health spa, acupuncture programs, mud slides and skiing, mud body painting, swim in a big pool of mud, and a photo competition, all consummation in a marvelous mud firecrackers show and dance parties.
4. Bangladesh (Asian Tourism Fair): A stage that gives a colossal chance for tourism purchaser and sellers from Asian nations to come and demonstrate their brand new product and services. It also aims to serve as a valuable advancement tool for spreading information for conservation, culture, as well as motivate community tourism in various countries and help each other regarding tourism destinations.

And many more events in various Asian countries to attract tourism. Source: https://www.google.com/search?biw=1366andbih=654andei=UaEqXofkCZiS9QPOh5_oDgandq=list+of+Event++in+asian+countries+for+touristandoq (Accessed on 24th Jan. 2020)

21.6 AN APPROACH FOR SUSTAINABLE GROWTH OF EVENT TOURISM

1. Local government and public agencies should likewise be counseled and dedicated to event tourism.
2. The event and tourism industry is very competitive and to attract an international tourist, one must invest in developing the proficiency, capability, and professionalism of event organizers.
3. While organizing an event for tourist, try to strengthen and meet the environmental protection standards.
4. There must be a strategic combination between marketing and branding of host destination and the kind of event to be organized.
5. Communicate about an event and tourism destination through international media coverage.
6. Try to feature the way of life, custom, and tradition, heritage of the country through an opening ceremony of an event to national and international tourist.
7. Try to build and manage the event stages with recycled materials so as to set aside the manufacturing cost.

8. Reprocess the reusable ingredients such as refreshment bottles, packaging bags, squander plastics or glasses, or waste paper in order to streamlining waste treatment framework.
9. Last however not least, it is also important to engage and enlighten the community about the advantages of event tourism.

21.7 CONCLUSION

Asia is a composition of the human evolution. With the global spread out of easily reachable tourism destinations, people are more and more exposed to and influenced by number of events. Events these days are innermost stages that not only highlight professional to symbolize their country but also provide host nations a legitimate method to introduce and embrace their national personalities and societies on an overall scale. To maximize the tourism capability of an event, it is important that tourism impacts are planned appropriately. Events are the important drivers in the tourism business. As a result, tourist destinations not only in Asia but around the world had realized that events are the essential part in attracting tourist whether it is a conference, a trade show, a music or art festival, a sport event, a wedding, or a fashion show. So if these events are organized properly, they endows with many benefits to communities and the host country, such as generating new revenue, generating employment, maintaining public facilities, and increasing country reputation. Also to ensure local support for hosting any event for the tourist, neighboring authorities and society leaders should be invited to unite as a team to assist in planning and making decisions related to organizing an event.

KEYWORDS

- **event**
- **tourism**
- **sustainable growth**
- **event tourism**

REFERENCES

Byrd, E. T., Bosley, H. E., and Dronberger, M. G. (2009): "Comparisons of stakeholder perceptions of tourism impacts in rural Eastern North Carolina". Tourism Management, 30, 693–703. doi:10.1016/j.tourman.2008.10.021.

Dwyer, L., and Edwards, D. (2010): "Sustainable tourism planning. In understanding the sustainable development of tourism"; Liburd, J.J., Edwards, D., Eds.; Good fellow Publishers: Woodeaton, UK, 2010; pp. 19–44, ISBN 978-1-906884-13-0.

Eck, G. V. (2018): "The role of events on tourism," A post on BizCommunity, Retrieved from https://www.bizcommunity.com/Article/1/595/185051.html, Accessed on 27th Jan. 2020.

Getz, D. and Page, S. J (2016): "Progress and prospects for event tourism research," Progress in Tourism Management, 52, 593–631. doi:10.1016/j.tourman.2015.03.007, Elsevier.

Jianna, L. (2019): "Asia fast turning into a sports hot spot" in China Daily, Retrieved from https://www.chinadaily.com.cn/a/201901/17/WS5c3fbbc0a3106c65c34e4e54.html, Accessed on 23rd Jan. 2020.

Lee, T. H. (2013): "Influence analysis of community resident support for sustainable tourism development". Tourism Management, 34, 37–46. doi:10.1016/j.tourman.2012.03.007.

Mihajlović I., and Vidak M. (2017): "The importance of local events for positioning of tourist destination," European Journal of Social Sciences Education and Research, 4(4). http://journals.euser.org/index.php/ejser/article/view/2432

Zlatanov, S. (2015): (2015): 89f eevents in tourism development,Bizinfo Blace, 6(2), 89), 89DOI: HYPERLINK "http://dx.doi.org/10.5937/BIZINFO1502083O" 10.5937/BIZINFO1502083O

Press Release on 17th October 2019: "Asia remains the largest tourism growth market," Retrieved from https://www.hospitalitynet.org/news/4095502.html, Accessed on 21st April 2020.

Sable, K. (2019): "Allied Market Research," Retrieved from https://www.alliedmarketresearch.com/asia-pacific-MICE-industry-market, Accessed on 23rd January 2020.

Seraphin, H., Platania, M., Spencer, P., and Modica, G. (2018): "Events and tourism development within a local community: The case of Winchester (UK)," MDPI, Sustainability 2018, 10, 3728.

TWC India Edit Team (18th December 2019): Retrieved from https://weather.com/en-IN/india/news/news/2019-12-17-india-first-asian-country-host-international-geological-congress, Accessed on 23rd January 2020.

INDEX

A

Aboriginal
   arts, 77
   cultures, 78
   tourism, 74, 75, 77, 268
Academic Search Engines, 221
Academy of Country Music (ACM), 108
Acquaintance, 18, 30, 297, 319, 320
Acrobatic feasts, 80
Acupuncture programs, 390
Administrative
   economic functions, 30
   methods, 33
Agriculture sector, 250
Ahare Bangla, 179
Akbank Jazz festival, 48
ALLEN, 139–143, 146, 148
Alternative tourism, 3, 39, 40, 68, 257
Altınözü olive and olive oil festival, 54
Ankara
   governorship, 51
   international jazz festival, 50
   metropolitan municipality, 51
Annual
   conferences, 119
   global value, 107
   religious festivals, 312
   thematic festivals, 17
Antalya
   golden orange film festival, 55, 56
   international
      choir festival, 58
      folk music and dance festival, 58
   metropolitan municipality, 47, 56
   state opera and ballet festival, 58
Apatani community, 271
Application program interface, 192
Archeological sites, 15, 16
Architectural objects, 15, 16
Artificial intelligence, 381
Artisan workshops, 33

Asian
   biggest regatta, 6
   countries, 4, 5, 7, 142, 153, 373, 381, 386, 390
   European continents, 39
   games, 6
Asia-Pacific region, 154
Aspendos
   ancient theater, 55
   international opera, 55
Asrlar Sadosi festival, 16
Association of Southeast Asian Nations (ASEANs), 6
Atatürk commemoration, 67
Attukal Pongala Mahotsav, 316
Australian Institute of Sport (AIS), 107
Authentic
   image, 30, 279
   Sri Lankan cuisine, 153
Azerbaijan, 22, 24

B

Backward-linked sectors, 129
Bahiroba, 79
Ballet, 55, 62
   festival, 55
Baneshwar, 73, 79–81
Bangladesh, 5, 154, 271, 327, 329, 331–340, 342–348, 350–355, 390
   Institute of Development Studies (BIDS), 345
   super league, 337
   travel and tourism fair, 332
Bankruptcy, 33
Bansal classes, 140
Başpehlivan, 60
Beijing Olympics, 224
Bergen conference, 237
Berlin film festival, 257
Beykoz Kundura factory, 47
Bhil, 79–81
   tribe, 79

Bhili, 79
Bibi Khanum mosque, 15
Biennale destination, 242
Bing, 184
Blackwell, 210, 215
Blueprint, 3
Bodrum International
  Ballet Festival, 58
  yacht show, 52
Boğaziçi intercontinental swimming races, 60
Boro Din, 333
Boshonto utshob, 334
Bosphorus intercontinental swimming race, 60
Bottom-up approach, 229
Brahmacharini, 317
Brainstorming, 222
Brand comprehension, 207
Brides, 87, 90, 94, 95
British, 79, 252, 268, 322
Broadcasters, 107
Bruised passport, 195
Buddhism, 21, 322
Budget allocation, 94, 351
Bukhara region, 15, 17
Bundi festival, 364, 366–369, 371
Business
  environment, 158
  events, 100, 104, 116–121, 123, 126, 133, 134, 332, 386
  index, 159
  machines, 50
  operations, 7
  tourism, 115–123, 126, 128, 130, 132–134, 166
  tourists, 115, 120–123, 128
  travel, 158, 167
    showcase, 5, 388

C

Camel wrestling, 63
Camialti shipyard, 47
Capital
  intensive projects, 32
  investment, 131
Cappadocia music festival, 50
Carlson Wagonlit travel (CWT), 201
Carnatic vocalist, 244
Carnivals, 224, 329

Catastrophic impacts, 101
Catering, 27, 30, 92
Caucasian dances, 52
Cemil Topuzlu open air stage, 47
Central
  administrative apparatus, 28
  Asian (CA), 289, 296
Ceremony, 49, 58, 63, 82, 87, 88, 90, 92–95, 109, 296, 298, 334, 364, 390
Christian, 106, 333
  orthodox, 66
Christianity, 239, 322
Chronic diseases, 176
Chronicles, 313
Chronological heritage, 77
Cochin Metro Rail Corporation Limited, 245
Collaborative projects, 194
Colombo art biennale, 238
Commemoration, 58, 62, 67
Commercialization, 225, 362
Commodification, 75, 82, 225
Commonwealth
  countries, 10
  games, 2, 6, 227
  of independent states (CIS), 12–14, 293, 294, 299
Communal celebrations, 312, 321
Communication infrastructure, 39
Community tourism, 361, 390
Computable general equilibrium model, 133
Congress tourism, 43, 65, 66, 68
Conspicuous consumption, 189
Consumerism, 90, 95
Content communities, 194
Cooperative learning, 143
Corel watching, 153
Coronavirus (COVID-19), 6, 7, 97–109, 219, 220, 225, 229, 327, 329, 331, 342–346, 348, 350, 351, 355
  economic impacts, 344
  environmental impacts, 350
  overview, 99–101
    award functions, 108
    geopolitical events, 108
    impacts, 104
    religious events, 105
    sports events amidst, 107
  pandemic, 105, 108, 109, 219, 327, 329, 331, 342–344, 346, 351, 355
  sociocultural impacts, 344

Craftsmen, 17, 365
Cricket world cup, 7, 337
Crime and vandalism, 225
Criticism, 219–222, 228, 230, 231
Critique, 221
Crony capitalism, 219, 220
Cross-sectoral cultural events, 34
Crowd surge, 230
Crowding-out, 228
Crystal palace exhibition, 237
Cuisine tourism, 172
Culinary
  heritage, 176
  tourism, 172, 175, 176, 180
Cultural
  awareness, 100
  centers, 77
  community potential, 323
  diversification, 151, 169
  enriching sessions, 147
  events, 16, 17, 34, 151, 167, 168, 225, 267, 268, 270–275, 278, 279, 282, 333
  exploration, 173
  familiarity, 5
  forms, 83, 84
  genocide, 278
  group, 22
  heritage, 17, 20, 22, 24, 28, 34, 47, 167, 175, 297, 354, 367
  monuments, 9, 19
  programs, 239
  resources, 11, 74, 77, 154, 167
  richness, 78, 81, 354
  sites, 15, 16, 20–25, 27, 32, 167
  support, 145
  tourism, 9–11, 17, 21, 23, 25–27, 129, 151, 167, 273, 310, 354, 370
    events, 167, 169
  traditions, 77, 322
  values, 78, 89, 255, 298
Customary living styles, 81, 83
Customer
  relationship management (CRM), 202
  retention, 89

D

Dan flying solos, 195
Dark tourism, 166

Data
  accuracy, 124
  collection, 31, 123
  distortion, 31
Decentralization, 236, 238
Decision
  makers, 362
  making, 204, 208–210, 213, 229, 363, 378
Deepdan ceremony, 364
Demand-supply perspective, 274
Demographic factors, 19, 35, 122
Destination
  marketing organization (DMO), 212, 340
  standpoint, 172
Dhaka
  art summit, 238, 332
  league, 337
  world music festival, 336
Digital
  clients, 378
  platform, 331, 373–376, 381, 382
  transformation, 373, 380–382
Digitalization, 379, 381
Direct-to-consumer communication, 196
Dissemination, 30, 31, 229
District governorship, 54
Diversification, 4, 117, 260
Diversifying tourism, 40
Diwali, 312
Domestic
  airline, 134
  foreign tourism activities, 40
  service, 32
  tourism, 6, 11, 12, 28, 228, 354
Double-digit growth, 118
Dravidian language, 79
Dussehra, 80, 315

E

East Mediterranean International Tourism and Travel Exhibition (EMITT), 41, 42, 64
Easter Sunday attack, 159
Eastern Mediterranean International Tourism and Travel Fair, 64
E-commerce, 184, 201
Economic
  assessment models, 132, 134
  criticisms, 222

development, 40, 73–75, 78, 82, 91, 106, 249, 250, 252, 254, 255, 258–261, 294, 331, 340, 385
  event tourism role, 258
  initiatives, 75
distress, 281
empowerment, 50
factors, 259
health, 363
impact assessment, 116, 124–130, 132, 134, 221–224, 339, 340, 344, 347
  direct negative and positive economic effects, 127, 128
  indirect negative and positive economic effects, 126, 129
  induced economic effects, 129
  multipliers effect, 129
  tourism satellite account, 131
incentives, 235, 236, 239–241, 245
indicators, 291
leakage, 223, 229
mechanism, 11, 27, 31, 33
resilient builder, 152
sectors, 6, 129, 362, 373
spheres, 12
standards, 168
Ecotourism, 74, 75, 380
Education
  city, 83
  driven society, 147
Effective tourism initiatives, 363
Electro-music, 46
Electronic entry visas, 12
Employment
  generation, 241
  multiplier, 130
Engel, 184, 209, 210, 215
English Olympiad, 338
Entrepreneur, 78, 319
Entrepreneurial activities, 78
Entrepreneurship, 78, 169, 318
Environmental
  cost, 226
  criticisms, 226
  degradation, 127, 219, 220
  dimension, 253
  pollution, 226, 350
  sustainability, 159

Ephesus congress center, 66
Esma Sultan Mansion, 47
Ethnic
  identity values, 270
  tourism, 268
Ethnocultural distinction, 269
Ethnoculture, 295, 304
Ethnography, 304
Ethnosport, 295, 296, 304
Eurasia
  boat show, 65
  marathon, 60
European
  commission, 131
  distinguished destinations, 59
  festivals association (EFA), 47, 55
  jazz
    festival association, 48
    network (EJN), 48
Eurostat, 131
Eurovision song contest, 40, 42
Event
  management, 3, 44, 91, 97, 99, 148, 166, 219, 221, 272, 328, 330, 339, 341, 342, 346, 347
  tourism
    activities, 40
    Akbank Jazz festival, 48
    Ankara accessible film festival (AFF), 57
    Ankara shopping festival, 51
    Antalya international golden orange film festival, 55
    Aspendos international opera and ballet festival, 55
    business-based events, 331
    camel wrestling, 63
    challenges, 350
    chill-out festival, 49
    classification, 329
    community engagement, 341
    congress and meeting events, 65
    contributions, 338
    culture and art festivals, 55
    development, 163
    economic impacts, 339
    educational and scientific events, 338
    entertainment-based events, 335

Index

environmental impacts, 340
fairs and exhibitions, 63
faith events, 66
festivals and culture-based events, 332
future challenge, 6
gastronomy events, 52
growth, 5
Hatay gastronomy activities, 54
impact, 388
international Antalya piano festival, 47
international Gaziantep gastronomy festival, 52
international Istanbul biennial, 57
international Istanbul theater festival, 56
Istanbul coffee festival, 53
Istanbul intercontinental swimming race, 60
Istanbul international dance festival, 52
Istanbul international gastronomy festival, 53
Istanbul international music festival, 46
Istanbul international puppet festival, 51
Istanbul international short film festival, 56
Istanbul jazz festival, 47
Istanbul marathon, 60
Istanbul shopping festival, 51
Izmir European Jazz festival, 48
Izmir international fair, 50
Kirkpinar oil wrestling championship and festival, 59
Konya international mystic music festival, 49
Manisa Mesir paste festival, 62
market, 40
music festivals and concerts, 45
national holidays, 66
presidential cycling tour, 59
regional effects, 256
Rock'n coke music festival, 46
SEB-I ARUS, 58
segment, 7
shopping and life festivals, 50
sociocultural impacts, 339
sports events, 58, 337
traditional Turkish festivals, 61
Urgup international grape harvest festival, 54

Excursion services, 28
Exogenous factors, 27
Exotic regions, 77
Exposhipping, 65
External
  stimuli, 210, 276
  stress buster, 152

F

Facebook, 104, 106, 109, 184, 186, 187, 190, 193, 194, 196, 200, 201, 213, 346
Farm tourism, 40, 172
Federation of International Filmmakers Associations (FIAPF), 56
Festivalization, 225
Festivities, 2, 315, 318, 323, 363
FIFA World Cup, 40, 227, 330
Film screenings, 48, 57
Financial
  resources, 34, 294, 369
  stabilization, 310
Flower festivals, 16
Folk
  dances, 82
  music, 365
Folklore recognition, 239
Food
  festivals, 100, 177, 179, 224
  tourism, 171–175, 179, 180
    authenticity, 174
    culture and heritage, 173
    destination orientation, 174
    management and marketing, 174
    marketing tools, 175, 180
    motivation, 173
    themes, 173
Football world cup, 287
Foreign
  citizens, 12–14, 17, 34, 299, 300
  enterprises, 33
  tour operators, 15, 17
Fourfold outcome, 160

G

Gair, 79
Galata Greek primary school, 53
Gallipoli marathon, 61

Galo people, 271
Gambling, 271
Game developers conference, 104
Ganapati Utsav, 312
GastroAntep gastronomy festival, 52
Gastronomy, 51–54, 172, 174
  festival, 53, 54
Gaziantep, 41, 48, 50, 52, 53
  development foundation, 53
  metropolitan municipality, 53
Gazprom sport complex, 302
General
  machinery, 50
  purpose maps, 280
  tourism, 9
Generation Z, 159
Geo-cultural attachment, 278
Geopolitical implications, 98
Giffin goods, 189
Gina historical attractions, 19
Global
  business events, 120
  crisis, 109
  economy, 116, 289, 361
  elitist appetite, 236
  joint ventures, 91
  media, 4
  power structures, 219, 220
  standards, 49
  tourism, 169
  trade fairs, 7
  travel
    indicators, 152
    tourism competitiveness, 159, 169
Globalization, 10, 319, 328, 336
Golden temple, 354
Golgappa-gulping competitions, 178
Google, 103, 104, 109, 184, 185, 187, 188, 205, 211, 221, 346
  meet, 109
  webmaster guidelines, 188
Googling, 186
Gourmet tourism, 172
Government expenditure, 131
Gowli
  community, 316
  women, 315
Grammy award ceremony, 40

Grandiose country project, 295
Grape molasses, 54
Gray literature, 99
Great
  Indian food festival, 178
  silk road, 14, 15
Gross domestic product (GDP), 4, 11, 97, 100, 106, 116, 120, 123, 131, 153, 224, 291, 301, 302, 319, 345, 351, 360, 374, 387
Grub
  fest, 178
  mile, 178
Guest-host perspective, 274
Guggenheim Bilbao, 239
Guinness book, 316
Gujarati food festival, 178
Gülbank prayer, 58
Gümüşlük international classical music festival, 50

H

Habitual bearers, 278
Hadoti region, 83
Hafsa Sultan, 62, 63
Hagia Eirene museum, 47
Hajj pilgrims, 105
Hallmark events, 91
Handmade artifacts, 364
Hangout, 109
Hardcore Biennale services, 241
Hashtags, 190, 196, 213
Haydarpaşa Station, 53
Health tourism, 40
Hezarfen airport, 46
High-class tourists, 32
Hindu religious festivals, 312
Hinduism, 82, 322
Historic cosmopolitan legacy, 242
Historical and cultural
  center, 27, 34
  potential, 11, 23, 27, 34
  sites, 21, 23
  tourism, 9, 10, 21, 23, 26, 35
    main trends analysis, 11
    potential analysis, 17
  tourist, 20, 21
  value, 22, 24
Holy artisan, 346

Horse-racing
  competitions, 365
  hippodrome, 302
Hospitality associations, 5
Howard Sheth model, 206, 215
Human civilization, 295

I

Imaging, 267, 268, 273, 276–282
Impact analysis for planning (IMPLAN), 133
Inbound tourism, 11
Income multiplier, 130
Incredible tiffin, 175
Indian
  cuisines, 177, 179
  culinary classes, 176
  premier league (IPL), 102, 103, 107
  tourism, 180
Indigenous
  celebrations, 310
  cultural event, 267–282
  festivals, 77
  tourism, 74–77, 268, 273
Indo Aryan language, 79
Industrialization, 76, 251, 252, 258
Inflation, 127, 224, 228, 229, 288
Influx, 5, 26, 33, 345
Information and communication technologies, 11, 34
Infrastructural
  constraints, 228, 275
  criticisms, 221, 227, 230
Inhabitants, 80, 177, 278, 282, 314
Innovative
  development, 10
  entrepreneurial growth, 311
Input-output coefficient, 131
Instagram, 184, 200, 213
Intangible
  cultural heritage representation list of humanity, 59, 63
  heritage, 24, 171
  tribal heritage, 74
Integration, 30
Intercultural dialogue, 296
Interdisciplinary approaches, 269
Internal stimuli, 210

International
  affairs, 28
  agenda, 268
  air transportation association, 374
  Ankara music festival, 50
  Antalya
    film festival, 55
    piano festival, 47
  Aspendos opera, 55
  conference, 121
  congress, 43, 118
    convention association (ICCA), 42, 43, 117, 118, 121
  convention centre, 43
  council Vesak, 107
  economic
    activity, 115, 116
    relations, 12
  emporium, 238
  events, 6, 15, 227
  exhibition logistics associations, 102
  folk festival, 336
  Gaziantep opera and ballet festival, 50
  groups, 131
  isolation, 24
  Istanbul
    biennial, 57
    cuisine days, 53
    puppet festival, 51
  Jazz festivals association, 47
  magnificence venue, 6
  mango festival, 178
  Manisa Mesir paste festival, 63
  media, 259, 278, 390
  mystic music festival, 49
  Olympic committee (IOC), 60
  openness, 155, 159
  organization, 14, 43, 131
  soloists, 47, 49
  standards, 11, 32, 294
  tourism, 98
  visitors, 53, 361
Internet
  internet of things (IoT), 381
  research firms, 185
Intersectoral
  cooperation, 10
  coordination, 29, 34
  relations, 17

Islam, 21, 105, 322, 334, 345, 347, 354
Istanbul, 41–44, 46–48, 50–53, 55–58, 60, 61, 65
  archeology museums, 47
  boat show, 52
  coffee festival, 53
  design week, 52
  fashion week, 52
  foundation for culture and arts (İKSV), 46, 47, 57, 58
  international
    opera festival, 58
    puppet festival, 52
  Jazz festival, 47
  Karagöz puppet foundation, 51
  Lutfi Kırdar International Convention and Exhibition Centre, 43
  marathon, 60, 61
  metropolitan municipality, 60
  music festival, 46, 47
  shopping fest, 51
  theater festival, 57
Izmir
  European Jazz festival, 48
  international
    fair, 50
    film festival, 58
    puppet festival, 52
    short film festival, 58

J

Jankunwari, 79
Janmashtami, 312, 333
Jazz
  audiences, 48
  festivals, 48, 336
  music, 48
  musicians, 48
Jet blue, 198

K

Kanhoba, 79
Katmandu international arts festival, 238
Kazakhstan, 19–21, 24, 290, 299, 300
Key tourism product, 4
Khandoba, 79
Kırkpınar, 59, 60
  oil wrestling, 59, 60
Knowledge transmission, 311

Kochi
  Biennale foundation, 238
  Muziris Biennale (KMB), 235, 236, 238, 240–246
Konya
  Metropolitan Municipality Mevlana Culture Center, 49
  mystic music festival, 49
Kota
  carnival, 139, 142, 144
  city, 83, 141, 142
  coaching, 139, 148
Kunefe, 54
Kyrgyz
  republic, 287–296, 298–302, 305
  tourism industry, 291
Kyrgyzstan, 24, 287–296, 298–306

L

Landscaping, 33
Lantern festivals, 4
Large-scale
  advertising campaign, 17
  event, 287, 288, 295, 303, 305, 306, 330
  organizations, 288, 298
  positive information flow, 34
Learning construct, 209
  perceptual defense/perceptual blocking, 209
  selective
    attention, 209
    exposure, 209
Leisure tourists, 121–123, 133
Life festivals, 50
Light-manufacturing sector, 319
Lillehammer Olympics, 223
Limited problem solving, 205
Little-known destination, 267, 268, 272, 274, 280–282
Live programs, 365
Livelihoods, 76, 78, 344, 364, 370
Local
  cultural tours, 134
  desserts and local soups competition, 54
  economic incentives, 235, 240, 246
Lockdown, 343, 345, 350, 354
Long-term
  development, 212
  environmental aspirations, 361
  memory, 184
Lord Shiva, 79, 81

M

Macau, 4
Maha Kumbh Mela, 2
Mahligai creative weddings, 91
Malaga economy, 106
Malay
  community, 87, 91, 93, 94
  contemporary society, 90
  modern society, 87
  wedding, 89–91, 95
    culture, 90
Malaysian context, 133, 134
Man-made environments, 226
Maqom international festival, 16
Marathas, 79
Marathon, 61
Marginal economic viability, 362
Marmara tour, 59
Marriott group, 202
Mass
  media, 17
  transmission, 220
Massive
  parade disembarks, 82
  tourism promotion, 168
Mastercard, 380
Mausoleum, 15
Mazhar Fuat Özkan (MFÖ), 46
Media exposure, 2, 4, 328, 338, 388
Medieval eastern architecture, 15
Mediterranean coastline, 55
Medium-term development, 29, 32
Meetings, incentives, conferences, and exhibitions (MICE), 4, 5, 83, 101, 116, 117, 119, 121, 123, 127, 133, 163, 166, 331, 340, 345, 346, 350, 352, 353, 355, 387, 388
Mega-event, 2, 106, 219–221, 223–225, 227–231, 235
  tourism, 221
Mehboob memorial orchestra, 244
Mei Ram-ew, 177
Melon festival, 17
Mersin international music festival, 50
Mesir paste, 63
Mesopotamia, 52
Metamorphoses, 193
Micro expenses, 125

Microblogging, 193, 201
Middle
  east and central Asia, 22, 23, 27
  eastern countries, 30
Millennials, 159
Ministry of,
  foreign affairs, 12, 29
  internal affairs, 29
Mobile world congress (MWC), 104
Modern
  communication technologies, 18
  dance groups, 52
  wedding industry players, 90
Modernization, 32, 76, 78, 88–93, 95, 237, 243, 251
  wedding
    attires, 93
    packages, 94
    rituals, 93
Modhu Purnima, 333
Momentum, 179, 220, 292, 385
Monetary
  advantages, 6
  development, 6
Money generation model (MGM), 129, 133
Monopolization, 30
Moscow Aeroflot, 27
Motivation-based perspective, 172
Moustache competition, 364
Movie screenings, 52
Mughals, 79, 322
Music festivals, 39, 45, 46, 49, 50, 336
Muslim, 66, 105, 244, 333, 353
  pilgrimage, 294
Mutual functions, 29
Muziris, 235, 236, 239, 242, 246
MySpace, 186
Mystic music festival, 49

N

Naari Puja, 317
National
  Association of Travel Agents Singapore (NATAS), 102, 108
  company, 27, 30
  dishes, 17
  economic growth, 355
  economy, 10, 288

emergency, 212
films, 56
holidays, 16, 66
horticultural board, 178
level officials, 129
policy framework (NPF), 160, 163
statistic committee, 291, 299–301
street food festival, 177
Natural
   cultural resources, 167
   destination, 341
   resources, 32, 35, 77, 155, 158, 159, 226, 255, 341, 355
Navaratri, 312
Negative environmental impacts, 227, 340, 341
Nehru trophy boat race, 242
Neo-liberalistic method, 229
Networking events, 88
Niche market, 77, 159
Nimble management tools, 378
Nomad games, 295, 300, 301
Nomadic
   civilization, 296, 304
   peoples, 296–298, 303, 305
Nonadoption, 368
Nongovernmental organizations, 43, 54
Nonprofit institutions, 3
Northeast Asia, 5
Nutraceutical value, 176

O

Objective
   database, 31
   evaluation tools, 236
   interpretation, 275
Off-peak season, 121
Olympic games, 2, 6, 40, 287, 296, 337
One love festival, 50
Online
   communities, 184, 196
   recommendations, 196
   social travel agency, 192
Open sessions, 139, 142, 147
Oral instructive worth, 323
Organization for Economic Co-Operation and Development (OECD), 131
Organizational units, 28

Oriental
   cuisine, 17
   sweets, 17
Oscar award ceremony, 40
Output
   indicators, 133
   multiplier, 130
Oxford economics, 100

P

Pahela Baishakh, 333
Palate fest, 178
Patriotism, 305
Payas Caravanserai festival, 54
Pekmez, 54
Pet boys shop, 46
Photography competitions, 58
Pilgrimage tourism, 11
Pinterest, 193, 194, 213
Plethora, 184, 185
Policymakers, 105, 159, 381
Portfolio approach, 272
Positive
   economic effects, 125
   image, 33, 205, 257, 338
Post-COVID-19, 6
Post-business trip expenditure activities, 123
Postmodern travel modes, 74
Post-pandemic period, 354
Potential
   consumers, 187, 275
   limiting factor, 27
Pre-Christian era, 268
Pre-pandemic era, 354
Presidential cycling tour, 59
Price competitiveness, 155, 156, 159
Primary data, 84, 132, 146
Problem-solving framework, 34
Professionalism, 98, 277, 390
Provincial culture and tourism directorate of Konya governorship, 49
Pseudo image, 280
Psychographic segmentation, 180
Public
   sector intervention, 338
   transport, 32, 228, 230, 360
Purnima, 333
Pushkar mela, 3
PWA World Windsurf competitions, 61

Q

Quality
　management certificate, 55
　tourism infrastructure, 160
Quantitative measurement, 246
Quinquennials, 236
Quran, 58

R

Raksha Bandhan, 312
Ramadan bairam, 66
Random effects model (REM), 133
Real-life travelers, 192
Referral rewards systems shape (RRSS), 377
Regional events, 3
Registan architectural ensemble, 15
Religious
　events, 40, 66, 67, 105, 109, 224, 332, 353, 354
　practice, 315
Republic of
　China, 19
　Kazakhstan, 12
　Tajikistan, 12
　Turkmenistan, 12
　Uzbekistan, 12, 14, 17, 27, 28
Return on investment (ROI), 126, 188
Right-policy mix application, 168
Rio carnival, 257
Rites de passage, 89, 90, 95
Ritualistic practices, 318, 321
Rock'n coke festival, 46
Roll ball world cup, 337
Routinized response behavior, 205, 206
Rural/urban tourism, 172
Russian Federation, 19, 21

S

Saharana, 81
Sahariyas, 81, 82
Samarkand
　breads, 17
　craftsmen, 17
　region, 15, 17
Sanitation, 180
Sao Paolo Biennale, 237

Saud Arabian pilgrims, 105
Scattering ceremony, 63
Scholars, 10, 77, 166, 219, 220, 237, 268, 270
Seclusion, 105
Second World War, 42, 250
Secondary
　data, 84, 146, 151, 219, 240, 365
　economic impacts, 130
　images, 277, 279
　sources, 146
Self-administrative expenditure, 124, 133
Sermons, 106
Severe acute respiratory syndrome coronavirus 2 (SARS-CoV-2), 97, 100, 329
Shab-e-Baraat, 333
Shab-e-Qadr, 333
Sharavana, 79
Shareholder meetings, 88
Sharq Taronalari music festival, 16
Shivratri, 79
Shopping festivals, 39, 50, 67
Short-term impact, 239
Siena Jazz foundation, 48
　Siena summer jazz master classes, 48
Sightseers, 3, 6
Sign language, 57
Silk road
　approach, 30
　office, 28
　restoration program, 28
Sirtaki, 52
Skill development program, 244
Small-scale
　employment areas, 366
　sectors, 241, 319
Snapchat, 193, 200
Social
　accounting matrix, 133
　ancient rarity, 174
　and cultural activities, 40, 322
　bookmarking, 193
　celebrations, 5
　community relationships, 92
　cultural discourses, 239
　distancing, 105, 347
　during trip phase, 212
　exclusion, 74
　groups, 18

isolation, 77
media, 88, 90, 183, 185, 188–194, 196, 197, 200, 201, 210, 211, 213–215, 331, 337, 370, 377, 380
   advertising, 194
   campaigns, 197, 200
   group, 189
   knowledge, 189
   marketing, 188, 215
   strategies
   travel campaigns, 198, 200
network, 17, 106, 190, 194, 377
networking sites (SSNs), 190, 194, 196, 213
post-trip phase, 213
pre-trip phase, 210
sharing, 189, 196, 197
stimuli, 207
Socialization, 270, 271, 273, 282, 381
Societal connectivity, 309, 312
Sociocultural
   criticisms, 224
   diversities, 310
   events, 224, 270
   impacts, 224–226, 229, 344
   traditions, 92
Sociodemographic characteristics, 18
Socio-economic
   context, 83
   development, 17, 34
   inconveniences, 275
   status, 78
Soft loans, 12
Solar energy, 230
Solitary travelers, 159
Space optimization, 241
Special
   interest tourism (SIT), 76, 77
   tourism investment zones, 380
Spiritual heritage, 24
Sports tourism, 40
Spring-summer tourist season, 15
Srauta ritual, 315
Sri Lanka tourism, 151, 152, 158, 163
Staffing, 31
Staged authenticity, 225
Stakeholders, 75, 76, 100, 151, 169, 230, 241, 242, 255, 260, 261, 328, 338, 341, 346, 375, 381, 388

Standard operating procedure (SOP), 350
Standardization, 28, 133
State
   border service, 299
   committee for tourism development, 16, 28
   opera and ballet, 55
   units, 28
Statistical error, 19
Stereotyped takbirs, 58
Stilt-walkers, 271
Sultan
   complex, 63
   mosque, 62, 63
Sunnah feasts, 62
Super spreading, 101
Superstructures, 39, 289
Supply
   factors, 9, 126
   side constraints, 274
Surfing, 153
Sustainability, 75, 76, 156, 158, 159, 219, 221, 228, 230, 231, 249, 250, 253, 255, 256, 261, 280, 338, 355, 386
Sustainable
   development, 3, 16, 153, 154, 252, 253, 255, 260, 268, 282, 369
   growth, 391
   inherent quality, 83
   local economic development, 359
   tourism, 75, 255, 280, 338
SWOT, 368, 369

T

Tashkent international
   film forums, 16
   photo exhibition, 16
   tourism fair, 15
Tax revenue, 120, 126, 129
Taxation, 130
Telecommunications, 50
The weather channel (TWC), 387
Theater festivals, 16, 55
Theory of spatiality, 19, 20
Therapeutic capacity, 159
Third-party organizations, 211
Tianmen massacre, 238
Topography, 173, 174
Tour operator association of Bangladesh (TOAB), 346

Index

Tourism
  activities, 28, 29, 31, 34, 39, 63, 64, 67, 68, 74, 77, 100, 126, 249, 256, 258, 259, 279, 281, 328, 339, 351
  behavior, 208
    Howard Sheth model, 202
  business, 9, 25, 99, 344, 345, 391
  characteristic products, 132
  competitiveness, 151, 153, 154, 167, 168
  connected products, 132
  culture, 11
  destination, 289
  development, 3, 10, 11, 14, 28, 29, 31–34, 40, 75, 82, 84, 126, 154, 158, 160, 163, 166, 168, 169, 178, 255, 256, 287–289, 292, 306, 340, 361, 363, 368, 370
  driver, 268
  enterprises, 29, 31, 34
  entities, 33
  future challenges, 376, 382
  income, 2, 42, 257, 299
  infrastructure, 11, 160
  management, 3, 29, 166, 169, 174, 219, 221
  market, 18, 32, 33, 35, 41, 43, 64, 66–68, 109, 120, 228, 267, 268, 280
  marketing, 40, 129, 188, 191, 257
  media group, 44
  opportunities, 19, 39, 382
  potential, 9, 11–13, 17, 19–27, 32, 34, 39, 41, 104, 268, 272, 289, 291, 292, 301, 304
  products, 26, 74, 98, 119, 125, 168, 257, 258, 289, 353, 363
  revenues, 40, 168, 260
  satellite account (TSA), 122, 131, 132
  season, 40, 249, 257, 259
  sector, 4, 14, 29, 98, 101, 153, 241, 250, 254–256, 259–261, 289, 291, 292, 294, 295, 302, 305, 328, 343–346, 351, 352, 355, 360, 362, 363, 365, 366, 373, 374, 376–378, 380, 386
  specific products, 132
  training, 281
  vouchers, 12
Tourist
  accommodation, 23
  activities, 10, 28, 77, 261, 370
  arrival, 11, 115, 134, 152, 159, 163, 360
  behavior, 183, 185, 186
  expenditure, 130, 220, 223
  factors, 24
  generating regions, 242
  imaginative acts, 77
  impressions, 30
  infrastructure, 27, 160
  potential, 9, 15, 20, 22–24
  reception infrastructure, 33
  resources, 23, 28, 33
  service, 30, 301
    cycle, 33
    infrastructure, 156
  trap, 225
  trips, 25, 29
  vouchers, 14
Trademark, 30
Traditional
  cultures, 89
  mystical music, 49
  ritualistic practices, 315, 318
Traffic congestion, 225, 230, 288
Transport
  equipment rental, 132
  supporting services, 132
Transportation, 27, 128, 178, 245, 362
Travel
  and tourism competitiveness, 151, 153, 155, 156, 158, 160, 167, 169, 291, 292, 360
    index (TTCI), 153–155, 157–159, 163, 164, 167
  bloggers, 195
  blogs, 211, 380
  expenditure, 122
  industry, 1, 116
Tribal
  cultural diversities, 73
  culture, 76
  diversities, 78
  fairs, 73–75, 82, 83
  festivals, 73, 75, 78, 83
  groups, 82
  population, 74
  tourism, 74, 78, 82
  traditions, 83
Tribe, 73, 76, 79–81, 83, 84, 258
Trilogy, 39

Trip planning tools, 192
TripAdvisor, 186, 194
Trouble-free access, 274
Turban tying, 364
Turkey
  cycling federation, 59
  National Olympic Committee (TOC), 60
Turkish
  Airlines Euroleague basketball, 61
  cinema, 55
  cuisine, 53
  festivals, 67
  lira (TL), 42
  sign language, 57
Türkiye Odalar ve Borsalar Birliği (TOBB), 64
Twitter, 193, 194, 200, 201, 213

U

UEFA champions league, 40, 41
Umrah pilgrimage, 103
Union
  cycliste internationale (UCI), 59
  of chambers and commodity exchanges of Turkey, 64
Unique
  architectural monuments, 15
  information system, 31
Uniqueness, 30, 93, 167, 180, 273, 310
United
  Arab Emirates, 12
  Kingdom, 73, 100, 103, 154, 191, 194, 327, 343
  Nations, 10, 43, 103, 107, 115, 118, 131, 260
    creative cities network, 52–54
    Educational, Scientific and Cultural Organization (UNESCO), 24, 25, 43, 53, 54, 59, 63, 152, 294, 334, 354
    world heritage, 15, 28, 294, 354
  World Tourism Organization (UNWTO), 5, 6, 10, 11, 14, 98, 115, 118, 119, 121, 131–133
    Regional Office, 14
Untapped potential, 151, 169, 351
Upavaas, 315
Urban communities, 177
Urgup international grape harvest festival, 54

Urosh, 333
User-generated content (UGC), 184, 186, 192, 211, 213, 375
Uzbek
  families, 26
  tourism, 27, 28, 30
    National Company, 28
Uzbekistan, 9–18, 20–29, 32–34, 290, 299, 300

V

Vacationers, 5, 6, 299, 310
Vadapav-eating competitions, 178
Vaghdev, 79
Valia Amma, 317
Venetian art, 236
Venice Biennale, 237, 243
Ventilation, 230
Versatile organization, 48
Virtual
  advertisements, 193
  communities, 194
  conferencing software, 346
  events, 7, 331
  social network, 185
Visa-free regime, 12
Visitation, 172, 240, 241, 267, 274–279
Visitor economy, 4, 328, 338, 388
Voluntarism, 338
Voluntary organizations, 312
Vratas, 312, 315

W

Web 2.0, 183–185, 191, 192, 215
Wedding
  attires, 90
  ceremonies, 89, 93
  dreams, 87, 90
  packages, 89, 90, 94
  party, 89
  planners, 88–90
  rituals, 90
Women solitary travelers, 159
World
  Association of Chefs' Societies (WACS), 53
  Chess Olympiads, 41

cinema, 56
class
　convention center, 65
　services, 180
community, 27, 34
economy, 11
food travel association, 172
health organization (WHO), 100, 101, 105, 107, 118–120, 225
nomad games (WNG), 287–289, 295–300, 302–306
　indirect impact, 303
red cross congress, 42
tour, 59
tourism
　and tourism council, 11
　forum and fair, 64
　market, 27, 29, 34, 289, 294
　mobility, 40, 67
　organization (WTO), 10, 98, 115, 118, 131, 254, 255, 260, 268, 289, 295, 300
　trade organization, 255
　travel and tourism council (WTTC), 98, 116–118, 131, 343
water forum, 41
wide web, 17, 183
Worldwide
　economy, 117, 118
　scale celebrations, 4
　tennis tournaments, 6
Wrestlers, 60
Wrestling, 59, 60, 63, 271, 390

Y

Yahoo, 184
YouTube, 109, 184, 186, 194

Z

Zeytinli rock festival, 50
Zoom, 109, 346